YACHTMASTER
FOR SAIL & POWER

OTHER TITLES OF INTEREST

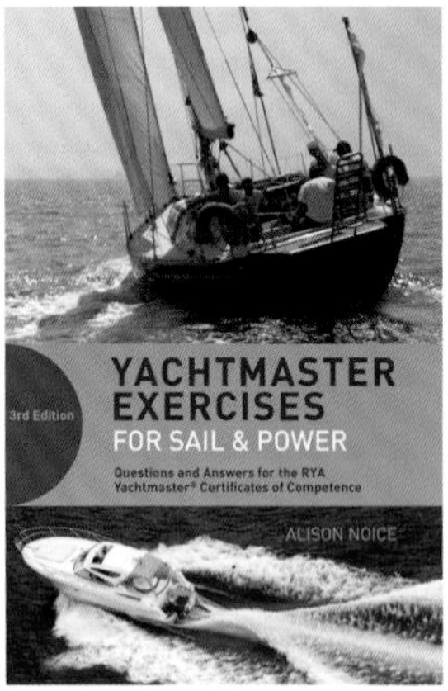

Yachtmaster Exercises for Sail & Power

3rd edition
by Alison Noice
ISBN 9781408178102

This companion volume to *Yachtmaster for Sail & Power* provides further navigation practice for anyone studying for the RYA Yachtmaster and Day Skipper qualifications. It is packed with exercises and answers and comes with a free practice chart for plotting practice. Completely updated, rewritten and redesigned to modernise and revitalise this essential course book for a new generation, this is an invaluable textbook and exam revision guide for anyone studying for the RYA exams or simply brushing up on their navigation skills.

The Adlard Coles Book of the International Certificate of Competence

3rd edition
by Bill Anderson
ISBN 9781408122754

Anyone hoping to take their boat to the inland waterways of Europe needs to pass the International Certificate of Competence test – and this book will show you how. It explains the syllabus in detail, outlines what skills you will need to demonstrate, and includes collision regulations and CEVNI, as well as boat handling skills. Revision notes are provided on all the subjects in the test, as well as a set of self-test questions and answers at each stage to help you take the ICC test with confidence.

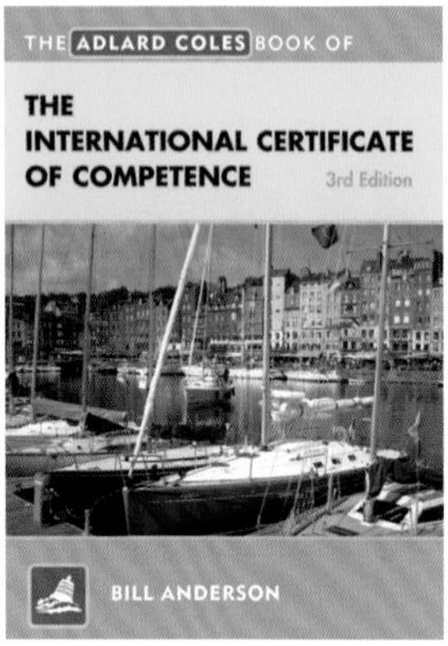

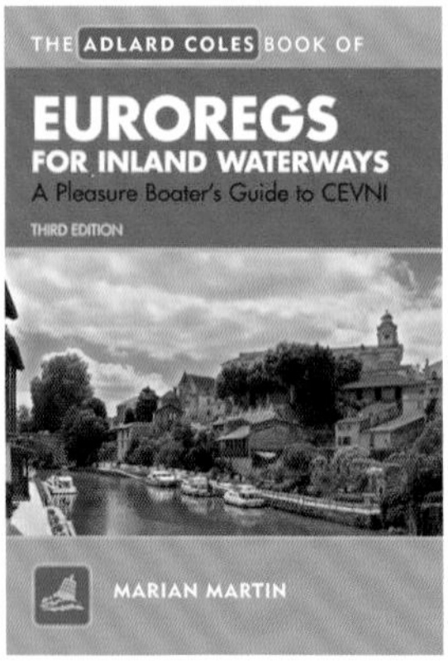

The Adlard Coles Book of EuroRegs for Inland Waterways

3rd edition
by Marian Martin
ISBN 9781408101414

In order to safely navigate Europe's major waterway routes, all boaters need to know CEVNI – the Waterway Code. This book has been written especially for pleasure craft users, setting out the rules in an easy-to-follow format. It covers waterway signs, signals, flags and lights, markings on vessels, procedures in tunnels, locks and weirs, overtaking rules, berthing, and explains buoyage and landmarks. It forms the basis of the RYA test for the ICC and is accepted by European countries as the obligatory rules book that must be carried on all small craft.

ALISON NOICE

YACHTMASTER
FOR SAIL & POWER

4th edition

A Manual for the RYA Yachtmaster®
Certificates of Competence

ADLARD COLES NAUTICAL
BLOOMSBURY
LONDON • NEW DELHI • NEW YORK • SYDNEY

Adlard Coles Nautical
An imprint of Bloomsbury Publishing Plc

50 Bedford Square
London
WC1B 3DP
UK

1385 Broadway
New York
NY 10018
USA

www.bloomsbury.com

First edition published 2004
Second edition 2010
Third edition 2012
Fourth edition 2015

British Library Cataloguing-in-Publication Data
A catalogue record for this book is available from the British Library.

Library of Congress Cataloguing-in-Publication data has been applied for.

ISBN 978-1-4729-2549-7
ePDF 978-1-4729-2551-0
ePub 978-1-4729-2550-3

2 4 6 8 10 9 7 5 3 1

Typeset in 9 on 11pt Trade Gothic by Susan McIntyre
Printed and bound in China by C & C Offset Printing Co., Ltd

CONTENTS

ACKNOWLEDGEMENTS

MY GRATEFUL THANKS to the following people and companies who gave permission for me to use their material:

Adlard Coles Nautical
Avon Inflatables
BBC Weather
Bruce Anchors
C-Map software
Crewsaver
Firdell Radar Reflectors
Firemaster Fire Extinguishers
Hamble School of Yachting
HM Customs & Excise
Imray Charts
International Maritime Organisation
Lewmar
Longbow Sail Training
Maritime & Coastguard Agency
McMurdo
Meteo France
Neptune Software
Premier Marinas
Raymarine
Reeds Nautical Almanac
Sue Fletcher
RFD Beaufort
Rick Tomlinson
Roger Seymour
Royal Yachting Association
Sea Pro Software
Simrad
UK Hydrographic Office
UK Met Office
USAF Sembach, Germany

A very special thank you to Peter Noice for most of the photographs, sound advice, constant technical support and never-ending patience.

INTRODUCTION

BY THE TIME YOU READ *Yachtmaster for Sail and Power* you will probably already have joined the ever growing number of enthusiasts who find pleasure in cruising Europe in leisure craft, both power and sail. You may be working through the RYA Yachtmaster training scheme or just wishing to learn more about navigation and seamanship, but whatever your aim, I hope you find what you are looking for in this book.

You are obviously wise enough to realise that it is not prudent to place blind faith in all the superb electronic equipment available, without a basic understanding of seamanship, meteorology and navigation. The RYA/DoT Yachtmaster syllabus covers all the subjects that are needed for safe, sensible cruising using a combination of electronic and traditional methods in harmony, and they have all been included in the book.

The subjects are arranged in a logical sequence and to make them as understandable as possible many illustrations have been used to clarify the text. A full copy of the collision regulations has been included so that those studying for the Yachtmaster Offshore exam do not have to buy an additional book.

Happy learning and good cruising.

Alison Noice

RYA SAIL CRUISING SCHEME

Course (and duration)	Suggested minimum pre-course	Assumed knowledge	Course content	Ability after course
Start Yachting Practical (2 days)	None	None	Introduction to sailing & seamanship	Basic sailing experience
Essential Navigation and Seamanship* (16 hours)	None	None	Introduces navigation & safety	Basic knowledge of navigation & safety
Competent Crew Practical (5 days)	None	None	Basic seamanship, helmsmanship, navigation & meteorology	Useful crew member
Day Skipper Shorebased* (40 hrs plus exam)	Some practical experience desirable	None	Basic seamanship & introduction to seamanship & navigation	Knowledge to skipper a small yacht in familiar waters by day
Day Skipper Practical (Yacht)** (5 days)	5 days sea time 100 miles 4 night hours	Navigation to Day Skipper Shorebased & basic sailing ability	Basic pilotage, boat handling & watch organisation	Skipper a small yacht in familiar waters by day
Watch Leader Practical (Sail training) (5 days)	5 days sea time 100 miles 4 night hours	Navigation to Day Skipper Shorebased & basic sailing ability	Navigation, seamanship & meteorology	Take charge of a watch on a sail training vessel

Coastal Skipper/ Yachtmaster Offshore Shorebased* (40 hrs plus exam)	Day Skipper Shorebased course	Navigation to Day Skipper shorebased standard	Offshore & coastal navigation, pilotage, coastal & offshore passages	Background knowledge to skipper a yacht on coastal passages by day & night
Coastal Skipper Practical** (5 days)	15 days sea time (2 days as skipper) 300 miles 8 night hours	Navigation to Coastal Skipper Shorebased standard. Sailing to Day Skipper Practical standard	Skippering techniques & planning	Skipper a yacht on coastal passages by day & night
Yachtmaster Ocean Shorebased course	Coastal & offshore sailing	Navigation to Skipper & Yachtmaster Coastal Offshore standard	Astro-navigation & ocean meteorology	Background knowledge to skipper a yacht on ocean passages

* Syllabus is the same for sailing and motor cruising
** Different courses for tidal and non-tidal waters

RYA MOTOR CRUISING SCHEME

Course (and duration)	Suggested minimum pre-course	Assumed knowledge	Course content	Ability after course
Essential Navigation & Seamanship* (16 hours)	None	None	Introduces navigation & safety	Basic knowledge of navigation & safety
Helmsman (2 days)	None	None	Boating safety, helmsmanship & boat handling. Intro to engine maintenance	Competent to handle motor cruiser of specific types in sheltered waters
Day Skipper Shorebased course*	Some practical experience desirable	None	Basic seamanship & introduction to seamanship & meteorology	Knowledge to skipper a motor cruiser in familiar waters by day
Day Skipper Practical** (4 days)	2 days	Basic navigation & helmsmanship	Pilotage, boat handling, seamanship & navigation	Skipper a motor cruiser in familiar waters by day
Coastal Skipper & Yachtmaster Offshore Shorebased course *	Day Skipper Shorebased course	Navigation to Day Skipper Shorebased standard	Offshore & coastal navigation, pilotage & meteorology	Background Knowledge to skipper a motor cruiser on coastal passages by day & night

Coastal Skipper Practical** (5 days)	15 days (2 days as skipper) 300 miles at sea 8 night hours	Navigation to Coastal Skipper Shorebased Standard. Boat handling to Day Skipper	Skippering techniques & passage planning	Skipper a motor cruiser on coastal passages by day & night

Yachtmaster Ocean Theory Shorebased** (5 days)	Coastal & offshore passages	Navigation to Coastal Skipper & Yachtmaster Offshore standard	Astro navigation & ocean meteorology	Background knowledge to skipper a yacht on ocean passages

* Syllabus is the same for sailing and motor cruising
** Different courses for tidal and non-tidal waters

YACHTMASTER COASTAL CERTIFICATE OF COMPETENCE (POWER)
YACHTMASTER COASTAL CERTIFICATE OF COMPETENCE (SAIL)

The Yachtmaster Coastal has the knowledge needed to skipper a cruising boat on coastal cruises but does not necessarily have the experience needed to undertake longer passages.

◆ Pre-exam requirement

To take the practical examination, candidates must be aged 17 or over and require:

- *Radio Operator's Qualification* A Restricted (VHF only) Radio Operator's Certificate or a GMDSS Short Range Certificate or higher grade of marine radio certificate.
- *First Aid* A valid First Aid Certificate. First Aid qualifications held by Police, Fire and Armed Services are also acceptable.
- *Seatime* 800 miles logged within 10 years prior to examination, 30 days living on board, 2 days as skipper and 12 night hours.

  For holders of the Yachtmaster Coastal Practical Course Completion Certificate, the seatime requirement is reduced to: 400 miles, 20 days living on board, 12 night hours, 2 days as skipper.

◆ Exam duration

The exam will take about 6 to 10 hours for one candidate and 8 to 14 hours for two. Candidates will be set tasks to demonstrate their ability as a Yachtmaster Coastal and may also be asked questions on any part of the syllabus for all practical and shorebased courses up to Yachtmaster Coastal.

YACHTMASTER OFFSHORE CERTIFICATE OF COMPETENCE (POWER)
YACHTMASTER OFFSHORE CERTIFICATE OF COMPETENCE (SAIL)

The Yachtmaster Offshore is competent to skipper a cruising boat on any passage during which the vessel is no more than 150 miles from harbour.

◆ Pre-exam requirement

To take the practical examination, candidates must be aged 18 or over and require:

- *Radio Operator's Qualification* A restricted (VHF only) Radio Operator's Certificate or a GMDSS Short Range Certificate or higher grade of marine radio certificate.
- *First Aid* A valid First Aid Certificate. First Aid qualifications held by Police, Fire and Armed Services are also acceptable.
- *Seatime* 50 days, 2,500 miles, including at least five passages over 60 miles measured along the rhumb line from the port of departure to the destination, acting as skipper for at least two of these passages and including two which have involved overnight passages. Five days experience as skipper.

◆ Exam duration

The Yachtmaster exam will take about 8 to 12 hours for one candidate and 10 to 18 hours for two. Candidates will be set tasks to demonstrate their ability as skipper of an offshore cruising boat and may also be asked questions on any part of the syllabus for all courses except Yachtmaster Ocean.

1 CHARTS & POSITIONS

THIS CHAPTER WILL BE REVISION for some readers but possibly completely new to others, so we shall begin with some historical background and then go on to look at charts, both paper and electronic.

Mariners have been making and using crude charts since man invented paper, but charting developed dramatically when the sixteenth-century chartmaker Gerardus Mercator devised a sound method for projecting spherical Earth on to flat paper, a method still being used today for coastal passage charts.

Captain James Cook was the next major player when he surveyed parts of north-east Canada, New Zealand, Australia and some of the Pacific islands during the mid eighteenth century. Admiral Francis Beaufort later made a major impact and became the hydrographer to the Navy in 1829. Not satisfied with devising his famous wind scale, he went on to introduce Admiralty Tide Tables, Notices to Mariners and also the use of the Greenwich meridian as the prime on British charts. Nowadays the UK Hydrographic Office keeps over 3,000 worldwide charts in stock to make them the most respected chart-producers in the world.

As the Earth is an oblate spheroid and not a perfect sphere, chartmakers have always had a problem calculating the exact centre of the Earth, and the charts they made contained small inaccuracies when charting land masses. When satellite mapping became widespread, these errors became very apparent. Indeed, when the Scilly Isles were resurveyed by satellite, it was found necessary to move them about

Fig 1.1 The chart on the left is from a 1914 survey of the Channel Islands showing the depths in fathoms and feet. The northern coast of Brecqhou shows a promontory whereas the 2003 highly coloured chart, on the right, does not. Other minor differences are also clearly noticeable.

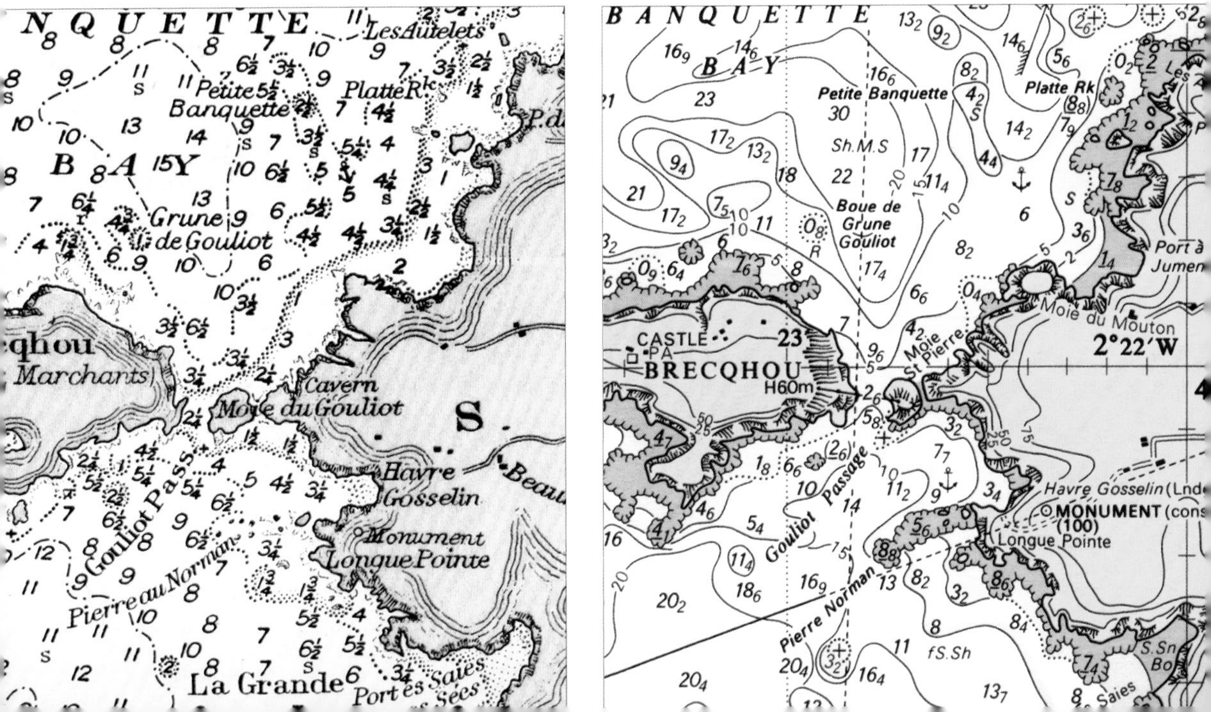

a hundred metres. Perhaps this was a contributory factor to the wrecking of the British fleet on the Bishop and Clerk rocks in 1707, when charting was still in its infancy.

The advantages of using satellite surveys become obvious when a comparison is made between old and new charts, as shown in Figure 1.1. The grey chart of Sark and Brecqhou dates back to 1914 whereas the full colour metric chart was printed in 2003.

LATITUDE AND LONGITUDE

For position-fixing purposes the Earth is divided into an internationally understood geometrical grid system that uses parts of a sphere as its basis. The co-ordinates of this grid are called **latitude** and **longitude**.

◆ Latitude

Latitude uses the Equator as the reference point and the location of a place is expressed as being an angular measurement, either north or south of this great circle that divides the Earth into the southern and northern hemispheres. The diagram in Figure 1.2 shows how these angles are formed using the centre of the Earth, the Equator itself being the 0° line and the Poles at 90°. Imaginary circles, that run east to west, are parallel to the Equator and decrease in size, as they get closer to the Poles.

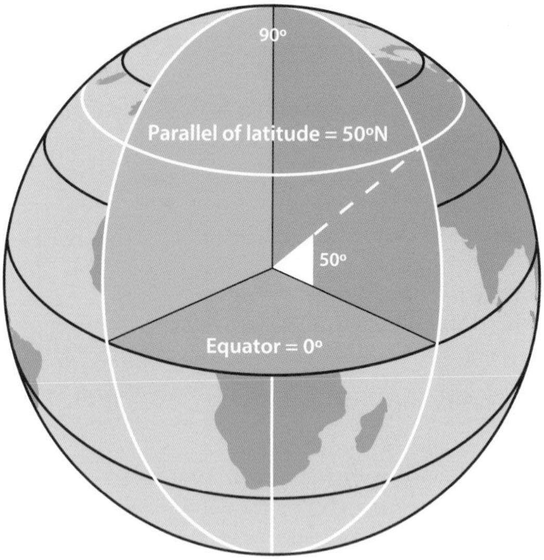

Fig 1.2 Parallels of latitude.

- **Each degree is divided into 60 divisions called minutes.**
- **Each minute is a nautical mile.**
- A **nautical mile** is **1,852 metres** in length. Each nautical mile is divided into tenths of a mile on large-scale charts and into fifths of a mile on the smaller-scale ones.
- **One tenth** of a nautical mile is called a **cable**.
- A **cable** is **185 metres**.

In Figure 1.3, the latitude is being measured with a pair of dividers. The position is 49 degrees (°) and 43.2 minutes north of the Equator, which is written as **49° 43'. 2 N**.

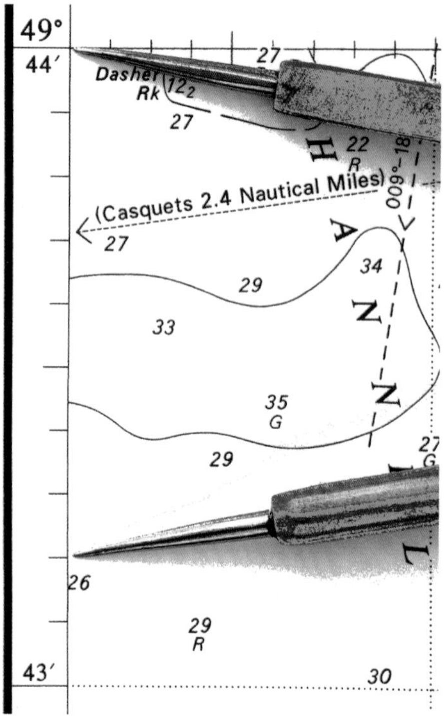

Fig 1.3 Measuring latitude. Each nautical mile is divided into tenths.

◆ Longitude

Longitude is the location of a place either east or west of one of the half circles joining the Poles, a line called a **meridian**.

The Equator, being the greatest circle on the globe, more or less elected itself as the reference for latitude but selecting what is known as the *prime meridian* for the measurement of longitude was more difficult and for hundreds of years each nation chose its own, usually passing through its capital city! However, the matter was resolved in 1884 when an international prime meridian passing through the Greenwich Observatory was agreed upon.

Longitude is measured in angles 0° to 180° east or west of Greenwich. The line at 180° is called the *International* **Date Line.** The longitude in Figure 1.5 is: **2°13'. 2 W.**

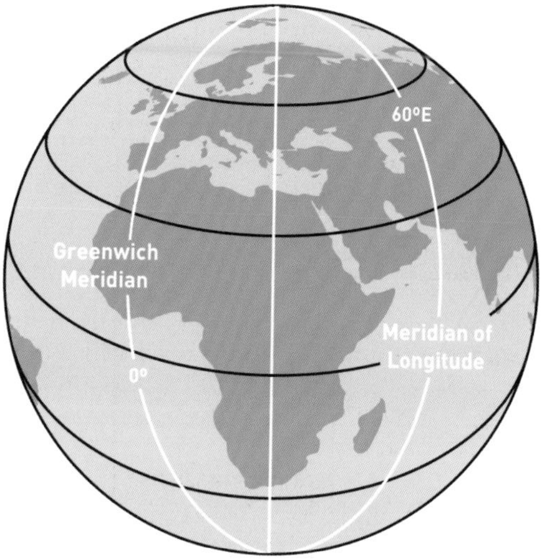

Fig 1.4 (right) Meridians of longitude with the prime meridian at Greenwich.

Fig 1.5 (below) Measuring longitude. The position is 2°13'. 2 W of Greenwich.

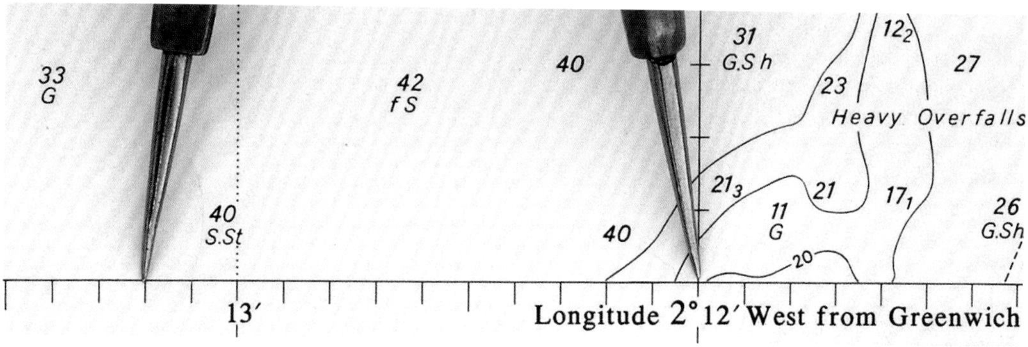

MERCATOR PROJECTION

Projecting an accurate image of the Earth onto flat paper was interesting to a host of early mathematicians and geographers, many of whom produced solutions to the problem. However, it was Mercator who produced a usable projection for position fixing and distance measurement.

Mercator gave us a mathematical solution which is more easily understood if we imagine a globe with a light source at its centre. A piece of paper is then wrapped around the globe and the light projected onto the plain material. The meridians of longitude appear as vertical parallel lines and the parallels of latitude as horizontal parallel lines cutting each other at right angles as shown in Figure 1.6.

When using Mercator charts today, we see that the longitudinal scale is constant at all latitudes, while land masses in northern latitudes appear distorted and far larger than they really are. The latitude scale is expanded the further away from the Equator you get and this is why it is essential to measure distance on either the left-hand side or right-hand side of a Mercator chart. The longitude scale should only be used when expressing position in degrees east or west of Greenwich, as the unit along the bottom of the chart is not the length of a nautical mile.

Another property of the Mercator projection is that a straight line drawn from A to B is not the shortest distance; it is a curved line in reality. This is why the Mercator projection is used for medium-scale charts covering a maximum of a few hundred miles, so that the error during a passage is no more than a mile or so. A straight line on a Mercator chart is called **a rhumb line**.

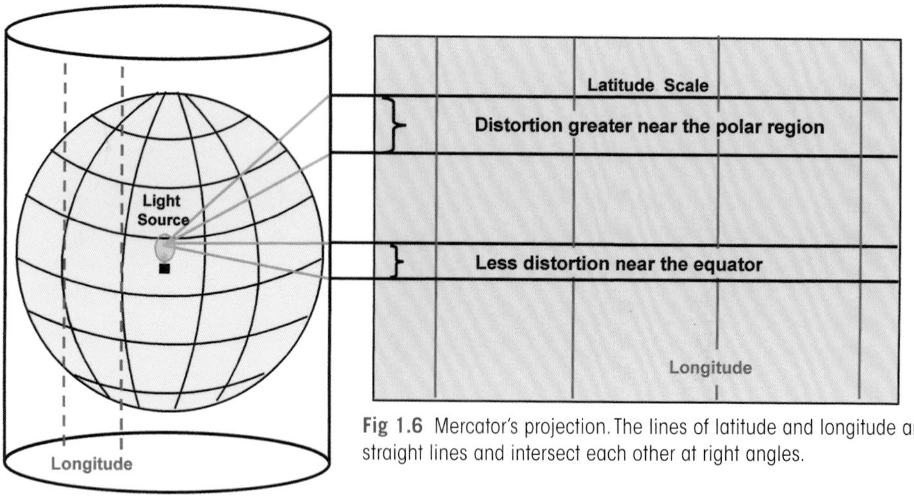

Fig 1.6 Mercator's projection. The lines of latitude and longitude are straight lines and intersect each other at right angles.

◆ Transverse Mercator

This is a variation on the normal Mercator projection where the cylinder is rotated by 90° relative to the Equator so that the projected surface is aligned to a central meridian instead of to the Equator. There is little distortion and the projection is ideal for mapping regions with narrow countries on a north/south line like Chile, New Zealand and the UK. It is the method recommended for large-scale harbour plans as the land suffers minimal distortion.

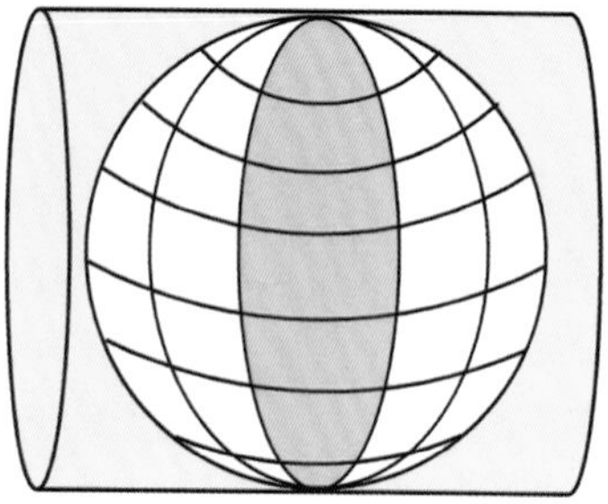

Fig 1.7 Transverse Mercator.

GNOMONIC PROJECTION

For longer voyages, it is important that the shortest distance is sailed so the charts used are to a different projection – called gnomonic. Once again, visualise that a flat sheet has been placed at a tangent to any point on the Earth's surface and the light projected through the globe onto the paper. For most practical purposes the paper is placed at one of the Poles (Figure 1.8).

As charts using the gnomonic projection give the shortest routes, these are used for planning long ocean voyages; a straight line drawn on this type of chart *is* the shortest distance and approximates a *great circle route*.

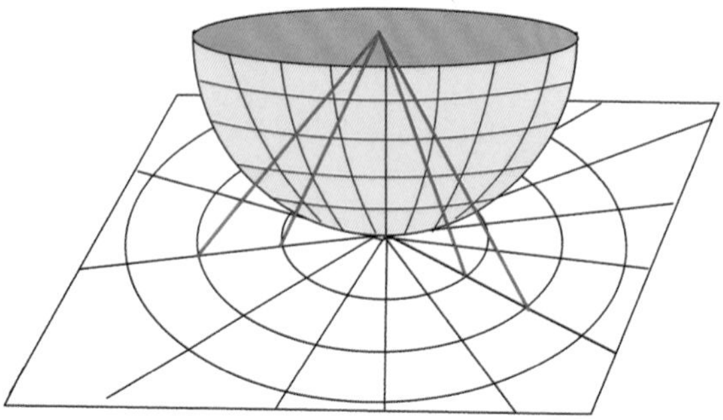

Fig 1.8 Gnomonic projection.

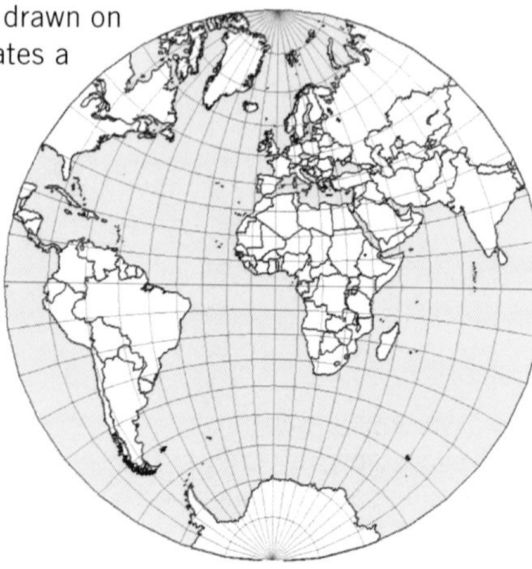

Fig 1.9 A straight line drawn on this gnomonic chart is a *great circle* – the shortest distance from A to B.

HORIZONTAL DATUMS

International co-operation has never been easy and in the days before nation began to speak to nation, cartographers and geographers were busy producing their own charts. As each had his own idea of the Earth's actual shape, this made any conformity extremely difficult and hundreds of datum points are known to be in existence.

Eventually, international agreement was reached and the standard datum WGS 84 was adopted. All UK Hydrographic Office and Imray charts use this datum (or one that is compatible) and charts are clearly labelled as shown in Figure 1.10. GPS sets default to the WGS 84 datum but most of the better sets can be altered to use alternative datums if required. This may be necessary if charter boats overseas use charts based on the local datum. Check the chart when taking over the boat and if necessary go into the 'set-up' mode of the GPS, find '*datums*' and then set the GPS receiver to the datum appropriate for the chart. Alternatively, apply a correction similar to the one shown in Figure 1.11 if the GPS is a basic handheld model with no adjustments.

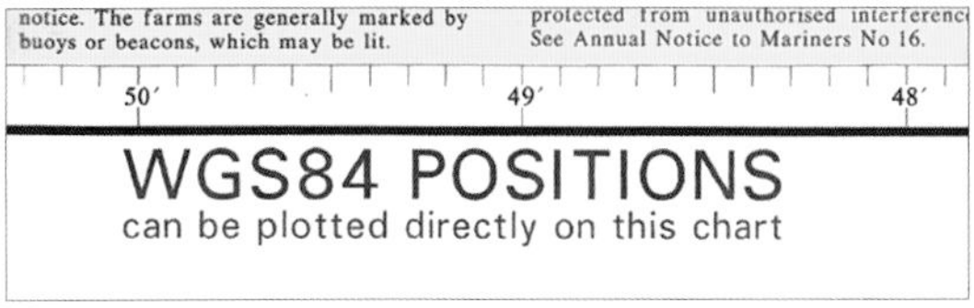

Fig 1.10 Most of the nautical chart publishers in the world use this datum.

SATELLITE-DERIVED POSITIONS
Positions obtained from satellite navigation Systems, such as the Global Positioning System (GPS), are normally referred to the World Geodetic System 1984 Datum. Such positions must be adjusted by 0·06' minutes NORTHWARD and 0·08' minutes EASTWARDS before plotting on this chart.

Fig 1.11 Horizontal datum correction for Chart SC2613.

TYPES OF CHART

There are two suppliers of charts in the UK – the UK Hydrographic Office and Imray. Both provide paper and electronic charts. Electronic charts and chart plotters are great to use but it is always wise to carry some paper charts in case of plotter or power failure.

UK Hydrographic Office

The UKHO's Leisure products department supplies over 20 different paper chart folios of popular sailing areas around the British Isles, Channel Islands and Ireland. The folios were designed by yachtsmen for yachtsmen and are a perfect size for the average chart table in a small boat. Packed in strong plastic wallets and containing numerous charts, they are very competitively priced and can be corrected.

The Admiralty ARCS 'Skipper' series of electronic charts are no longer available and corrections for them are not supplied.

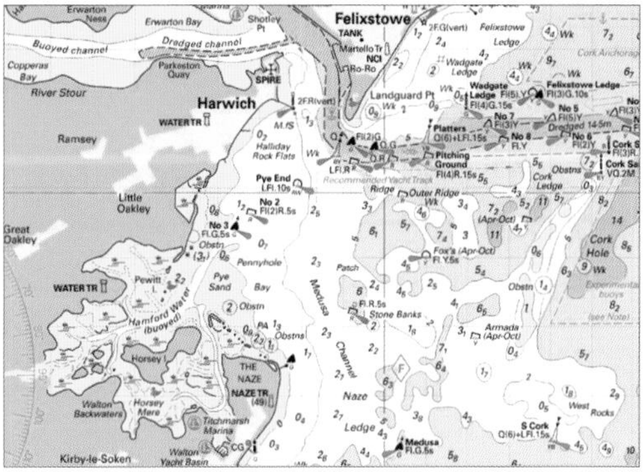

Fig 1.12 An Imray chart.

Imray

Imray also supply paper and electronic charts. Again, chart-table sized folios are available for popular sailing areas as well as many larger-scale single charts. The charts are waterproof but can be drawn on with pencil or ballpoint pen.

The colours are user-friendly and the arcs of major lights are shown in colour. To complement these there is a series of well-illustrated pilot books.

Electronic chart apps are available for iPhone and iPad – a great innovation.

◆ Foreign charts

Some excellent charts are produced by other national hydrographic offices. When cruising abroad and hoping to explore some of the lesser creeks and anchorages, the best and most up-to-date charts will most likely be the ones printed locally.

There is much co-operation between the hydrographers of Europe, and many of the UKHO's charts of France are almost entirely based on data supplied by France and vice versa. The UKHO chart of Cherbourg to Fécamp carries the crests of the International Maritime Organisation (IMO), the French Hydrographic Office and the British Admiralty.

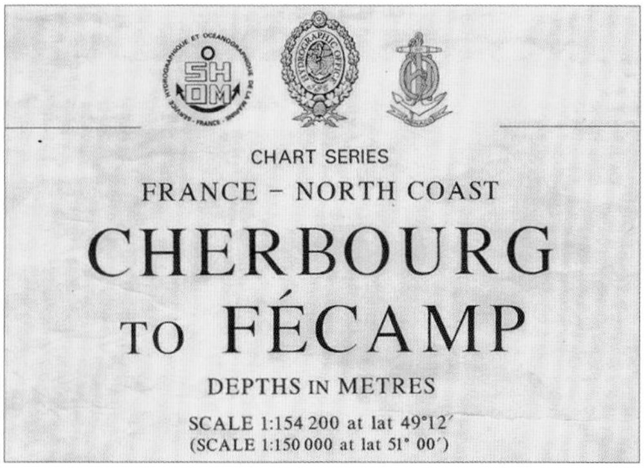

Fig 1.13 Title panel from Admiralty passage chart SC 2613.

◆ Scales

All chart publishers provide charts in a range of scales but the following will act as a rough guide when you are buying charts.

- **Passage planning** 1:325 000 to 1:150 000
- **Coastal passage** 1:25 000
- **Harbour plans** 1:5 000 or 1:7 500

◆ Depths and heights

Depths and heights will be covered in Chapter 5 – Tidal heights.

◆ Navigational marks

These are covered in Chapter 9 – Lights & buoyage.

◆ Source data

Parts of Admiralty Chart SC2613 were surveyed by lead lines as long ago as 1833 and some inshore areas frequently used by recreational craft on the eastern side of the Cherbourg Peninsula have not been surveyed since 1922 (see Figure 1.14.)

However, old lead line information from areas that change little over the years can be very reliable and survey ships tend to concentrate on portions of the coastline where there is continual shifting of the seabed.

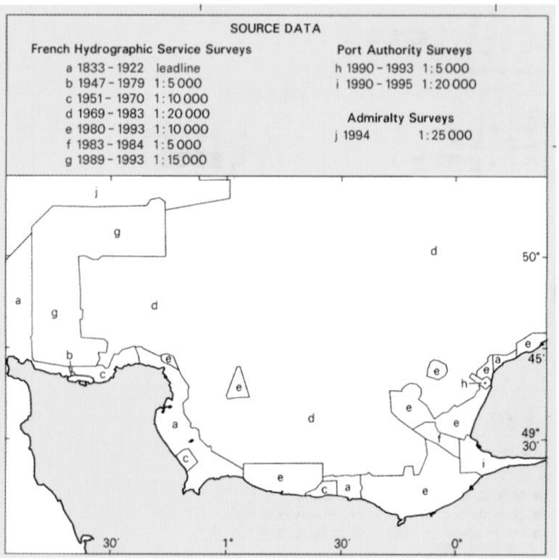

Fig 1.14 Source data diagram from Chart SC2613.

CORRECTING PAPER CHARTS

One great advantage of electronic charts is that keeping them up to date is fairly easy. However, if you are still doing it manually with pen and ink, then corrections can be downloaded free of charge from the Admiralty Leisure website which is part of the UKHO's main site at www.ukho.gov.uk, or found in some boating magazines.

The advice here is to do the corrections as often as possible. It can be daunting to spend an entire winter weekend ploughing through a whole year's worth of corrections. Often, when faced with such a prospect, the job does not get done.

Most of the small corrections are done with a fine pen in waterproof magenta ink and a stencil of chart symbols greatly assists neatness. For major changes, high-resolution blocks are supplied to perfect scale and are then glued to the chart to cover old information. Figure 1.15 shows one of these blocks and 1.16 a correction which would be done in ink. When the correction has been entered on the chart a note is made in the footer on the bottom left hand corner of the chart.

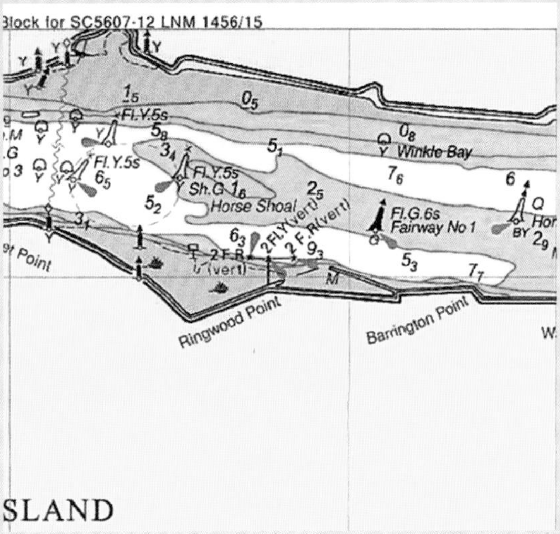

Fig 1.15 (right) Notice to mariners. A block for Chart SC 5607/12.

L1456/15 ENGLAND — East Coast — River Crouch — Wallasea Island N — Buoyage. Swinging circle.
Source: Crouch Harbour Authority

Chart: SC5607·12 (panel A, Rivers Crouch and Roach) ETRS89 DATUM
Insert the accompanying block, showing amendments to buoyage and swinging circle, centred on: 51° 36′ ·9N. , 0° 50′ ·8E.

Fig 1.16 Chart correction for Chart SC 5607/12.

ELECTRONIC CHART PLOTTERS

A few die-hards may still grumble that no good can possibly come from anything that relies on electricity but you only have to use a chart plotter for an afternoon to appreciate how useful and versatile they are. Not only are they here to stay but they are developing so fast that it is hard to keep up with the new developments – touch-screen, multifunction displays showing a chart, radar, AIS, thermal images and a fish finder. And if this were not enough we could add port information, aerial photos and tidal heights to the list.

If a simple chart plotter is a requirement, there are now many ways of displaying the information once the software has been bought from software houses such as Chersoft, Imray and Navionics. Laptops, tablets and mobile phones are all capable of doing the job – but some people like to see the bigger picture rather than fighting with a small mobile screen.

Fig 1.17 This wheelhouse installation is rugged and weatherproof with a chart plotter and a second multifunction screen.

◆ Dedicated chart plotter

This equipment is purpose built to withstand the rigours of marine life, and is usually robust and waterproof. It can be attached to a bulkhead near the yacht's chart table or close to the helm position. Plotters with large screens are very expensive and, although one gets used to the small-screen variety quite quickly there is a tendency to lose the overall picture of the route unless there is a paper chart close by for reference.

The software is supplied as **Firmware** as it is electronically installed before purchase but the chart software packs are an extra so that you can select your area of coverage. The plotter in the illustration Figure 1.18 is the Lowrance HDS5M.

Fig 1.18 Lowrance HDS5M.

◆ Laptop computer

More and more people are taking laptop computers to sea so that electronic charts may be displayed on the large screen rather than investing in a more expensive dedicated chart plotter. GPS data is easily fed in using a serial or USB port and, as a bonus, personal e-mail may also be collected with the aid of an iPhone.

Care needs to be taken to stow the computer in a dry place.

Fig 1.19 Laptop computer with Sea-Pro chart software.

◆ Electronic chart formats

Computerised charts are supplied in two different formats: **raster** and **vector**.

Raster charts A raster chart uses the same technology as your digital camera. It is nothing more than a photograph of the original chart with the picture broken down into millions of very small blocks called **pixels**, each of which can be portrayed in a vast number of colours. When the photograph is printed on paper at normal scale, the pixels are not apparent but when displayed on a computer screen at high magnification they are very obvious. Figure 1.20 shows a small area of chart sufficiently magnified to show the pixels.

The Admiralty were the trail blazers in electronic charting when they digitised their paper charts and launched the Admiralty Raster Chart Service towards the end of the last century. Displaying the charts took a lot of computer memory which was difficult at that stage of computer development. Manufacturers of dedicated chart plotters sought a different format that was not so power hungry and came up with the vector format.

Now that flash drives can store so much material in something smaller than a matchbox, the raster chart is still used for the electronic Admiralty Leisure charts which are most often displayed using laptops. Note that these charts are no longer available to buy.

Vector charts Whereas the pixel can be thought of as a complete piece of a very much bigger jigsaw puzzle, the analogy for the vector chart is more like one of those small children's books where turning each successive page takes you further into the rabbit warren giving you more and more detail as each layer is uncovered.

Making charts in this way is more complicated at the initial stage but they are more versatile than raster charts and a large number of folios may be stored on a small memory card. The format stores the chart as a series of co-ordinates for each line and groups the information such as coastline, depth contours, buoyage and light sectors which can be shown selectively. This data may be enlarged without degrading the picture – pixelation does not occur. It also allows the same information to be used to provide an audible alarm if the boat strays into areas that are considered too shallow for safety. It is for this reason that the IMO favour vector charts and since 2002, commercial ships using them have not been required to carry paper charts as a backup. Those using raster charts are not granted this privilege.

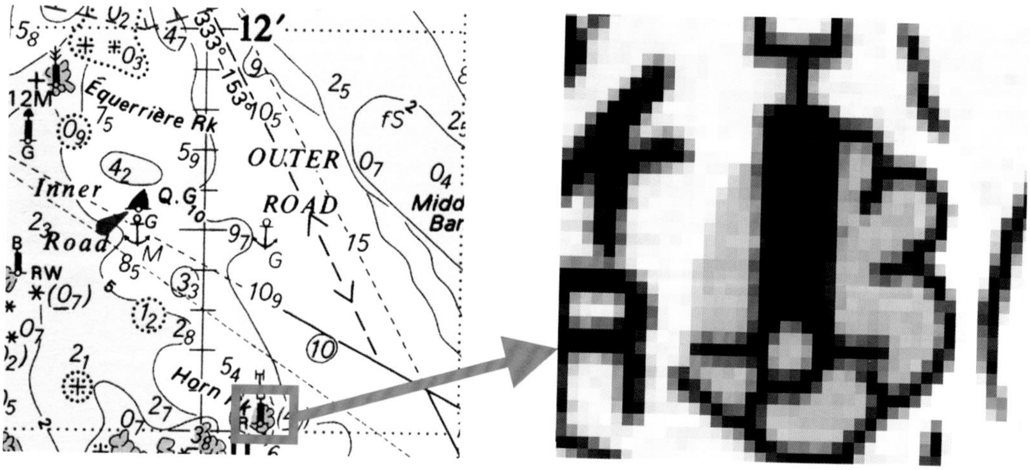

Fig 1.20 This simulation of a raster chart demonstrates the result of zooming in on the small area outlined in red. It is now possible to see the individual pixels which make up the picture.

Another advantage of vector is that when the display is set to small scale the screen is not cluttered with harbour information that is unnecessary when well offshore. As the coast is closed and larger scale is chosen, more detail is revealed.

The UK Hydrographic Office launched their worldwide vector chart service (AVCS) in 2008 for commercial shipping and defence agencies. These charts conform to IMO Rule S-57, the rule regarding the standard of charts for commercial shipping. Some leisure-market chart plotters use vector charts but do not comply with IMO regulations.

Fig 1.21 The C-Map NT software and chart package.

◆ Correcting electronic charts

Vector charts may be corrected but each software house uses a different method. Some offer free downloads on the Internet and C-Map cartridges need to be taken to a stockist for updating.

The Admiralty ARCS Skipper charts are no longer supported so corrections are not available.

MEASURING ANGLES ON A PAPER CHART

It is now time to draw some lines on a chart but first you must gather together the tools of a well-organised navigator. In addition to a chart you will require:

- **At least two soft 2B pencils** Soft pencils may give a dark line but it is very easy to erase after use and does not gouge lines in the surface of the paper. Charts are expensive and deserve to be looked after.
- **A good quality eraser** Plastic erasers are kindest to the chart. Those on the end of pencils are seldom adequate.
- **Pair of dividers** The dividers in Figure 1.22 are well constructed with an adjustment screw at the end and may be opened and shut using one hand. Straight ones that require two hands will be adequate but all dividers should have shafts of at least 20cm in order to be of use on most scales of chart.
- **A notebook** is essential, as scribbling in the margin of the chart does not give you credibility as a tidy navigator.
- **A pencil sharpener** 2B pencils get blunt very quickly.
- **A calculator** for the numerically challenged.
- **A plotting instrument** of your choice. The one shown in the illustration (Figure 1.22) is of the Breton type; it is ever popular because it is easy to use, has no protruding plastic arms to get

broken and any bearings that are set, when the central dial is turned, remain set until the dial is turned again. We will see how the plotter may be used to:

– **Measure the angle of a line drawn on the chart.**

– **Draw a line for a given angle.**

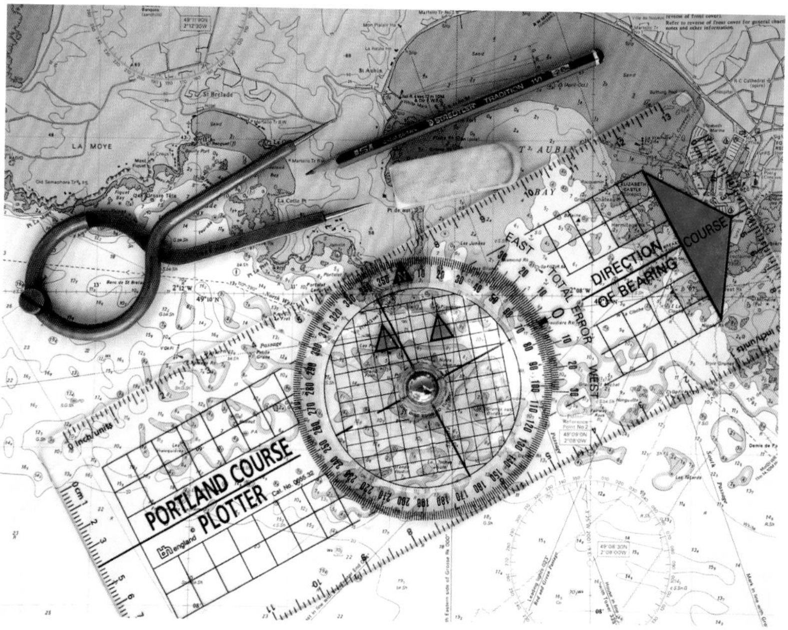

Fig 1.22 Chart and plotting equipment.

CHART SYMBOLS

Just like land maps, marine charts use symbols and abbreviations to describe features at sea, on the shore, navigational buoys and lights. Individual chart publishers are not bound to follow the International Maritime Organisation's (IMO) recommended symbols but most of the non-standard ones used are intuitive and easily understood.

The UKHO print a splendid chart booklet 5011 containing all the symbols used on their charts and all the more important ones are illustrated in Figure 1.27 (page 14).

This is a 'must have' book and deserves to be kept in the chart table so that it can readily be consulted when an unknown hieroglyphic is found on the chart. It would be impossible to memorise every symbol in the book but it would be prudent to learn those for rocks and wrecks and any hazards that have the potential to take the bottom out of your boat!

USING THE PORTLAND PLOTTER

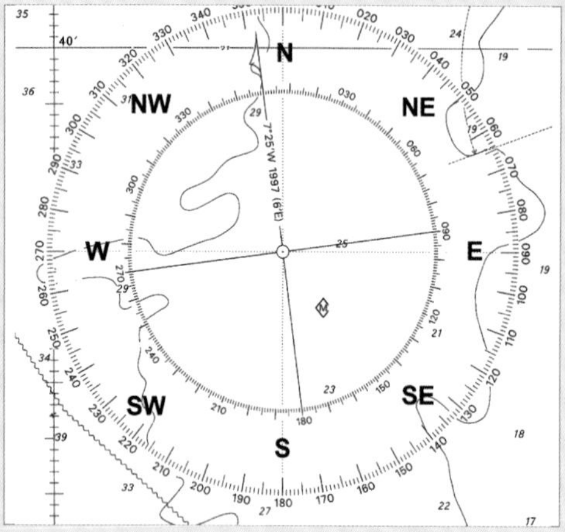

Fig 1.23 Compass rose on chart. Annotated with points of the compass.

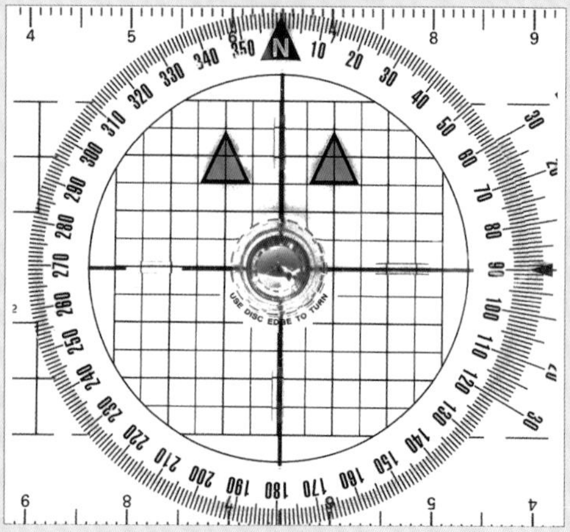
Fig 1.24 Compass rose on plotter.

Each chart is printed with a device for measuring angles called a **compass rose** which is illustrated in Figure 1.23. In fact, there are usually two or three compass roses dotted over the chart but they are not always exactly where they are needed. The plotter (not to be confused with the electronic box of the same name) simulates the compass rose but can be moved around the chart and placed where it is required (Figure 1.24).

Using the Portland Plotter to determine the angle of a drawn line.

The order of working which follows is shown in Figure 1.25:

1 A line running from south-west to north-east is drawn close to the Island of Alderney and the plotter is held firmly on the line.
2 The plotter is placed in such a way that the **large green arrow**, labelled **COURSE**, is pointing in the direction of travel.
3 The rotating compass rose is aligned with the **two small green arrows** pointing towards the top of the chart ie north. This can be achieved by aligning the grid lines on the rotating rose with lines of latitude and longitude on the chart (highlighted in red in the illustration).
4 Finally read off a bearing of 063° from the rose.

Using the Portland Plotter to plot a given angle

In the last example we laid the plotter along the drawn line and swivelled the dial until it was in line with lines on the chart.

This time we are going to set an angle on the dial and swivel the body of the plotter to do the lining up. Figure 1.26 shows the steps.

1 Set the angle you require, in this case 063°, in line with the zero mark on the plotter. We will not be moving the dial again.
2 Place the plotter so that the **large green arrow** points approximately north-east (the angle 063° is close to north-east on the compass rose).

3 Move the whole plotter so that the long edge is over the position where you wish to draw the line making sure that the **small green arrows** point towards the north.
4 Still moving the body of the plotter, not the dial, make last small adjustments to bring the grid on the dial to line up with horizontal or vertical lines on the chart.
5 Check that the edge is still over the start position.
6 To finish the job, draw the line.

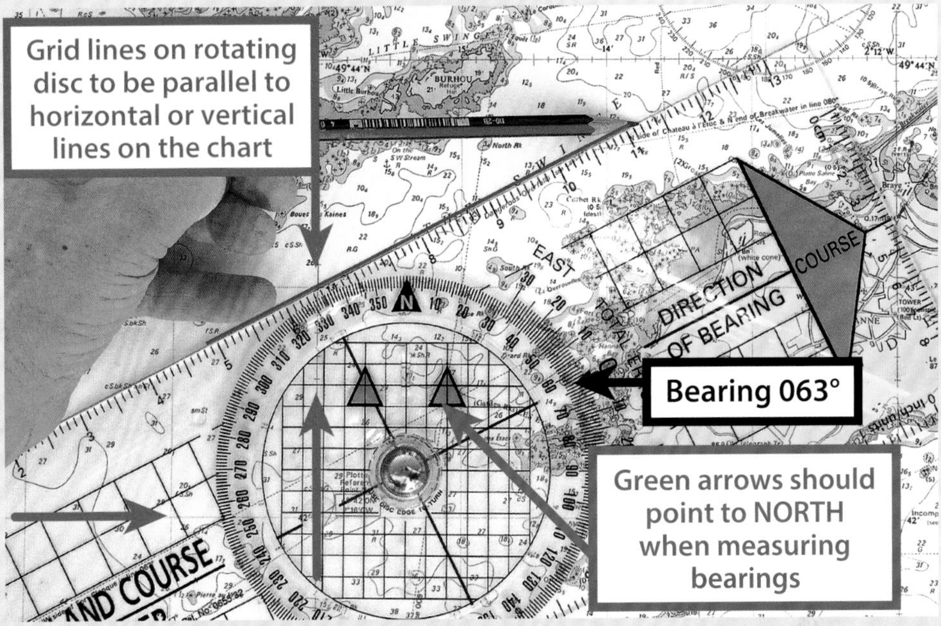

Fig 1.25 Determining the angle of a line drawn on the chart.

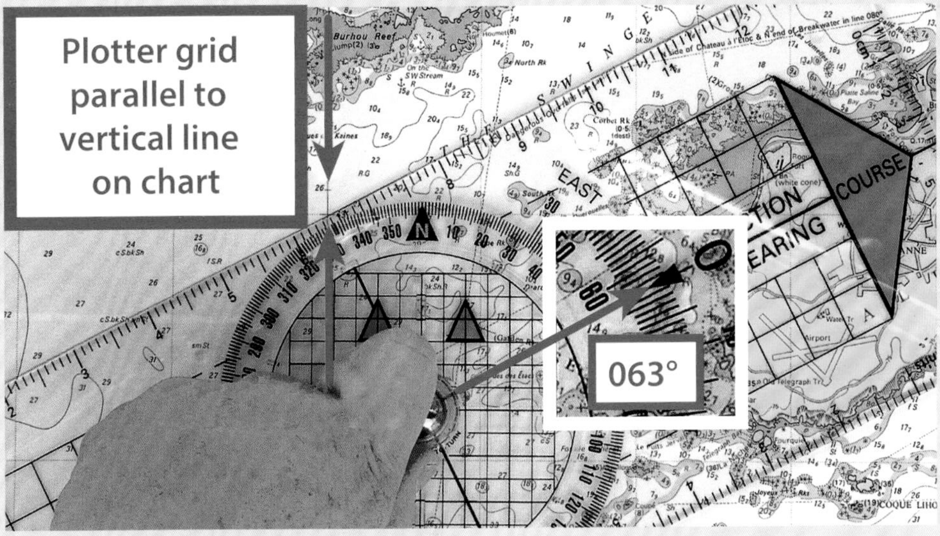

Fig 1.26 The angle 063° is set on the dial then the main body of the plotter is moved to align the grid with the vertical line of longitude on the chart.

Symbols and abbreviations used on charts

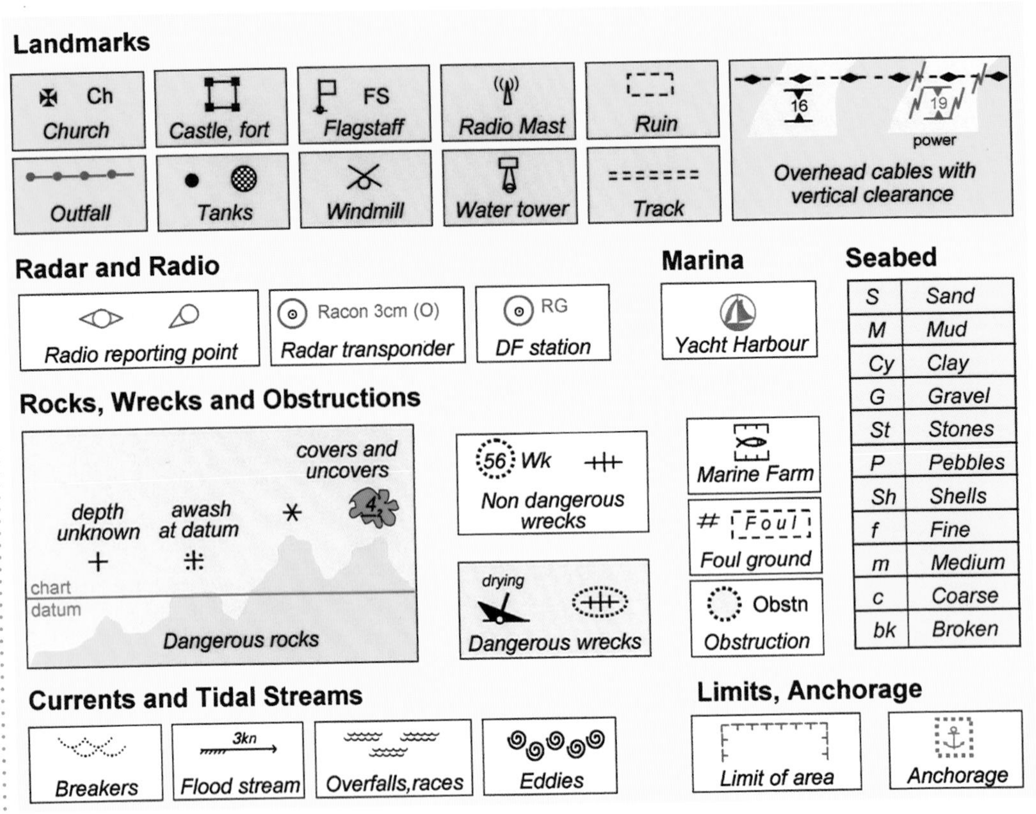

Fig 1.27 Some commonly used chart symbols.

OTHER PUBLICATIONS

◆ Yachtsman's Almanacs

Almanacs like the one in Figure 1.28 are published specifically for skippers of small craft and are jam-packed with information including tide tables, waypoints, tidal stream atlases and port information for harbours in much of northern Europe. Whatever the query, the answer is usually tucked away somewhere in the book. It is a large book, admittedly, but still takes up less space than a pile of individual books covering the same subjects.

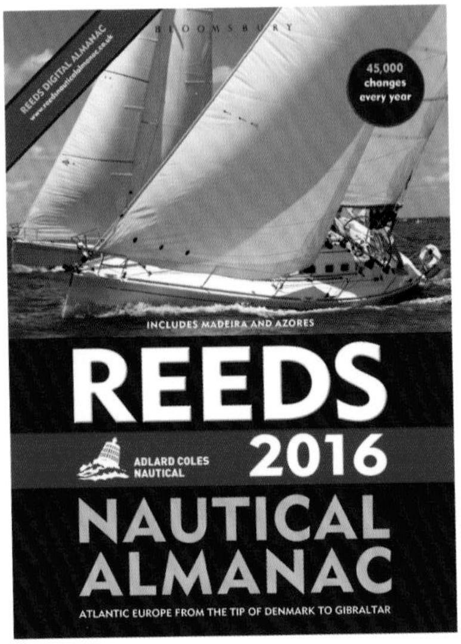

Fig 1.28 *Reeds Nautical Almanac.*

◆ Pilot books

Pilot books (Figure 1.29) are most useful when they give a large scale harbour plan and an aerial photograph to go with it. Most give historical information and advice on the best places to visit and also good details of hazards en route to the port. Content varies from book to book so browse the chandlery bookshelf until you find a suitable one.

Fig 1.29 A selection of popular pilot books.

QUESTION PAPER 1 – CHARTS & POSITIONS

1.1 Why is the transverse Mercator projection used for harbour plans?

1.2 In which publication would you expect to find a full list of all chart symbols used on UKHO charts?

1.3 What is now the international standard horizontal datum for charts?

1.4 What are the main differences between raster and vector charts?

Answers at the back of the book

2 THE COMPASS

A GOOD COMPASS is top of a navigator's wish list. Used in conjunction with the distance log and tidal stream information, a compass is paramount if the boat is to arrive at the correct destination.

Since the Vikings began to use lodestone, or magnetite, to navigate worldwide, magnetic compasses have been using the Earth's magnetic field to determine direction. The majority of small sailing and motor boats still use this type of compass and, in addition to the main steering compass, will also carry a small portable one for fixing and collision avoidance and an electronic (fluxgate) compass for autopilots and radar. Apart from the fluxgate compass, they use the principal that a free swinging magnet will turn to point to magnetic north.

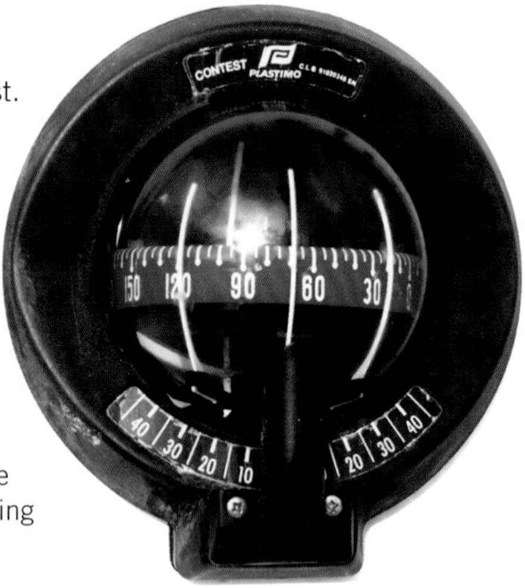

Fig 2.1 The Plastimo Contest porthole compass.

STEERING COMPASS

The instrument consists of a bowl, part of which is transparent, filled with liquid and containing a graduated card mounted on a pivot. Attached to the compass card are either several magnets or one shaped in a ring. The graduations on the card may vary; on older types the cardinal points (**North**, **East**, **South** and **West**) are marked but it is now more usual to divide the card into 360° as shown on the porthole compass in Figure 2.1. The lines marked on the fixed part of the compass are lubber lines and, for accuracy, the centre one must lie on the fore-and-aft line of the vessel.

The porthole compass is designed for sailing yachts fitted with a tiller and is one of a pair mounted through the bulkhead on either side of the cockpit. One or the other can be viewed from a level position whichever tack the yacht is on. When the course is altered the boat swings around the compass; the card itself does not move.

Larger sailing yachts and motor cruisers with wheel steering have the steering compass mounted in a special housing directly forward of the wheel as in Figure 2.2.

Fast motor boats require a compass that is well damped so that the card will not spin when the boat turns quickly or pitches bow-down into a wave; those intending to embark on a voyage to the southern hemisphere will need to fit a compass that is balanced to

Fig 2.2 A binnacle-mounted compass used in a boat with wheel steering.

compensate for 'dip' – the downward magnetic force that would otherwise cause the card to tilt at locations south of the Equator.

As most boats are designed for, or supplied with, a steering compass there is seldom any choice where it is sited. For preference it should be where it can best be seen without parallax and where it cannot easily be damaged.

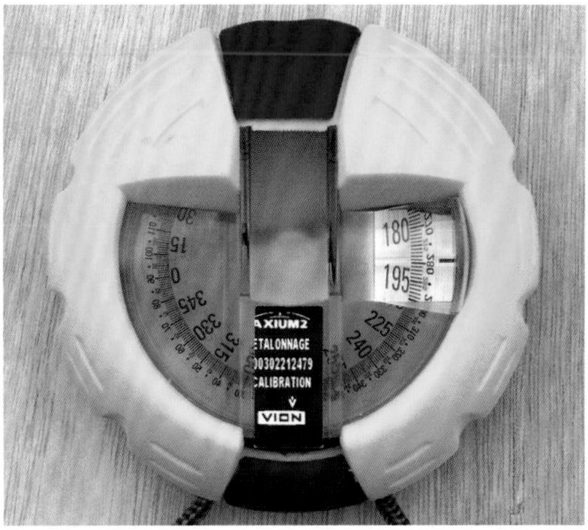

Fig 2.3 This hand bearing compass is protected with a rubber ring and sited on infinity.

HAND BEARING COMPASS

A portable compass may be used for taking bearings of ships to ascertain whether a risk of collision exists, for fixing the boat's position and for clearing dangers.

The most useful type is protected by a rubber cover and well damped. A lanyard is attached so it can be worn round the neck for safe keeping and it is fitted with an infinity prism which makes sighting easier. The mini compass shown in Figure 2.3 has a phosphorescent lighting system that is charged by exposure to strong light.

THE FLUXGATE OR ELECTRONIC COMPASS

A fluxgate compass can sense the direction of magnetic north without any moving parts. The small sensor unit uses at least two coils of wire surrounding magnetic material to sense the direction of the Earth's magnetic field. The unit, two examples of which are shown in Figures 2.4 and 2.5, should be mounted amidships and as close to the centreline of the boat as possible. Heading information is sent in electronic form to instruments such as radar, chart plotter and wind instruments. Once installed, it requires calibration so that it automatically compensates for the boat's own magnetic signature, *deviation*.

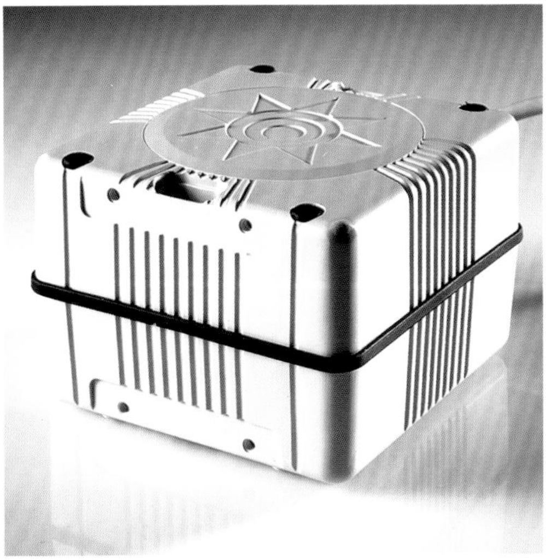

Fig 2.4 The Simrad fluxgate compass sensor.

Fig 2.5 The workings of the Raymarine fluxgate compass.

VARIATION

Both magnetic and fluxgate compasses sense the magnetic north pole, which is approximately 500 miles away from the geographical pole. Unfortunately, the magnetic pole moves each year so our compass needle points to a moving target! The Canadians have been responsible for tracking its position as until recently the pole has lain in their Arctic Territory. Since 2010 the annual change has increased considerably and in 2015 the pole was plotted at 86.3° 160.0°W.

It would be very inconvenient if charts were aligned to magnetic north and had to be reprinted every year as the pole moves and it is for this reason that a static reference point is used for charts – **True north**.

The angular difference between True and **Magnetic north** is called **variation**. Figure 2.6 shows how this angle alters at different locations on Earth. For example:

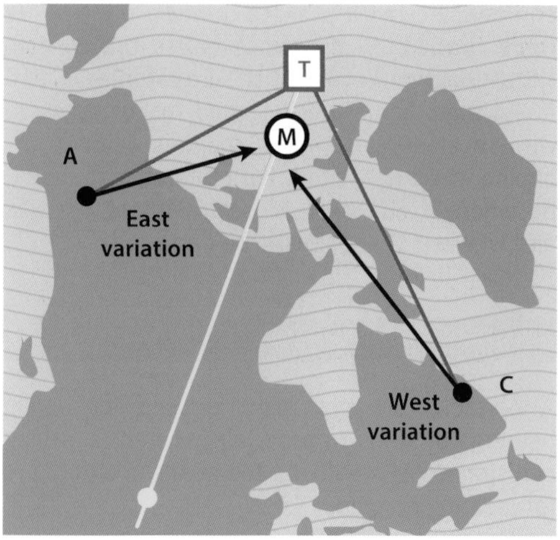

Fig 2.6 Variation. At point A the Magnetic pole is to the EAST of True, at point C it is to the WEST and at B there is no variation.

- From observer point A the Magnetic pole lies to the east of True north.
- At point B True and Magnetic north are directly in line so there is no variation.
- At point C Magnetic north lies to the west of True north.

As a consequence, any reading taken from a compass needs to be corrected before a line is drawn on the chart; the relevant correction is printed on each chart in the middle of the compass rose.

Figure 2.7 shows a correction for 2015 but we shall assume that it is now 2017. In the two-year interval the variation will have decreased by 16 minutes so the new value is 2° 09'W. For all practical purposes we can round down to the nearest whole degree and use 2°W.

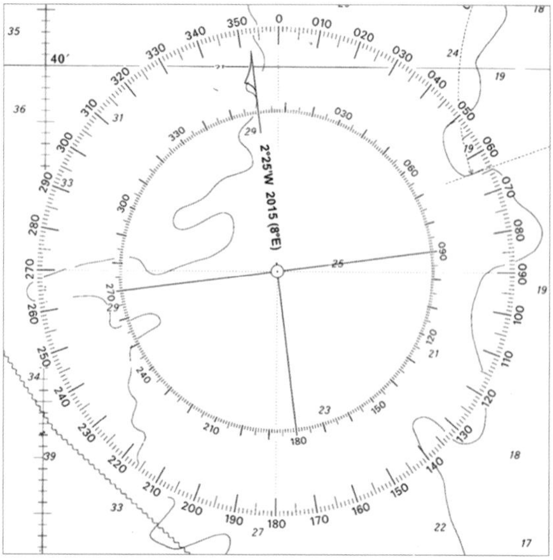

Fig 2.7 A compass rose can be found in various positions on navigational charts. The variation is shown for the year 2015 and is decreasing by eight minutes per annum (8'E).

◆ Correcting for variation

When the helmsman tells us what course he has been steering, we need to convert it from a **Magnetic** bearing before it is plotted as **True** on the chart.

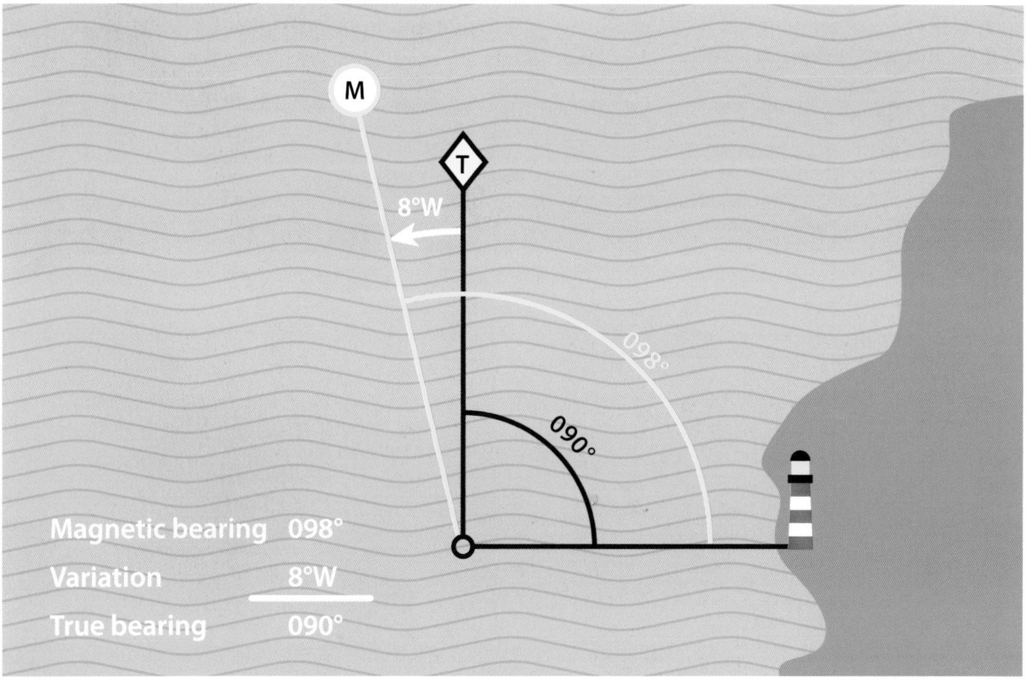

Fig 2.8 The variation is 8° W so the compass will measure an angle larger than the one entered on the chart.

Figure 2.8 shows a variation of 8° W. The compass measures the larger bearing so we need to SUBTRACT 8° to convert it to True.

To reverse the process and convert **True** to **Magnetic** we ADD the 8° W.
There are cunning rhymes to help you remember whether to add or subtract:

If the error is WEST then the compass reads best (greater)
If the error is EAST the compass will read least
or
C A D E T: Compass – Add East – True

DEVIATION

Unfortunately, the ship's compass is also to some extent affected by any magnetic materials in the boat itself. When engines are manufactured the parts are turned on a lathe and this magnetises component parts; ferrous metal, loudspeakers, analogue instruments, electric motors and electrical wiring are all either magnets in their own right or can generate magnetic fields. Any of these placed too close to the compass can cause it to be **deviated**.

The compass in Fig 2.10 was deviated by no less than 60° when a mild steel screwdriver was placed close by. Using the binnacle frame as a safe resting place for a mobile phone could make the difference between arriving in Le Havre or Cherbourg!

Loudspeakers carry large magnets and should be sited well away from the compass.

A VHF radio antenna cable installed near the autopilot and transmitting on 25 watts is sufficient to drive the craft around in circles.

Fig 2.9 The compass reading accurately.

Fig 2.10 This compass has been deviated 60° by the tool.

Compasses require a light for night passages and if DC current is used it is important that the twin wires to the bulb are twisted to reduce unwanted magnetic influence on the compass.

Minimise compass errors by making sure that all equipment likely to cause deviation is installed according to the manufacturer's instructions; most recommend at least one metre from any compass, be it magnetic or electronic. If deviation is found after all precautions have been taken it is often possible to reduce errors by placing small correcting magnets at the base of the compass. However, this is not a job for amateurs and a compass adjuster should be employed to do this specialist job which, in the hands of an expert, is usually completed in a surprisingly short time and at reasonable cost. With a fibreglass boat he will often be able to reduce the deviation to a negligible amount but it is a lot more difficult with a steel or ferro-cement hull.

Before calling on this expert we can easily check whether there is substantial deviation.

◆ Deviation check

Leading lines (objects in line/transit) Most harbour authorities use conspicuous shoreside features to lead seafarers safely into the haven. By day it is necessary to steer a course to keep two of the objects in line to avoid dangers as in Figure 2.11. Provided that there is a slack tidal stream and no cross wind the leading line may be used to check the compass. The true bearing is always written on the chart so it will be possible to calculate what the magnetic bearing should be as you enter the harbour. If this is compared with the actual reading on the compass then deviation can be calculated.

Example using Fig. 2.11 As we enter this small harbour for the night, we notice that the steering compass reads 323°M when the leading lights are in line.

The chart gives the True bearing as:	315°
Magnetic variation is given as:	+ 4° W
Add west variation:	319° M
Compass reads:	323°
Therefore there is an error of:	**4° W**

Later in the chapter we will look further into the calculations for deviation.

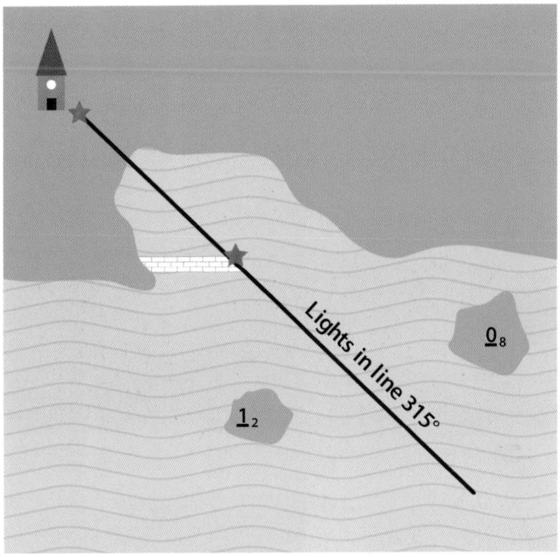

Fig 2.11 Leading lights into a harbour.

Hand bearing compass error It is impossible to accurately estimate the deviation suffered by a hand bearing compass as it is easily moved closer to, or away from, magnetic influences. If deployed away from the cockpit and the stern (where there could be an outboard motor with a strong magnetic field) it can be used to check for deviation on the steering compass.

Forward of the non-ferrous mast and rigging, but away from cables inside the mast and anchor chain at the bow, is an ideal place to be positioned.

Steering compass deviation can be checked with the GPS by comparing the course over ground in still water with the compass heading. The hand bearing compass can also be used in the same way but the GPS will be more reliable.

◆ Correcting for deviation

Deviation does not remain constant – it changes with an alteration of heading, causing the compass needle to be deviated either east or west. It is therefore necessary to check the compass on a number of different headings. Using the same leading line and a bearing astern would give us an additional check.

A compass adjuster will use known transits to check for error on numerous headings then supply a deviation card which shows the corrections to be applied on each heading. Figure 2.12 shows a card which will be used to answer questions at the end of the chapter.

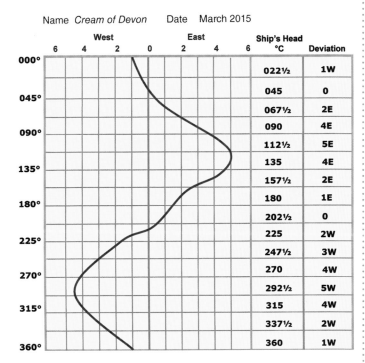

Name *Cream of Devon* Date March 2015

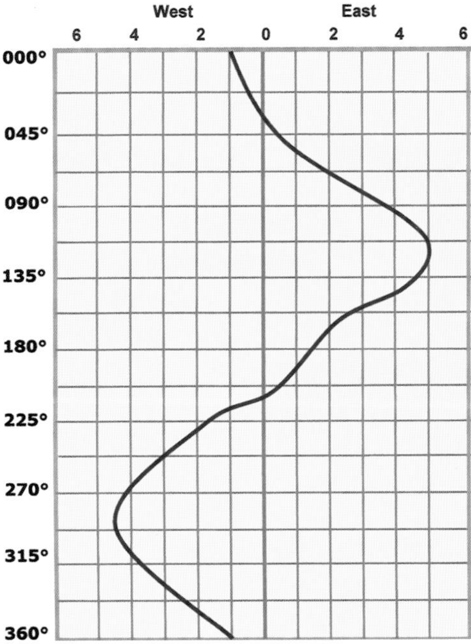

Ship's Head °C	Deviation
022½	1W
045	0
067½	2E
090	4E
112½	5E
135	4E
157½	2E
180	1E
202½	0
225	2W
247½	3W
270	4W
292½	5W
315	4W
337½	2W
360	1W

Fig 2.12 The deviation card for *Cream of Devon*.

MAGNETIC ANOMALIES

In some areas, a magnetic substance, such as an iron ore deposit, can occur quite naturally on the seabed; the Plateau de Roches Douvres on the north coast of Brittany is a good example (Figure 2.13).

This material can influence compass readings on the surface and where there are known errors, a note is made on the chart by the hydrographer. There is no correction for them – just be aware that the compass may be deviated. This may be particularly important when in close pilotage situations.

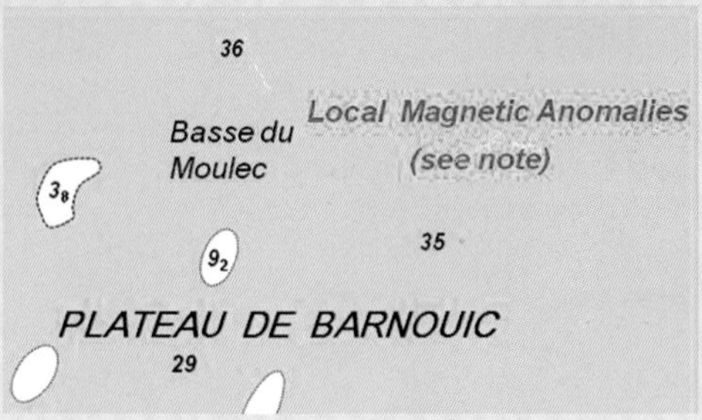

Fig 2.13 Magnetic anomaly near North Brittany.

APPLYING VARIATION AND DEVIATION

Variation and deviation are both applied in the same way so the aides-mémoires: **Error west – compass best. Error east – compass least** and **CadET** can both be used. It must be remembered that deviation varies with the ship's heading so there is a very definite order in which the calculation has to be worked.

◆ Converting True to Compass

Suppose for example, we used the chart to work out the True course to a harbour entrance and wanted to give our helmsman the compass course to steer. We must convert it to a magnetic heading (variation is 4°W) before correcting for deviation. The order of working is:

True (°T) +W/- E Variation = Magnetic (°M) +W/– E Deviation = Compass (°C)

A quick memory jogger for this is:

True **V**irgins **M**ake **D**ull **C**ompany

If the arithmetic is laid out in a logical order it is easier to follow:

True course	065° (T)
Variation (+ W)	4° W
Magnetic Course	069° (M)
Deviation from Fig. 2.12	2° E
Course to steer (- E)	**067°(C)**

Because the magnetic errors in this calculation are small it would still be reasonably accurate to combine them with a little mental arithmetic. For example: plus 4° W minus 2° E = 2° W.

◆ Converting from Compass to True

Still using 4°W variation, if the course we have steered needs to be plotted on the chart the order of working is reversed.

Compass (°C) +E/-W Deviation = Magnetic (°M) +E/-W Variation = True (°T)
The aide-mémoire now reads:
Cadbury's **D**airy **M**ilk **V**ery **T**asty

Compass course	250° (C)
Deviation	- 3° W
Magnetic	247° (M)
Variation	– 4° W
True course	**243° (T)**

HEELING ERROR

A change in deviation may occur when a yacht is heeled. This is due to the fact that features such as the cast iron keel and metal engine take on a different position relative to the compass. The error will also be different on each tack so it is extremely difficult to calibrate the error accurately.

Comparison between steering and hand bearing compass readings will give a ball park figure and when approaching harbour well heeled, a known transit can be used to compare the main compass heading with data on the chart. Make sure that the results are noted in the ship's log book or on the bottom of the deviation card.

QUESTION PAPER 2 – THE COMPASS

2.1 You wish to find out the variation for a specific area. Where would you look?

2.2 Where should an electronic compass sensor be installed?

2.3 Convert the following True courses to Magnetic

- **a** 178°T Var. 3°W
- **b** 345°T Var. 7°W
- **c** 245°T Var. 5°E
- **d** 002°T Var. 9°E

2.4 Convert the following Magnetic courses to True:

- **a** 086°M Var. 4°W
- **b** 235°M Var. 10°E
- **c** 358°M Var. 6°E
- **d** 000°M Var. 3°W

2.5 Are electronic compasses affected by deviation?

2.6 Using the deviation card in Figure 2.11, what are the Magnetic courses for the following?

- **a** 038°C
- **b** 000°C
- **c** 242°C
- **d** 190°C

Answers at the back of the book

3 ELECTRONICS

THE GLOBAL POSITIONING SYSTEM

YOU MAY TRAVEL BY CAR, PLANE OR FERRY but whichever method you choose GPS will have had an influence on them all. Even the wheat for the cereal you ate for breakfast will have been cut by combine harvesters guided by this amazing navigation system.

Before we learn about its many functions we will first take a look at the satellites which make it all possible.

◆ The Satellites

Since the first Navstar GPS satellites were launched in 1978 by the US Military, a series of further improved ones have been sent into space to replace older failing ones. In March 2015 there were 31 active satellites with further ones held in reserve.

The satellites are spaced so that at least four are visible to a receiver anywhere on the Earth at any time. Using a super accurate atomic clock, the satellites transmit perfectly synchronised time data which enables GPS receivers to calculate the distance to each visible satellite. These distances are received as ranges which give a 'circle of position' on the Earth's surface. Using the data from more than one satellite will give a number of spherical position lines and the boat will be positioned where these lines intersect (Figure 3.2). A very accurate position can be calculated using data from up to 12 satellites.

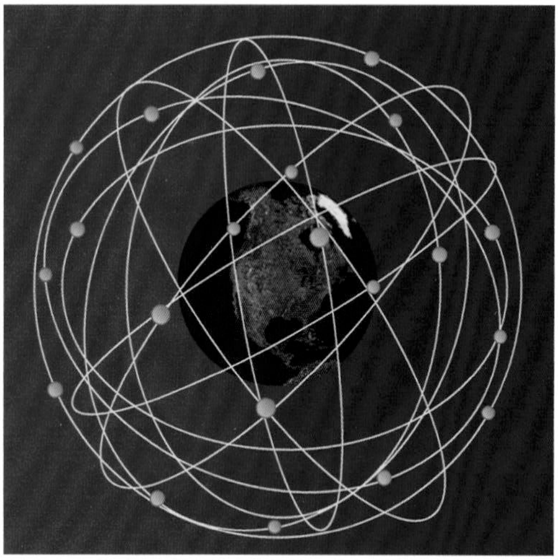

Fig 3.1 A network of orbiting satellites provide accurate positioning on the Earth's surface.

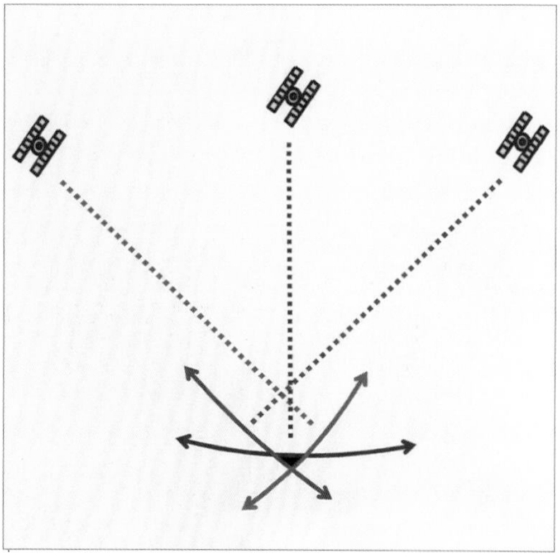

Fig 3.2 A fix obtained from three satellites.

◆ GPS Receivers

Fig 3.3 (left) Garmin Montana rugged GPS available with Blue Chart marine charts.

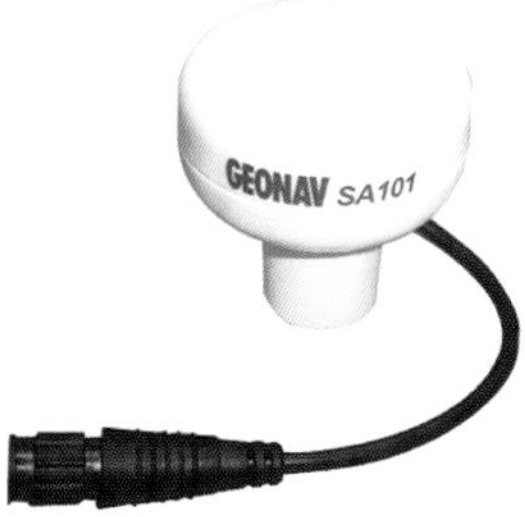

Fig 3.4 (below) GPS antenna.

GPS receivers come in all shapes and sizes, those for marine use being either handheld or fixed. Some give a simple numerical display but most now incorporate a chart plotter. Both fixed and handheld digital selective calling VHF radios also have inbuilt GPS.

Fixed installations will require a reliable power source and a dedicated GPS antenna similar to the one in Figure 3.4. The antenna should be mounted low down, away from damage and with a clear view of the sky – many are installed on the stern pulpit rail. Antennas mounted on top of the mast can suffer course and speed over ground errors due to excessive movement at the top of the mast.

SATELLITE BASED AUGMENTATION SYSTEMS – WAAS AND EGNOS

When the Global Positioning System was first introduced by the USA, it gave an accuracy of about 15 metres for 95% of the time. While this level of accuracy was acceptable for offshore shipping, it was not suitable for landing commercial aircraft safely in poor visibility. As a result, a method was devised for refining the given GPS positions by using a network of ground stations and satellites to provide GPS signal corrections. This system is known as the Wide Area Augmentation System (WAAS) which claims a position accuracy of 3 metres 95% of the time.

When the European Space Agency introduced its own system, Galileo, it was decided that it would be under civilian control so that it could not be switched off or downgraded in the event of war. As of April 2015 there are eight of the intended 30 satellites in orbit.

Galileo also has a position correction service, the European Geo-stationary Navigation Overlay Service (EGNOS), which uses the ground station/satellite combination which is currently giving an accurate position to between 10 and 15 metres. When all 30 satellites are in orbit, this will be reduced to mere centimetres.

All the main players in the marine chart plotter industry are producing equipment that uses WAAS, EGNOS and a Japanese system, MSAS.

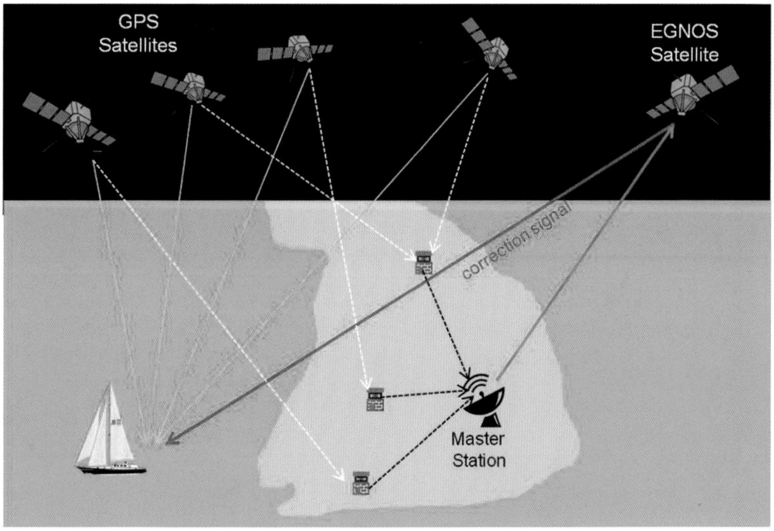

Fig 3.5 The EGNOS satellite correcting the GPS signals to obtain greater accuracy of position.

GPS FUNCTIONS

A GPS receiver can use the series of accurate positions it is given to perform certain tasks. Most mariners will have bought the set because they do not want to get lost on the open sea when out of sight of land, so we will look at position fixing first.

◆ Latitude and Longitude

As mentioned in Chapter 1, portable GPS sets and chart plotters use WGS84 as the default datum. Positions are given to two or three decimal places as shown in Figure 3.6. Note that this is a chart of the Harwich area which is east of the Greenwich Prime Meridian.

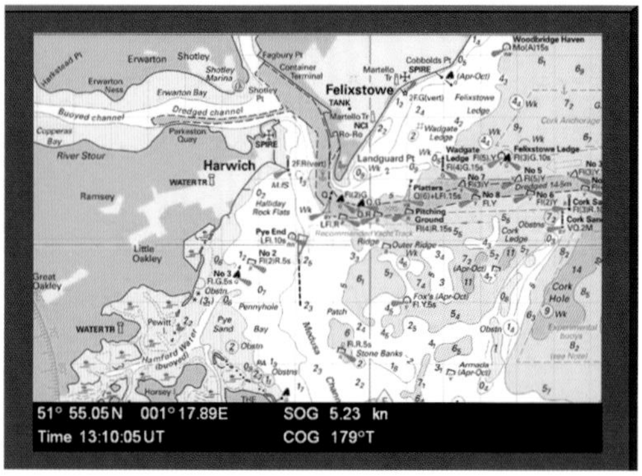

Fig 3.6 Chart plotter using Imray charts.

◆ Speed Over Ground (SOG) and Course Over Ground (COG)

As the GPS fixes the boat's position every few seconds it is possible for it to quickly compute the SOG and also the course it has followed. In Figure 3.6, the red triangle shows the boat's position, and the dotted line ahead of the vessel is a projection of its future COG provided that the course steered, speed through the water and tidal stream remain constant.

◆ Waypoints and Routes

State-of-the-art GPS sets and chart plotters are capable of storing thousands of positions which could be used as turning points when you are planning routes to a known destination. The set will always give the bearing and distance TO a chosen waypoint and how long it will take to get there; Figure 3.7 shows that waypoint 1 is 3.42 miles away and that it will take 36 minutes to arrive there. The waypoint has been placed to one side of the buoy in order to avoid anyone's hitting the buoy in fog! Note that the bearing to the waypoint is the same as the COG which means that the vessel is following the route exactly.

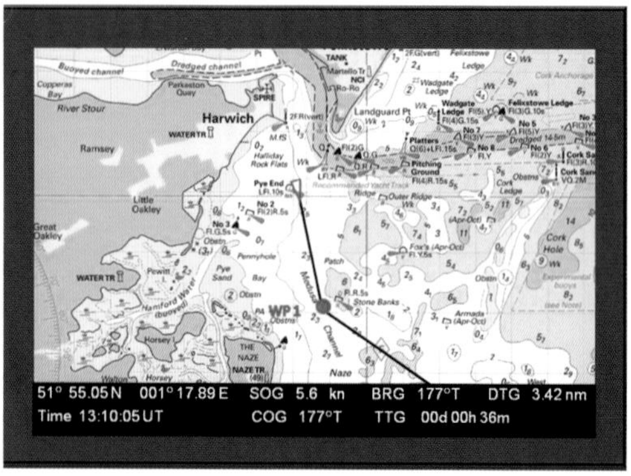

Fig 3.7 A waypoint entered as a turning point in a calculated route is known as 'a route point'.

◆ Man Overboard

Most sets have a MOB button that can be pressed if one of the crew falls in the water. A position is automatically set and the bearing and distance to that waypoint is displayed on the screen. No allowance is made for tidal set and drift but it makes it possible for the navigator to work out the casualty's position at any time.

◆ Cross Track Error (XTE)

Cross track error is another feature. It shows the distance the boat is off its intended course over the ground and the bearing to the waypoint. In Figure 3.8 the boat needs to alter course to port to bring the boat back to the intended track.

Fig 3.8 The boat is 0.4 miles off track.

If the bearing to waypoint were the same as the 'track' then the boat would be on the intended course over the ground.

SPEED AND DISTANCE LOGS

◆ Paddle wheel

When you take over any charter boat you can be almost sure that it will be fitted with a paddle wheel log.

The log is normally mounted just forward of the keel and consists of a small paddle wheel mounted at the end of a cylindrical probe. This then passes through the hull in a tube that is about 3cm in diameter. One of the paddle wheel blades is fitted with a magnet (Figure 3.9), which produces an electrical pulse each time the wheel revolves. This pulse is used to calculate the distance run and, by adding time, the log can display the speed.

Fig 3.9 Through-hull speed and distance transducer

The principle is simple but these logs require calibration for accuracy and they need to be cleaned regularly to keep the wheel turning. The probe should be withdrawn into the boat when the boat is in harbour so that seaweed and orange jelly-like substances do not grow on the paddle. Some newer systems provide an automatic shutter which blanks off the hole when the probe is withdrawn for cleaning which prevents water going into the bilge (and up your shirt sleeve).

◆ Log calibration

A hull-mounted log is affected both by the shape of the underwater hull and any build-up of weed on the hull and log impeller. Rough seas may cause the hull to occasionally lift out of the water and this will affect the accuracy of the log reading. It is therefore necessary to calibrate the log on first fitting and at intervals thereafter. The manufacturer of the equipment will have provided details indicating how an electronic correction can be applied to the log.

A few local maritime authorities provide measured distances ashore for this purpose. They normally consist of two pairs of transits, one on the shoreline, the second a hundred metres or so inland with a distance of one mile between the pairs. These will be marked on the chart as a *measured distance* and will indicate the correct course to steer.

In still water the procedure is simple. Settle the boat at a steady speed on the course specified. Note the time when crossing the first transit and record the log speed at intervals of about 15 seconds. Note the time when crossing the second transit. Average the indicated speed-readings. Calculate the true speed:

Speed in knots = Distance in miles ÷ Time in hours

Compare this with the average indicated speed and adjust the log accordingly.

Unfortunately, the water doesn't remain still for any period of time when in tidal waters so it is normally necessary to allow for the tidal stream. To do this, two runs in opposite directions have to be made at a time when the stream is running at a steady rate.

Using the above formula calculate the true speed over the ground for each run then add the two resultant speeds together and divide by two to find the average speed. Compare this with the average of the displayed readings that were taken every 15 seconds and correct the log.

A common mistake that is often made is to add the *times* for the two runs together and use this to calculate the speed over a two-mile distance – this gives an incorrect result. The calculation for each run must be made separately and the two *speeds* averaged to give the correct answer.

Alternatively, the log can be checked by comparing GPS fixes with estimated positions that have been worked up during a longer passage.

DEPTH SOUNDERS

A simple depth sounder works by sending out a single pulse downwards to the seabed, then timing how long it takes for the sound to be reflected back to the instrument. The result of its labours is displayed on a dedicated instrument as shown in Figure 3.10. The best return of signal is from hard sand or rock and the worst from soft mud when the pulse can penetrate down into the ooze. When close to a ship's wake where there are a large number of bubbles present the display may not give a depth reading at all.

The new generation of sounders use two frequencies to give much greater clarity to images which are displayed on multi-function screens. It is possible to pick out the shape of small fish and determine the orientation of wrecks, as shown in Figure 3.11. This is called CHIRP sonar and some of the more advanced equipment also sends a pulse sideways to give a 3D effect to the extremities of a channel.

Figure 3.12 demonstrates the clarity that can be achieved using a sideways pulse.

Fig 3.10 Simrad depth sounder display.

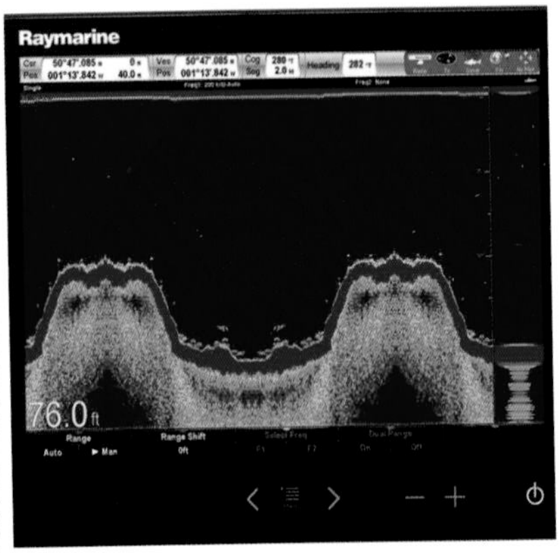

Fig 3.11 Display of a Raymarine instrument using CHIRP sonar.

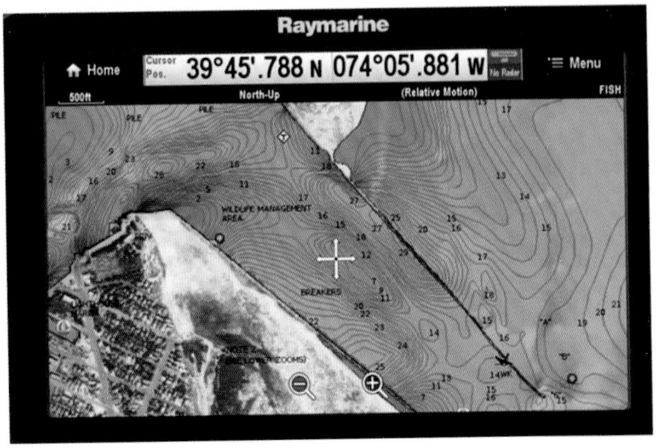

Fig 3.12 Pilotage into this harbour would be easy using this much detail.

◆ Offset

As supplied, the sounder will display depth below the transducer, which may be more than a metre below the waterline. Most sounders have an offset adjustment so that the depth can be displayed as *below the keel* or *below the waterline*. The setting is a matter of personal preference but for some illogical reason it always seems preferable to run aground when the sounder reads zero rather than have it happen unexpectedly when it reads 1.2m, which is the depth below the transducer!

◆ Deep and shallow alarms

Many sounders can be set to ring a strident alarm when the depth reaches a minimum acceptable level. Again, the safety margin is set at the skipper's discretion and will probably depend on the nature of the seabed. Deep alarms are particularly useful for pilotage in restricted visibility when it is the aim to remain in shallow water to avoid commercial shipping (Figure 3.13). Both shallow and deep alarms can be used to check that the boat has not drifted off station whilst anchored overnight. Figure 3.13 shows deep and shallow alarms on a Simrad sounder.

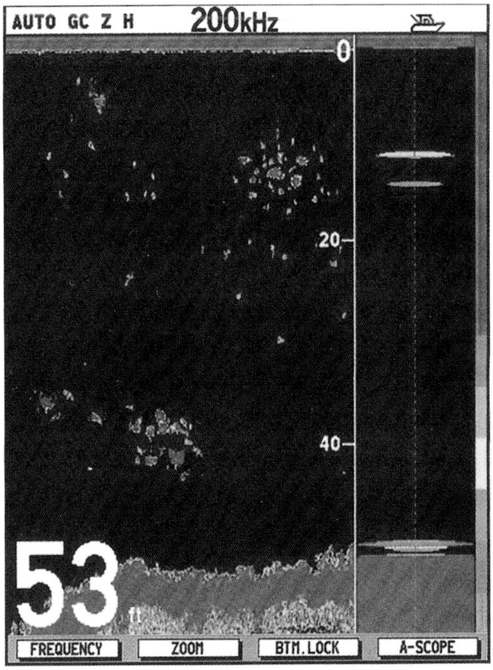

Fig 3.13 Depth sounder showing a depth of 53ft with shoals of fish clearly visible at 15ft and 40ft.

RADAR

Many will argue that radar is more useful than GPS as it may be used for navigation, position fixing and collision avoidance. In the last few years radar has become more attractive to the small boat owner as sets use flat screen colour technology, take up less space and are not so power-hungry. Radar images may be overlaid onto an electronic chart and an automatic radar plotting aid can monitor whether a risk of collision exists with other vessels. Many sailing yachts are now fitted with displays which may be viewed by the helmsman – once a privilege only available to motor yachtsmen using the inside helm position. All in all, radar is a very powerful navigational tool. I am going to give just a very brief introduction to it here but I hope it will tempt you to attend an RYA Radar course at a later date.

◆ How radar works

The user will think of the radar 'package' as having two parts – the display unit and the scanner.

1. **The display unit** houses all the control buttons and displays the picture. Depending on the make of the set it will also contain the receiver, the transmitter and a one way valve which separates the transmitter and the receiver.
2. **The scanner** which is mounted where it has a clear view of the horizon.

◆ The scanner

The scanner revolves at about 25 revolutions per minute and sends out short bursts of microwave energy known as the radar 'beam'. If this beam is interrupted by a solid object the beam is reflected

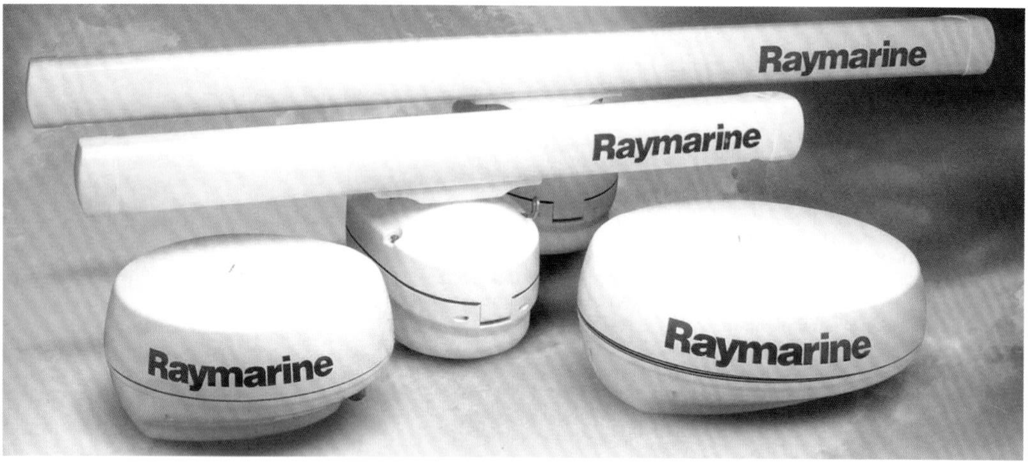
Raymarine
Raymarine
Raymarine
Raymarine

Fig 3.14 Radome and open array radar scanners.

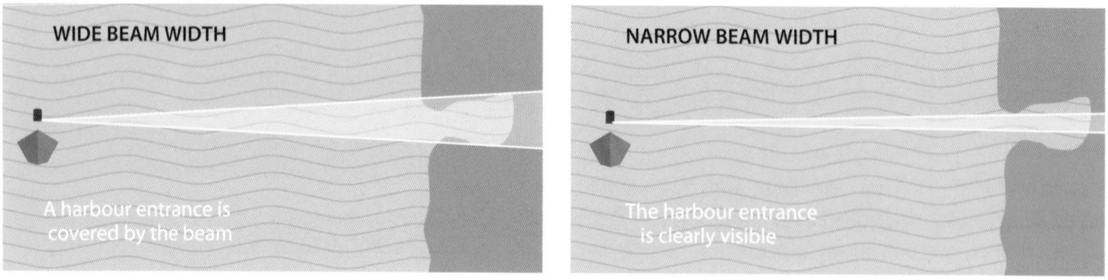
WIDE BEAM WIDTH
A harbour entrance is covered by the beam
NARROW BEAM WIDTH
The harbour entrance is clearly visible

Fig 3.15 The boat with the wide beam radar cannot see the harbour entrance as the beam covers the cliffs on either side. The narrow beam boat can see the entrance because the beam does not touch the cliffs on both sides simultaneously.

back to the set where it is enhanced and displayed as a contact on the display screen. The contact's distance and bearing relative to the ship's head is also given.

The scanner is available either as an 'open array', which is the long horizontal strip in Figure 3.14, or enclosed in a fibreglass radome. Sailing yachts obviously favour the enclosed radome as a revolving object and sails are not compatible but motor yachts are able to use an open array, which is considered more efficient.

The length of the scanner controls the width of the beam that is transmitted, and the narrower the beam the more the set can discriminate between objects. Short scanners can only transmit beams that are wide – a typical small boat radar with a short scanner has a beam width of between 5° and 6°. The size of the scanner is often not a matter of choice – it would not be possible to attach an enormous scanner to the mast of a small boat but users should be aware of the limitations of wide beam width. The illustrations in Figure 3.15 show how a wide beam may 'hide' a harbour entrance if both sides of the beam extend to cover the land on either side of the harbour entrance.

◆ What makes a good reflector?

This will depend on a number of things:

1. **Size** Large targets are generally best.
2. **Material** *Poor conductors*: wood, fibreglass.
   Good conductors: aluminium, seawater, and steel. (Your engine is probably the best radar reflector you have except that, in most small boats, it is mounted too near the waterline to be of much use).

3 **Shape** A slab sided object such as the side of a ship will reflect well whereas a cylindrical object will reflect only the angle that is square to the beam – a conical buoy will be a poor reflector even though it is made of metal.
4 **Texture** A rough surface with multi-faces will scatter the radar beam but those that are bounced back to the receiver will give a steady return.
5 **Aspect** An angled or multi-angled object will reflect the energy in the wrong direction, which is why 'stealth' aircraft have no two angles the same over their entire surface so that they remain almost invisible!

◆ Controls

When radar is first switched on it goes into *warm up mode* so that the magnetron heats itself slowly. When this process is complete, the screen will display the fact that it is now in *standby* and will remain that way until told to *transmit*.

We will look at some of the more important controls, one or two of which are recognisable from the television set at home. Most current sets on the market have an 'Auto' mode for the controls shown below but user preference will dictate whether slight alterations are made.

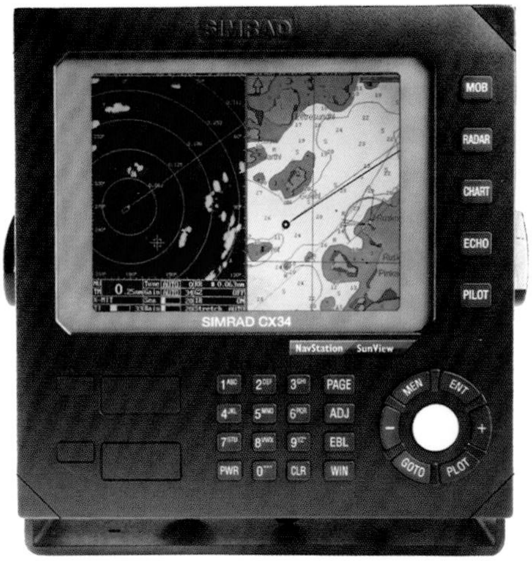

Fig 3.16 Simrad CX34 combined radar and chart plotter.

Brilliance controls the whiteness or brightness of the screen and is very much a matter of personal preference.

Contrast controls the blackness of a liquid crystal display and is adjusted in conjunction with the brilliance.

Gain regulates the sensitivity of the set and how it displays weak echoes. If it is not turned up high enough, the echoes will be lost. If it is too high then the screen will be covered in white speckles and any proper echoes will be smothered. It should be adjusted so that the speckles just fade except for the ones in the centre of the screen.

Tuning Most modern radars now have automatic tuning but you will still find a tuning control on older sets.

Sea clutter control takes the speckles out of the centre of the picture, which are always a lot worse when the sea is rough – you will remember that seawater is an excellent reflector of radar beams and wave fronts appear as contacts. This is probably the most dangerous control on the set because whilst you are removing the speckles any contact muddled in with them gets wiped away as well. Turn it fully up and you can make all the land disappear as well. Treat it with great caution – it is scary stuff!

RADAR DISPLAY

◆ Display

It is traditional for your own boat to be in the centre of the screen but on some sets you can be offset to one side or at the bottom. This last option can be particularly useful to fast powerboats who need to see further in front of the boat. In Figure 3.17, the boat is in the centre of the screen.

The screen in the illustration shows the heading as 235° True and the heading marker can be seen pointing towards the south-west in the bottom left-hand corner.

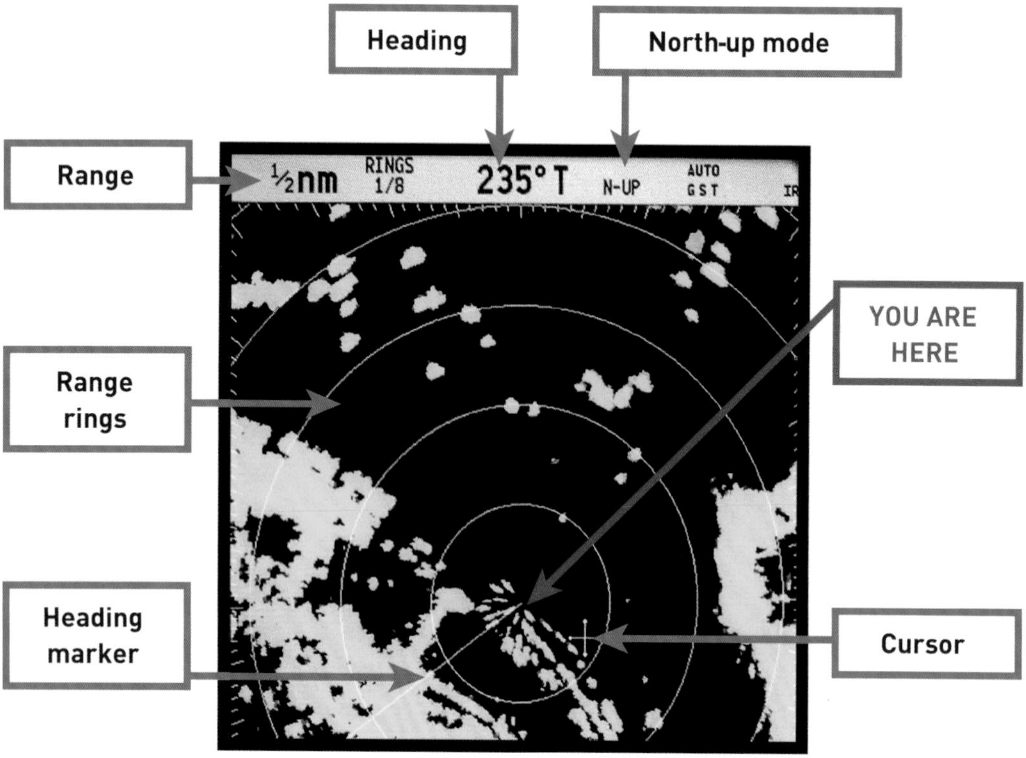

Fig 3.17 Features on the screen of the Raymarine RL80C.

This set is interfaced with a remote electronic compass which 'stabilises' the picture to reduce the effect of yawing and allows it to be displayed with north at the top of the screen, the same orientation as paper or electronic charts. This mode is generally called 'north-up'. For collision avoidance many skippers prefer to be in the 'head-up' mode as it is considered easier to keep a radar plot of the conflicting vessel.

Older sets which cannot be interfaced remain in the 'head-up' mode and are described as being un-stabilised. Un-stabilised displays swing from side to side when the boat yaws and rolls in a choppy sea which makes it more difficult to keep an accurate radar plot.

A stabilised 'head-up' display is often called 'course-up'.

◆ Range and range rings

Radar beams travel in straight lines, just like VHF radio waves. If the scanner is high enough it will be able to see further over the horizon so it is useless to buy a 48 mile radar set and mount a scanner 2 metres above the waterline because an object like a small buoy would be slipping below the horizon at a distance of 3 miles.

For collision avoidance offshore, most small boat skippers find that the 8-mile range setting is ideal but the one in Figure 3.17 is assisting with close quarter's pilotage into harbour, using the half mile scale. Features on the shore like the marina are clearly visible. The rings can be shown or hidden according to preference; in close-quarters they are useful because you have a consistent reminder how close things are to you!

◆ Variable Range Marker and Electronic Bearing Line (VRM and EBL)

The displays have one or two additional range rings that can be moved out from the centre of the screen in increments so that the range of a particular contact can be measured.

In addition, an extra bearing line can be moved around the circle to determine the bearing of the echo. If the bearing remains constant, then a risk of collision exists.

◆ Cursor

In addition to the VRM and EBL there will be a cursor which may also be used to measure the bearing and distance of any feature. As the cursor is moved around the screen, a caption will inform you of its bearing and distance from the boat. In Figure 3.18 the cursor is in the right-hand side of the picture and the centre of the screen is to the left of it. The range is 0.1 nautical mile and the cursor bears 242° RELATIVE to the boat's head – don't forget that the boat is travelling from the centre in a direction just off south-west and all the motion is relative to your boat.

◆ Position-fixing with radar

The variable range marker or cursor may be used for position-fixing provided that you know what you are looking at and that the features are shown on the chart. The next chapter covers all aspects of position-fixing but a radar fix is best taken using range as the basis, not bearings. Figure 3.19 shows a fix using ranges off three prominent headlands.

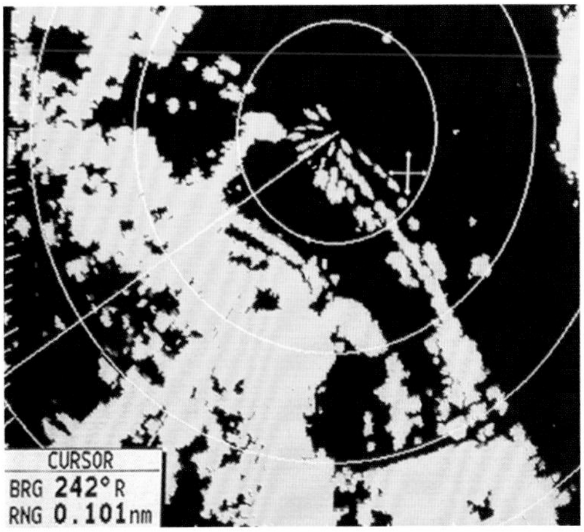

Fig 3.18 Range rings, heading marker and cursor on a radar display.

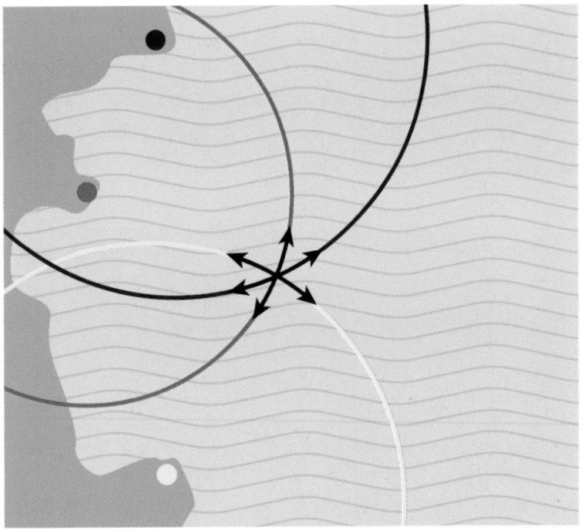

Fig 3.19 Fix of position using radar ranges.

QUESTION PAPER 3 – ELECTRONICS

3.1	Does the GPS show speed through the water or speed over the ground?
3.2	What is the meaning of the following: **a** XTE? **b** TTG?
3.3	There are a number of factors that affect how an object will reflect radar pulses. Name five.
3.4	Is it more accurate to fix position using radar bearings or radar ranges?
3.5	What is the meaning of the following: **a** VRM? **b** EBL?

Answers at the back of the book

4 FINDING THE POSITION – where are we?

BEFORE WE CAN CALCULATE THE COURSE to our destination or work out the route we have travelled, we have to know the starting position. If close to home, this may be found with a quick glance at the local landscape and, if in unfamiliar waters, a slightly longer stare at the GPS or chart plotter. Even if we are navigating electronically it is prudent to check the position visually or by traditional methods. I certainly get a great kick and gain confidence when the calculations my father used are found to work perfectly.

USING GPS TO FIX POSITION

We looked at GPS background and features in Chapter 3; now we will see, in detail, how versatile it is for position fixing.

◆ Latitude and longitude

As soon as the GPS has been switched on and has locked onto satellites, it will display the position of the boat in latitude and longitude. This is the universal way of expressing position and is easiest to plot using a pair of dividers for one of the co-ordinates and a plotter for the other. The secret is to find a rough position first so that you choose the closest margin. Having done this, check whether the nautical mile graduations are divided into five or ten parts. The illustration in Figure 4.1 shows the mile divided into tenths but Figure 4.3 has 0.2M divisions.

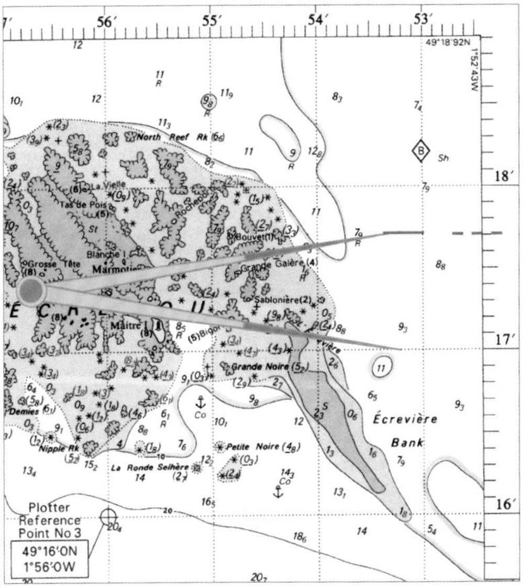

Fig 4.1 Latitude has been measured with dividers and is 49° 17′. 7N.

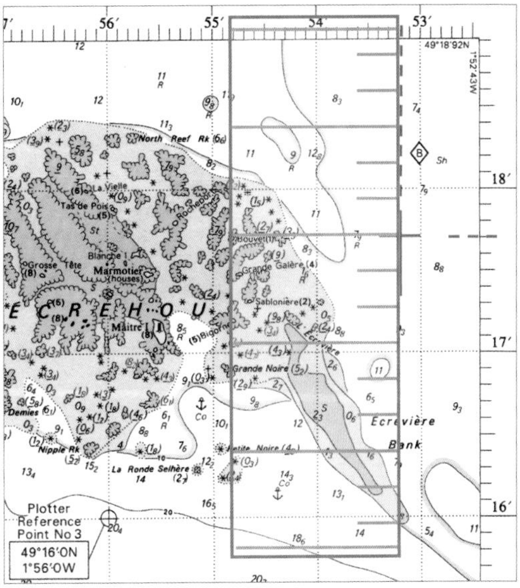

Fig 4.2 Longitude has been measured as 1° 53′. 2W.

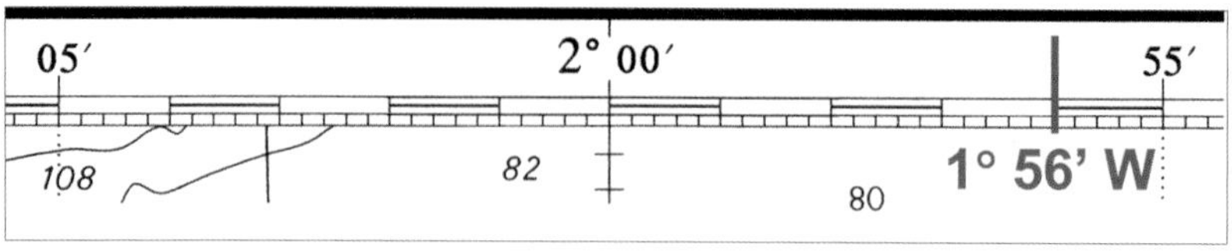

Fig 4.4 This position can erroneously be read as 2° 04′ W instead of the correct longitude.

It is extremely easy to make mistakes when plotting latitude and longitude and great care should be taken. The most common problem is the transposition of numbers, for example, 49° 41'. 4N is plotted as 49° 44'. 1N as it has been in Figure 4.3.

Errors also occur when plotting longitude west of Greenwich when the degrees ascend from right to left instead of in the normal direction for reading a page. In Figure 4.4, for instance, the longitude could be read as 2° 04' W by mistake.

As the potential for error when plotting latitude and longitude will be greater in times of high workload, it will save time in the long run if you study the GPS instruction book to learn how to enter a waypoint. Waypoints can be used very effectively to plot a position quickly and accurately.

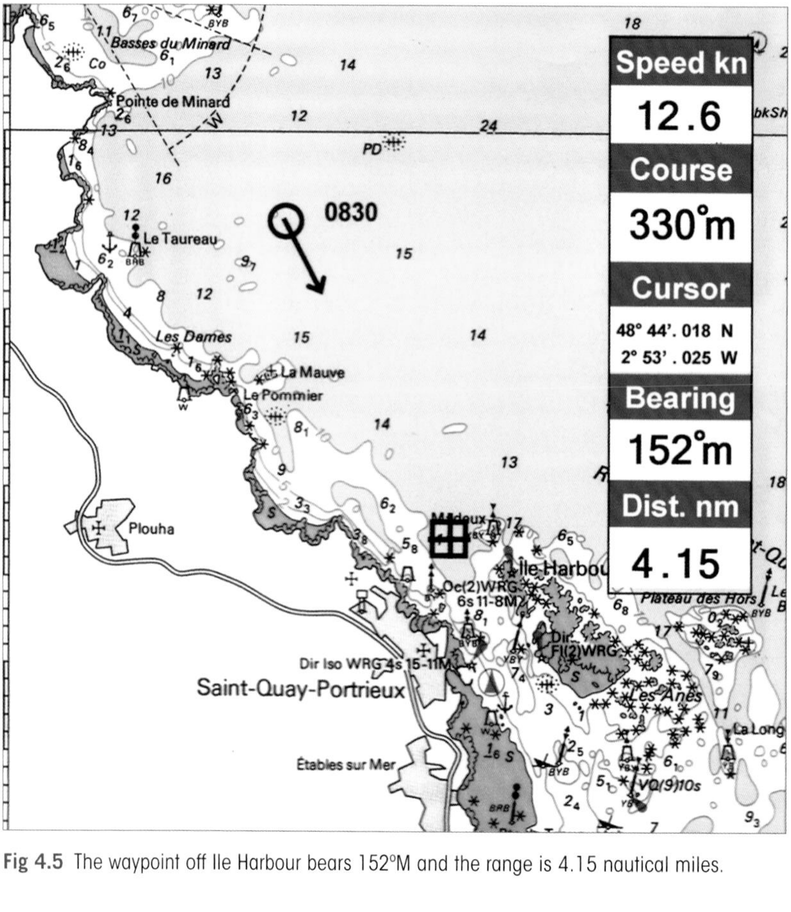

Fig 4.5 The waypoint off Ile Harbour bears 152°M and the range is 4.15 nautical miles.

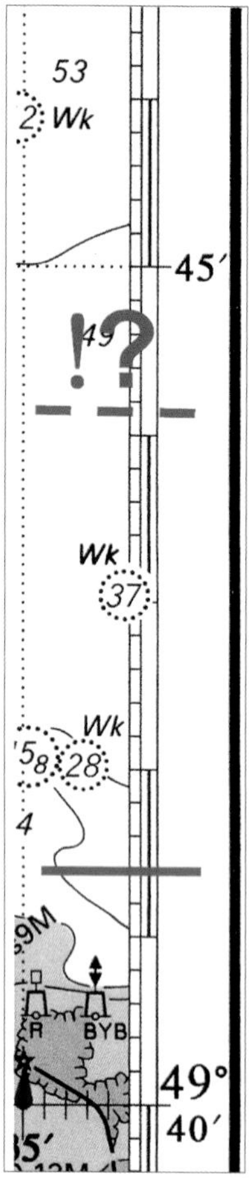

Fig 4.3 Latitude scale with 0.2M divisions to the mile.

◆ Range and bearing to a waypoint

In Figure 4.5 the yacht *Merlin* has entered a waypoint just north-west of St Quay-Portrieux and is using it to plot the position. The bearing shown is always **to** the waypoint, in this case 152°M at a distance of 4.15 miles.

Merlin's skipper has chosen to display a Magnetic bearing on the GPS so that it mimics the steering compass but most navigators work only in True – it is personal preference.

If *Merlin* was on a longer passage he may choose to use a convenient central point from which to plot a bearing and distance. A compass rose situated somewhere in the middle of the chart is ideal for this purpose. Admiralty Leisure Folio charts show the latitude and longitude of the centre of the rose so that this can be entered into the GPS as a *special waypoint.*

To plot the bearing, a straight edge is aligned to pass through the centre of the rose and the appropriate angle. The ruler in Figure 4.6 is plotting a bearing of 315°T, which means that the position is to the south-east of the rose.

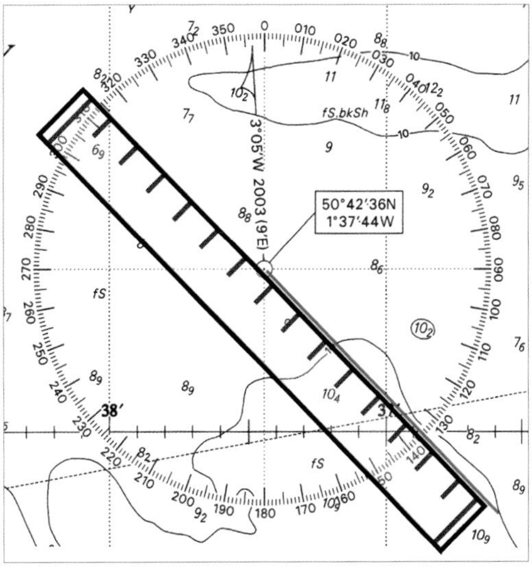

Fig 4.6 The GPS will show the bearing **to** the waypoint as 315°. The position will be to the south-east of the rose centre.

◆ The 'Spider's Web'

When navigating at high speed, the sea state and motion of the boat may make plotting almost impossible; especially if the chart is resting on the navigator's lap as is likely to be the case in a fast semi-rigid inflatable boat. Pre-planning is a must in this situation and, if a 'spider's web' similar to the one in Figure 4.7 is drawn for the approach to a waypoint, the position can be plotted speedily. If the chart is in a protective polythene cover a chinagraph crayon can be used to mark the position on the cover.

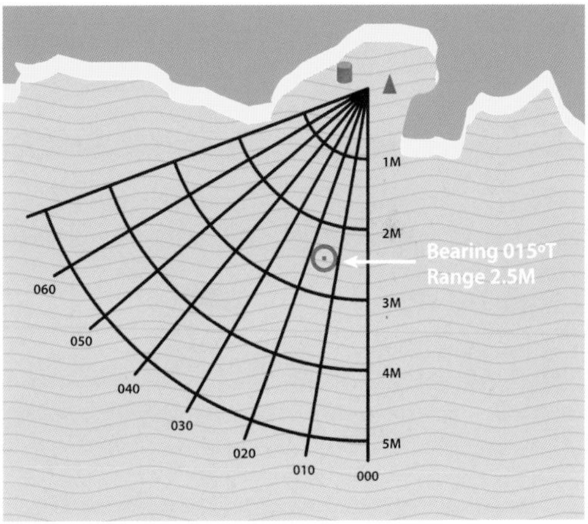

Fig 4.7 The Spider's Web is a useful way of plotting position when navigating at high speed.

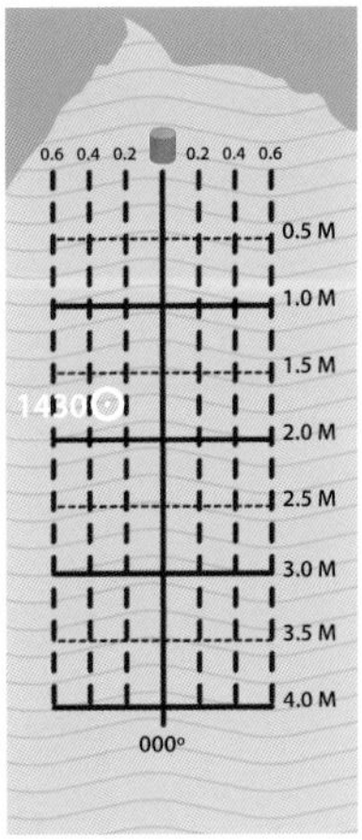

◆ Cross track error and range

As part of the passage planning, a cross track error ladder can be drawn on the chart to help cut down the workload at busy times. In Figure 4.8 *Merlin*'s navigator has used a ladder for his final approach into the coast.

At 1430, the GPS tells him that the boat is 1.75M from the waypoint but 0.3M to port of track. He has obtained a position quickly and can see at a glance that he needs to take corrective steps to regain track.

Fig 4.8 A cross track error (XTE) ladder.

◆ Chart plotters

Chart plotters are a 'must' for most skippers and it is not hard to see the reason why. Most have built-in GPS and use electronic chart folios to continuously show the GPS position on a moving chart. Figure 4.9 shows a colour plotter, which is displaying the depth measured by the echo sounder in addition to the standard GPS information.

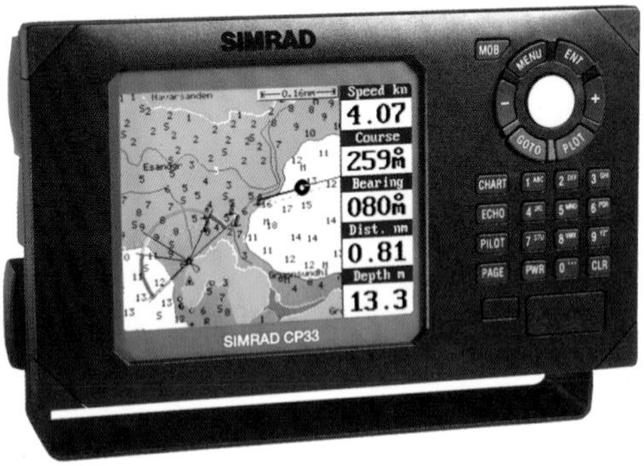

Fig 4.9 Simrad CP33 colour chart plotter.

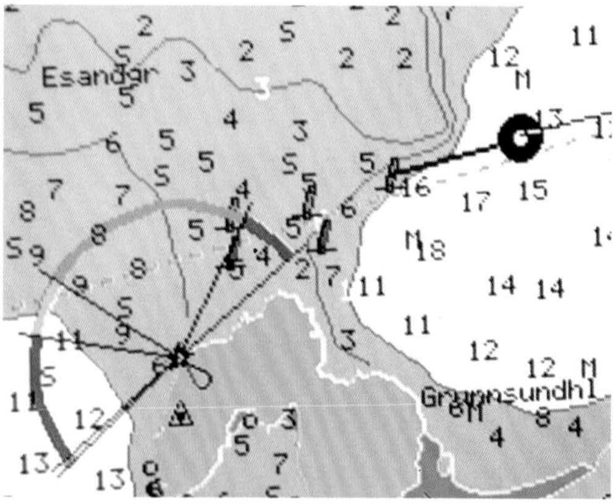

Fig 4.10 Enlarged display of the Simrad CP33. The amount of information shown can be reduced or increased as desired.

TRADITIONAL METHODS FOR FIXING POSITION

Each time an electronic fix is taken, the navigator should confirm its accuracy by using one of the more traditional methods, which have kept seafarers safe for hundreds of years. Mostly, this can be a quick gathering of visual evidence as a backup: 'If I am here then the depth sounder should read 15m – does it?' or 'If I am here then, on the beam, there should be a flagstaff almost in line with a chimney on the shore – is it there?'

If we are out of sight of land, we cannot do this and would have to plot an estimated position, which will be covered in Chapter 7. In the meantime we will look at other well-tried and tested ways of fixing the position of the boat.

◆ Position lines – transits

When two charted features are in line, one behind the other, (known as being 'in transit'), an accurate line of position can be drawn on the chart – the observer must be on an extended line joining the two features. The chart extract in Figure 4.11 shows a conspicuous transit at Portsmouth. If the War Memorial is kept in transit with the south-east corner of the building behind, a safe passage between Spit Bank and Hamilton Bank can be found.

In photo 1 the War Memorial appears on the right-hand side of the building, which means that an alteration of course to starboard must be made to regain the transit and find deeper water. Photo 2 shows the two in transit affording a safe passage through the Swashway Channel.

In any pilotage situation, use transits wherever possible because you can be in the cockpit and in full command of the situation instead of burying your head over the chart table down below.

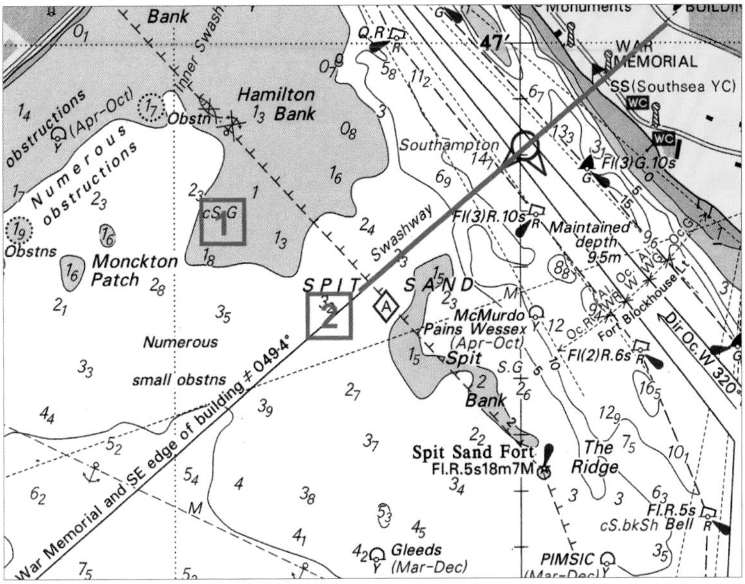

Fig 4.11 This transit at Portsmouth leads craft between two shallow banks.

◆ Three-point fix

The transit gave us a single line of position but no clue to our actual position on it. For this we need to use the handbearing compass to obtain a second and a third position line to check where we are on the first. This method requires little equipment and is time honoured but if success is to be guaranteed certain procedures should be followed.

Features The bearings we take are going to be drawn on the chart so first of all we must check that the chosen landmark is actually on the chart. Chimneys, monuments, flagstaffs and church spires are usually prominent but on some coastlines, particularly in Brittany, there are so many water towers and churches that it is sometimes impossible to be certain which is the correct one. Prominent headlands are often in silhouette and if they are 'steep to' they can be used for bearings. If a feature is wide, like Spit Sand Fort in Figure 4.15, then the side should be used and recorded in the log book.

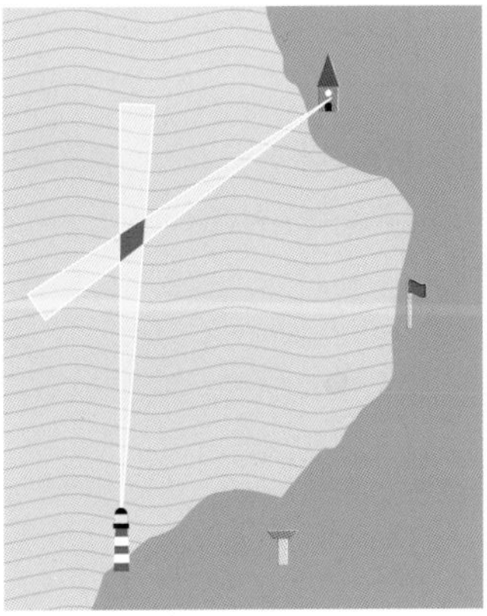

Fig 4.12 The area of uncertainty is small as there is a good angle of cut between the two features.

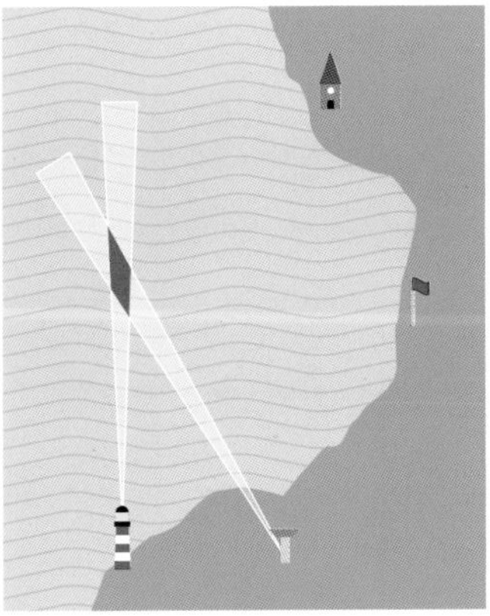

Fig 4.13 The cut is narrow which gives a greater area of uncertainty.

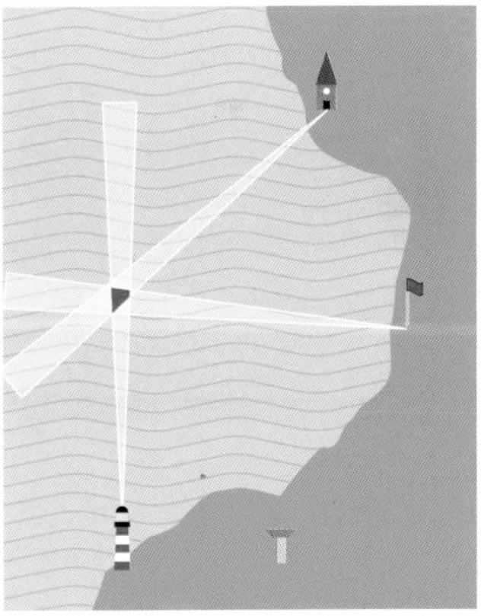

Fig 4.14 The area of uncertainty is further reduced by the third bearing.

The features should not be too close together as this will compromise the accuracy of the fix. The movement of the boat may give an error of plus or minus 5 degrees for each of the bearings taken but if there is a good angle of cut between the bearings, as there is in Figure 4.12, the area of uncertainty can be reduced. In Figure 4.13, the angle between landmarks is narrow and the uncertain area, which is marked in red, is much larger.

A third bearing should be taken as a check on the other two (Figure 4.14) and the last one should be the one that is changing most quickly. This is likely to be the feature that is either closest to or on the beam. Close bearings are often difficult to take because they move quickly but those taken at a distance are never as accurate.

Taking the bearings Before taking the bearings, check for a safe position away from all magnetic influences. The companionway is undoubtedly the most comfortable and secure but could be too close to analogue instruments or a repeater loudspeaker for the VHF, all of which contain magnets. Many people go to the stern of the boat where they are protected by the stern pulpit rail, but make sure that there is not an outboard attached there. Wedge yourself in firmly, wait for the compass needle to settle and take the bearings in quick succession.

It will reduce the workload if you ask a member of the crew to write down the bearings for you, but ask them to label whether they are written in Magnetic or True.

Fig 4.15 The navigator has fixed position near Portsmouth using three charted features on the shore. The left-hand side of Spit Sand Fort has been used.

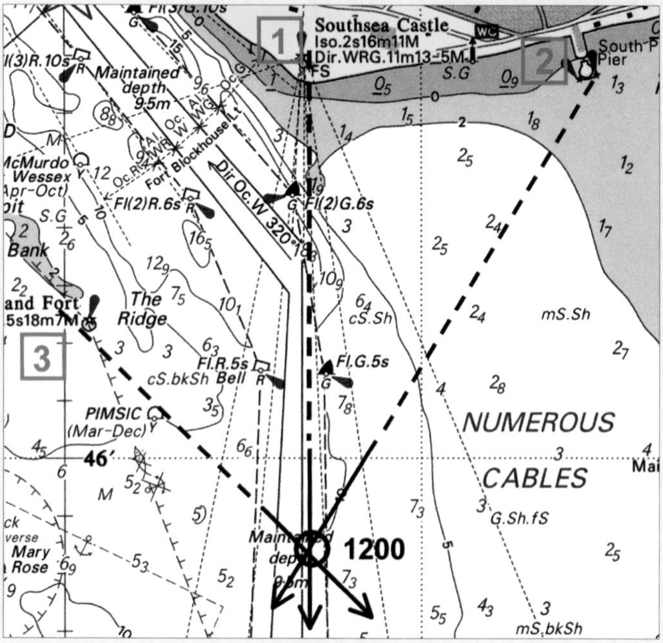

Plotting the fix In Figure 4.15, the fix has been plotted and the lines do not quite meet – a cocked hat has been formed. The hat is small and the landmarks are close so this fix should be fairly reliable. If there is any doubt, take the fix again to be sure. The depth at the plotted position is greater than in the surrounding water and this could be used to check accuracy.

◆ Depth and bearing

A single position can be used together with a sounding to get a fix (Figure 4.16) provided that the height of tide is known and depth sounder reading is reduced to chart datum. In areas where serious silting or scouring occurs this fix should be regarded with suspicion.

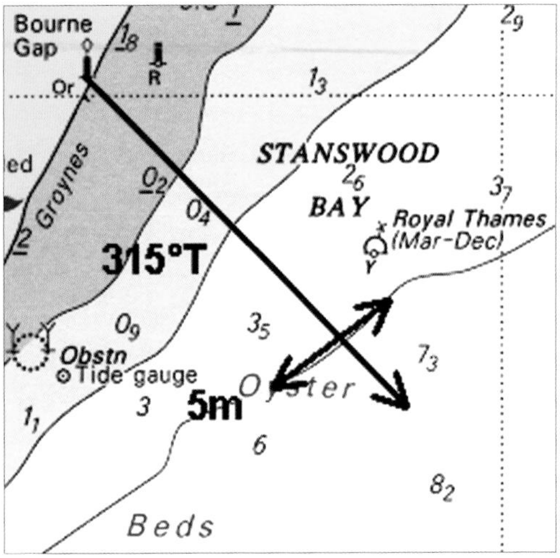

Fig 4.16 A fix with a single position line and a depth.

QUESTION PAPER 4 – FINDING THE POSITION

Use Variation 3°W in questions 2, 3 and 4.
Plot your answers on the chart extract in Figure 4.17 (page 42).

4.1 Plot the following fix taken at 0800 when the log reads 27.2M.Le Grand Jardin lighthouse bears 170°M. Depth 28m. Height of tide 8.0m.

4.2 At 1300 the following 3-point fix was taken in the area to the west of St Malo.

S Lunaire Water Tower	129°M
BRB Beacon near Ile des Hebihens	185°M
Les Bourdinots BYB buoy near St Cast	253°M

4.3 At 1800 the following fix is taken in the area to the north-east of St Malo. YBY Beacon Tower near Rochefort rock in transit with the BYB buoy. Spire in St Malo 166°M.

4.4 Name three methods of fixing position using the GPS.

Answers at the back of the book

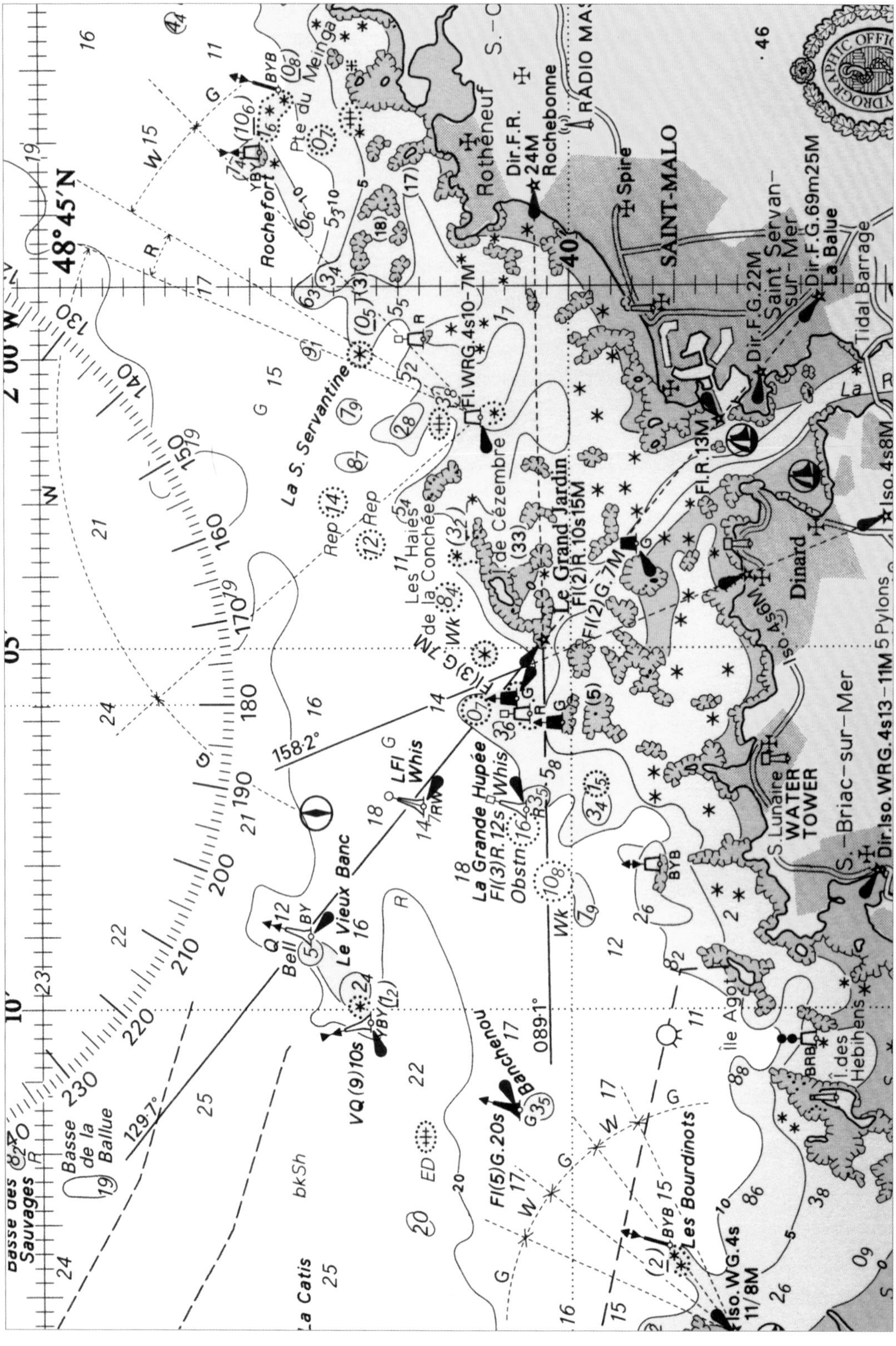

Fig 4.17 Plot your answers on this chart extract.

5 TIDAL HEIGHTS – will we stay afloat?

IN NORTHERN EUROPE, 'Will we go aground?' is probably the most frequently asked question, because the rise and fall of the tide here influences just about everything we do on the water. Having the ability to work out how high the tide is at any given time, and subsequently how fast the water is moving, is vital for successful navigation and pilotage.

Tidal theory is very complicated and there are many aspects that even the experts fail to understand, so when we talk about the causes of tides in this chapter it is with a very simplistic view. Fortunately, because things astronomical are so very predictable, there is much reliable data to assist with any calculations.

SPRING AND NEAP TIDES

The Earth's surface is covered by an immense amount of water which is moved vertically by the gravitational pull of the Moon as it revolves around our globe. The Moon's gravity acts unevenly on the Earth and as the surface facing the Moon is most affected, the water on that side is pulled upward, creating an area of deeper water (a high tide). There is also a bulge of water on the other side of the Earth as the Moon pulls the Earth away from the distant water.

The Sun also exerts gravitational pull but to a lesser extent because it is so much further away than the Moon.

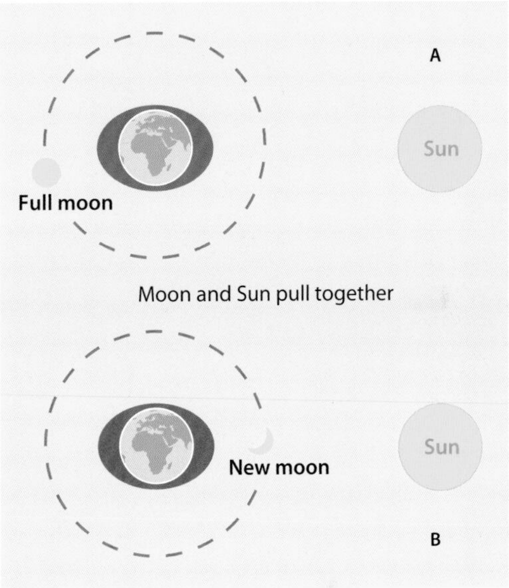

Fig 5.1 Spring tides: the gravitational effect of the Moon and Sun working together.

When the Sun and Moon and Earth are all in line with one another (A & B in Figure 5.1), their gravitational forces are at their maximum and this causes the greatest rise of the water known as a **spring** tide, when the high water is higher and the low water is lower than on other occasions. The numerical difference between high and low water is known as 'the range' and the range is at its greatest just a couple of days after the full moon.

When the Sun and Moon are at right angles to the Earth (C & D in Figure 5.2), the forces oppose one another so that the tides are far less extreme. These are called **neap** tides, when the high water is not as high and the low water is not as low as it is at springs.

Springs occur shortly after the new and full Moon and neap tides shortly after the quarter Moon (which, when viewed from the Earth, looks like a half Moon). During the lunar month, which is actually 29 days, there are two spring tides and two neap tides.

In the UK we have what are called 'semi-diurnal' tides – that is a complete tide cycle every half day. If the flow of water is not restricted by headlands or funnelling it will take the tide approximately 6 hours 12 minutes to rise and the same time to fall. In a 24-hour period this should take 24 hours 48 minutes, which is why the time of high water (HW) is later every day.

THE LANGUAGE OF TIDES

Some of the terms and definitions used in tidal calculations were learned in Chapter 1 but revision is always a good thing, and the illustration in Figure 5.3 will act as an aide-mémoire.

◆ Chart Datum (CD)

Chart datum is a level to which the tide will seldom, if ever, fall and corresponds to the Lowest Astronomical Tide (LAT). It can be thought of as 'The *Zero Level*' because any height given in the tide table is above this level and any depth shown on the chart is below it. In areas where the land is slowly sinking, there are some instances of the tide being below datum, but in general terms it stays above it.

When determining chart datum, the hydrographers take only astronomical factors into consideration, not meteorological. Strong winds and tide surges can raise the level of the water and high pressure will depress it by up to half a metre.

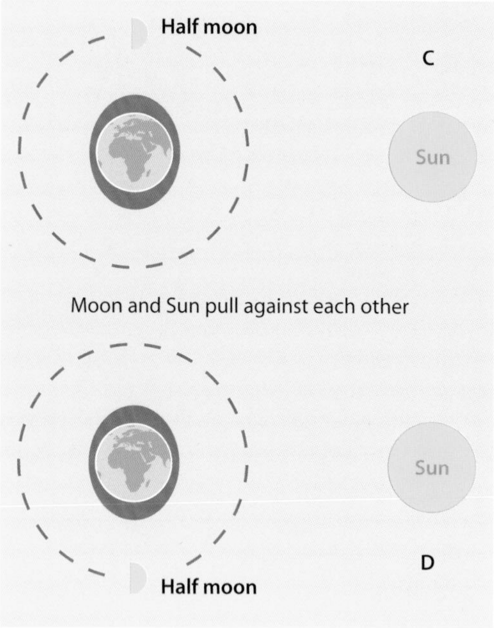

Fig 5.2 Neap tides – the pull from the Moon and the Sun are in opposition.

◆ Mean High Water Springs (MHWS)

This is the average height of all the high waters at spring tides.

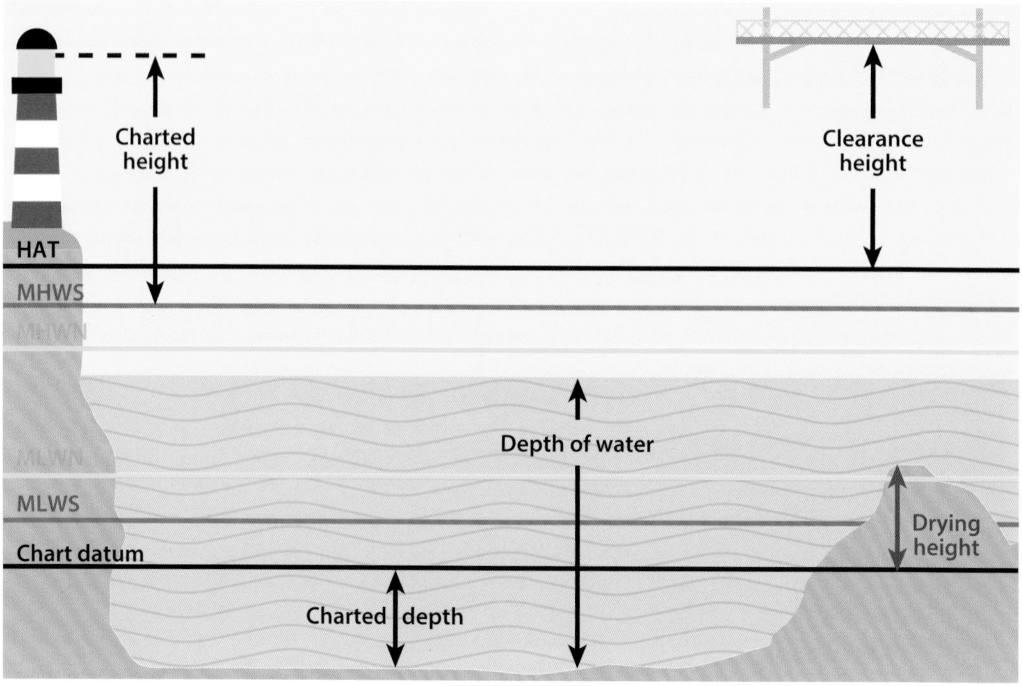

Fig 5.3 Tidal levels.

◆ Highest Astronomical Tide (HAT)

This level is set at a level that the tide will seldom, if ever, reach and is used for clearances under bridges and power cables. It is therefore the minimum clearance one would expect in normal conditions. The HAT for standard ports (but not secondary ports) is shown at the bottom of each tide table page in Reeds Nautical Almanac.

Remember that when you're passing under a power cable, a gap of at least 4.0 metres should be left above the top of the mast.

Standard Port ST HELIER

Height (metres)			
MHWS	MHWN	MLWN	MLWS
11·0	8·1	4·0	1·4

Fig 5.4 Mean heights above chart datum at St Helier.

◆ Other mean levels

Almanacs, pilot books and charts give details of other mean levels such as Mean Low Water Springs (MLWS), Mean High Water Neaps (MHWN) and Mean Low Water Neaps (MLWN) for many different ports.

The extract in Figure 5.4 is from an almanac and gives levels for St Helier on Jersey whilst Figure 5.5 shows data taken from Admiralty Chart 5604/2 of the Channel Islands area. Similar tables can be found on most Admiralty Charts.

Tidal Levels referred to Datum of Soundings

Place	Lat N	Long W	Heights in metres above datum MHWS	MHWN	MLWN	MLWS
Cherbourg	49°39′	1°38′	6·4	5·0	2·5	1·1
Goury	49 43	1 57	8·1	6·6	3·5	1·4
Alderney - Braye	49 43	2 12	6·2	4·7	2·5	0·9
Jersey - St. Helier	49 11	2 07	11·0	8·1	4·0	1·4
Carteret	49 22	1 47	10·6	8·1	3·7	1·3

Fig 5.5 Mean levels for Jersey and Alderney.

◆ Charted depth

The amount of water that will still be present in a position if the tide level falls to zero is known as the *charted depth*. The black oval, in Figure 5.6, shows a charted depth of 14.3 metres.

◆ Charted height

The height of a feature, measured above MHWS is the *charted height*. This measurement is used in calculations to determine the distance from the feature using a sextant or the '*dipping distance of lights*' table. The fort which is highlighted in purple in Figure 5.6, is 14m above MHWS.

◆ Drying height

This is an area that is uncovered when the tidal height is 0.0m and covered at MHWS. The red circle marks a rocky patch, which dries 3.4 metres above datum.

◆ Clearance height

This measurement is taken from the Highest Astronomical Tide (HAT) and is used to determine the clearance under an overhead cable or bridge.

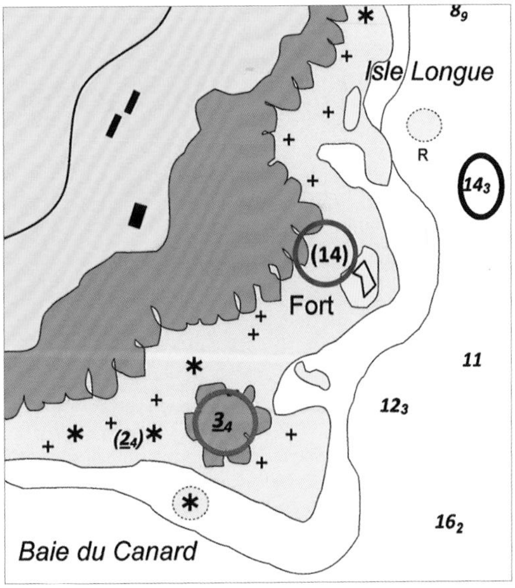

Fig 5.6 A drying height of 3.4m, a charted depth of 14.3m and a charted height of 14m at Alderney.

◆ Equinoxes

Twice a year, around 21 March and 22 September equinoxes, the Sun is directly over the Equator. At these times, larger than normal spring tides occur and are referred to as equinoctial springs. Running aground at HW on an equinoctial spring tide could mean that you will be stranded for up to six months!

◆ Tidal range

The difference in metres between the height of high water and the previous, or next low water is the *tidal range*.

The difference in height between MHWS and MLWS is called the *mean spring range* and the difference between MHWN and MLWN, the *mean neap range* (see Figure 5.7).

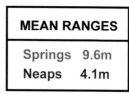

MEAN RANGES	
Springs	9.6m
Neaps	4.1m

Fig 5.7 Mean ranges at St Helier.

TIDE TABLES

Tables listing the times and heights of high and low water are available from a number of sources. For those going into deep water the Admiralty print tide tables for the whole world in a number of different volumes, but owners of smaller recreational boats usually choose those printed in nautical almanacs or ones available on computer software.

Full tables are printed for the larger, commercial ports, which are known as **standard ports**. Harbours and havens which are likely to be visited by motor boaters or yachtsmen are considered to be **secondary ports**, which are discussed later in the chapter. Our old friend St Helier is a standard port and the tide table in Figure 5.8 is taken from *Reeds Almanac*.

If we look at the morning of 3 April the information it gives is:

Low water (LW) is at 0321 Universal Time which is Greenwich Mean Time (GMT) under another name. We must add one hour to this time because by 2 April the clocks have gone forward an hour. The tide tables remind us of this by changing the shading on the page and printing a reminder at the top of the page.

The LW height is 1.5m above chart datum and HW is at 0957 BST with a height of 10.4m. The range is 8.9m and if you look at Figure 5.7 you will see that this range is nearer to springs than neaps.

ST HELIER LAT 49°11'N LONG 2°07'W

TIMES AND HEIGHTS OF HIGH AND LOW WATERS

Dates in red are SPRINGS
Dates in blue are NEAPS

YEAR 2010

e m	FEBRUARY Time m	Time m	MARCH Time m	Time m	APRIL Time m	Time m
1 2.3 2 10.2 2 2.1	1 0215 0.6 0751 12.0 M 1443 0.3	16 0206 1.8 0744 10.6 TU 1424 1.6	1 0111 0.6 0649 11.9 M 1339 0.3	16 0111 1.8 0648 10.5 TU 1329 1.6	1 0212 0.6 0747 11.6 TH 1432 0.8	16 0147 1.6 0722 10.6 F 1402 1.6

JANUARY Time m	Time m	FEBRUARY Time m	Time m	MARCH Time m	Time m	APRIL Time m	Time m
1 0046 1.7 0626 11.0 F 1316 1.3 1858 10.9	16 0121 2.3 0702 10.2 SA 1342 2.1 1922 10.0	1 0215 0.6 0751 12.0 M 1443 0.3 2018 11.6	16 0206 1.8 0744 10.6 TU 1424 1.6 1959 10.4	1 0111 0.6 0649 11.9 M 1339 0.3 1915 11.7	16 0111 1.8 0648 10.5 TU 1329 1.6 1903 10.5	1 0212 0.6 0747 11.6 TH 1432 0.8 2006 11.4	16 0147 1.6 0722 10.6 F 1402 1.6 1935 10.7
2 0137 1.4 0715 11.3 SA 1406 1.0 1947 11.1	17 0154 2.2 0734 10.3 SU 1414 2.0 1953 10.1	2 0259 0.5 0833 11.9 TU 1524 0.5 2058 11.4	17 0234 1.8 0812 10.6 W 1451 1.7 2026 10.4	2 0157 0.3 0732 12.1 TU 1422 0.1 1956 11.8	17 0142 1.6 0718 10.7 W 1359 1.5 1932 10.6	2 0248 0.9 0823 11.1 F 1505 1.3 2039 10.8	17 0218 1.6 0755 10.5 SA 1433 1.7 2007 10.6
3 0225 1.2 0803 11.5 SU 1454 0.9 2033 11.1	18 0224 2.2 0805 10.3 M 1444 2.0 2022 10.0	3 0339 0.8 0913 11.5 W 1602 1.0 2136 10.9	18 0301 1.9 0840 10.4 TH 1518 1.9 2053 10.2	3 0238 0.3 0811 12.0 W 1500 0.4 2033 11.6	18 0211 1.6 0747 10.7 TH 1427 1.5 2000 10.6	3 0321 1.5 0857 10.4 SA 1535 2.1 2111 10.1	18 0250 1.8 0829 10.2 SU 1506 2.1 2042 10.2
4 0311 1.2 0849 11.4 M 1540 1.0 2118 10.9	19 0253 2.2 0835 10.2 TU 1513 2.1 2051 9.9	4 0416 1.4 0950 10.8 TH 1637 1.7 2212 10.1	19 0328 2.2 0906 10.1 F 1544 2.3 2120 9.8	4 0315 0.6 0848 11.5 TH 1535 1.0 2107 11.0	19 0239 1.7 0816 10.6 F 1454 1.7 2028 10.4	4 0352 2.3 0929 9.5 SU 1603 2.9 2143 9.3	19 0325 2.2 0906 9.7 M 1541 2.6 2120 9.7
5 0356 1.4 0933 11.1 TU 1623 1.4 2201 10.4	20 0321 2.4 0904 10.0 W 1541 2.4 2120 9.7	5 0451 2.2 1027 9.9 F 1710 2.6 ◑ 2249 9.3	20 0355 2.6 0934 9.6 SA 1612 2.8 2149 9.3	5 0348 1.3 0923 10.7 F 1605 1.8 2140 10.2	20 0307 1.9 0844 10.2 SA 1522 2.1 2056 10.1	5 0424 3.1 1004 8.6 M 1634 3.7 2221 8.4	20 0404 2.7 0950 9.1 TU 1624 3.1 2208 9.1
6 0439 1.9 1016 10.5 W 1706 2.0 2244 9.8	21 0350 2.7 0932 9.6 TH 1611 2.7 2150 9.3	6 0528 3.1 1107 8.9 SA 1749 3.5 2335 8.5	21 0425 3.2 1007 9.0 SU 1646 3.4 2228 8.7	6 0420 2.2 0955 9.7 SA 1633 2.8 2212 9.3	21 0336 2.4 0914 9.7 SU 1552 2.7 2127 9.5	6 0504 3.9 1052 7.8 TU 1720 4.4 ◑ 2322 7.7	21 0455 3.2 1050 8.5 W 1723 3.6 ◐ 2316 8.6
7 0522 2.5 1100 9.8 TH 1750 2.7 ◑ 2331 9.2	22 0420 3.1 1003 9.2 F 1642 3.2 2223 8.9	7 0617 3.9 1203 8.0 SU 1847 4.3	22 0507 3.7 1055 8.3 M 1736 4.0 ◐ 2328 8.2	7 0451 3.1 1031 8.7 SU 1704 3.7 ◑ 2251 8.4	22 0409 2.9 0950 9.0 M 1628 3.3 2208 8.9	7 0608 4.4 1220 7.3 W 1845 4.9	22 0607 3.5 1213 8.2 TH 1846 3.8

Fig 5.8 Tide table for St Helier. Times are given in universal time (GMT) which means that one hour has to be added between the months of April and October.

This is the information we will need every time we wish to find out when the water is at a specific height or what height of tide we require to enter a harbour.

In addition we will also use the **tidal curve** for St Helier, which can be found in Figure 5.10 and, in real life, close to the tables in the Almanac. It is in two halves, the curved part on the right and the straight linear graph on the left.

The curved part of the drawing shows the pattern of the rise and fall of the tide. You will notice that there are two curves, one dotted for neaps and the solid one for springs. There are boxes underneath the curve and we shall be entering the St Helier HW time in the centre box and preceding hours in the others. The left-hand side of the graph is there is to help you with the calculations.

FINDING A TIME FOR A GIVEN HEIGHT

Let us assume that it is Saturday 3 April and we wish to anchor for breakfast in a sandy bay that has a drying 3.4m rock at the entrance. We are in a boat with a draught of 1 metre and, to be prudent we require at least 1 metre of water under the keel as we pass over the rock. This means that the tide must be at least 5.4m above datum to give us this clearance. It is a good idea to draw a diagram similar to the one in Figure 5.9 just to check that all our deliberations are correct.

Now go to the tidal curve for St Helier at Figure 5.10 and follow the steps.

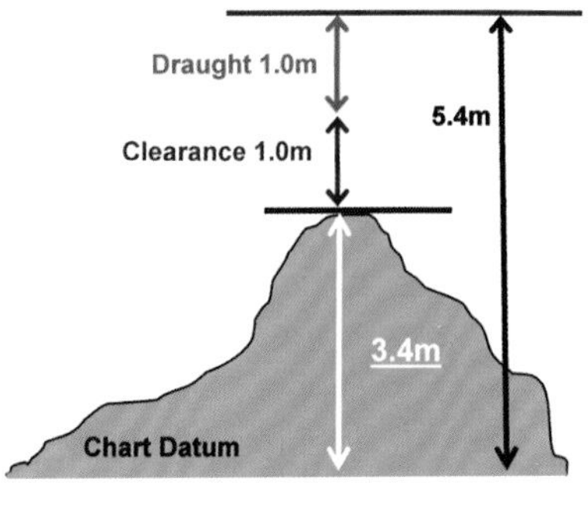

Fig 5.9 The height of tide required is 5.4m.

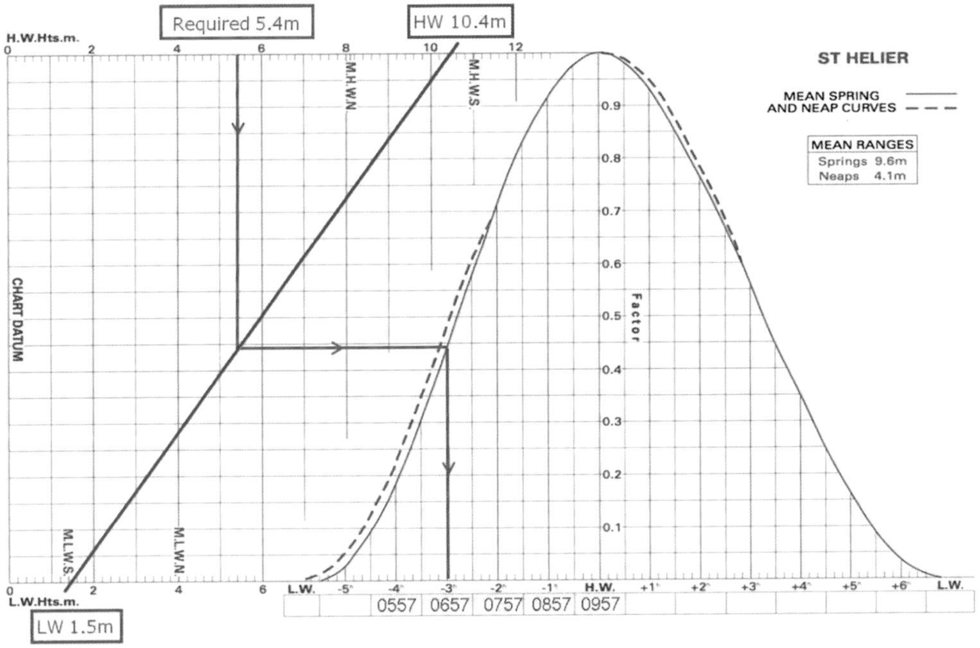

Fig 5.10 There is sufficient water to enter the bay just a few minutes before 0700. Best not to try it any earlier if a sure clearance of one metre is required.

1 Enter the morning HW height on the top line of the straight graph and the LW height on the bottom line. Join these two points.
2 Enter the HW time in the centre box and previous hours to the left. (You are entering the bay on a rising tide.)
3 Enter the required height of tide on the top line ie 5.4m.
4 Draw a perpendicular downward to meet the diagonal height line.
5 From here, trace a horizontal path until you come to the solid line of the spring curve.
6 Lastly draw another perpendicular line down to your time line to get the answer 0650 BST – just in time for a well-earned breakfast!

FINDING A HEIGHT FOR A GIVEN TIME

What is the height of tide at 1240 UT on Sunday 7 March at St Helier?

This time we start with a proposed time but we still need to complete steps 1 and 2 as before.

- Remember that we don't have to add an hour to the time because March is in the shaded area of the tide table.
- The range is close to the neap range, so use the neap curve on the graph.

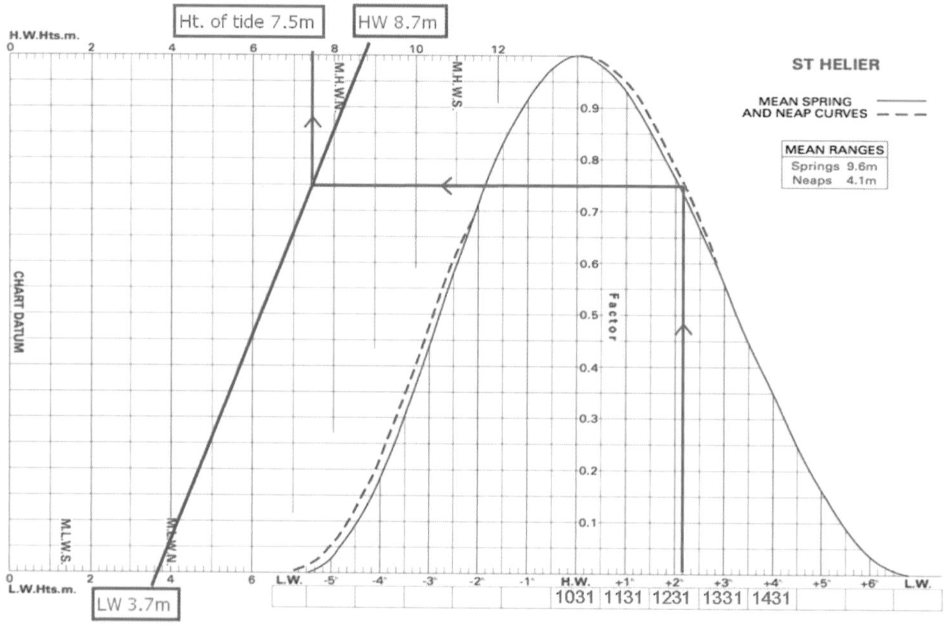

Fig 5.11 Calculating the height of tide for a given time.

St Helier HW 1031 UT 8.7m LW 3.7m Range 5.0m Near neaps

Repeat steps 1 and 2 from the last example.
3 Take a line upwards from 1240 until it meets the dotted neap curve.
4 Track left until the diagonal line is reached.
5 Take a further line upward to find the answer of **7.5m** on the top line.

COMPUTER SOFTWARE FOR CALCULATING HEIGHT OF TIDE

If you are able to take a laptop computer to sea, then a wonderful array of software is available to calculate the tidal heights for you. Check that the program is reliable before you buy – some require you to update the software annually which can be unsatisfactory.

Figure 5.12 shows tidal height predictions for St Helier for a week in October 2009 using the UKHO's 'Easy-Tide' facility. This information is currently free for the current week but with a small fee for future predictions for both standard and secondary ports.

If more detailed information is required, the Neptune Software program is very comprehensive and gives far more in-depth information.

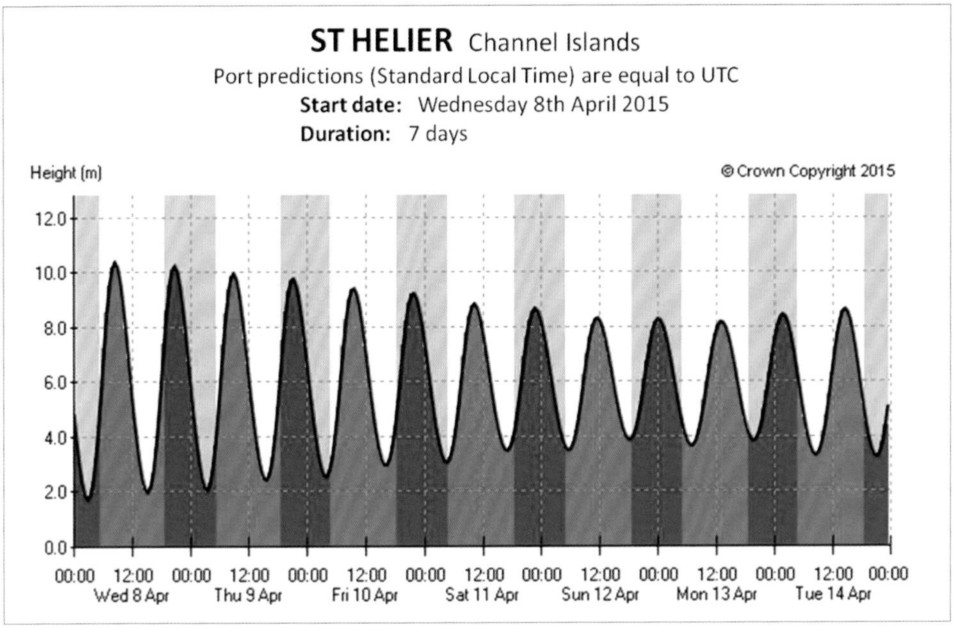

Fig 5.12 Tidal height predictions for St Helier using 'Easy-tide' from the Hydrographic Office.

SECONDARY PORTS

The tide tables in the almanac are given in full for the busier commercial or naval ports – there is simply no room in the book to give full information for the surrounding small harbours. Larger harbours are designated as Standard ports and their satellites as Secondary ports. When the almanac gives port information about a secondary port it will show tidal corrections which have to be applied to the standard port tide tables.

Let us assume that we wish to go into Lézardrieux on the north coast of Brittany on 18 May. The box on the lower right hand corner of Figure 5.13 shows that it is a secondary port of St Malo. HW is at 0951 French Standard Time, the time zone on which Lézardrieux corrections are based. Eventually we will have to convert to French Summer Time but not until the corrections have been applied. We will look at both HW and LW time corrections before we look at the heights.

Now look at Figure 5.14 and you will see that the different sections of it have been divided into coloured boxes. We will begin with the red box.

ST MALO

LAT 48°38´ N LONG 2°02´ W

TIMES AND HEIGHTS OF HIGH AND LOW WATERS

TIME ZONE –0100
Subtract 1 hour for UT
For French Summer Time add
ONE hour in non-shaded areas

Dates in red are SPRINGS
Dates in blue are NEAPS

MAY

Day	Time	m	Day	Time	m
1	0323	1.5	16	0259	1.8
	0846	11.8		0825	11.8
SA	1537	2.0	SU	1516	2.0
	2101	11.9		2040	12.0
2	0356	2.0	17	0339	1.9
	0921	11.3		0906	11.6
SU	1608	2.6	M	1556	2.2
	2136	11.3		2122	11.8
3	0427	2.6	18	0421	2.2
	0956	10.7		0951	11.2
M	1638	3.2	TU	1639	2.6
	2211	10.6		2208	11.4
4	0500	3.3	19	0506	2.6
	1034	10.0		1040	10.7
TU	1711	3.9	W	1726	3.1
	2250	9.9		2301	10.8
5	0538	3.9	20	0557	3.1
	1118	9.3		1138	10.2
W	1754	4.6	TH	1823	3.6
	2341	9.2			

JUNE

Day	Time	m	Day	Time	m
1	0409	2.6	16	0423	1.7
	0941	10.7		0951	11.7
TU	1621	3.1	W	1641	2.1
	2155	10.8		2207	11.9
2	0443	3.0	17	0510	2.0
	1018	10.3		1039	11.4
W	1655	3.5	TH	1729	2.4
	2232	10.3		2257	11.5
3	0519	3.5	18	0558	2.4
	1056	9.8		1129	10.9
TH	1733	4.0	F	1819	2.8
	2313	9.8		2349	11.0
4	0600	3.9	19	0650	2.8
	1139	9.4		1224	10.4
F	1818	4.4	SA	1914	3.3
◑			◐		
5	0001	9.3	20	0047	10.5
	0649	4.2		0746	3.3
SA	1233	9.1	SU	1325	10.1
	1915	4.7		2016	3.5

JULY

Day	Time	m	Day	Time	m
1	0427	2.6	16	0504	1.3
	0957	10.7		1025	11.9
TH	1638	3.0	F	1720	1.7
	2209	10.8		2241	12.1
2	0458	2.9	17	0546	1.8
	1029	10.4		1109	11.4
F	1709	3.4	SA	1803	2.3
	2242	10.3		2326	11.4
3	0530	3.3	18	0628	2.5
	1102	10.0		1154	10.8
SA	1743	3.8	SU	1848	3.0
	2317	9.9	◐		
4	0606	3.7	19	0014	10.6
	1141	9.6		0714	3.3
SU	1823	4.2	M	1246	10.1
◑				1942	3.7
5	0000	9.5	20	0113	9.9
	0649	4.0		0811	3.9
M	1230	9.2	TU	1353	9.6
	1915	4.5		2049	4.0

Fig 5.13 St Malo tide tables with additional information about Lézardrieux, one of its secondary ports. Notice that the tide table is in French Standard Time which is one hour ahead of Universal Time.

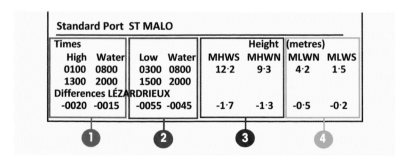

Standard Port ST MALO

Times				Height (metres)			
High Water		Low Water		MHWS	MHWN	MLWN	MLWS
0100	0800	0300	0800	12·2	9·3	4·2	1·5
1300	2000	1500	2000				
Differences LÉZARDRIEUX							
-0020	-0015	-0055	-0045	-1·7	-1·3	-0·5	-0·2
1		2		3		4	

Fig 5.14 Time and height differences for Lézardrieux.

(1) This is the HW 'package'. If HW is at, or very close to 0100 or 1300 then Lézardrieux HW will be 20 minutes earlier than St Malo. On the other hand, if St Malo HW is at 0800 or 2000 the Lézardrieux HW will be 15 minutes earlier.

On 18 May HW St Malo is at 0951, which falls between the times mentioned above so some interpolation is required between the two columns.

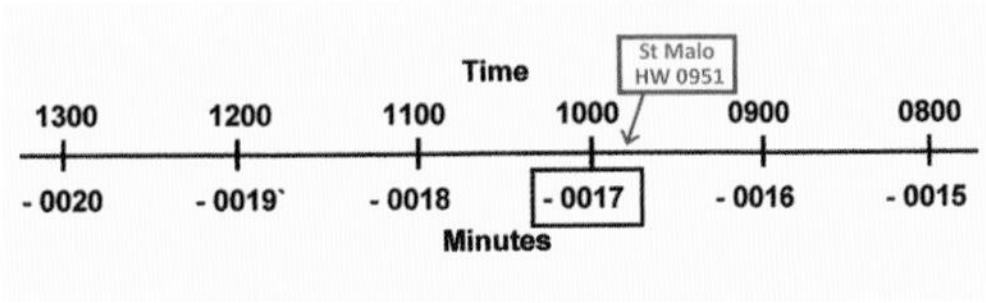

Fig 5.15 Lézardrieux HW is 17 minutes before HW St Malo.

If you enjoy using numbers you can probably do this problem in your head but laying out the figures on a linear scale may help the more artistic.

Looking at the scale we see that 0951 is very close to 1000 and the correction for that time works out neatly at minus 17 minutes, at 0934 Standard Time. Now, we add the hour for summer time to make it **1034 French Summer Time**.

2 We will do the same thing for the LW time but this is for interest only because it is not needed to enter the tidal curve. However, it is always useful to know when the water is at its lowest.

We see from the scale in Figure 5.16 that LW is 52 minutes before St Malo, which makes it at **1647 French Summer Time**.

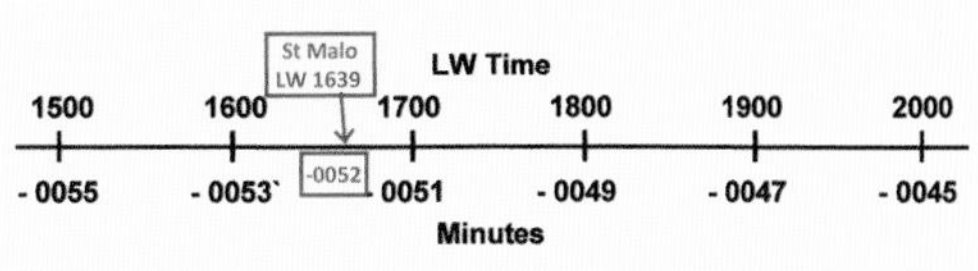

Fig 5.16 Lézardrieux LW is 52 minutes before HW St Malo.

At this stage we are going to make sure that all this information is noted down logically. Experience has shown that the tidier you are with the arithmetic the easier it is – odd jottings on scraps of paper usually result in dismal failure!

18 May French Standard Time			Range 8.6m		
St Malo	HW	0951	11.2m	LW 1639	2.6m
Diff. Lézardrieux		–0017	??	–52	??
Lézardrieux +1 hr		**1034**	**??**	**1647**	**??**

3 Now we come to the height information in part 3 of Figure 5.14. The height of HW at St Malo on the morning of 18 May is 11.2m. Looking at the blue box we see that today's tide is lower than the MHWS height and higher than the one for MHWN, so some interpolation is necessary. On this occasion we are going to calculate the difference geometrically, using what is known as a 'tidal crocodile', which is a different way of working through the maths.

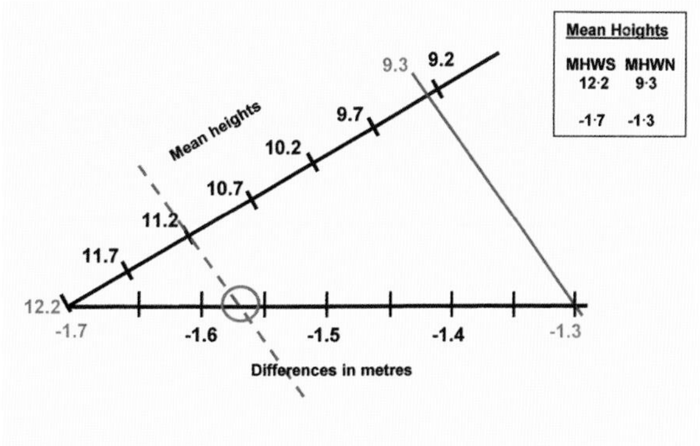

Fig 5.17 The tidal crocodile marked up for Lézardrieux differences.

a) Draw a horizontal line and a second one at an acute angle to the first.

b) Mark a regular scale along each line – about eight graduations will do. Figure 5.17 shows a typical construction.

c) Starting at the left-hand end of the 'mouth' mark in the differences along the bottom line and the mean heights along the top making sure that, in this case, the 12.2m is grouped with the minus 1.7m as it is in the small inset box. It is very easy to transpose the figures by mistake so be especially careful here.

d) Draw a line to complete the third side of the triangle by joining the 9.3m to the 1.3m (the right-hand solid line in Figure 5.17).

e) Lastly draw a line parallel to this line but this time passing through the 11.2m mark which was the height of HW at St Malo.

f) Read off the difference on the bottom line. The answer is closest to 1.6m; there is no need to work to two decimal places.

4 Try to work through the LW calculation by yourself. Hopefully the final answer is now:

St Malo	HW 0951	11.2m	LW 1639	2.6m
Diff. Lézardrieux	–0017	–1.6m	– 52	–0.3m
Lézardrieux + 1 hr	**1034**	**9.6m**	**1647**	**2.3m**

Only very occasionally are tidal curves for secondary ports included in the nautical almanac so the tidal calculation for Lézardrieux would be completed using the St Malo curve.

TIDAL ANOMALIES – SWANAGE TO SELSEY

Tides along the south coast of England between Swanage and Selsey Bill do not conform to the general pattern due to the geography of the area and the presence of large expanses of shallow water.

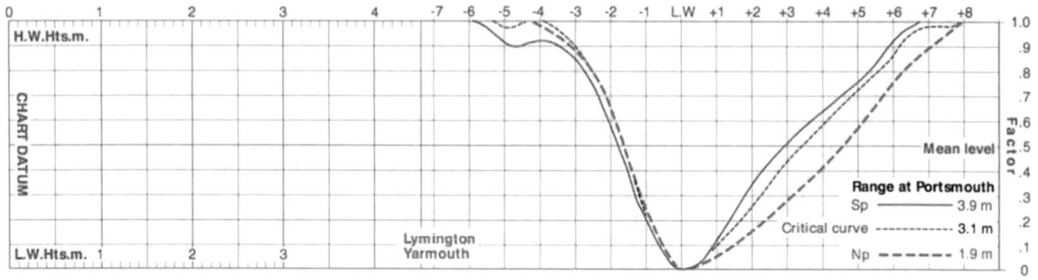

Fig 5.18 Tidal curve for Lymington and Yarmouth.

In some areas the high tide stands for one to two hours whilst at other places a second high water occurs. It is therefore easier to calculate times and heights in these areas using the LW time as a reference and 'upside down' tidal curves similar to the one for Yarmouth and Lymington in Figure 5.18. Note that a third curve has been added for use when it is between springs and neaps. This is because the pattern of rise and fall varies so much during the tidal cycle.

Where two high waters occur, use the height of the higher one to find the range.

◆ Calculating the minimum depth in which to anchor at Lymington

A yacht drawing 1.8m approaches an anchorage off Lymington at 2100 on Wednesday 17 July. What is the minimum depth of water in which to anchor at 2100 to give a clearance of 1.0m under the keel at the next low water?

Follow through this worked example for Lymington.

ENGLAND – PORTSMOUTH

LAT 50°48′N LONG 1°07′W

JULY						AUGUST					
	Time	m		Time	m		Time	m		Time	m
1	0305	4.0	**16**	0315	4.4	**1**	0351	3.9	**16**	0440	4.1
	0842	1.4		0855	0.9		0917	1.7		1018	1.4
M	1546	4.1	TU	1554	4.5	TH	1624	4.0	F	1714	4.2
	2107	1.7		2122	1.2		2148	1.8		2256	1.6
2	0349	3.9	**17**	0408	4.3	**2**	0440	3.8	**17**	0546	3.9
	0927	1.6		0948	1.1		1009	1.9		1129	1.7
TU	1632	4.0	W	1649	4.4	F	1716	3.9	**SA**	1825	4.0
	2158	1.9		2220	1.3		2250	2.0			
3	0439	3.8	**18**	0507	4.1	**3**	0542	3.7	**18**	0016	1.7
	1019	1.8		1048	1.3		1118	2.0		0711	3.9
W	1723	3.9	TH	1749	4.3	**SA**	1821	3.9	**SU**	1251	1.8
	2258	1.9		2326	1.5					1947	4.0

Fig 5.19 Portsmouth tide tables.

LYMINGTON

Standard Port PORTSMOUTH (⟶)

Times				**Height (metres)**			
High Water		Low Water		MHWS	MHWN	MLWN	MLWS
0000	0600	0500	1100	4·7	3·8	1·9	0·8
1200	1800	1700	2300				
Differences LYMINGTON							
−0110	+0005	−0020	−0020	−1·7	−1·2	−0·5	−0·1

Fig 5.20 Lymington differences. Note that the HW time difference is 1 hour and 10 minutes NOT 110 minutes.

Standard Port	**Portsmouth**	**17 July**			
Portsmouth UTC	HW 1649	4.4m	LW 2220	1.3m	Range 3.1m
Difference	- 10	- 1.5m	- 20	- 0.3m	(mid range)
Lymington BST	**1739**	**2.9m**	**2300**	**1.0m**	

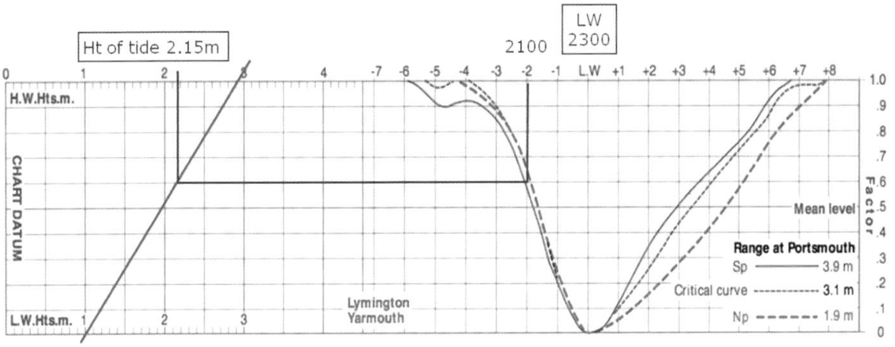

Fig 5.21 The range at Portsmouth is 3.1m so the green dotted curve is used to determine the height of tide. At 2100 the blue and the green lines have merged.

Using the curve in Fig 5.21: Height of tide at 2100	= 2.15m
Fall to LW (Height of tide at 2100 – LW height)	= 1.15m
Draught of 1.8m	= 1.8m
Clearance of 1.0m	= 1.0m
Amount of water required (Fall + Draught + Clearance)	= **3.95m**

RULE OF TWELFTHS

If you need to make a quick approximation of the tidal height and are in an area where the rise and fall pattern is fairly regular over the six-hour period, then it is possible to use the 'Rule of Twelfths' to get a quick answer.

This rule assumes that the rise starts slowly, speeds up and then slows down again towards the end of the period. The arithmetic is fairly simple if the range is first divided into twelve parts. In the example in Figure 5.22, the range is 6m so one twelfth is 0.5m. By the end of the third hour the tide will therefore be 3m above low water.

It should be stressed that this method would not be accurate for areas such as the Solent with its asymmetric curve.

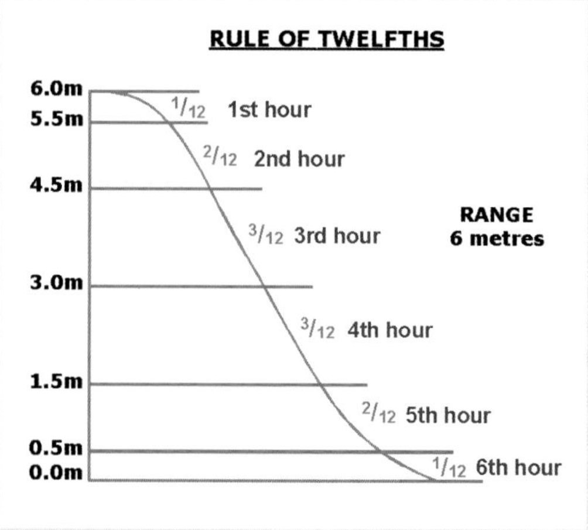

Fig 5.22 The tide falls three twelfths of its range in its third and fourth hour.

QUESTION PAPER 5 – TIDAL HEIGHTS

5.1 What height of tide will be required for a boat drawing 2.0m to cross a drying patch of 2.3m with a 1.0m clearance?

5.2

Tide levels					
	HAT	MHWS	MHWN	MLWN	MLWS
St Malo	13.6	12.2	9.3	4.2	1.5

Use the tidal information for St Malo to solve the following:
What clearance will there be if a yacht with an air draught (height of the mast above the waterline) of 18.5m is taken under a power cable with a clearance height of 20 metres near St Malo? It is MHWN.

5.3 St Malo HW 0800 French Standard time. Using the table in Figure 5.13 what is the time of HW at Lézardrieux?

5.4 LW Portsmouth is 1.6m. Use the figures in Figure 5.20 to calculate the height of LW Lymington.

5.5 Use the data in Figure 5.11 to answer the following question.
What clearance under the keel will there be at the next low water if a yacht drawing 2.0m anchors in 6.8m of water at 1240 BST at St Helier?

Answers at the back of the book

6 TIDAL STREAMS

IN THE LAST CHAPTER we calculated a height of tide for St Helier and saw that the water around the island of Jersey is raised and lowered by as much as 10 metres at spring tides when the gravitational forces of the Moon and Sun are at the maximum. Obviously this amount of water cannot simply disappear and re-appear – it has to physically move from one place to another. This horizontal movement, known as tidal stream does not always run parallel to the coast and does not do an 'about turn' after running for six hours in one direction. Neither does its change of direction always coincide with the time of high or low water. The two diagrams below illustrate this point and Figure 6.1 shows an almost circular motion around Alderney at the time of the direction change. In South Brittany the streams run into and out from the coast for four hours out of every six (Figure 6.2).

A river will naturally flow towards the sea but once it becomes influenced by tide the ebb stream is enhanced by the natural flow and runs more fiercely than the flood. The direction of stream usually follows the line of the river or small estuary.

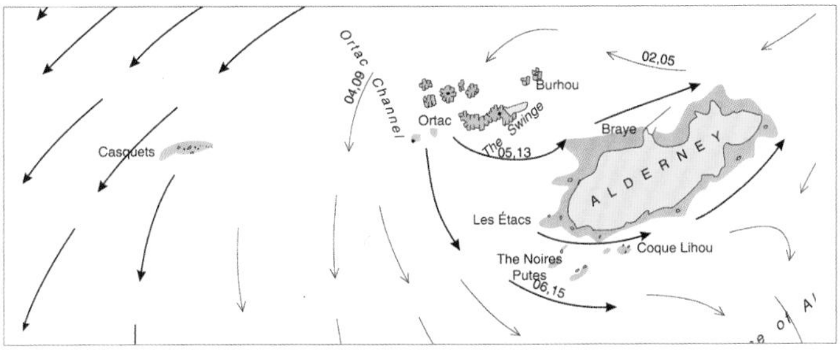

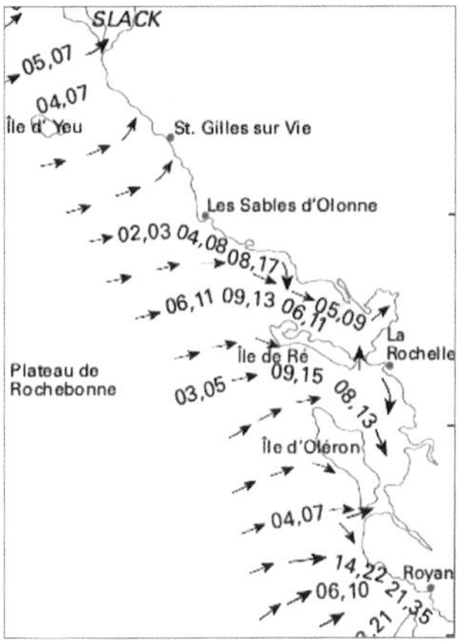

Fig 6.1 (above) As the tidal stream changes direction it becomes almost circular around the island of Alderney.

Fig 6.2 (right) In South Brittany the flow is into and out from the coast for most of the time.

FACTORS AFFECTING THE SPEED OF THE STREAM

◆ Tidal races, rips and overfalls

Where the water gets funnelled between land masses and has to make a detour around islands and headlands, the speed of the stream will increase.

When a narrowing gap is combined with a marked change of direction around a headland, as it is between France and Alderney in the Channel Islands, the flow can be extremely powerful running at up to nine or ten knots (Figure 6.3). As the nature of the seabed is very uneven around these headlands, the sea will be tumbled causing overfalls or a *tidal race* as water moves swiftly across it.

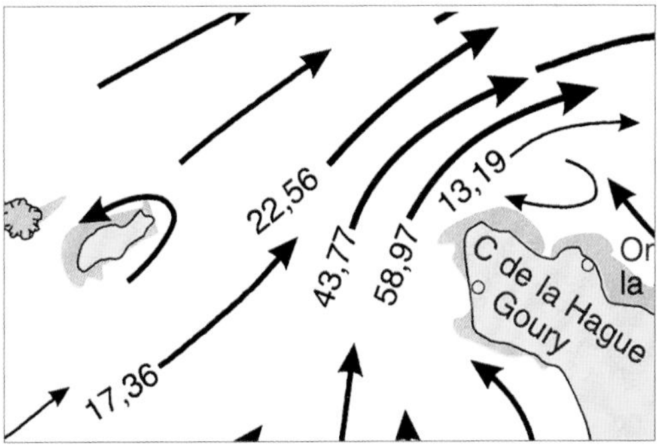

Fig 6.3 Tidal streams off the coast of Northern France.

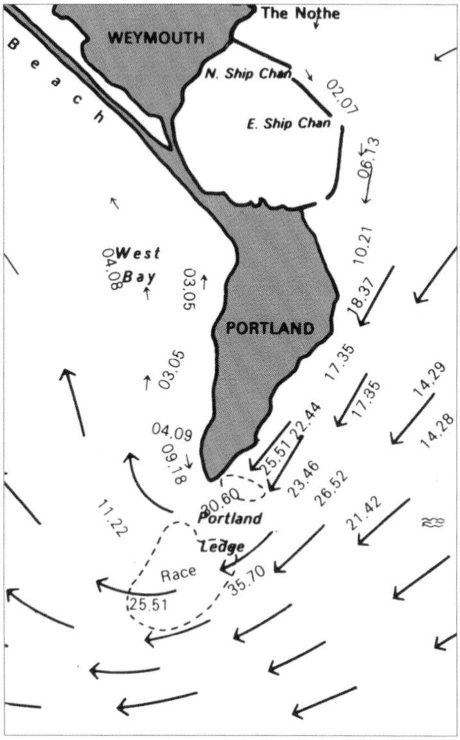

Fig 6.4 The tidal race off Portland Bill.

One of the most notorious races is off Portland Bill in Dorset where severe disturbance can be felt up to six miles offshore (see Figure 6.4). The areas of rough water alter position as the flow direction changes; tidal stream diagrams should be studied closely before you round 'The Bill'.

When the fast stream of up to seven knots is moving in a direction contrary to the wind the area becomes dangerously rough to both large and small craft. Wise, experienced seafarers will only negotiate such an area at slack water when it is at its most benign.

◆ Shallow water effect

In shallow water, close to the coast, the water will run more slowly due to the frictional effect of the land underneath and, at the end of the tidal cycle, will also change direction earlier as the tide slackens. If making a passage against an adverse stream, more forward progress will be made by staying inshore in waters less than 10 metres deep.

These streams are predictable and knowledge of them can assist us when making a passage.

TIDAL DIAMONDS

Magenta diamonds with capital letters in the centre are inserted on Admiralty and Imray charts at regular intervals and these refer the navigator to a table somewhere near the edge of the chart which gives tidal stream information; Imray charts use circles instead of diamonds but the information given is similar.

The correlation between tidal heights and tidal streams becomes obvious when looking at the table in Figure 6.5.

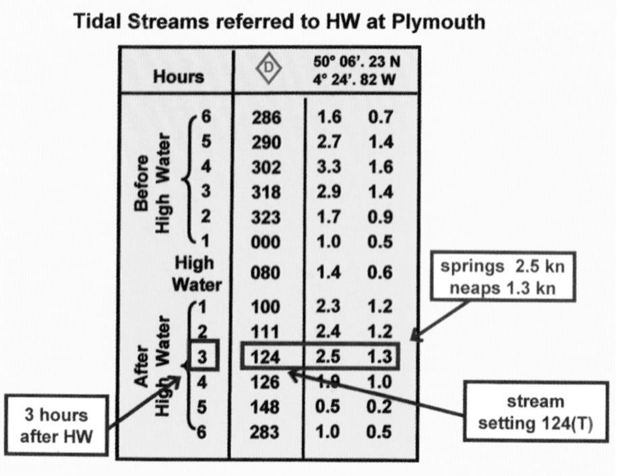
Tidal Streams referred to HW at Plymouth

Hours		D	50° 06'. 23 N 4° 24'. 82 W	
Before High Water	6	286	1.6	0.7
	5	290	2.7	1.4
	4	302	3.3	1.6
	3	318	2.9	1.4
	2	323	1.7	0.9
	1	000	1.0	0.5
High Water		080	1.4	0.6
After High Water	1	100	2.3	1.2
	2	111	2.4	1.2
	3	124	2.5	1.3
	4	126	1.9	1.0
	5	148	0.5	0.2
	6	283	1.0	0.5

Fig 6.5 Extract from a tidal diamond table which is shown on the chart.

It shows direction and rate of the stream for each of the six hours before and after high water in much the same way that the tidal curve does with heights. The stream sets *towards* the stated direction; at 3 hours after HW the water is running south-eastwards. The rates are given in knots, the larger being the spring rate.

One advantage of tidal diamonds is that all the stream information is given on the chart and no other publication is needed. However, they are presented in tabular form in small print and it is easy to read off the wrong line and even to use data from the wrong diamond by mistake, especially when you are cold, wet, tired and slightly seasick!

TIDAL STREAM ATLAS

The same data is presented pictorially in tidal stream atlases and you saw examples of these chartlets at the beginning of the chapter. Instead of the data table, twelve or thirteen small charts are used where arrows show the direction of the stream. The thick black ones depict strong stream and the thinner, shorter ones the weak stream.

At first glance the rates in Figure 6.6 look amazingly fast but then we realise that they are given in tenths of a knot with the neap rate shown first. The numbers just north of Braye harbour read: **08,17**. This means rates of: **0.8 knot at neaps** and **1.7 knots at springs**. The comma between these two figures is the data collection point, which corresponds with the position of a tidal diamond on the chart.

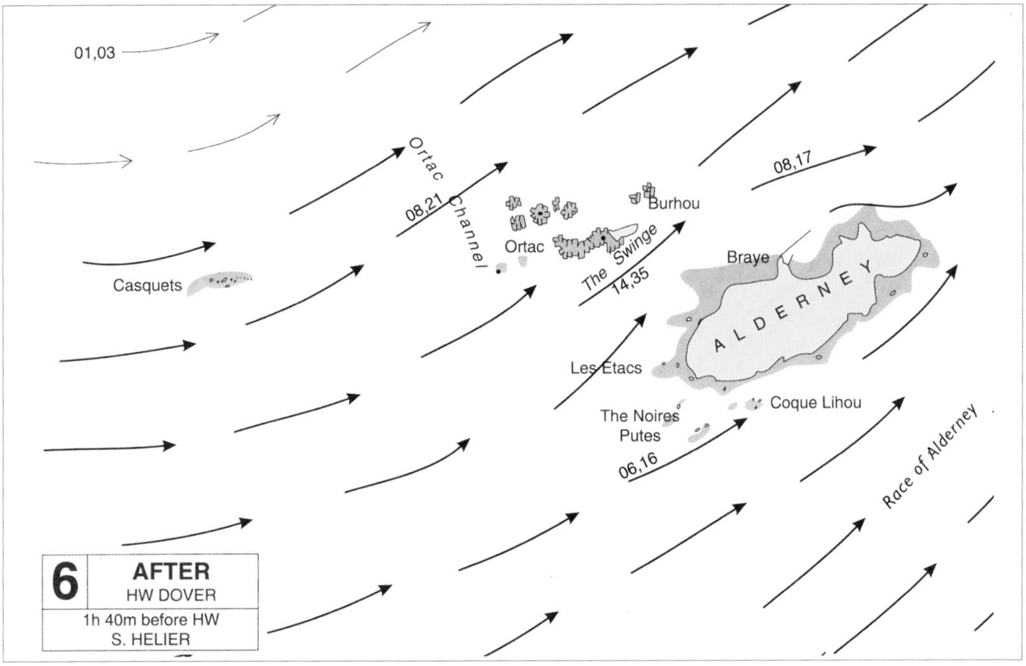

Fig 6.6 Weak streams shown in the top left corner of the chart but much stronger in The Swinge.

The tidal stream atlas is particularly useful when passage planning as it allows the whole tide cycle to be viewed all at once. The times can be entered on the top of each page as part of the passage planning procedure (see The 'Tidal Hour' later in this chapter). A mistake is far less likely when the information is presented pictorially.

INTERPOLATING – RATE OF STREAM

Both the diamonds and the stream atlas give us the rate of the stream for the mean spring and mean neap ranges only. When the actual range differs from these values we will need to adjust the figures accordingly – we will need to interpolate or extrapolate to find the actual rate for the day.

A quick and easy way of achieving this is to use the **Computation of Rates** table which is shown in Figure 6.9 and may be found inside the front cover of an Admiralty Tidal Stream Atlas or in the Tides section of *Reeds Nautical Almanac*. To use this table we need some other information first and for this example we will assume that we are calculating the direction and rate of the stream off Plymouth at **1300 BST** on a day when **HW Plymouth is at 1600 BST** and the **range is 4.2m**.

EXAMPLE

1 Check the mean ranges for Plymouth which can be found in a text box alongside the tidal curve. From Figure 6.7 we see that the 4.2 range is less than the mean spring range so some interpolation is required.
2 Referring to the tidal diamond table in Figure 6.8 we find the rates for 3 hours before HW Plymouth are 2.9 knots at springs and 1.4 knots at neaps.
3 Now look at the table in Figure 6.9. Down the left hand side you will find the range line in metres. Make a light pencil mark against 4.2 metres on this line.
4 Locate the red spring range line and make a mark at 2.9 knots. Notice that the speed is marked in tenths of a knot.
5 Drop down to the blue neap line and make a mark at 1.4 knots.
6 Now join the two marks extending the line beyond the mean lines.
7 Draw a horizontal line from the range margin to where it meets the diagonal line and then strike a perpendicular either upwards or downwards to the rate line. The rate of the stream = 2.6 knots.
8 Had the range been 5.2m, then extrapolation is needed. Following the same procedure gives a rate of 3.2 knots.

MEAN RANGES	
Springs	4.7m
Neaps	2.2m

Fig 6.7 Mean ranges – Plymouth.

Tidal Streams referred to HW at Plymouth

Hours		◇D 50° 06'. 23 N 4° 24'. 82 W		
Before High Water	6	286	1.6	0.7
	5	290	2.7	1.4
	4	302	3.3	1.6
	3	318	2.9	1.4
	2	323	1.7	0.9
	1	000	1.0	0.5

Fig 6.8 Extract from tidal diamond table.

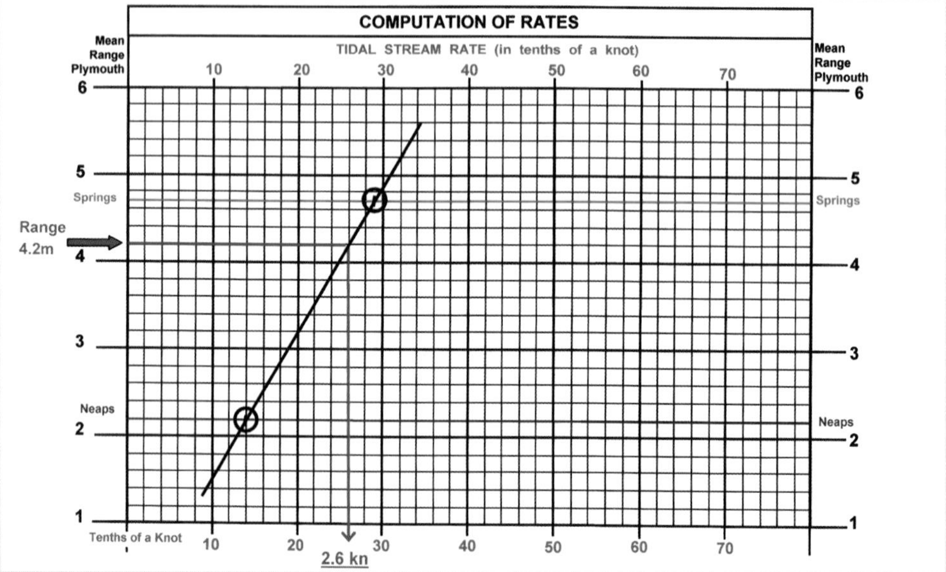

Fig 6.9 Computation of rates table for calculating the rate of the stream for intermediate ranges.

INTERPOLATING FOR A POSITION BETWEEN TWO DIAMONDS

On some charts there are few diamonds and they are a long way apart so it will be necessary to interpolate between two diamonds for an intermediate position. If your position is equidistant from both diamonds you will have to do some careful approximation. Using the arrows in the tidal stream atlas will probably give a more accurate result than using the tidal diamonds.

Remember that all tidal stream predictions are just what they say they are – predictions. The figures can be altered by the vagaries of both wind and weather; over-reliance on the information in a close-quarters situation could be a great mistake. The stream will sometimes turn over an hour early and observation of features around the boat is important.

COMPUTER SOFTWARE FOR CALCULATING TIDAL STREAM

The on-board laptop computer can be used to give almost instant tidal stream information when using programs like Neptune's stream and passage planning package, an example of which is shown in Figure 6.10. The package is very comprehensive, easy to use and extremely useful for calculating best use of streams and the optimum time for departure.

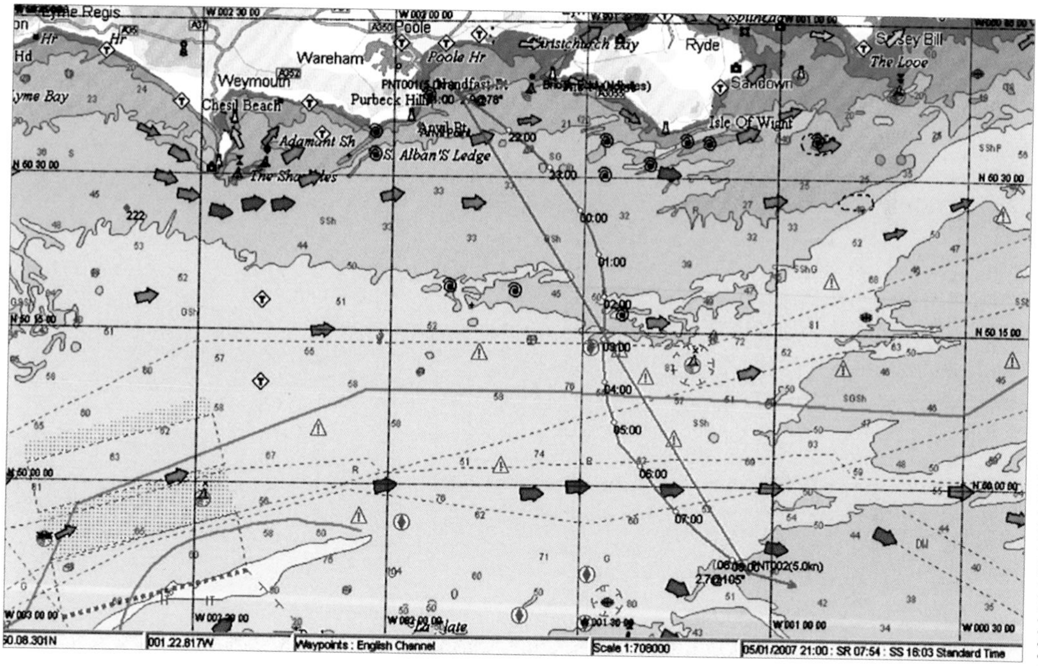

Fig 6.10 Data taken from Neptune tidal stream program.

OBSERVING THE FLOW

Fig 6.11 (top left) Buoy leaning to a strong tidal stream.

Fig 6.12 (above) The weak tidal stream is flowing from left to right. The small pick-up buoy is lying on the downstream side.

Fig 6.13 The yacht is lying downstream of the mooring buoy.

THE 'TIDAL HOUR'

When we look at the predictions in both the tidal stream atlas and the tidal diamonds, we are always referred to a set number of hours relative to the HW time, whereas in reality the stream is constantly changing over the full tidal cycle. The compilers have therefore averaged out the movement for each hour.

They have asked us to assume that the information given is valid from half an hour before to half an hour after the given time.

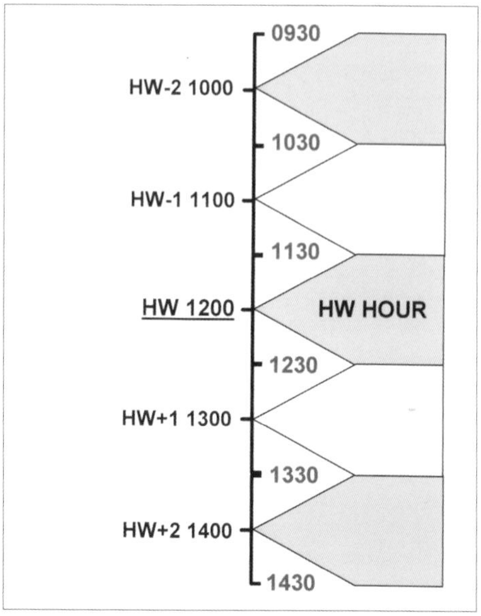

Fig 6.14 Tidal hour diagram.

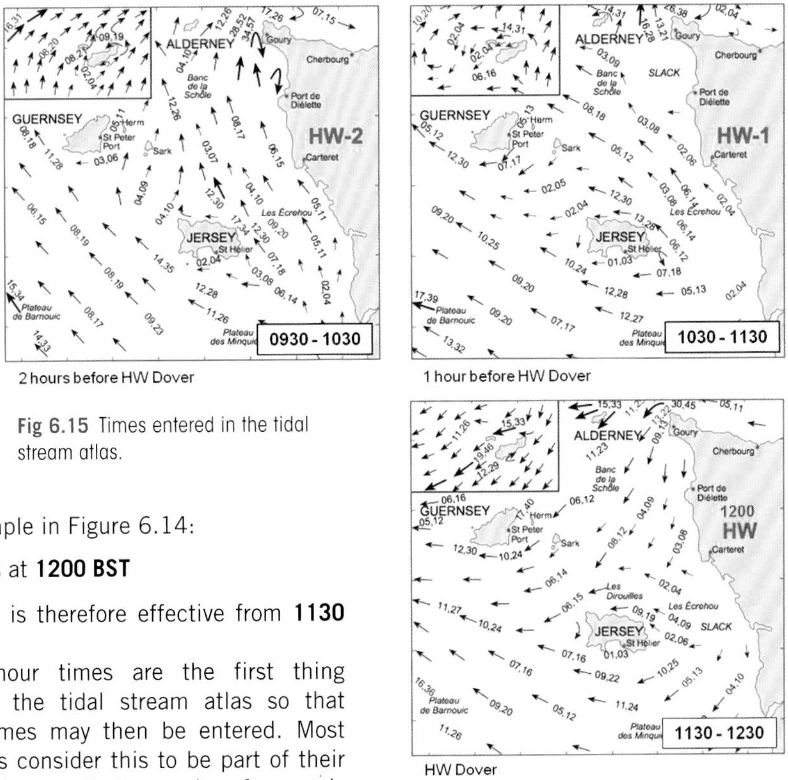

Fig 6.15 Times entered in the tidal stream atlas.

From the example in Figure 6.14:

HW Dover is at **1200 BST**

The HW value is therefore effective from **1130** to **1230**.

The HW hour times are the first thing we write into the tidal stream atlas so that subsequent times may then be entered. Most wise navigators consider this to be part of their passage planning, so that a ready reference is available should it be needed to work up an EP or plot a course to steer to counteract the effect of the stream. The times have been entered on to the charts in Figure 6.15.

QUESTION PAPER 6 – TIDAL STREAMS

6.1 Refer to the table in Figure 6.5 for Questions 1 & 2.
What will be the direction and rate of the tidal stream 4 hours after HW at neaps?

6.2 Divers require slack stream to dive safely. If HW Plymouth were at 0900 between what times could they be in the water?

6.3 Use the computation of rates table in Figure 6.9 for this question.
What would be the rate of the tidal stream if the range were 2.8m?

6.4 Using the tidal stream chartlets in Figure 6.15: What would be the direction and rate of the spring stream off the south-west corner of Jersey at 0715 if HW Dover were at 0930?

6.5 Does the tidal stream run strongest in deep or shallow water?

Answers at the back of the book

7 ESTIMATED POSITION – where we think we are

THE NAVIGATOR OF A CRAFT in coastal waters will seldom be required to work up an estimated position (EP) on the chart because most use the GPS to give an accurate position. Confirming that the GPS is correct is a simple matter of checking the depth sounder or scanning local landmarks.

Away from the coast, rather than putting blind faith in an electronic box, we work up an EP as our check. We might also use the method to ascertain whether we will clear a hidden danger if we continue on our present heading.

DEAD RECKONING POSITION (DR)

This position is found using three factors only: course steered, distance run and leeway.

Firstly, we need to know our starting position and plot it on the chart. At the same time we should note the log (tachometer) reading in the log book (the ship's record book) or jot it on the chart. This is vital otherwise subsequent plotting becomes impossible.

The distance run requires simple arithmetic; the log reading from the starting position is subtracted from the log reading at the end of the run. Note that this is distance through the water – not over the ground.

The course steered is the one taken from the steering compass then corrected for magnetic variation, deviation and any *leeway* (the sideways push that the wind has caused).

When these corrections have been made, the line can be plotted on the chart and is often called the *water track*. Figure 7.1 shows a DR plot (with no leeway) for half an hour during which time the boat has travelled 3.4 miles through the water.

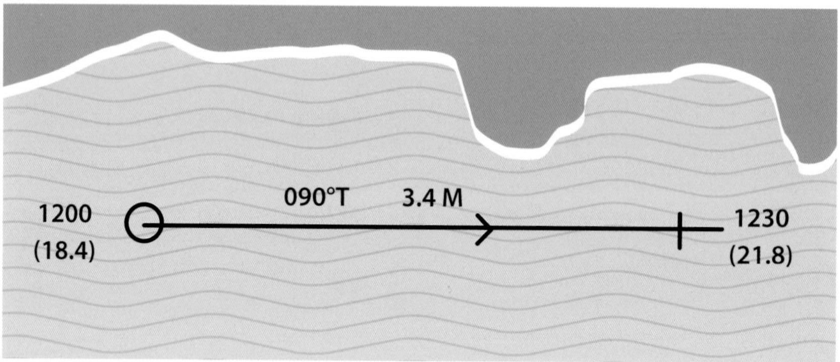

Fig 7.1 Plot for a dead reckoning position at 1230.

LEEWAY

Leeway is a sideways movement that is caused by the wind and affects both sail and power driven craft.

◆ Power

Shallow-draught motor cruisers usually have high topsides and little form under water; when taking the wind on the beam they slide sideways easily. The leeway angle can be 20 degrees at low speeds.

◆ Sail

Deep draught yachts running downwind will make no leeway, whereas a shoal-draught bilge keel yacht, sailing hard on the wind with a high angle of heel, could make up to 15 degrees. When the toe rail is dragging in the water, it may give the illusion that the boat is going as fast as possible but it usually pays to reef down to keep it upright; side slip downwind will be far less at lower angles of heel.

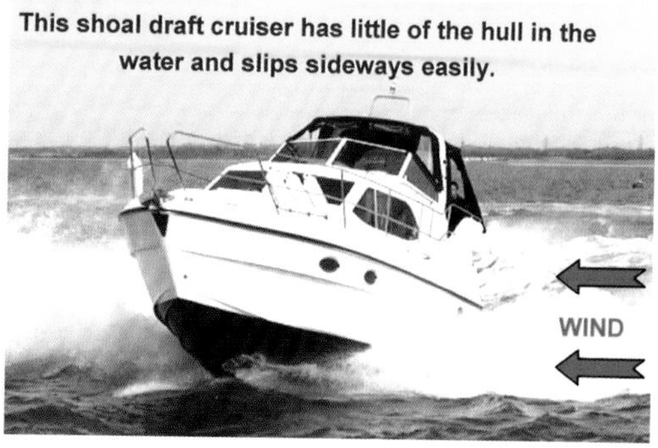

This shoal draft cruiser has little of the hull in the water and slips sideways easily.
WIND

Fig 7.2 With the wind on the beam, the shoal-draught cruiser makes leeway.

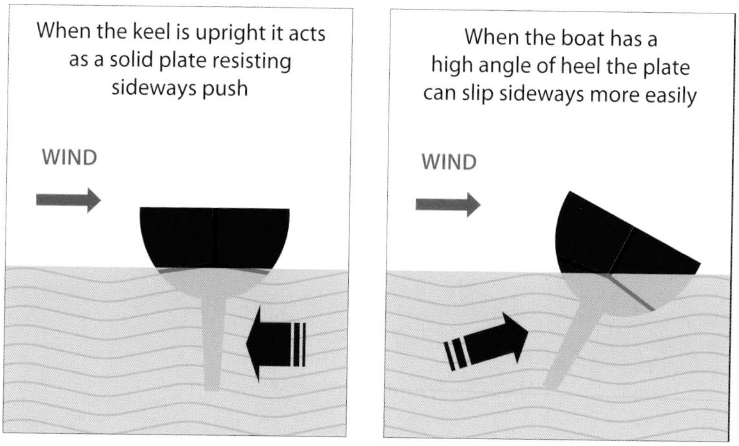

When the keel is upright it acts as a solid plate resisting sideways push
WIND
When the boat has a high angle of heel the plate can slip sideways more easily
WIND

Fig 7.3 With the boat upright the keel offers greater resistance to sideways push. As the boat heels, the draught is reduced and there is less resistance.

◆ Allowance for leeway

Suggestions for assessing the leeway angle are numerous and none is guaranteed completely accurate. Comparing the wake angle to the heading works quite well in lighter winds but when the wind is strong, the surface of the water is blown by the wind and the angle becomes exaggerated.

One respected sailor and instructor used to say that one degree of leeway is made for each force of wind up to force 4 but when force 5 is reached it should be 2 degrees for each force. This theory has been put to the test on many occasions and found to be generally very reliable.

GPS can be used very effectively by comparing the heading with the course over ground. Allowance for any tide will have to be made, but if the tidal set appears to be a lot more than

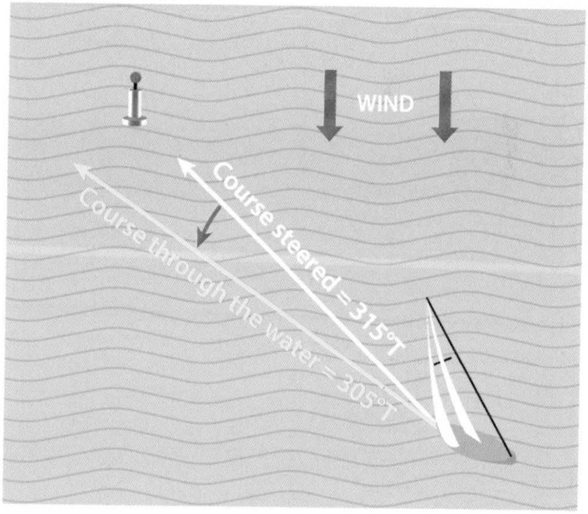

Fig 7.4 This yacht is making 10° leeway. The 305°T course is the one plotted on the chart.

expected, some of it is most likely to be leeway. Never be afraid that you are overestimating for leeway. Any overestimation will put you upwind of your destination which means that you will be able to bear away and not come hard on the wind late in the day.

◆ Plotting when there is leeway

The first thing we must do is to correct the course we are steering for deviation. In the example below we are steering a course of 265°C and the deviation card in Chapter 2 shows that the deviation is 4° West on this heading. Subtract this to give a magnetic heading of 261°M.

Next, correct for leeway – we are being pushed to port by the wind so subtract 10° to make 251°M. Finally subtract a further 2° for the variation.

Remember that we are plotting what has happened to the boat – if we have been heading in a northerly direction with wind on the port side we will have been pushed to starboard so the angle will have increased. The following examples give the workings for wind on both port and starboard sides.

WIND NW **Leeway 10°** **Variation = 2°W** **Deviation from card in Chapter 2**

Starboard tack		Port tack	
Course steered	265°C	Course steered	005°C
Deviation	– 4°W	Deviation	– 1°W
	261°M		004°M
Leeway	–10°	Leeway	+10°
	251°M		014°M
Variation	– 2°W	Variation	– 2°W
COURSE TO PLOT	249°T	COURSE TO PLOT	012°T

THE ESTIMATED POSITION

When experiencing tidal stream, a DR position cannot be accurate so we work up an estimated position, which takes tide into account. Before we can get busy on the chart we need to get a few things prepared first.

◆ Preparation

Let us assume that the Yacht *Merlin* fixes position at 1320 BST on Sunday 16 June and then continues on course for a further hour. At 1420, the skipper asks for an estimated position to be plotted. The navigator has ready:

MEAN RANGES	
Springs	6.0m
Neaps	3.2m

Fig 7.5 Dover mean ranges.

ENGLAND – DO

LAT 51°07'N LONG 1

TIMES AND HEIGHTS OF HIGH AND

TIME ZONE (UTC)	SPR
For Summer Time add ONE hour in **non-shaded areas**	Date Dat

JUNE

	Time	m		Time	m		Tin
1	0249	5.9	**16**	0218	6.1	**1**	03
	0954	1.8		0940	1.5		10
SA	1513	5.9	SU	1450	6.2	M	15
	2220	1.8		2211	1.4		22
2	0343	5.5	**17**	0320	5.9	**2**	03
	1037	2.0		1033	1.6		10
SU	1606	5.6	M	1551	6.0	TU	16
	2314	2.0		2310	1.5		23

Fig 7.6 HW Dover is at 1550 BST.

a) The relevant chart of the area.
b) The tide table and mean range information (Figures 7.5 and 7.6). HW is at 1550 BST and the range 4.7m, which is very close to mid-range.
c) The tidal stream atlas, which is referred to Dover.

Before the EP can be plotted, the tidal hour must be calculated and the period 1320 to 1420 uses the 2 hours before HW page in the atlas (Figure 7.7).

The figures given are 2 knots at springs and 1 knot at neaps, which makes interpolation for the mid-range quite simple, 1.5 knots. The direction can be found using a plotter along the straight arrows, which we will use for this plot.

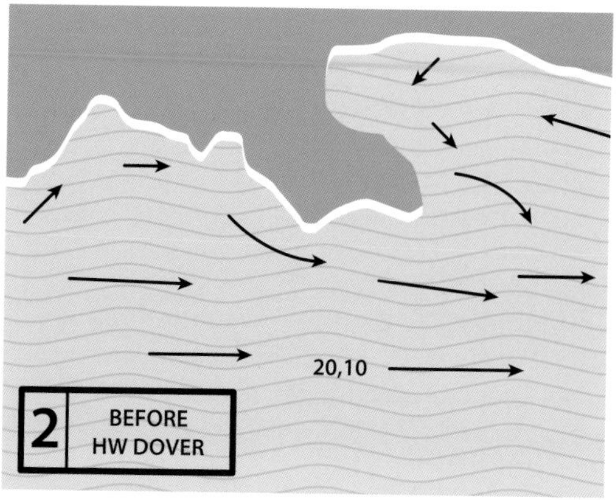

Fig 7.7 Tidal Stream is 090° 1.5kn.

◆ Plotting the position

In Figure 7.8 the position at 1320 is plotted, together with the log reading. From this position, the water track is laid off for the distance covered during the hour. Lastly, the tidal stream is added at the end and marked with a triangle, which is the EP symbol.

The white line represents the path that the boat has taken over the ground and if its length is measured, the speed over ground can be calculated.

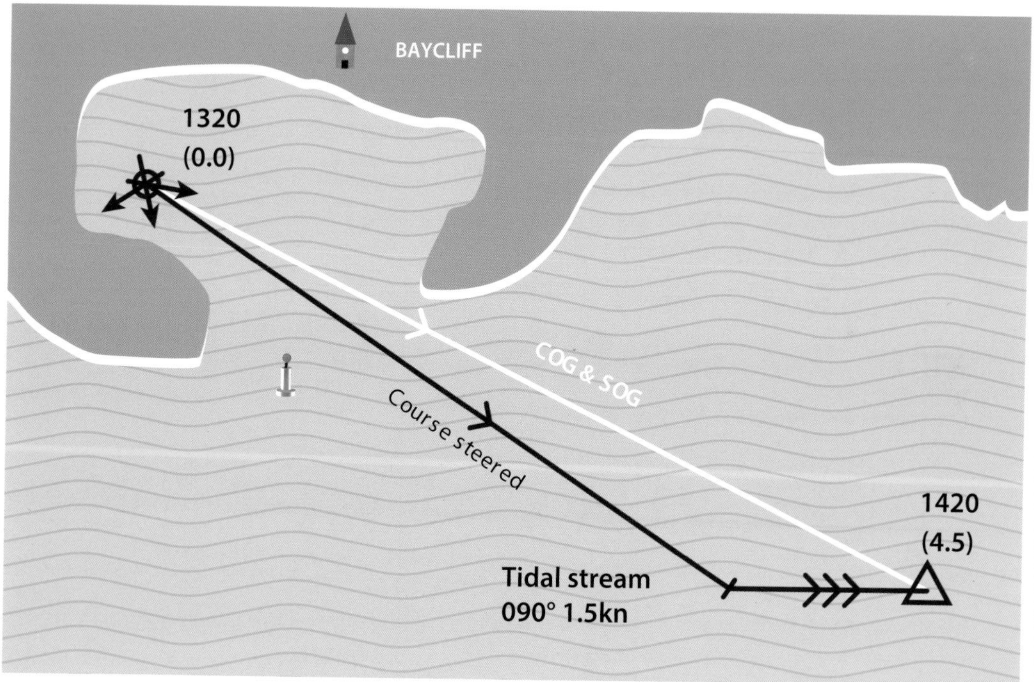

Fig 7.8 Plotting the estimated position for a one-hour run. The log is read at the beginning and end of the hour. The course steered is adjusted for variation, deviation and leeway before it is plotted. The white line is the course over the ground.

◆ The projected estimated position

If you are in open water, which is free from hazards, it is perfectly safe to follow a course and then work out where you have been afterwards but on many occasions you will want to work out whether the path you are intending to follow is a safe one. This is the one task that the average GPS is not very good at because it takes only the present course, speed and tidal data into consideration. A projection is what is needed and this can be plotted easily. The illustration in Figure 7.9 shows a projected estimated position, which has been plotted to determine whether the rocks will be cleared on the present course. Too close for comfort as we pass inside the danger limit line.

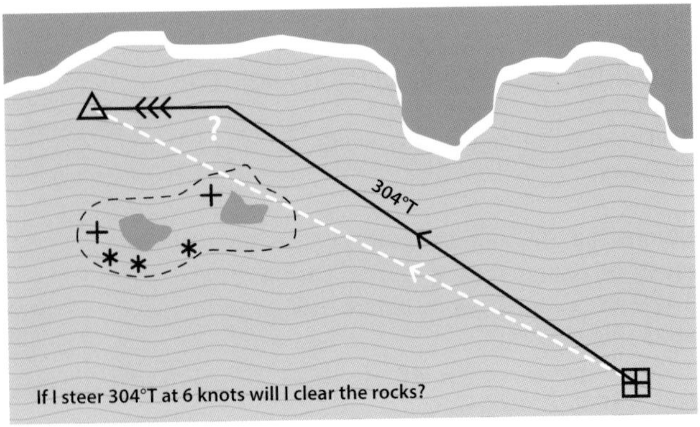

Fig 7.9 A projected estimated position to determine whether a hazard will be cleared safely.

◆ Estimated position when out of sight of land

When we are on passage out of sight of land, the GPS will give us a position fix whenever we require one and it will be one which is far more accurate than we really need. But if we don't have any landmarks to check our progress, can we be absolutely sure?

Most experienced navigators make sure that the position is plotted on the chart and recorded in the log book at least once an hour; and it is prudent to work up an EP of some description to check that the GPS genie is still earning its keep!

Figure 7.10 shows a plot which has been kept for a long cross-tide passage together with GPS fixes.

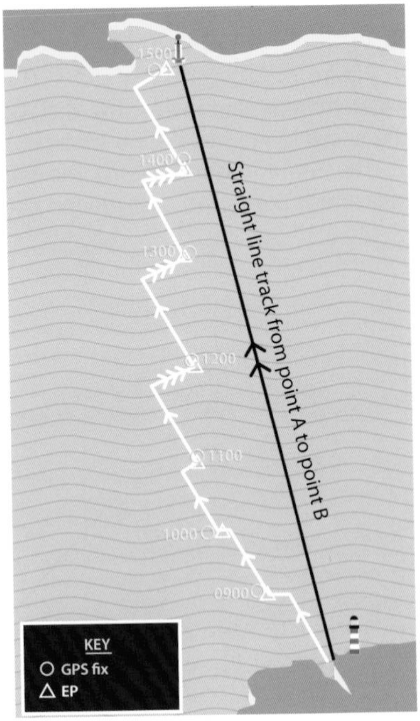

Fig 7.10 Plot for a cross-tide passage out of sight of land. The passage time is quicker if the yacht is allowed to wander off the track.

PLOTTING SYMBOLS

A number of chart plotting symbols have been used in this chapter. When navigational duties are being shared by crew members on a boat it is important that standard symbols are used so that no misunderstandings arise. Coming on watch in the middle of the night, and taking over a chart that has been left in chaos, can be exasperating at best and thoroughly dangerous at worst!

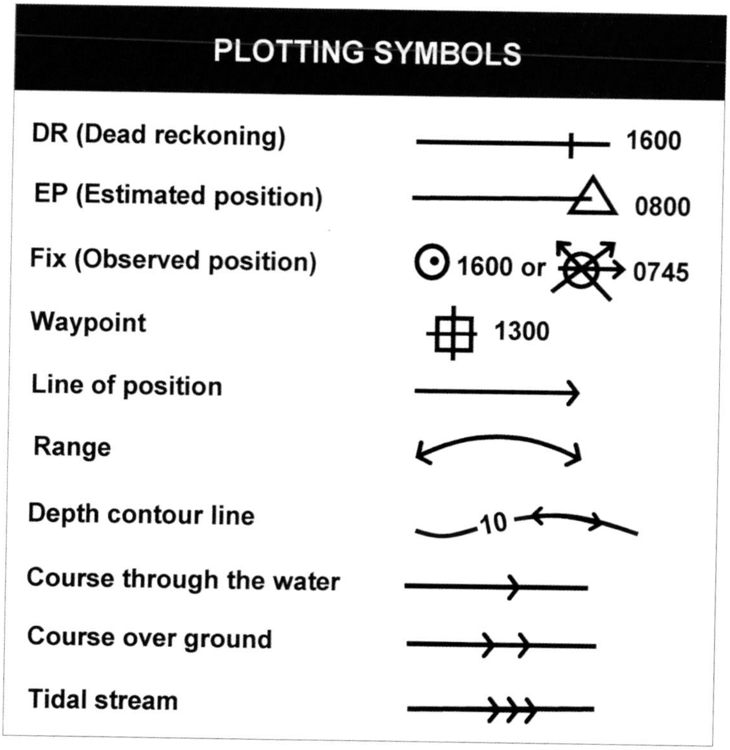

Fig 7.11 Standard chart plotting symbols.

QUESTION PAPER 7 – ESTIMATED POSITION

Plot your answers on the chart extract in Figure 7.12 (page 68). Variation 3°W with no deviation.

7.1 At 1430, when the log reads 14.5, a motor boat is in position 48° 50'N 2° 45'W steering 175°M. At 1530 the log reads 24.5 and the tidal stream is 130°T 2.5kn. Plot the estimated position at 1530 and give the COG and the SOG.

7.2 At 0830 a yacht is 0.5M west of Madeaux beacon just north of Ile Harbour. The wind is north-easterly and the yacht is making 5° leeway on a close-hauled course of 355°M. If the boat speed is 7kn and the tidal stream 315°T 1.8kn what distance will she be from the BYB post by Basse du Menard as she passes?

Answers at the back of the book

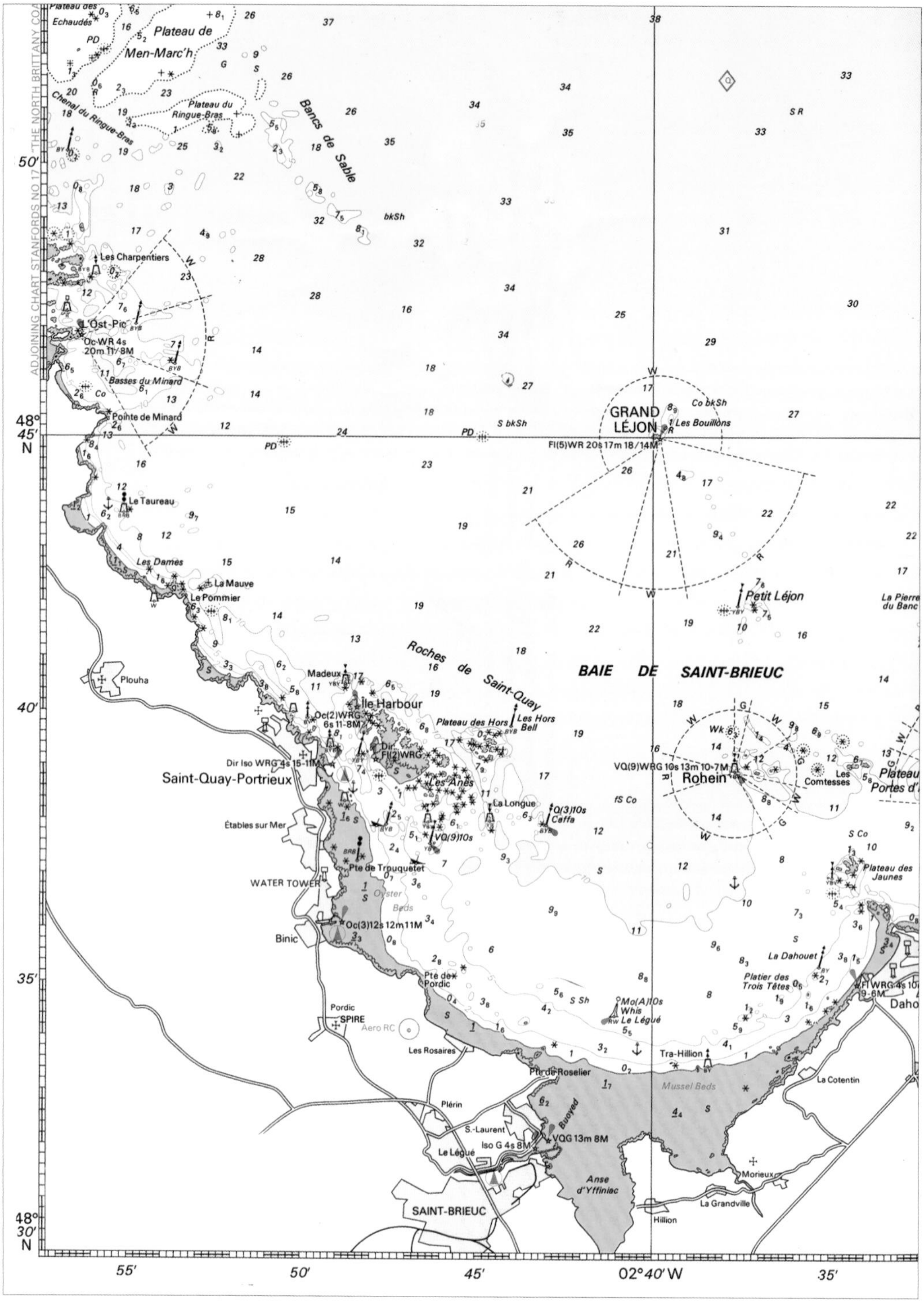

Fig 7.12 Plot your answers on this chart extract.

8 COURSE TO STEER – how do we get there?

IF YOU ARE CRUISING in an area where there is no current or tidal stream, getting from one place to another is very easy. Without tide you can depart when you feel like it, not when the stream dictates and provided the boat is not being pushed sideways by the wind, a simple line from A to B is all the chart work that is required. Throw tidal stream and leeway into the equation and things become a little more complicated!

We are going to look at two methods of compensation for these two forces; firstly the traditional way using the chart to plot a vector triangle and secondly the electronic method, using GPS.

SHAPING A COURSE TO STEER ALLOWING FOR TIDAL STREAM

In previous chapters we learned how to calculate the direction and strength of the tidal stream and the principle of the 'proportional triangle': if you plot a one-hour run you then plot one hour of tide; half an hour of run, half an hour worth of tide and so on.

We will continue to use this principle when shaping a course across a tide.

In Figure 8.1 we can see that Boat A is pushed sideways by the tidal stream whereas Boat B is correcting for it so that it remains on track. The vector triangle we are going to draw will decide by how may degrees we have to alter our course to stay on our drawn track and we will begin by assuming that we are not making any leeway.

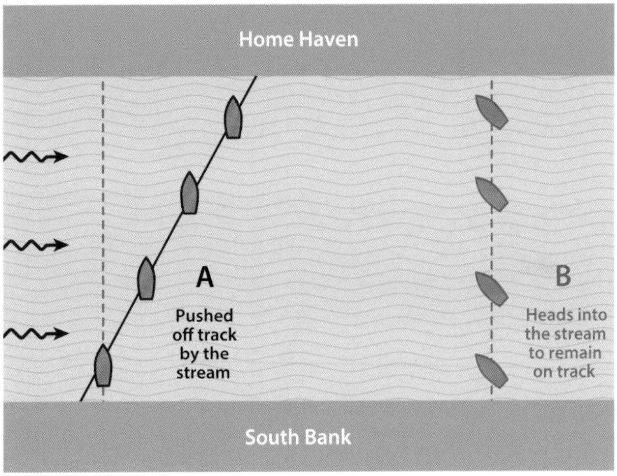

Fig 8.1 Boat A is being pushed sideways by the tidal stream. Boat B is aiming into the tide so that it remains on track.

PLOTTING THE VECTOR TRIANGLE

1 Draw a line from the departure point (A) through and beyond destination (B) making sure that there are no dangers on or close to the intended track. The reason for extending the line (shown in Figure 8.2) will become clear as we work through an example.

2 Extract tidal stream information from the diamonds or tidal stream atlas and plot the vector at your departure point. The whole aim is to correct for tide before you start the run and this may help you to remember on which end of the track the stream is plotted.

We are drawing a one-hour triangle because the passage will take roughly that time.

The illustration (Figure 8.3) shows that the spring rate has been used.

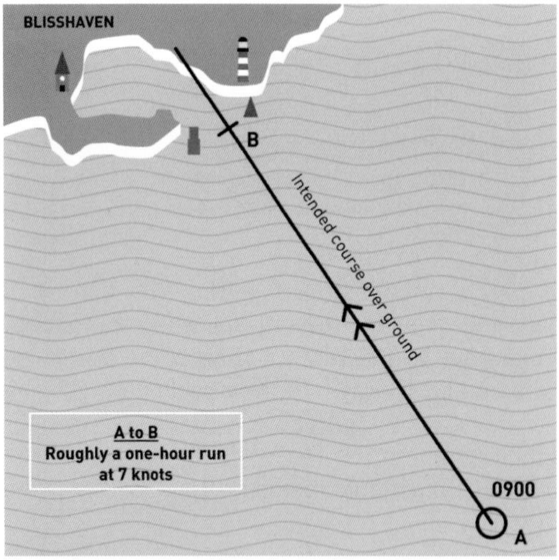

Fig 8.2 Plot a line from the point of departure to the destination and beyond.

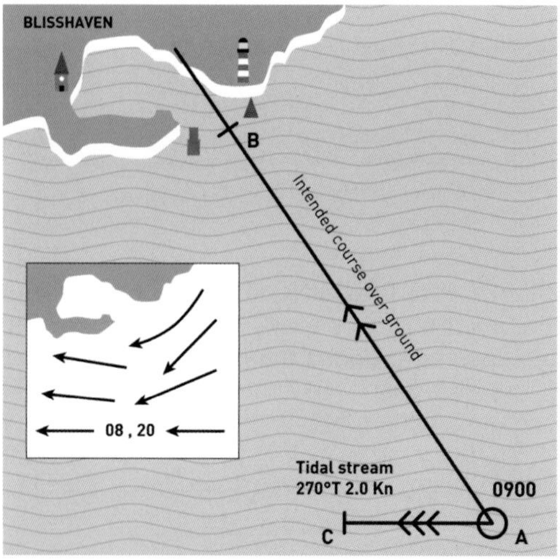

Fig 8.3 The tidal vector is plotted from the departure point.

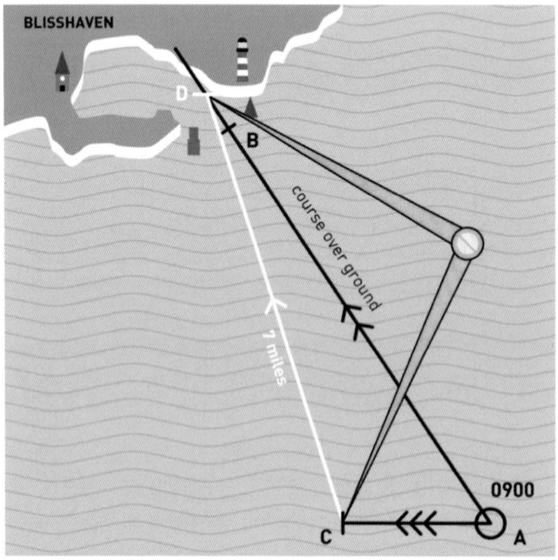

Fig 8.4 A line representing the distance run in one hour is drawn from the end of the tidal vector.

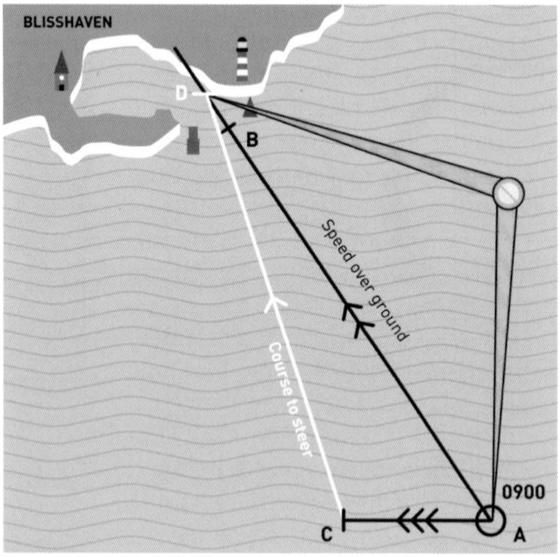

Fig 8.5 The distance A to D is measured to calculate the speed over the ground.

3 Now the third line of the triangle has to be drawn and this is where some guesstimation has to be used because we have to predict how fast we will go. Under power this is not a problem because we can set the revs for a chosen speed but under sail the speed varies during gusts and lulls. There is always a tendency to overestimate the average speed but a 9 metre boat should make a sustained 5 knots in moderate winds, provided that there is not a short, choppy sea. For our example, we are in a much faster boat which cruises at 7 knots.

The dividers should be opened to 7 miles and one point placed at the end of the tidal stream vector and the other point scribing an arc on the track as shown in Figure 8.4.

The line CD is then drawn and, assuming no leeway, becomes the course to steer when the angle is measured.

Until the concept of this triangle of velocities becomes fixed in the mind of the novice navigator, the temptation to join the end of the tidal stream vector to the destination must be resisted, which is why we extend the track line beyond the destination!

This triangle can be plotted using any scale – it is the proportions that matter and in our example we have used 2 units of tide and 7 of speed. The result would be identical had we halved or doubled both of the values.

4 Having drawn this line in, it is now a simple matter to estimate how long our run is going to take. The distance A to D is known as *speed over ground* and is the distance we will have actually covered in one hour; this, in turn, becomes directly convertible into knots.

Looking at Figure 8.5, and assessing by eye, it looks as if the journey to Point B will take us about 55 minutes.

CALCULATING ESTIMATED TIME OF ARRIVAL

If a more accurate ETA is needed, then the formula is:

$$\frac{\textbf{Distance to travel (A to B)}}{\textbf{Speed over ground (A to D)}} \times 60 = \textbf{Elapsed time in minutes}$$

Fig 8.6 Formula for calculating estimated time of arrival.

PASSAGES TAKING LONGER THAN ONE HOUR

When undertaking a passage which will take longer than an hour we have the choice of whether to plot our course to steer in successive individual hours or to work out a *composite course*. Before deciding on our course of action we need to study the chart to see whether there are any dangers that could become a problem if we wander off our intended track. If there are, then we should plot individual hours so that we stay as close to the track as possible, as in Figure 8.7.

PLOTTING COURSE TO STEER OVER A LONG CROSS-TIDE PASSAGE

With no hazards en route it is preferable to work up a composite course for a longer run of a few hours. There are numerous reasons for this:

1 The boat is kept on a steady course and, if sailing, on a steady point of sail.
2 The sailing time is shortened.
3 It is easier for the autopilot, and the helmsman is more likely to remember what course he is steering!
4 Off-watch crew don't grumble that they had just got comfortable when you changed course yet again!

Figure 8.8 shows how the vectors are drawn on the chart before departure. It is difficult to accurately estimate the speed you are likely to maintain but any plotted course is, at best, an estimation that will have be to constantly updated en route. It is very important to pre-plan the passage but only so much can be done in advance.

The course over the ground that is achieved when steering a composite course is shown in the illustration Figure 8.9.

When crossing the English Channel from Poole to Cherbourg, the boat is affected by a cross tide in each direction over the 60 mile passage. After 6 hours of tidal flow at springs, this means that the boat may be as much as 10 or 11 miles off the track drawn on the chart. In open sea where there are no hazards this is quite acceptable but not in restricted waters.

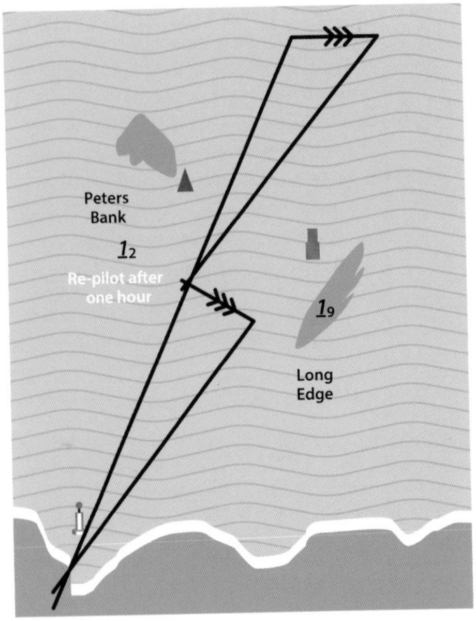

Fig 8.7 Plotting the course to steer every hour. The boat remains close to the intended track but the distance sailed through the water will be greater.

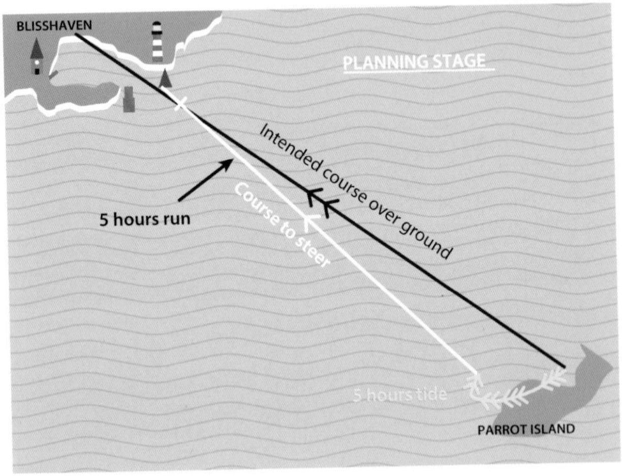

Fig 8.8 For this plot, tidal stream for each hour of passage is plotted at the departure point.

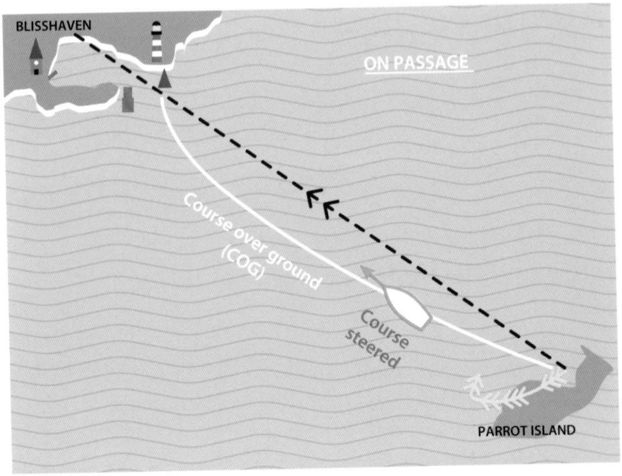

Fig 8.9 The boat slides sideways on the tide and gradually returns to the track by the end of the passage.

LEEWAY

When shaping a course to steer any correction for leeway is done after all other lines have been drawn on the chart. A small diagram as an aide-mémoire will assist us again here.

Do not worry if you feel you have overestimated the amount of leeway you will make. Overestimating will put you upwind of your destination so that you can turn downwind to coast home.

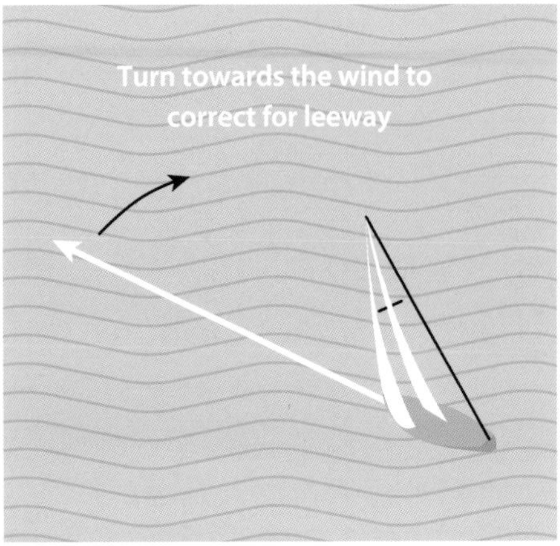

Fig 8.10 To correct for leeway alter course toward the wind.

USING GPS FOR COURSE TO STEER

Course over ground (COG)

GPS may be used very effectively for shaping a course to steer to a waypoint at the destination. In the situation in Figure 8.11 our boat is heading to Blisshaven across a tidal stream, and the bearing and distance to waypoint are shown in the lower half of the insert showing a chart plotter GPS display.

The 'course' is the course over the ground and it can be seen that the boat is tracking very close to the intended track as the bearing to waypoint and the COG are within just one degree of one another.

As the tidal stream will probably slacken as the boat gets nearer the land, the helmsman will need to adjust the course he is steering to make the bearing to waypoint and the course over the ground read the same.

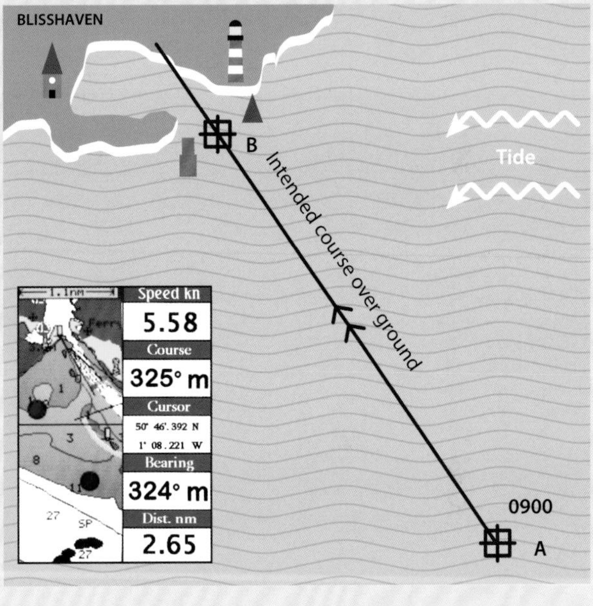

Fig 8.11 The heading, which is not shown, has been altered so that the course over the ground and the bearing to waypoint are as close as possible to each other.

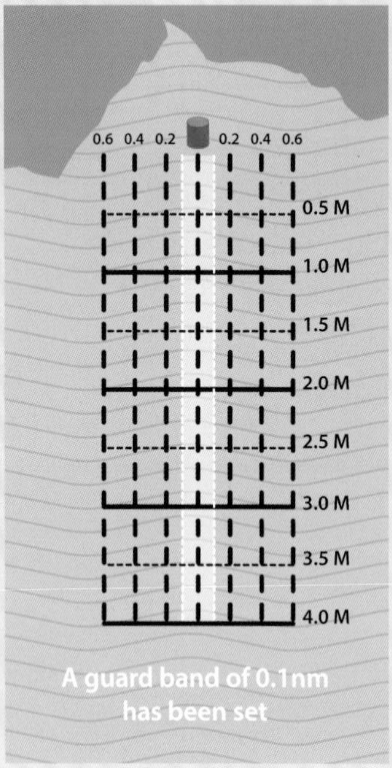

Cross Track Error (XTE)

The XTE display may be used in very much the same way as the COG and if an autopilot is being used it will steer the boat to the waypoint keeping the cross track error to a specified limit. The chart plotter can be set up with a 'guard lane' down each side of the intended track as in Figure 8.12. If the boat goes outside the pecked line, an off track alarm will sound.

Fig 8.12 XTE used for shaping a course to steer.

QUESTION PAPER 8 – COURSE TO STEER

Use the chart in Figure 8.13 (page 75) to plot answers. Use 3°W variation.

8.1 At 1400 a navigator fixes one mile due west of La Pierre Noire west cardinal buoy to the north-east of Cherbourg. Boat speed is 6 knots and there is no leeway.

a What is the Magnetic course to steer to the centre of Cherbourg eastern entrance with a tidal stream of 280°T 1.5 knots?

b What is the speed over the ground?

8.2 At 0900 a motor cruiser fixes position by GPS 49° 46'.0N 001° 46'.0W. Boat speed is 18 knots and the tidal stream 275°T 2.5 knots.

a What is the Magnetic course to steer to Cherbourg western entrance?

b What is the approximate ETA?

8.3 At 1930 a yacht is in position 0.5M north of Basse Bréfort buoy (approximately 8 miles to the west of Cherbourg) in a fresh southerly wind. Boat speed is 5 knots and the tidal stream is 095°T 2.0kn. What will be the Magnetic course to steer to a position 0.5M north of Raz de Bannes beacon if the yacht is making 10 degrees leeway?

Answers at the back of the book

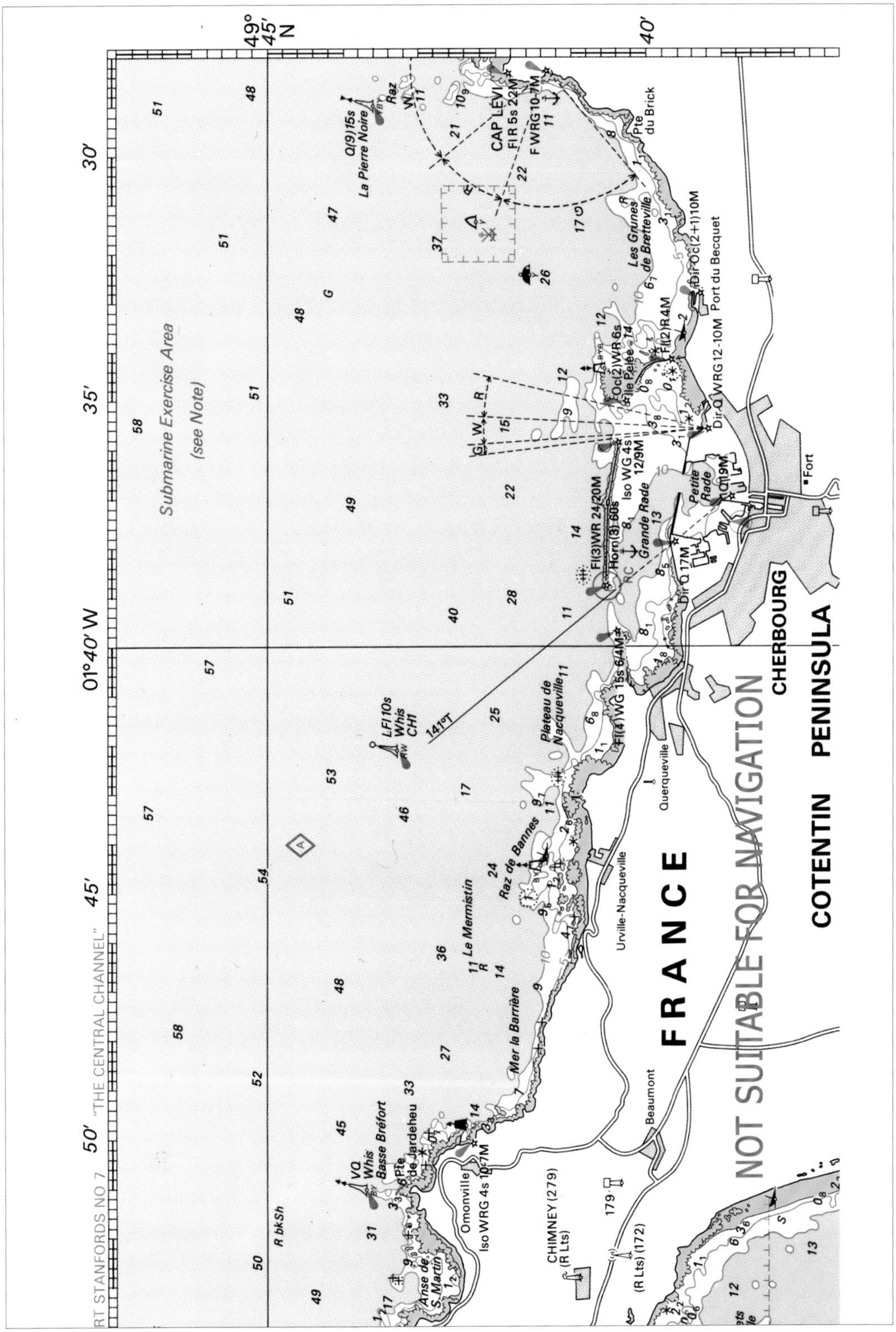

Fig 8.13 Plot your answers on this chart.

9 LIGHTS & BUOYAGE – the signposts

FOLK HAVE BEEN USING LIGHTS to guide sailors for thousands of years and often not for the best of motives. Searching for rich cargo, Cornish wreckers are said to have sent many a good ship on to rocks by moving marks and lights which should have led them through safe water.

Henry VIII founded Trinity House in 1514 and one of its early tasks was to establish a buoyage system in the Thames Estuary. It was Queen Elizabeth I who extended their duties to include the setting up of 'sea marks ashore' as an aid to navigation and, to this day, the Elders of Trinity House, together with the Commissioners of Northern Lighthouses and Commissioners of Irish Lights, remain responsible for lights and buoyage in the British Isles. Details of all lights around the British Isles, Ireland and the north coast of France are given in nautical almanacs and in *Admiralty List of Lights and Fog Signals Vol A*.

LIGHTHOUSES

Most lighthouses are great structures and to build one on an isolated rock required dogged determination and engineering expertise as Winstanley found when building his famous lighthouse on the Eddystone Rocks in the seventeenth century (Figure 9.1).

Modern lighthouses are now unmanned and sophisticated optics and computerisation keep the lights burning. A lighthouse of any merit is marked on the chart as a black star with a hole in the centre ✪ together with a magenta tear drop to show that it has a light.

The light at Casquets, to the west of Alderney is shown on the chart extract (Figure 9.2) and its light characteristics are adjacent to the feature:

Fl(5)30s 37m 24M Horn(2)60s

Let us analyse each part of this sequence:

- **Fl (5) 30s** A white light flashing in groups of five during a 30 second period.
  Note: If the colour of the light is not mentioned, it is always white.
- **37m** refers to the height of the light above **Mean High Water Springs**, which we need to know when estimating how far away we could see it.
- **24M** is the **nominal range** of the light in **nautical miles**. *Nominal range* is the distance that the light can be seen assuming clear (10 miles) visibility but taking no account of the observer's height of eye or the curvature

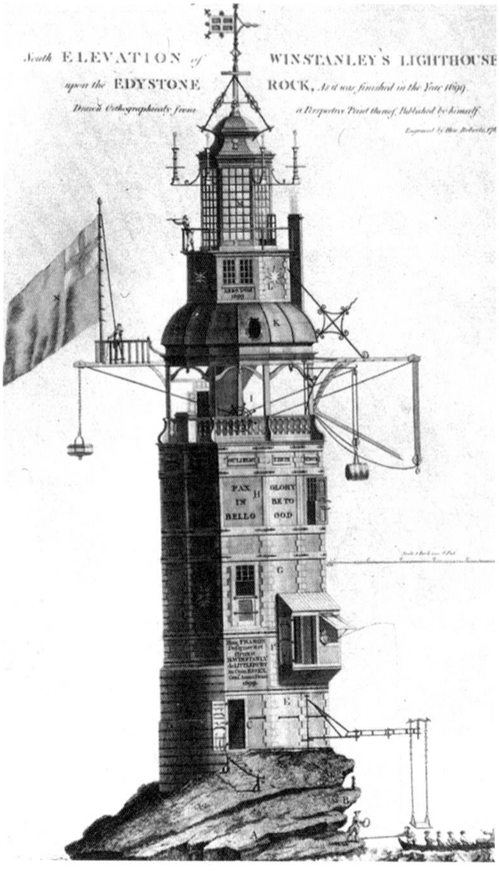

Fig 9.1 Winstanley's lighthouse on the Eddystone Rocks.

of the Earth. In other words, how far the light would shine if the Earth were flat; in the case of Casquets Light the light bulb is strong enough to shine 24 miles.

- **Horn (2) 60s** describes the fog horn which **gives two blasts every 60 seconds**.

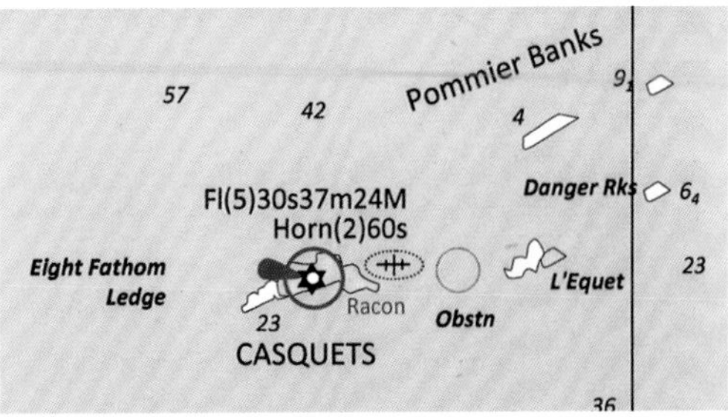

Fig 9.2 Casquets Lighthouse to the west of Alderney.

◆ Sectored lights

Most lighthouses sweep a beam of white light for a full 360 degrees but it is technically possible to change the colour of the light over certain arcs with the use of coloured filters. Red or green arcs may guard rocks or shoals and white sectors show a safe angle of approach.

The light at the entrance to Stonehaven (Figure 9.3) has three sectors, red, green and white. Boats entering the harbour remain in the white sector to ensure safe passage into the harbour.

If a green light is seen, then an alteration of course to port is required; if red, a change to starboard.

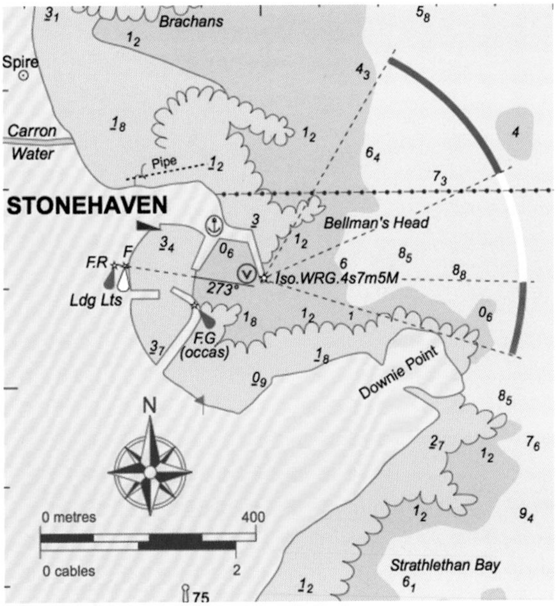

Fig 9.3 The sectored light at the entrance to Stonehaven.

◆ Directional lights (Dir)

Harbours with narrow, hazardous approach channels use directional lights similar to the one at L'Aberwrac'h in Figure 9.4.

These are very similar to sectored lights but the sectors are so narrow that they are drawn as a single line on the chart. Often these lights are intensified (Intens) and extremely bright when approaching at the correct angle.

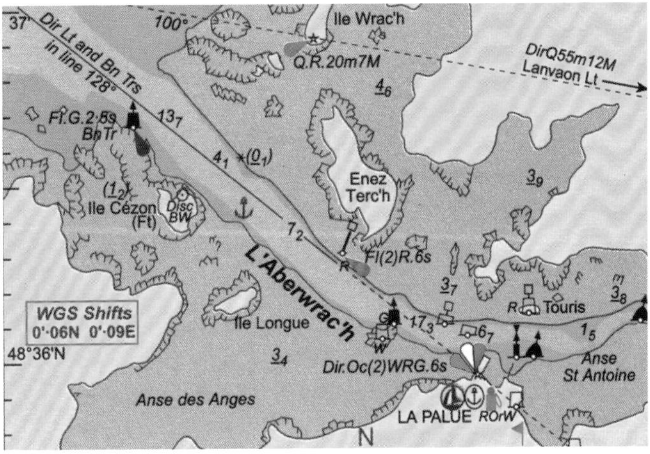

Fig 9.4 The directional light at L'Aberwrac'h leads craft into the narrow harbour.

RISING AND DIPPING DISTANCES

The range of a lighthouse can be used to calculate the distance from the light but this time the Earth's curvature is taken into consideration. If we know the height of the light and our height of eye, we can use a simple table to calculate the distance we are from the light as it rises above the horizon or dips down below it. It is important to wait until the actual light can be seen, not just the 'loom' and it is best to stand up in the cockpit to increase the height of eye above any waves. If a bearing of the light is taken at the same time the light is seen, a surprisingly accurate fix can be obtained – given a calm sea. Figure 9.5 shows a light rising above the horizon.

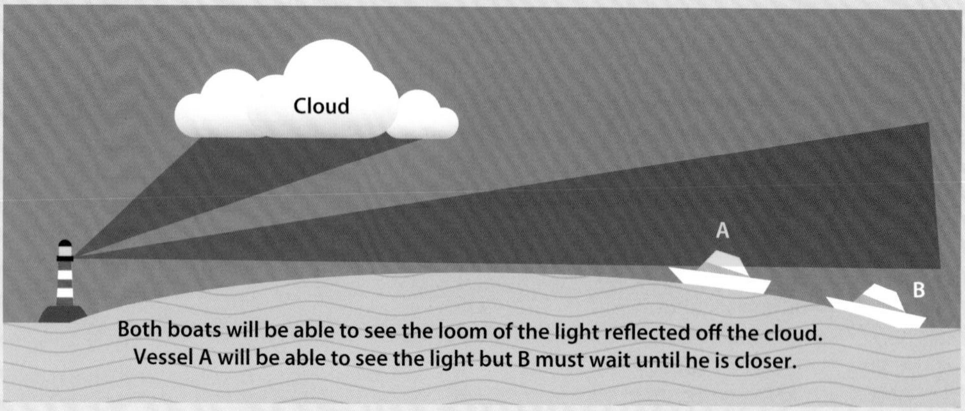
Cloud
A
B
Both boats will be able to see the loom of the light reflected off the cloud.
Vessel A will be able to see the light but B must wait until he is closer.

Fig 9.5 Vessel B will be able to see the loom of the light reflected off the cloud. Vessel A will be able to see the light on the horizon and be able to calculate the distance from the light.

Let us now assume that we need to know our distance from Point Corbière light on Jersey. It stands 36m above MHWS and our height of eye is 3 metres.

Method

Using the rising and dipping table (Figure 9.6) find 36m in the left-hand column then track across horizontally until the vertical 3m height of eye column is met.

An answer is quickly found: **16.1 nautical miles.**

Lights - distance off when rising or dipping

Height of Light		Height of Eye					
		metres	1	2	3	4	5
metres	feet	feet	3	7	10	13	16
10	33		8·7	9·5	10·2	10·8	11·3
12	39		9·3	10·1	10·8	11·4	11·9
14	46		9·9	10·7	11·4	12·0	12·5
16	53		10·4	11·2	11·9	12·5	13·0
18	59		10·9	11·7	12·4	13·0	13·5
20	66		11·4	12·2	12·9	13·5	14·0
22	72		11·9	12·7	13·4	14·0	14·5
24	79		12·3	13·1	13·8	14·4	14·9
26	85		12·7	13·5	14·2	14·8	15·3
28	92		13·1	13·9	14·6	15·2	15·7
30	98		13·5	14·3	15·0	15·6	16·1
32	105		13·9	14·7	15·4	16·0	16·5
34	112		14·2	15·0	15·7	16·3	16·8
36	118		14·6	15·4	16·1	16·7	17·2
38	125		14·9	15·7	16·4	17·0	17·5

Fig 9.6 A rising and dipping table for calculating distance off.

LIGHT CHARACTERISTICS

Lights are positively identified by three features:

1. **Colour** Red, green and white are usual but yellow is used for special marks.
2. **Period** The time it takes for the light to complete its identifying characteristics plus any time it is eclipsed.
3. **Character** The identifying rhythm of the light. Many combinations of rhythm are possible and the most commonly used ones are: flashing, occulting, isophase or fixed.

Flashing (Fl) Period of darkness is longer than the period of light

There can be a single flash within a time period but many major lights have the lights grouped for easy identification. Casquets (Figure 9.2) flashes in groups of five **Fl (5)** and the lighthouse on Alderney, 8 miles away is **Fl (4)**.

Some marks flash quickly **(Q)** at a rate of 50–79 flashes a minute and some very quickly at almost double the frequency **(VQ)** 80–159 per minute.

A long flash **(L Fl)** is one that lasts longer than 2 seconds.

Occulting (Oc) Period of light is longer than the period of darkness

As the occulting light is on for longer than it is off, it is often used for lighthouses near harbour entrances, leading lines and safe water marks. It is far easier to steer for a lit feature rather than a dark one! Both St Anthony Head light at Falmouth (Figure 9.7) and Needles light at the entrance to the Solent have occulting lights as do the leading lights into St Helier, Jersey.

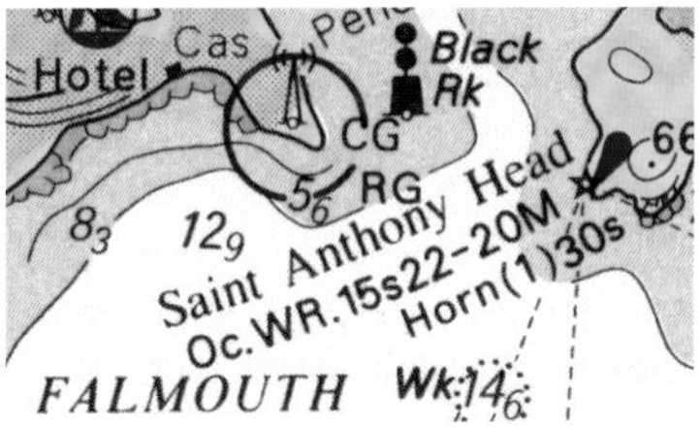

Fig 9.7 St Anthony Head has an occulting light.

Isophase (Iso) Equal periods of light and darkness

Isophase lights are occasionally used for lighthouses but more often for leading lights and safe water marks at the beginning of a buoyed channel.

Fixed (F) A light that is on all the time

Fixed lights are used on the end of jetties and similar features connected to the shore. The lights are mounted in pairs one below the other and usually green or red in colour: eg **2FG (vert)** on charts. Lights in the River Dart are shown in Figure 9.8.

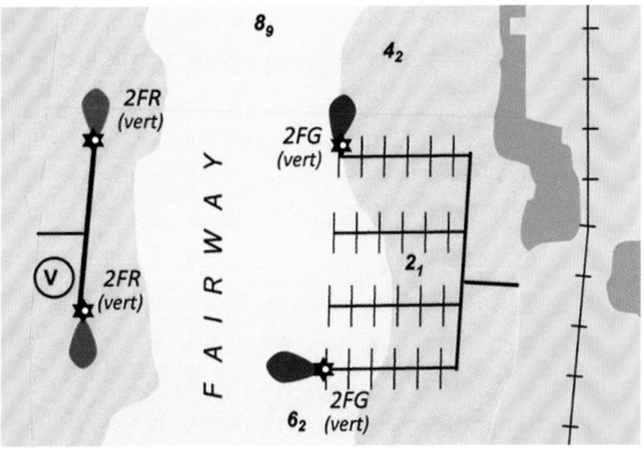

Fig 9.8 Fixed red and green lights marking solid structures are mounted in pairs vertically.

◆ Other characteristics

Morse (Mo) Light that flashes a Morse code letter ie Mo (U)

The international meaning of the single Morse U is 'You are running into danger' and this character is often used for offshore drilling platforms where there are prohibited zones around rigs.

Although knowledge of Morse is now no longer a requirement for the Yachtmaster Offshore exam, the letter U is a useful one to know. It has saved me the embarrassment of hitting a dredger's unlit mooring wire on a wet and wild night near Harwich entrance. Doing a quick 180° turn saved possible injury and damage.

Alternating (Al) A light which shows different colours alternately

Each colour shows in turn either as the light rotates or different colour filters are shown. Sometimes used for leading lights; the ones leading into Ardrossan are shown in Figure 9.9.

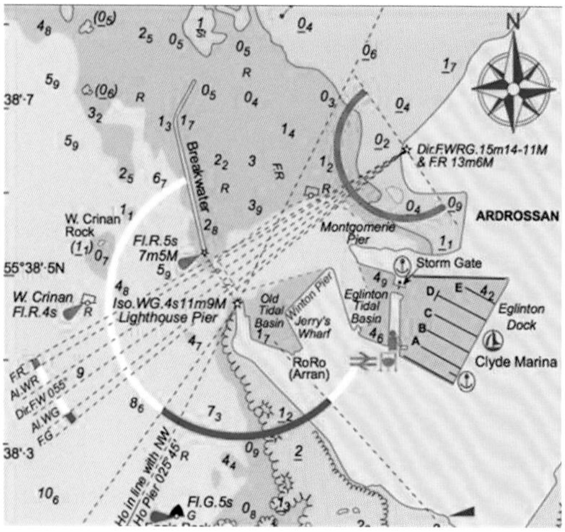

Fig 9.9 Leading lights at Ardrossan in Scotland show alternating lights in narrow sectors.

BUOYAGE: BUOYS AND BEACONS

The International Association of Lighthouse Authorities (IALA) have standardised world buoyage and two systems are currently used: IALA A and IALA B. The Americas, the Caribbean and some countries bordering the Pacific use IALA B and the rest of the world use A.

Buoyage is laid in a clockwise direction around land masses, or in the general direction when approaching from seaward (see Figure 9.10). The British Isles are considered to be part of the European continent so the general direction is from south to north.

Where there may be doubt, a magenta arrow is placed in a prominent position on the chart to clarify the situation (Figure 9.11). In an area where two directions conflict, such as the Solent, two arrows are used to avoid any ambiguity.

There are three main types of buoy: **lateral**, **cardinal** and **special marks**.

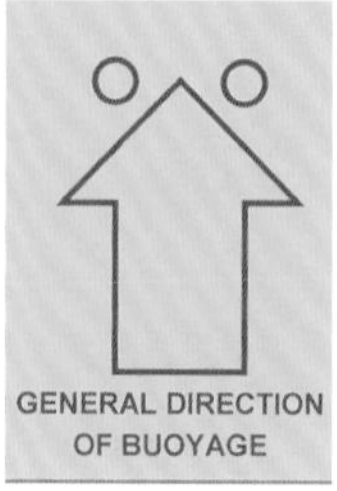

Fig 9.10 (above) Direction of buoyage around the United Kingdom and Ireland.

Fig 9.11 (left) Direction of buoyage symbol.

◆ Lateral marks (Region A)

Lateral marks are used to mark the port and starboard side of a channel and, when moving in the direction of buoyage, the green conical buoys pass down the starboard side of the boat and the red can-shaped ones down the port side.

Channels in small harbours and rivers may be marked with red and green posts or with 'withies' which are tree branches pushed into the mud as in Figure 9.14. Notice that the green post has a *green triangular topmark* whereas a red post would have a *red can-shaped mark*.

> ***Lights***
> *Port-hand mark* = Red light, any rhythm.
> *Starboard-hand mark* = Green light, any rhythm.
> The marks in Figures 9.12, 9.13 and 9.15 are all lit.

Fig 9.12 Port-hand buoy.

Fig 9.13 Starboard-hand mark.

Fig 9.14 Withy.

Fig 9.15 Starboard post.

Preferred channel marks

When a channel forks and it is unclear which one of the two is the major channel, a preferred channel mark is used at the junction. In Figure 9.16, the post on the chart is the port-hand mark for the main right-hand channel and the starboard-hand mark for the lesser one. It is, therefore, predominantly red in colour with a small green portion.

Shape Conical or can buoy or post.
Colour Green with red band or red with green band.
Topmark Triangular green or can-shaped red.
Light Green 2 +1 or Red 2 +1.

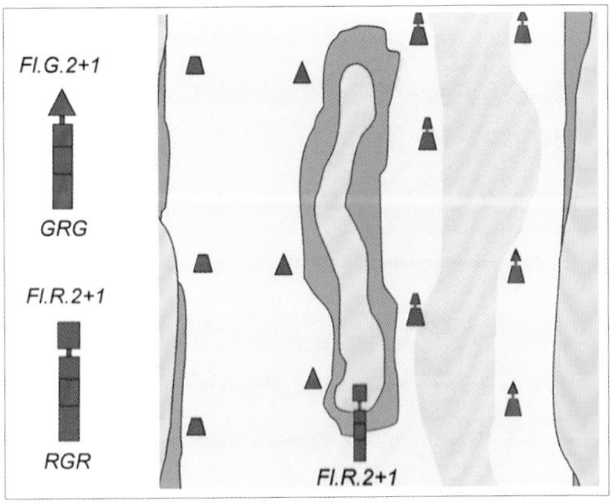

Fig 9.16 Preferred channel marker at the fork of a channel.

◆ Cardinal marks

The buoys are placed to the north, south, east and west of a danger and named after the four cardinal points of the compass; the buoys in Figure 9.17 guard a patch of dangerous rocks.

They are pillar-shaped buoys, their most distinguishable characteristics being their twin topmarks and black and yellow colouring. A buoy always lies to the side of the danger indicated by its name; for example: a north cardinal mark would be to the north of the danger. It will be seen from the illustration that the points of the triangles on the north cardinal point to the north and on the south cardinal they point to the south. The west cardinal could be thought of as 'wasp waisted' or looking like a wineglass; the east cardinal looks 'egg-shaped'.

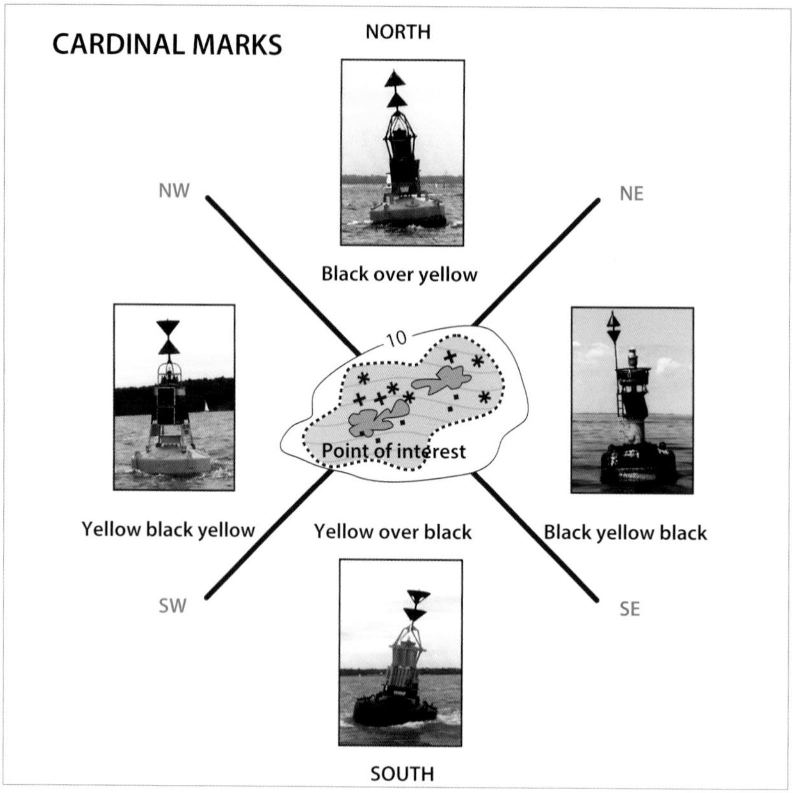

Fig 9.17 Cardinal marks positioned around a group of rocks.

Shape	Pillar or post	
Colour	(Note: points of triangles point to black on buoy.)	
	North	Black over yellow.
	East	Black, yellow, black.
	South	Yellow over black.
	West	Yellow, black, yellow.
Lights	(Sometimes likened to the clock face.)	
	North	Quick or very quick flashing white light.
	East	Quick or very quick white light flashing in groups of 3.
	South	Quick or very quick white light in groups of 6 plus long flash.
	West	Quick or very quick white light flashing in groups of 9.

◆ Safe water mark

This type of mark is most often used to inform those coming into a harbour from seaward that they are about to join the lateral system of buoyage. Called *landfall* or *fairway* buoys, they indicate that there is safe water around the mark. Figure 9.18 shows the Eastbourne Fairway buoy marking the beginning of the channel into the marina.

Shape	Pillar or spherical.
Colour	Red and white vertical stripes.
Topmark	Single red sphere.
Light	*Colour*: white *Character:* Long flash 10s, Isophase, Occulting, Morse A (short long).

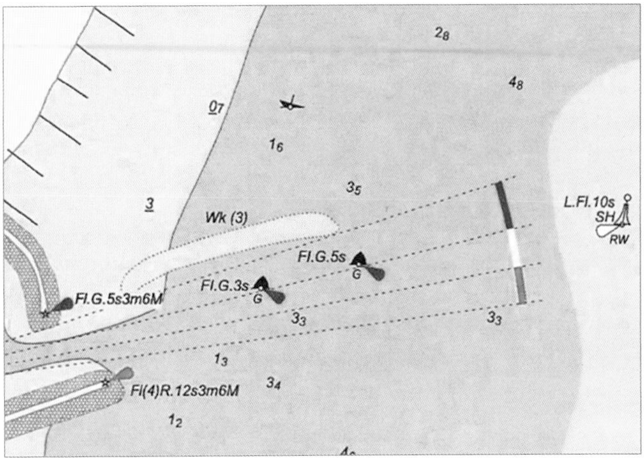

Fig 9.18 Eastbourne Marina channel with safe water mark.

Fig 9.19 Distinctive red and white stripes on safe water mark.

◆ Isolated danger

This type of buoy or beacon is more common on the Continent than in the British Isles and is used to mark isolated pinnacle rocks or wrecks. Generally beacons or posts are used in preference to buoys as these hazards are often close to the shore and in relatively shallow water. Figure 9.21 shows an isolated danger close to Granville.

Shape	Beacon, post or buoy.
Colour	Black and red horizontal stripes.
Topmark	Two black spheres.
Light	White light flashing in groups of two: Fl(2).

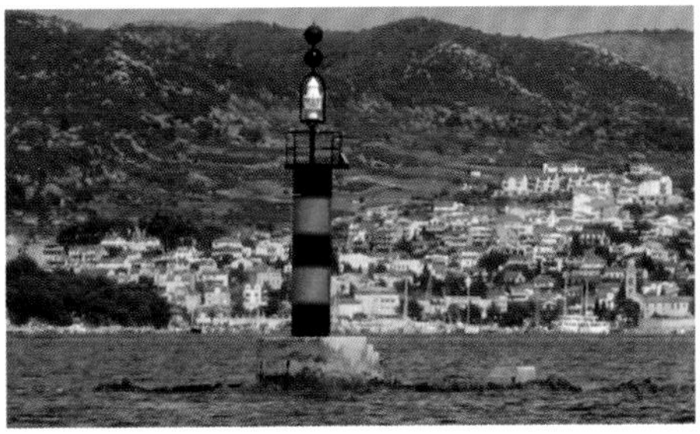

Fig 9.20 Isolated danger mark.

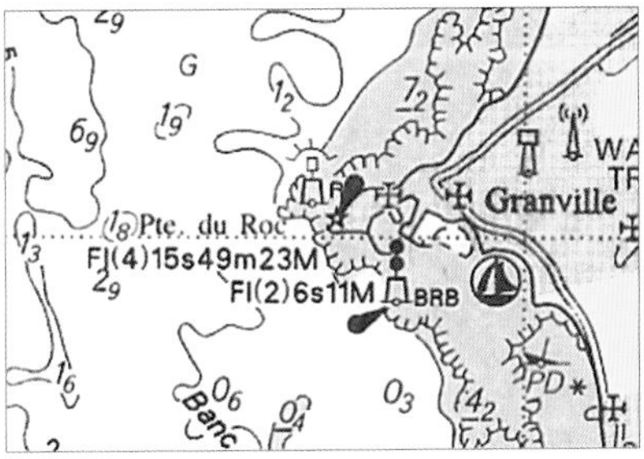

Fig 9.21 Isolated danger off Granville.

◆ Special marks

Whilst these are not navigational marks they are of special significance because they mark the boundaries of gunnery ranges and water skiing areas as well as being used for racing marks and large Admiralty mooring buoys. Very large yellow marks are used for collecting data on tidal streams and water temperature. The mark in Figure 9.22 is a Solent racing mark.

Shape Spherical, can-shaped or conical.
Although not primarily to assist navigation, these special marks are listed in booklet 5011 as coming under the IALA buoyage system. If the can shape is used to mark a restricted area then it should be left to port to remain clear when proceeding in the general direction of buoyage. The exact purpose will be shown on the chart.

Colour Yellow.

Topmark Yellow diagonal cross.

Light Yellow, any rhythm not used for a white light.
Although many special marks are unlit a yellow light is used for ones that are close to channels and liable to be hit at night.

Fig 9.22 Racing mark in the Western Solent.

◆ Temporary Wreck Buoy

In 2006 Trinity House introduced a very noticeable buoy to temporarily mark new dangerous wrecks which are close to shipping channels. It is blue and yellow in colour and has an alternating blue and yellow light. Some models are fitted with a yellow St George's cross topmark as shown in the illustration of THV *Alert* laying such a mark in the Harwich area (Figure 9.23).

Fig 9.23 Temporary wreck buoy.

QUESTION PAPER 9 – LIGHTS AND BUOYAGE

9.1 As you enter harbour at night, you see two fixed red lights mounted in a vertical line. Do you leave them to port or to starboard?

9.2 What is the topmark of a buoy with red and black horizontal stripes?

9.3 Which of the following is the correct light for a yellow buoy?

a Flashing 4 yellow
b Isophase yellow
c Flashing 3 yellow

9.4 What is the full meaning of the following when referring to a lighthouse?
Fl.(2)15s45m18M +F.R

9.5 You see a light which has a sequence of one long flash every ten seconds. What type of buoy is it?

Answers at the back of the book

10 PILOTAGE

WHEN CRUISING OFFSHORE, and out of sight of land, there is nearly always plenty of time to work up courses to steer and to keep a perfect navigational plot. As the land is closed there is a lot more to think about as the water gets shallower and we are faced with numerous buoys marking shoals and hidden hazards. The tidal stream pushes up the approach channel rather more quickly than anticipated and suddenly the unprepared navigator is floundering to keep pace with events. This is the time to use pilotage skills and a good aerial photo of the harbour (Figure 10.1) could have saved a thousand doubts!

Fig 10.1 Yarmouth, Isle of Wight.

Forward planning is the key to successful pilotage even if it means waiting outside the harbour while a plan is worked out for getting in. Always resist the temptation to 'wing it', hoping that you will be able to work things out as you go along – invariably you can't!

Most major harbours have deep unobstructed water all the way to a clearly marked breakwater or pier head; few pilotage techniques are needed to enter. However, many require all the weapons in the armoury to ensure that a safe line of approach is monitored and that all dangers are cleared.

BUOYAGE

Navigational buoys mark channels where there are no obstructions and, hopefully, sufficient water to remain afloat. They greatly assist with pilotage and it is therefore quite acceptable to hop from one buoy to another to find the way in, provided that we do not hog the deep water channel that larger ships require and that the buoys are counted off correctly. A word of warning – it is very easy to miss a buoy out, particularly when turning round a bend in a river.

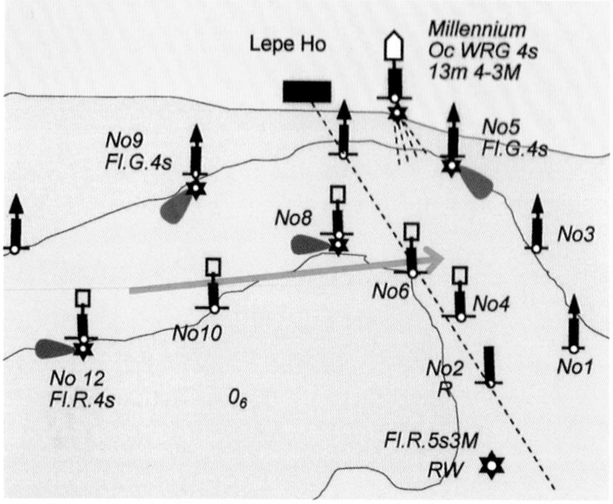

Fig 10.2 The orange arrow marks the straight line course when leaving the river. This course passes to the wrong side of post No 8 and a grounding is often the result.

The chart in Figure 10.2 shows a corner at the entrance to the River Beaulieu which frequently causes a problem when leaving the river under sail on the starboard tack. When a yacht is approaching post No 10, the next post is sighted in line and the helmsman steers to leave it to starboard. Unfortunately, he is looking at post No 6 as

No 8 is hidden under the headsail; he cuts the corner and the yacht runs aground on the drying bank.

A pilotage plan could have prevented this grounding. Without a plan, the navigator becomes overworked and stressed, making only occasional guest appearances on deck whilst the rest of the crew become apprehensive. It certainly pays to list all the posts and buoys together with bearings and distances between each so that even if the helmsman cannot see the next buoy, the boat can be turned on to a safe heading. Consult both pilot book and almanac for photographs and local information and calculate direction and rate of the tidal stream so that you have a rough idea how long it will take to reach the next buoy. If this is done, there is less chance of missing a buoy or reaching one before it is expected.

TRANSITS

See also Chapter 4.

Using a transit to keep a good approach line in a cross-tide situation means that the navigator doesn't have to be down at the chart table working out courses to steer when he should be on deck keeping an eye on progress.

The transit can be an official man-made one as it is at Beaucette Marina on Guernsey (Figure 10.10) or derived from local features such as an unusually shaped tree or a building on the shore.

Lymington, at the western end of the Solent, has a strong cross tide when approached from the south and a useful natural transit can be made by lining up the race-starting platform with a convenient tree behind as shown in Figure 10.3.

Fig 10.3 An effective transit has been made by lining up a prominent tree and the race-starting platform.

CLEARING BEARINGS USING THE HAND BEARING COMPASS

Some of the most peaceful anchorages may be found in rocky bays but without leading lines, the skipper is often reluctant to venture in for fear of grounding.

Let's assume that wind is in the north and that the recommended anchorage in Guernsey's Icart Bay will give us a calm anchorage for lunch (Figure 10.4). Unfortunately there is a large rock which covers and uncovers in the middle of the bay so this is where a *clearing bearing* will come to the rescue.

The first thing to do is to study the chart to find a feature on the shore such as a flagstaff or tower which could be used to take bearings. In the case of Icart Bay there is a convenient Martello Tower in the north-west corner. The safest approach line is to the west of the rock as there in another smaller rock to the east.

Fig 10.4 The Martello tower is used to provide a bearing to clear the drying rock.

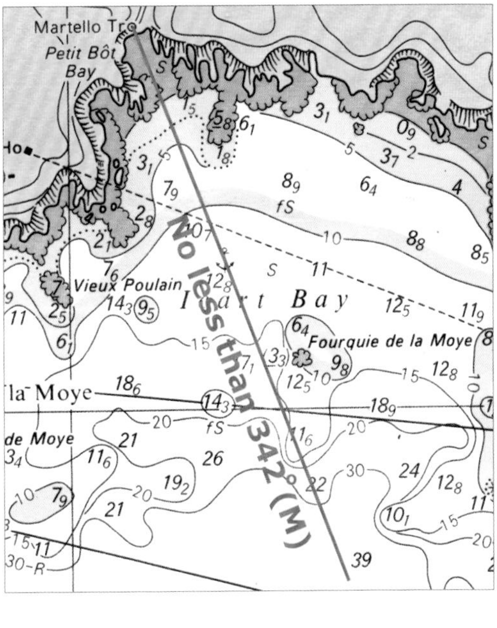

Draw a line from the tower past the western side of the rock, then measure the angle with a plotter. Conversion to magnetic is important at this stage because a crew member will probably be using the hand bearing compass to call out bearings to the navigator, and it is best that there is no ambiguity between Magnetic and True.

Now pretend that you are on the dangerous side of your drawn line. From that position, is the bearing of the tower less or more than 342°M? Obviously, it is less than the safe angle and so we label the line 'No less than 342°M' (sometimes abbreviated to read 'NL 342°M').

If the boat is to be anchored further into the bay, a second bearing would be required so that the drying ledge to port is cleared.

Note that this anchorage wouldn't be suitable for an overnight stay if a quick and safe exit were required in the dark.

In the second example, Boufresse Rock and Platte Boue have to be given a wide berth on the approach into St Peter Port from the north. Fortunately we have the prominent beacon tower on Tautenay, in the bottom left hand corner of Figure 10.5, which we can use for bearings.

In the situation shown, the bearing must be less than 216°M and has been drawn to give a good clearance as a strong tidal stream will push the craft sideways very quickly.

Clearing bearings are an important pilotage tool and easy to use. Other crew members can become interested and involved with taking the bearings and, if the navigator were to make a mistake, there is a second person to notice the error. Where pilotage is concerned the saying 'a problem shared is a problem halved' is very true.

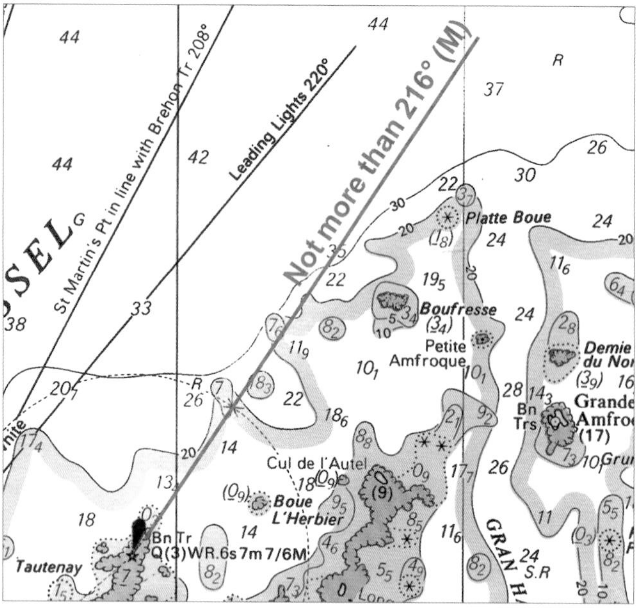

Fig 10.5 In an area with strong cross-tides it is prudent to use a clearing bearing to ensure safe pilotage. This bearing on Tautenay, off Guernsey, will keep the boat clear of Boufresse Rock.

CLEARING RANGES USING RADAR

Those navigators with radar can use it very effectively to avoid rocks and shoals off the coast. Instead of a clearing bearing, a clearing range may be used to perform a similar task provided that the coastline is reasonably straight, well defined and not low-lying. This method has the advantage that it can be used at night and in poor visibility which may make use of the hand bearing compass impossible.

In Figure 10.6 (opposite) you can see that the first part of the approach to the anchorage is on a northerly heading. To avoid the off-lying rocks it is necessary to remain at least 0.35nm off the coastline. Once the land ahead is between 0.5nm and 0.25nm away the helmsman can alter course to remain in the safe corridor to the anchorage.

The relevant distances should be marked on the chart and then constantly checked using the range rings or variable range marker.

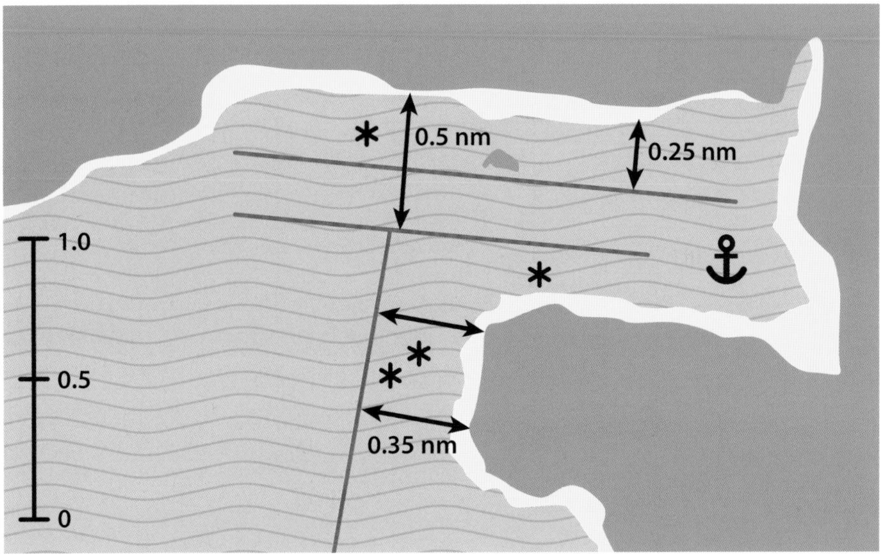

Fig 10.6 This skipper is using radar ranging to clear the rocks to starboard on the first leg. Later, on the second leg, he is staying no less than 0.3M off the land on the port side and no more than half a mile on the starboard side.

DEPTH CONTOURS

When in fog, some accurate blind pilotage can be achieved using the depth sounder. If shallow and deep alarms are set it is possible to stay in depths between 5m to 10m to stay clear of commercial vessels. Set a route where there are clearly defined contours to help check the position.

SECTORED LIGHTS

The use of light sectors for pilotage is discussed in Chapter 9 – Lights & buoyage.

LOCAL RULES & REGULATIONS

When completing a pilotage plan it is wise to study the almanac and pilot book to see if there are any special rules or restrictions for your destination. Most ports impose restrictions on vessels over 20m in length but smaller leisure craft are spared from having to call the harbour authorities on VHF before leaving or entering harbour. Naval and ferry ports are more closely regulated than small non-commercial ones but check to see which rules apply to small craft. It is possible that you may not be allowed to sail into a river or harbour. Flying a spinnaker is forbidden in many narrow rivers and in others it is mandatory to use an engine, if fitted, because of congestion.

Figure 10.7 shows the many rules in force in Portsmouth Harbour which has an entrance heavy with ferry and naval movements. Notice that small craft entering Portsmouth are restricted to a 'small boat channel' as the approach channel is narrow and very busy.

Always check on the port entrance signals as some harbours will exhibit a light or shape if entry is prohibited. See Figure 10.8.

PORTSMOUTH

Portsmouth is a major naval base and Dockyard Port; all vessels come under the Queen's Harbour Master's authority.

If more than 20m LOA, ask QHM's permission (VHF Ch11) to enter, leave or move in the harbour, especially in fog.

Fishing and anchoring in channels is prohibited.

Navigation Beware of:

1 Very strong tides in harbour entrance.
2 Commercial shipping and ferries.
3 Gosport ferry and HM ships.
4 High speed ferries operating within the area.

Small Boat Channel (SBC) is *mandatory* for craft under 20m LOA when entering or leaving harbour. It runs just outside the W edge of the main dredged channel from abeam No 4 Bar buoy to Ballast Beacon.

Craft may not enter harbour on the E side of the main channel and must not enter the SBC on its E side; craft may enter or leave the SBC on its W side.

Engines (if fitted) must be used when in the SBC between No 4 Bar buoy and Ballast beacon (*which should always be left to port*)

If crossing to or from Gunwharf Quays or to the Camber do so at 90° to main channel N of Ballast Bcn (with approval from QHM Ch 11).

If joining or leaving the SBC via the Inner Swashway, *BC Outer Bcn must be left to port.*

Speed limit is 10kn (through the water) within harbour and within 1,000 yards of the shore in any part of the Dockyard Port.

Fig 10.7 The nautical almanac and pilot books carry port information such as these rules for Portsmouth Harbour.

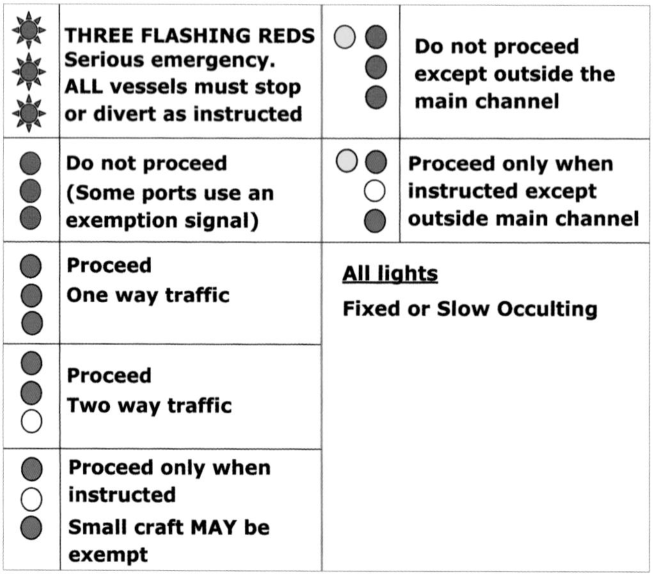
THREE FLASHING REDS
Serious emergency.
ALL vessels must stop or divert as instructed
Do not proceed except outside the main channel
Do not proceed
(Some ports use an exemption signal)
Proceed only when instructed except outside main channel
Proceed
One way traffic
All lights
Fixed or Slow Occulting
Proceed
Two way traffic
Proceed only when instructed
Small craft MAY be exempt

Fig 10.8 International port entry signals.

LOWER HEADS LT BUOY TO BEAUCETTE MARINA DURING THE MORNING OF FRIDAY 21 AUGUST

Fig 10.9 Beaucette Marina (courtesy of Premier Marinas).

Before setting out on the passage from Jersey to Beaucette we need to do some advance planning as the rocky area and strong tides around Guernsey need our full concentration when we arrive at the Lower Heads South Cardinal (see Figure 10.12).

The pilotage plan which follows addresses the factors that need consideration for a safe and enjoyable passage northwards through the Little Russel Channel to Beaucette Marina on the north-east corner of the island.

◆ Charts of the area

Admiralty folio charts 5604.9 and 5604.10 are ideal for the job as one gives an overall view of the east coast of Guernsey and the other, of larger scale, shows more detail.

The next task is to draw the route on the chart and measure the bearings and distances on each leg as shown in Figure 10.10 overleaf.

Features which will be clearly visible en route have also been circled. When the boat reaches the northerly turning point off Grune Fosse the small chart of Beaucette will be used.

It is approximately 4.5 nautical miles to Grune Fosse which, with a 5kn boat speed and a favourable stream, will take less than an hour.

◆ Pilot book

In the pilot book there are excellent aerial photographs of Beaucette and the Little Russel Channel as well as ones of Roustel beacon and Petite Canupe Lt. There is also a small chartlet of the area showing buoyage. Figure 10.9 shows boats safely berthed in the sheltered marina.

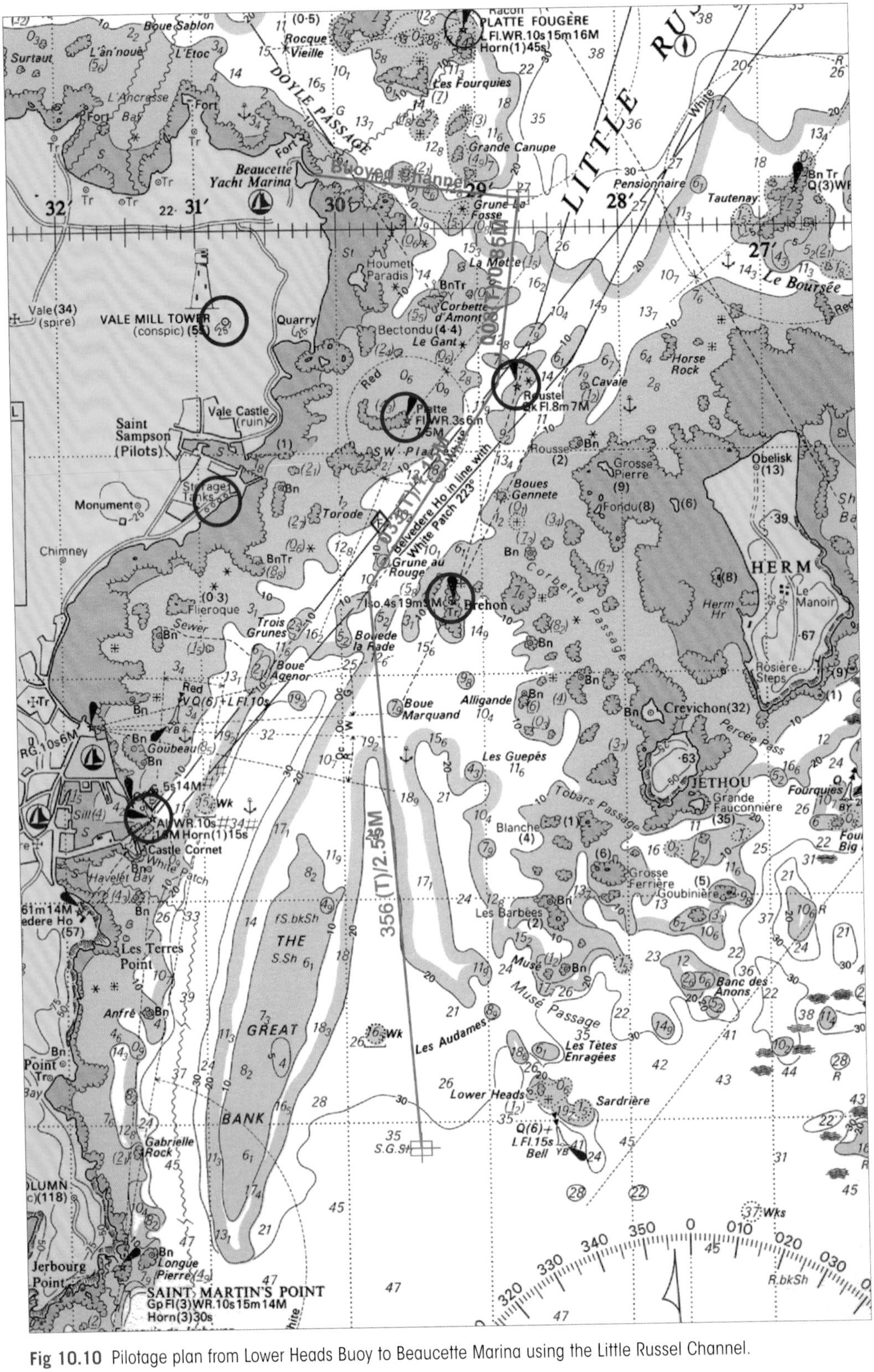

Fig 10.10 Pilotage plan from Lower Heads Buoy to Beaucette Marina using the Little Russel Channel.

◆ Almanac

Reeds is the almanac being used as it has a full section on Guernsey and a small chart of Beaucette (Figure 10.11).

It says that the marina has good shelter except in strong onshore winds and access for three hours either side of local HW. Waiting buoys are available if arriving too early for the sill and the dock-master listens on Channel 80 until late in the evening (Figure 10.12).

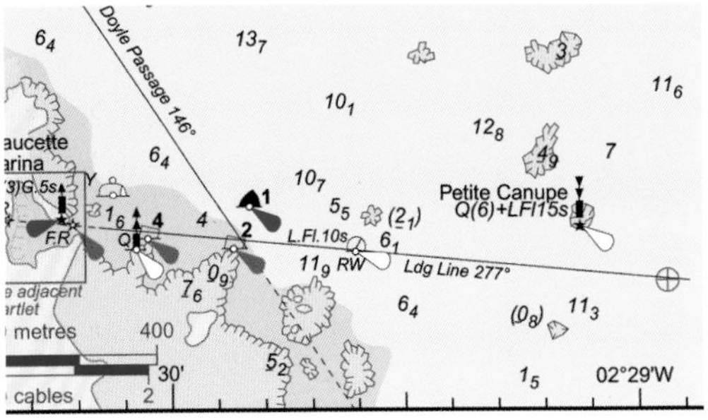

Fig 10.11 The well-marked channel into Beaucette Marina. Interestingly, the Admiralty chart gives the leading lights in line as 276°.

Fig 10.12 (right) Pilotage notes for Beaucette.

Extract from Almanac – Beaucette Marina

SHELTER

Excellent in Marina. Entry not advised in strong N to SE onshore winds.
R/T Ch 80 (0700 – 2200) for HM and water taxi.

FACILITIES

Marina sill dries 2.37m; access HW St Peter Port ±3. 6 Yellow waiting buoys lie outside the 8m wide entrance channel. For entry sequence and a berth it is essential to pre-call HM with boat details.

◆ Tides and Tidal Streams for 21 August

We require the tidal information for St Peter Port to determine the entry period for Beaucette Marina and Dover tide times so that we can use the tidal stream information in *Reeds Almanac*.

HW St Peter Port is at 1101 BST.
Entry times for Beaucette = 3 hours either side of HW St Peter Port **= 0801 until 1401**.

HW Dover is at 1529 BST. From the tidal stream atlas we see that it is close to neaps and the stream is setting north in the Little Russel until 1359.

Best to enter the marina by 1330 making sure that we avoid the rocks off: Brehon Tower, Platte Rock and Grune Fosse.

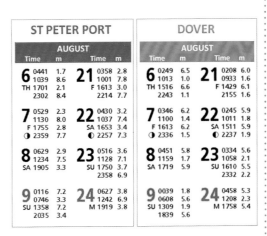

ST PETER PORT – AUGUST

	Time	m		Time	m
6	0441	1.7	21	0358	2.8
	1039	8.6		1001	7.8
TH	1701	2.1	F	1613	3.0
	2302	8.4		2214	7.7
7	0529	2.3	22	0430	3.2
	1130	8.0		1037	7.4
F	1755	2.8	SA	1653	3.4
	◑ 2359	7.7		◐ 2257	7.3
8	0629	2.9	23	0516	3.6
	1234	7.5		1128	7.1
SA	1905	3.3	SU	1750	3.7
				2358	6.9
9	0116	7.2	24	0627	3.8
	0746	3.3		1242	6.9
SU	1358	7.2	M	1919	3.8
	2035	3.4			

DOVER – AUGUST

	Time	m		Time	m
6	0249	6.5	21	0208	6.0
	1013	1.0		0933	1.6
TH	1516	6.6	F	1429	6.1
	2243	1.1		2155	1.6
7	0346	6.2	22	0245	5.9
	1100	1.4		1011	1.8
F	1613	6.2	SA	1511	5.9
	◑ 2336	1.5		◐ 2237	1.9
8	0451	5.8	23	0334	5.6
	1159	1.7		1058	2.1
SA	1719	5.9	SU	1610	5.5
				2332	2.2
9	0039	1.8	24	0458	5.3
	0608	5.6		1208	2.3
SU	1309	1.9	M	1758	5.4
	1839	5.6			

Fig 10.13 Tidal information for 23 August.

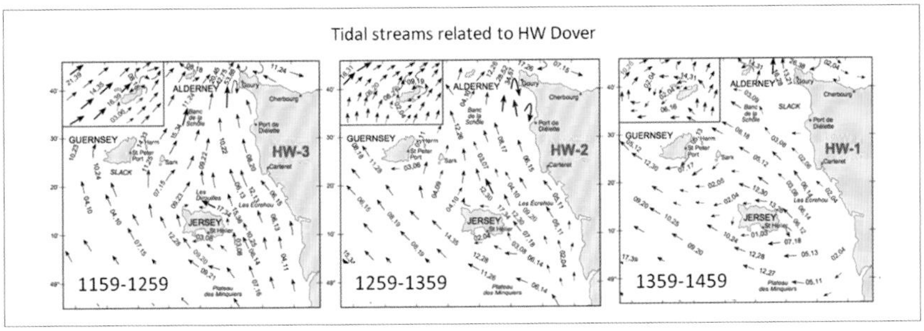

Fig 10.14 The tidal stream information for Guernsey.

◆ Landmarks

The circled landmarks will be useful to check on progress northward and the GPS waypoint off Grune Fosse is close to the transit into the Marina.

Bearings from landmarks to the track could also be drawn on the chart as a further visual position check. St Peter Port breakwater is shown in Figure 10.15.

Fig 10.15 St Peter Port entrance.

CHART PLOTTER PILOTAGE

See also Chapter 3.

Begin your preparations for entering harbour early. The main pilotage plan will probably have been done with the passage plan but the plotter can be used to give instant tidal height information if arrival is either early or late.

Study a very large-scale electronic chart of the port or marina. Plotter software often gives pontoon numbers and frequently marks visitors' berths. Notice where the fuel pumps are if refuelling is necessary. By placing the cursor over the port it should be possible to display a text database of other port information normally found in an almanac, such as harbour master's office, lift-out facilities, engine repairers and VHF channels used by harbour authorities.

Fig 10.16 Simrad CP33 Plotter.

Mark your ideal track up the channel and into the harbour by adding 'route points', normally done by just clicking the cursor. Establish how safe it is to deviate from this track and, for each leg, designate maximum safe cross-track error distances which will be marked on the plotter with parallel dotted lines, one on either side of the track.

Once the display is set up you can leave the chart table and assist with visual pilotage, briefly slipping down below to confirm each feature you pass and to verify that the depth is as you would expect. There should be no need, nor is it desirable, for you to sit at the chart table, even if it is warmer down below!

Navigators in motor cruisers and wheel-steered yachts often have the advantage that the plotter, or a repeater display, is situated near the wheel within sight of the helmsman. This makes life very easy for the skipper provided that the equipment has been properly set up in ample time.

◆ Will it go according to plan?

There are a number of things that could go wrong, the most likely being that bad visibility occurs unexpectedly, obscuring all marks. St Peter Port would be much easier to enter in poor visibility as it has few obstructions close to the entrance together with a powerful fog horn.

The boat may arrive after the stream has gone foul which would mean entering on a falling tide in the dark. The leading lights are lit and a good searchlight could pick out the approach buoys but it would be for the skipper to decide if St Peter Port would be a safer bet.

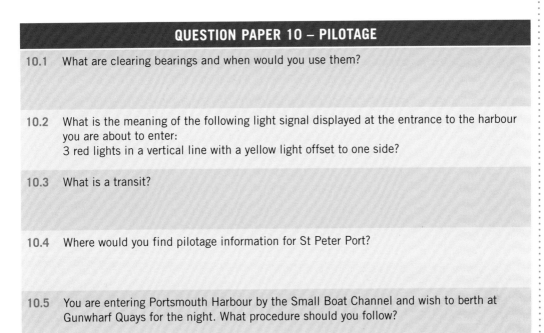

QUESTION PAPER 10 – PILOTAGE

10.1 What are clearing bearings and when would you use them?

10.2 What is the meaning of the following light signal displayed at the entrance to the harbour you are about to enter:
3 red lights in a vertical line with a yellow light offset to one side?

10.3 What is a transit?

10.4 Where would you find pilotage information for St Peter Port?

10.5 You are entering Portsmouth Harbour by the Small Boat Channel and wish to berth at Gunwharf Quays for the night. What procedure should you follow?

Answers at the back of the book

11 WEATHER TO GO – or not to go

THE WEATHER AND THE STRENGTH OF THE WIND affect every person who ventures on to the water. Small sailing dinghies capsize if there is too much wind but windsurfers won't bother to go until it is blowing half a gale. Racing powerboats break up in rough seas but sailors like Ellen McArthur pray for strong winds on record-breaking voyages. The average cruising man hopes for moderate winds, sunshine and relatively calm seas and he may not even leave the harbour if the forecast is for anything more.

Fig 11.1 Does this cloud formation show a quiet night watch or will it blow?

Old seafarers used to predict the weather by the state of the captain's rheumatism or the behaviour of the ship's parrot but now we are lucky enough to have satellites, computer models, electronic recording instruments and superb communications to assist a team of highly-trained professional meteorologists. We hear grumbles at the marina bar about a forecast that appeared to be badly wrong but most forecasts usually cover a large area; in the case of the forecast area 'Portland' (Figure 11.42) the same forecast is given for both Weymouth and St Malo, 150 miles apart, so it is not surprising that some variations occur.

Let us consider a beat to windward at six knots with a four-knot tide under us and the wind being funnelled or bent around a headland. In these conditions, a wind forecast for Beaufort force 5 (17–21kn) would be felt as a force 7 (28–33kn) or even more in the gusts. Familiarity with the local conditions and how the topography and tidal streams can modify them might save us from a rough trip.

However, it is necessary to look at the larger picture before local knowledge comes into play and this chapter attempts to explain basic principles so that there is greater understanding of meteorology – both local and global.

WEATHER BASICS

Oceans great and small and land masses, ranging in size from small islands to huge continents, cover our world. The Sun heats our globe unevenly because the Sun's rays hit the equatorial regions at 90° so that maximum heat is absorbed, whereas the Poles get a glancing blow of light and warmth (Figure 11.2). The Equator remains very much the same temperature all year round but the Poles get so little

Sun during their winter that it barely gets light, let alone warm.

Another complication is that the land and sea heat and cool at different rates. Land heats up and cools down quickly but the sea can take many months to gain or lose just 10° Celsius. Figure 11.3 shows the winter and summer temperature ranges in northern Europe where the variation is a lot greater over the land than at sea.

It is this differential heating that is the major ingredient for 'the weather recipe', and for those who have forgotten school physics, a little revision may assist.

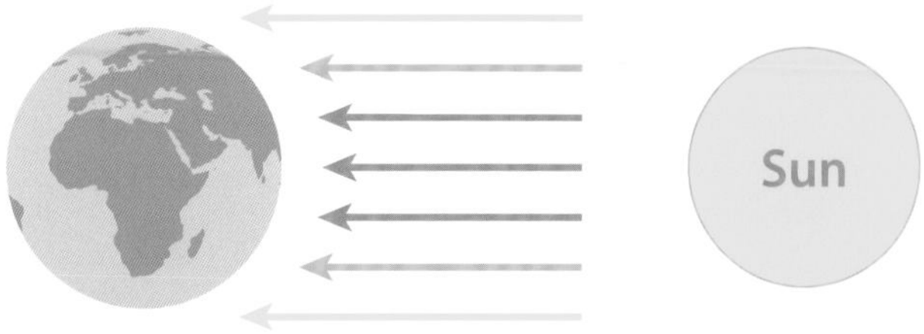
Sun

Fig 11.2 The Sun heats the equatorial region more than the Poles.

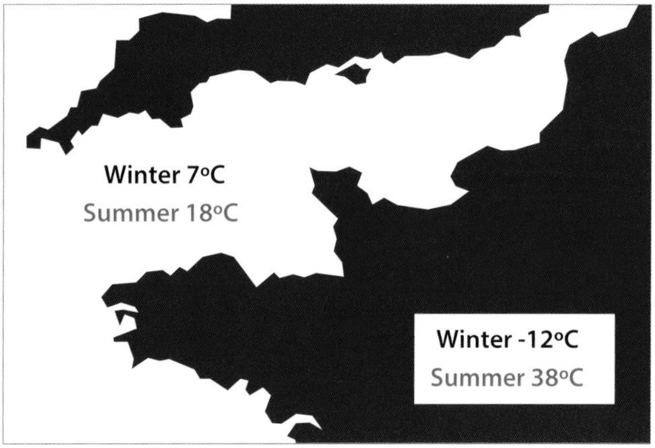
Winter 7°C
Summer 18°C
Winter -12°C
Summer 38°C

Fig 11.3 The sea temperature alters a mere 11°C throughout the year but the land mass can change by as much as 50°C.

HEAT & PRESSURE

The Sun heats the surface of the Earth that, in turn, warms the air above the surface. The warmed air becomes buoyant and rises, expanding as it gains height. As it expands, it cools and the higher it rises, the colder and denser it becomes until, because of its weight, it falls back down to Earth again. We can prove that cold air falls by looking at the open freezers in the supermarket and noticing that the ice cream remains frozen as the cold air sits in the freezer!

We can liken the whole process to a bonfire where a circulation is set up as it has been in Figure 11.4. Air rising from the fire creates an *area of low pressure* above the fire and the cool air subsiding from height, gives an *area of high pressure*. The air flows from the high-pressure area to the low-pressure zone, just as it does when a car tyre is punctured or a pressurised gas cylinder is opened!

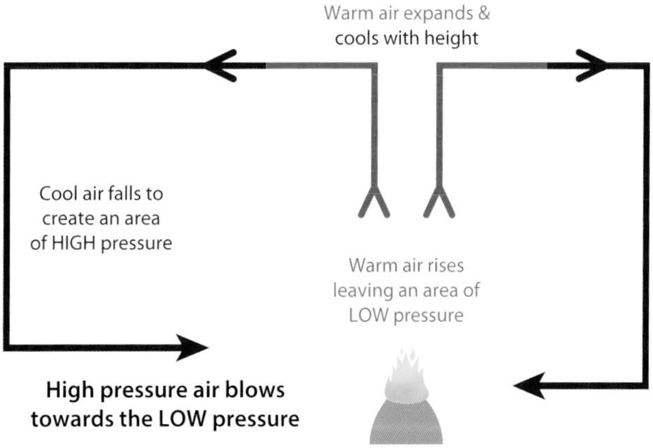
Warm air expands & cools with height
Cool air falls to create an area of HIGH pressure
Warm air rises leaving an area of LOW pressure
High pressure air blows towards the LOW pressure

Fig 11.4 The warm air that rises from the fire cools and falls back to ground level. An area of low pressure is formed at the fire and high pressure where the cold air is falling.

MOISTURE

When a mass of air blows over an ocean such as the Atlantic, it picks up moisture as it goes and is therefore quite damp by the time it reaches the British Isles. If the wind is from the south-west it will be warm and damp but if it blows from a Polar source, it will be cold and wet. As can be seen from Figure 11.5, air that comes up from the European continent will be warm and dry in summer and cold and dry in winter.

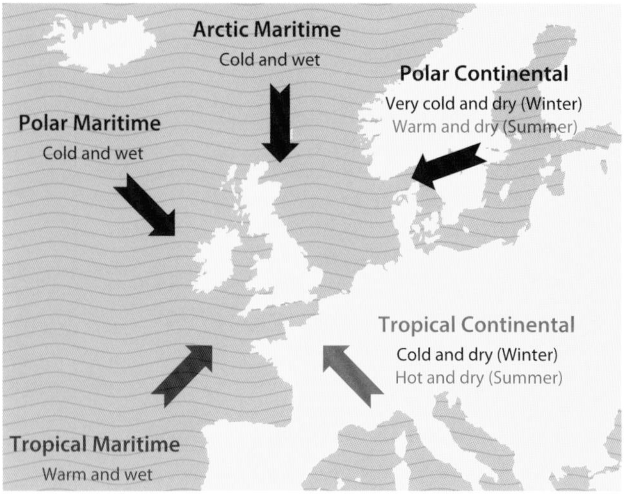

Fig 11.5 Air coming over the sea is damp. Continental air is cold in winter and hot in summer.

◆ Water vapour and dew point

Air contains water but you cannot normally see it – it is held as a vapour. The temperature of the air is important because the hotter it is, the more moisture it can hold invisibly. If a parcel of hot humid air is cooled down it is able to hold less water vapour; when it is holding all the moisture it can for a given temperature, it is said to have reached its *dew point*. Air at a temperature of 30°C can hold just over 30 grams of water vapour per cubic metre whereas at 10°C it can hold a mere 9 grams (Figure 11.6). With further cooling, condensation will occur and the moisture will become apparent as either fog, cloud, dew, rain, snow or frost.

It becomes fairly obvious why we get more rain in the winter when it is colder; water is still in the air during the summer, but is held as vapour due to the higher temperature.

With a few exceptions, weather generally passes over the British Isles from west to east. As moist air blowing off the sea passes over land, it is forced to rise over beaches and cliffs and is unable to retain its moisture as it cools, which is why west-facing coasts and hills of the British Isles and Northern Europe are always a lot wetter than those facing east (Figure 11.7). By the time air gets to eastern regions the water content is greatly reduced.

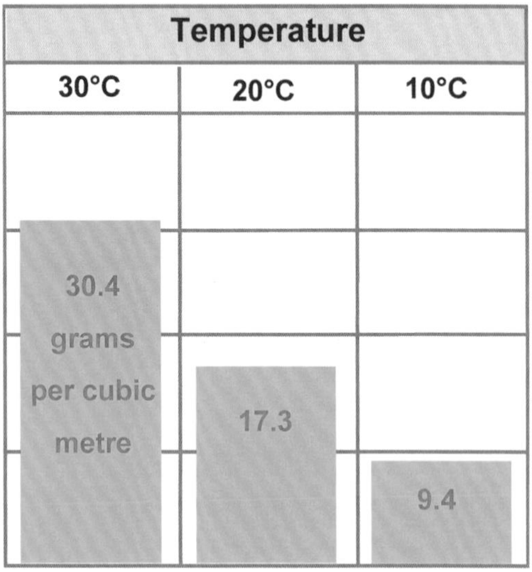

Fig 11.6 Air at 30°C can hold over three times the amount of water than it can at 10°C.

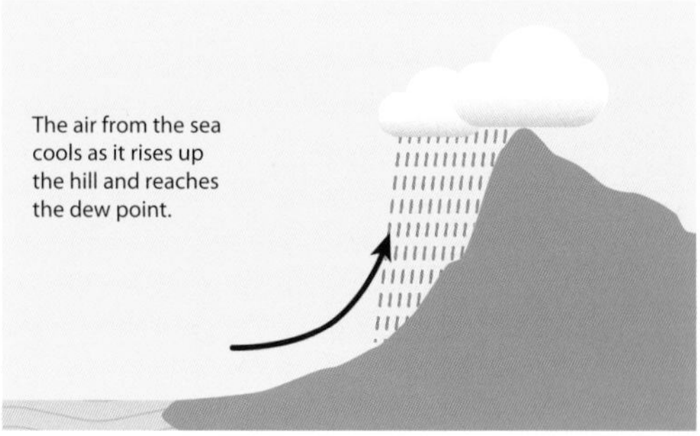

The air from the sea
cools as it rises up
the hill and reaches
the dew point.

Fig 11.7 Air blowing off the sea is damp and when forced to rise, will cool below the dew point and condensation will occur.

GLOBAL AIR CIRCULATION

Weather on a global scale is a continuous attempt for nature to even everything out – to equalise temperatures, pressure and humidity and the battle takes place in a relatively thin layer extending to about eight miles above the surface of the Earth, called the *troposphere*. This layer is a few miles higher at the Equator and its upper boundary is known as the *tropopause*. Weather activity as we know it stops at this level and we can actually see the tropopause, when there is a large squall cloud (cumulonimbus) in the sky. It forms an anvil at its top, which spreads out at the tropopause.

Fig 11.8 This well-developed cumulonimbus cloud 'tops out' at the tropopause, the upper boundary for our weather systems.

THE SPINNING GLOBE

At this stage we need to add the final ingredient to 'the weather pudding' – the fact that the Earth revolves and disturbs the air above it.

When studying global circulation, we see from Figure 11.9 that the warm air rises from the Equator leaving a low-pressure area at the surface. The risen air cools, and when it reaches the tropopause, spreads out towards the Poles just as it did with the bonfire in Figure 11.4. However, it is unable to travel as far as the Pole because it cools and gets more dense as it moves upward and northward. Eventually this cold air falls back to the surface again. In general terms the result is semi-permanent bands of high and low pressure in both hemispheres but, for clarity, the illustration shows just one side of the globe. On the surface the opposite is happening, the trade winds blow to replace the air rising away from equatorial regions and the air from the horse latitudes spreads northward to fill the low

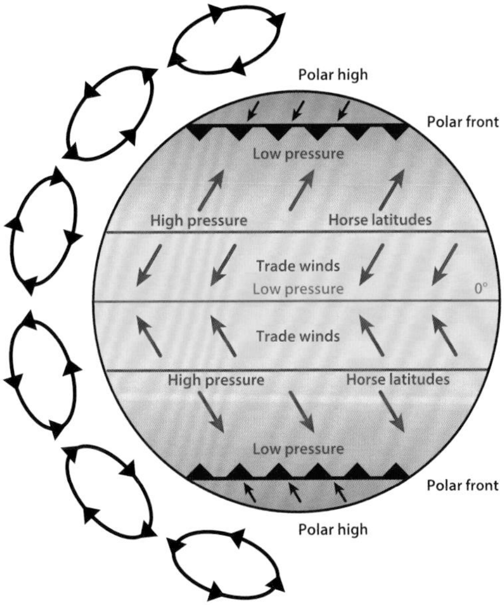

Fig 11.9 The warm air rises from the Equator, cools and moves northwards to join air already falling to the high-pressure area over the mid latitudes.

pressure in the North Atlantic. To complete the cycle, cold air spreads out from the Polar high and blows southwards.

◆ Convergence and divergence

As the warm air rises away from the surface of the Earth, as in Figure 11.10, the pressure aloft builds and the air moves outwards, some moving north and the rest southwards. This out-flowing is known as *divergence*.

Equatorial air moving northwards is joined by air from temperate latitudes and the two flows converge and subside back down to the surface. This is known as *convergence*.

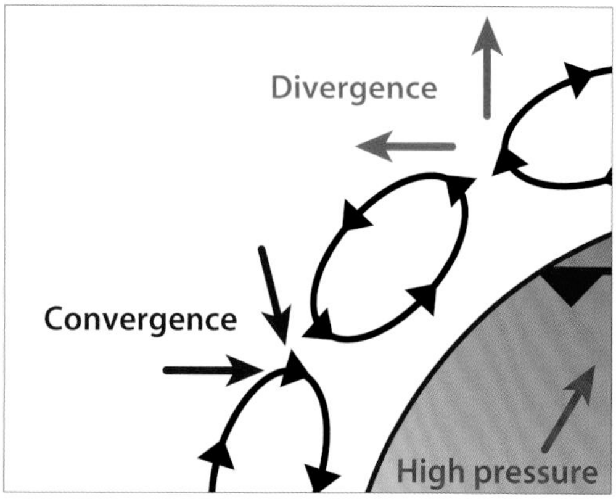

Fig 11.10 Convergence and divergence.

WIND FLOW AROUND CENTRES OF HIGH AND LOW PRESSURE

In the northern hemisphere, the Earth's rotation causes the wind to blow in a clockwise direction around an area of high pressure and anticlockwise around a low as in Figure 11.11. The high-pressure area is called an anticyclone.

This circulation around the semi-permanent air masses brings warm air northwards and cold air southwards to meet each other in 'the weather pudding mixing bowl' or more normally called the *Polar front*. The battle for equilibrium occurs along this leading edge of Polar air and it is here that depressions are born.

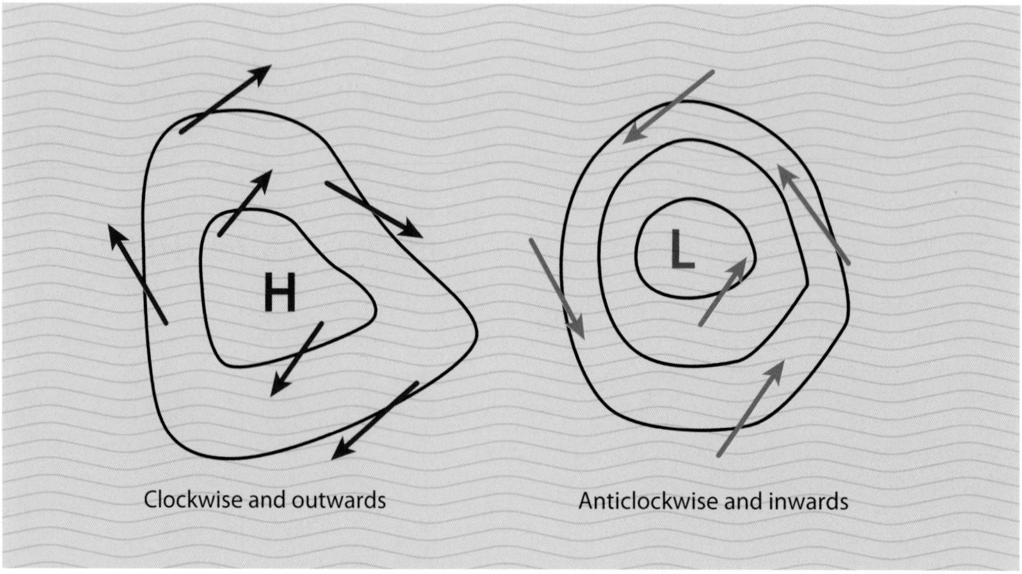

Fig 11.11 In the northern hemisphere the circulation of air is clockwise around high pressure and anticlockwise around low pressure.

DEPRESSIONS

◆ The birth

The first illustration (Figure 11.12) shows the birth of the depression, in this case in an area south-west of Iceland where the warm waters of the North Atlantic Drift supply fuel to stoke the fire.

The warm front is depicted in red with round symbols and the cold front is blue with spikes. Lines joining points of equal barometric pressure, the *isobars*, are drawn in black. The isobars are not close together which means that it is not windy. Later in the chapter we will learn how to determine wind speed from isobaric spacing.

◆ Early development

When two air masses with different temperatures converge and meet, the warmer air tends to over-ride the colder, heavier air, whilst the colder air undercuts the lighter warm air. This causes a disturbance that takes place along the leading edges of the air masses: the *fronts*.

In Figure 11.13, the warm air has begun to rise and has left an area of low pressure on the surface. A small bulge appears in the cold front and an anticlockwise rotation is established.

◆ Further development

The warm wedge of air, the bulge, continues to enlarge, accompanied by a further fall in pressure at the point of the bulge. These isobars near the centre now have a closed form and as pressure deepens, the wind strengthens.

The isobars in the warm sector are straight or nearly straight lines and the whole depression will move in a direction more or less parallel to the isobars; in the case of the depression in Figure 11.14 in an east north easterly direction, moving around the anticyclone which is pushing a ridge of high pressure ahead of the front. This ridge should give a period of fair weather for a time between fronts.

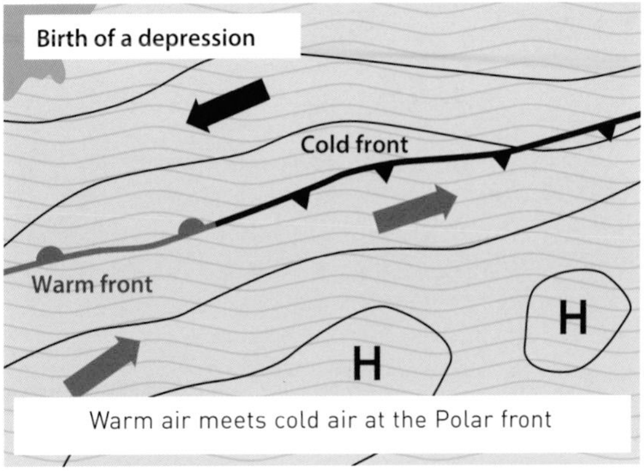
Birth of a depression
Cold front
Warm front
H
H
Warm air meets cold air at the Polar front

Fig 11.12 This chart shows a high-pressure centre and the lines of equal pressure drawn in black. The warm air blowing from the south-west is both warm and wet when it meets the cold Polar air.

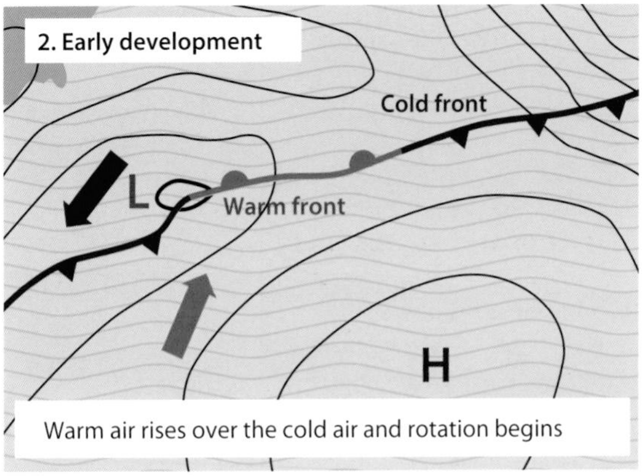
2. Early development
Cold front
L
Warm front
H
Warm air rises over the cold air and rotation begins

Fig 11.13 As the warm air rides over the cold air ahead of it, a circulation in an anti clockwise direction is established.

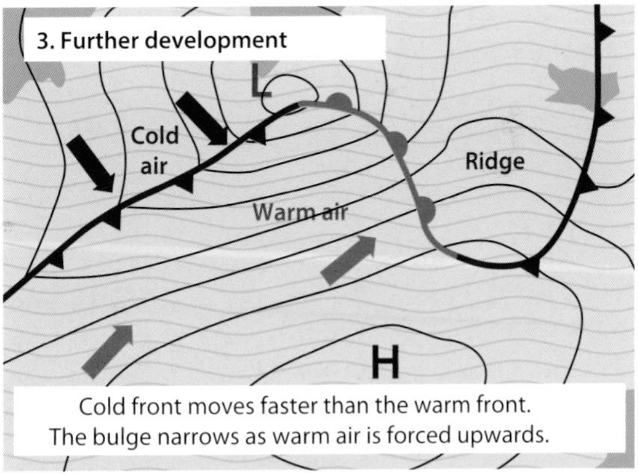
3. Further development
L
Cold air
Ridge
Warm air
H
Cold front moves faster than the warm front.
The bulge narrows as warm air is forced upwards.

Fig 11.14 The warm sector enlarges and the barometric pressure at the point of the bulge lowers. The cold air from the north pushes the warm air upwards.

◆ The fronts occlude

The weather system is now coming to the end of its life as the cold front pushes the warm air upwards. The bulge continues to narrow until the two fronts join at the tip of the warm sector. The warm air is no longer on the surface but there is still disturbance along the line and, in the early stages of occlusion, the depression will continue to deepen for a while. Activity will continue until the warm sector bulge is closed and the occlusion is no longer driven forward by the wind direction in the warm sector.

The occlusion in Figure 11.16 is accompanied by a 90° wind veer which, in open water with a long fetch, could cause confused seas and pyramid waves as the established wave pattern is altered by wind from the new direction.

The symbol for an occlusion is a combination of those used for warm and cold fronts and the line is coloured purple on most working charts. The weather experienced is also a combination of that found on each of the two fronts and will be discussed later in this chapter. However, before we leave illustrations 1 to 4, compare the first and last in the series and note the similarity in the situation. Another depression will surely form as the anticyclone continues to push warm damp air northwards.

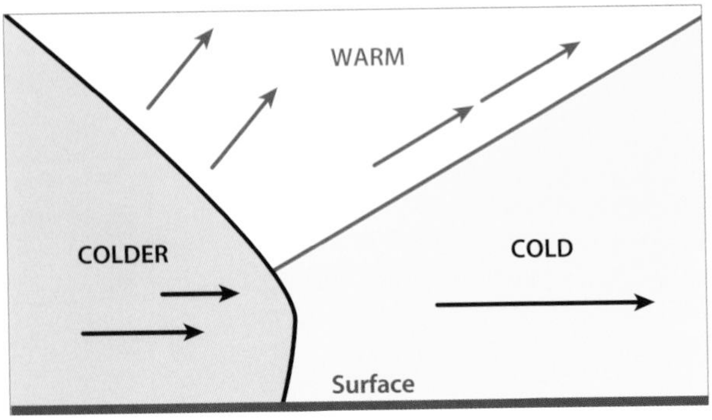
WARM
COLDER
COLD
Surface

Fig 11.15 An occluded frontal system.

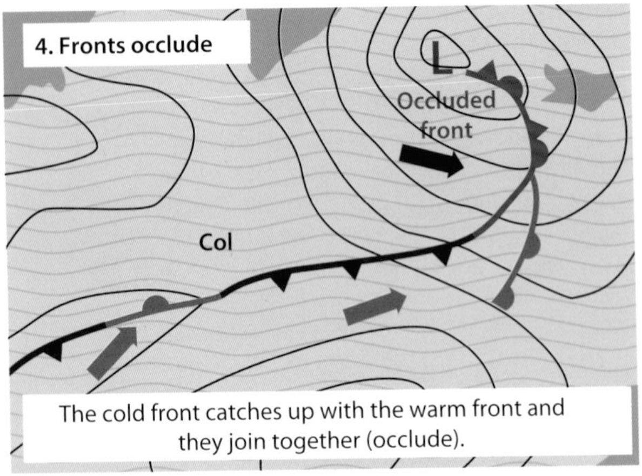
4. Fronts occlude
L
Occluded front
Col
The cold front catches up with the warm front and they join together (occlude).

Fig 11.16 The occluded fronts are marked in purple using a combination of the symbols used for the warm and cold fronts.

CLOUDS

Before studying the weather associated with a frontal system, it would be a good idea to take a quick look at some of the cloud types formed as a depression passes over us.

Clouds are classified by height and shape, whether they are broken, or carry rain. The names are in Latin but quite easy to remember:

CLOUDS

	heights	prefix
HIGH	5,000m - 11,000m	Cirrus or Cirro
MEDIUM	2,000m - 5,500m	Alto
LOW	Surface to 2,000m	No prefix

Fig 11.17 Clouds are classed as high, medium or low according to the height of their base.

Cumulus (Figure 11.18) This word means 'growing' or 'accumulating' and the clouds look a little like cauliflowers. They develop upwards because moist air is being pushed up by cold air or by surface heating. This type of cloud is a convectional cloud and shows instability in the atmosphere. (Stability and instability are explained in the next section.)

Stratus This type of cloud is flat and signifies stability. It forms when warm moist air is sliding upwards over cooler air or when fog has risen above ground level.

Nimbus is the Latin word for rain; any cloud with the prefix 'nimbo' means that it is rain-bearing. Nimbostratus cloud (Figure 11.19) is flat and bears rain, whereas cumulonimbus is heaped and rain-filled.

Fractus Means fractured or broken. Fractostratus is therefore a broken layer of cloud and, because it is not prefixed with the word *cirro* or *alto*, its base must be at a low level.

Cirrus Latin for 'thread' or 'hair'. High cloud, which consists entirely of ice crystals, is wispy and will be prefixed with the word *cirro*. Hooked cirrus similar to that shown in Figure 11.20 will be one of the first signs of an approaching front.

Stratocumulus (Figure 11.21) This is exactly what it says – it is flattish lumpy cloud! Typically it is found in the warm sector where the warm front stratus is beginning to be pushed upward by the approaching cold air. It can give intermittent rain and drizzle within the warm sector.

Fig 11.18 Cumulus cloud over Florida in summer. Within half an hour, this cloud developed to give a torrential shower.

Fig 11.19 Nimbostratus cloud. It is a low level, rain-bearing cloud that is found ahead of, and on, a warm front.

Fig 11.20 This cirrus cloud has become hooked in the upper wind and is one of the signs of an approaching warm front.

Fig 11.21 Stratocumulus cloud is found in the warm sector.

STABILITY AND INSTABILITY

The clouds we can see tell us how the air around us is behaving – whether it is rising or sinking and how buoyant it is. When weather forecasters talk about cumulus clouds 'bubbling up' they are describing air that is warmer than the air around it; it is buoyant and rising easily – *unstable air.*

The rising air takes the pollution up with it, so visibility is good in unstable conditions but as the air rises, it tumbles over itself, some coming back down. This causes gusty wind conditions, often with squally showers.

Stable air is air that is cooler than the air around it so remains on the surface. As there is no upward air movement the winds are steady and light and the pollution stays on the surface giving poor visibility and the risk of fog. If clouds form they are layer clouds with no vertical development – stratus clouds.

WEATHER SEQUENCE THROUGH A DEPRESSION

No two depressions are ever the same, but their weather is characteristically unsettled and usually wet and windy. They also vary widely in size, with their diameters being anything between 200 and 2,000 miles and it is not unknown for a depression centred over the north Atlantic to extend over the British Isles and the North Sea.

In the case of the depression in Figure 11.22, a wide belt of rain lies to the north and east of the warm front.

The next illustration (Figure 11.23) shows a cross section and the sequence of weather which could be experienced if an observer could walk from point A to point B in Figure 11.22.

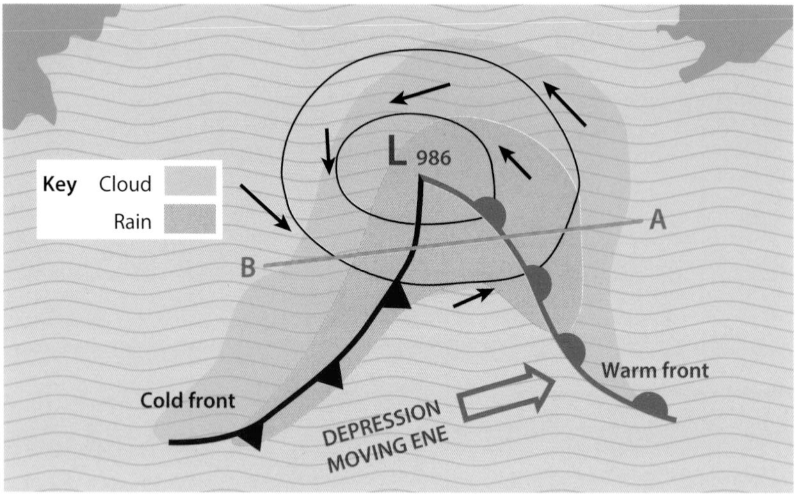

Fig 11.22 The area of the cloud bulges out in front of the warm front and the heaviest rain is closest to the centre of the depression. As there is an anticyclone to the south, the area of cloud in the warm sector is reduced.

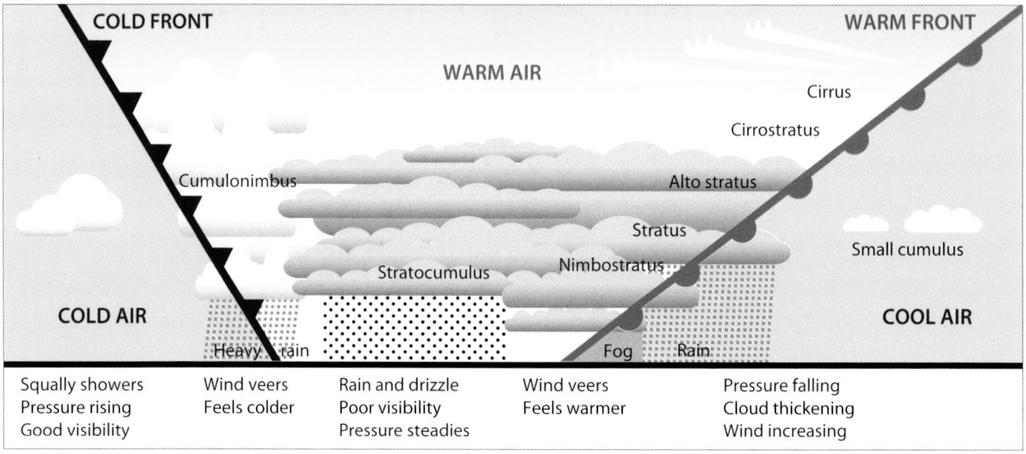

Fig 11.23 Cross section through a typical north Atlantic depression.

◆ Before the warm front

The first thing you may notice is some high cirrus cloud (Figure 11.20) and aircraft vapour trails that do not disperse; both mean that there is moisture aloft.

Another sure sign that there is moisture present is a ring or halo around the Sun. This is formed when the Sun's rays shine through the ice crystals of cirrostratus cloud (Figure 11.24).

As the approach continues, the cloud will continue to thicken and get progressively lower, first with altostratus (Figure 11.25) then stratus and nimbostratus.

Fig 11.24 Sun shining through a veil of cirrostratus cloud.

Fig 11.25 A very 'watery' sky with building altostratus.

The barometric pressure will fall, the wind will back and increase and it will begin to rain ahead of the front. If the pressure falls rapidly – at a rate of more than 6 millibars in 3 hours – find shelter quickly because a gale will come whatever the wind speed is at present.

◆ At the warm front

The temperature will rise as the front gets closer and a sign that it is very close is the presence of 'frontal fog' which is, in reality, cloud that is down to ground level.

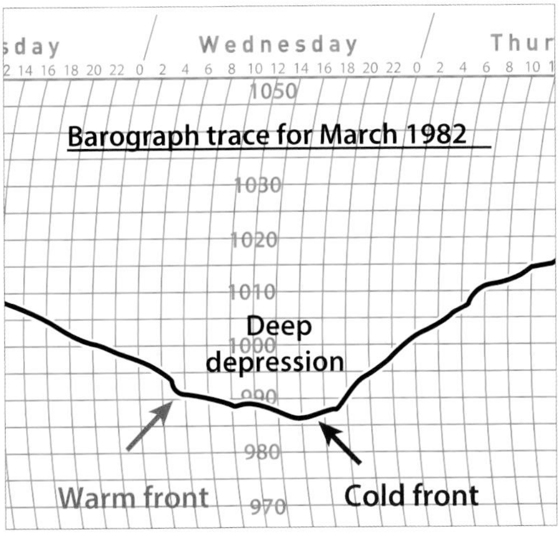

Fig 11.26 The barograph trace of a typical north Atlantic depression. This was recorded during a windy week at Portsmouth in March 1982.

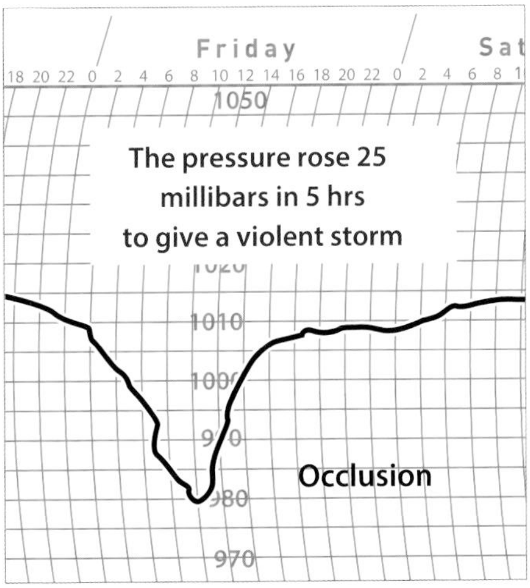

Fig 11.27 Portsmouth March 1982. This occlusion gave winds of over 60 knots – Beaufort force 11.

◆ In the warm sector

As the front passes, the wind will veer if the centre of the depression is to the north of the observer and be steady in direction and speed. The barometric pressure will either 'bottom out' or fall more slowly and generally the visibility will be poor in intermittent rain and drizzle. Figure 11.26 shows the pressure falling during a Tuesday night in March 1982 with a warm front going through the following morning at 0600. Note that the pressure rose quickly after the cold front went through on the Wednesday evening.

◆ The cold front

The cold front is the more dramatic of the two fronts and, as it approaches, cumulonimbus clouds form as the warm air is pushed forward and upward. A dip in pressure will occur and a short period of heavy rain will be followed by blue sky approaching from the west or north-west. As the sky clears it will feel cooler, the wind will veer and the visibility will become very good. The wind will increase for a time as the pressure rises quickly and squally showers will develop.

Gradually these showers will die down and the rise in pressure will slow to give clear periods and occasional showers.

BUYS BALLOT'S LAW

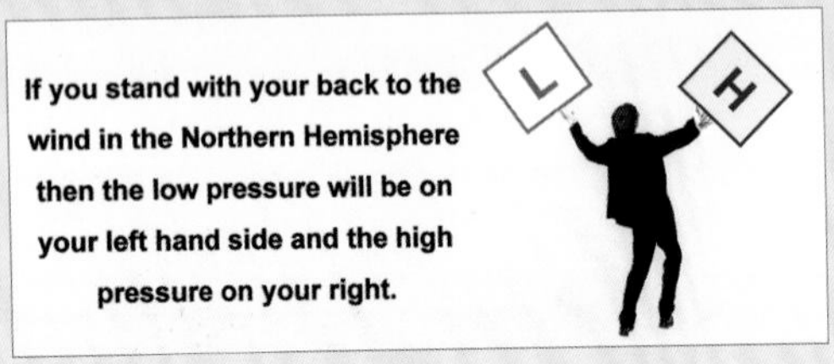

If you stand with your back to the wind in the Northern Hemisphere then the low pressure will be on your left hand side and the high pressure on your right.
L
H

In the 1850s the Dutch meteorologist Buys Ballot gave us a very useful way of telling in which direction the low pressure lies in relation to our own position. This information could be very useful when determining whether the wind will veer or back on the passage of a front.

SECONDARY DEPRESSIONS

Once the fronts of a depression occlude and the low weakens, it may deepen again if a second depression forms within the isobaric pattern of the *primary* low. This *secondary* forms at least 600 miles from the primary, either on the trailing cold front, or at the junction of the occluded, warm and cold fronts. As it deepens it can pivot on the primary or 'dumb-bell' around it and the winds in the secondary can be stronger than they were in the parent depression, although the winds between the two are usually light with widely-spaced isobars (Figure 11.28).

A secondary which forms on the trailing cold front usually tracks further towards the tropics than the primary and often results in the formation of a family of depressions coming one after another as in Figure 11.29. This is a common occurrence in springtime in the northern hemisphere when warm equatorial air is pushing northwards.

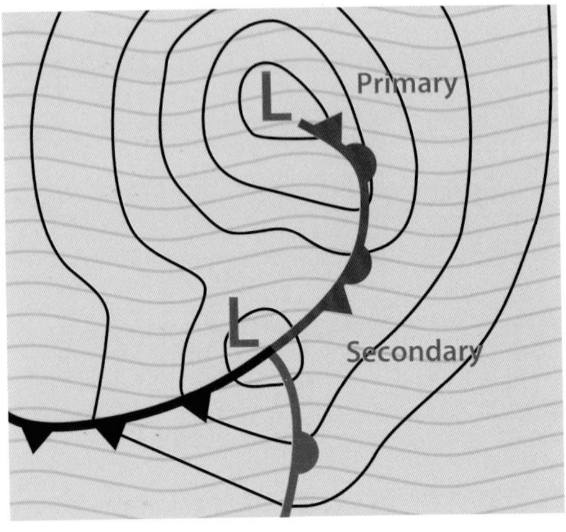

Fig 11.28 This secondary depression has formed at the tip of the warm sector bulge and may become the more dominant depression as it deepens.

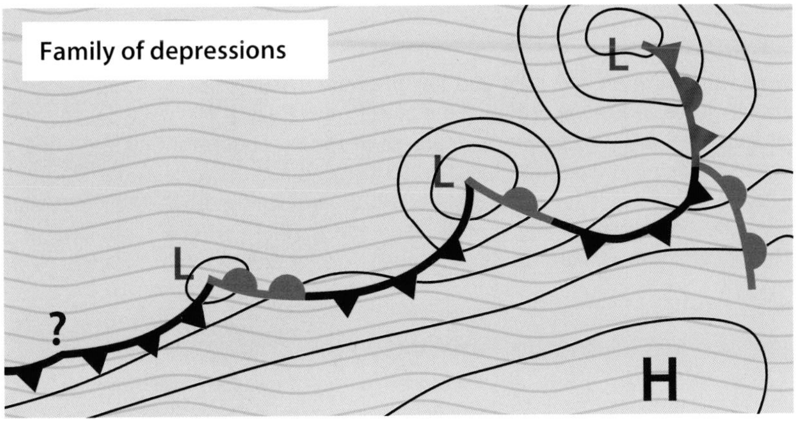

Fig 11.29 A family of depressions approaching the British Isles from the west will give unsettled weather with short fair periods as the ridges of high pressure pass over.

ANTICYCLONES

An anticyclone is an area of high pressure round which the wind blows in a clockwise direction in the northern hemisphere. It is surrounded by relatively low pressure, is often slow moving and has isobars that are widely spaced and roughly circular in shape. The weather in the centre of the high is usually dry and sunny in the summer months but it is often cloudy with rain at the outer extremities of the system.

In winter the weather may vary, depending on whether the air has travelled over sea and picked up moisture, or come from the Russian continent. If damp, the sky could be covered with low stratus cloud that persists for many days, known as *anticyclonic gloom*. Air from Siberia will give cloudless skies with sharp frosts at night.

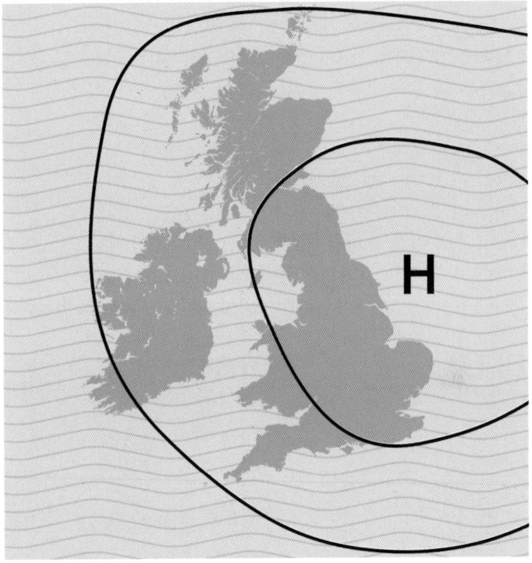

Fig 11.30 An anticyclone centred over the east coast in winter will often give cloudy skies in the south of England.

◆ Cold anticyclones

The Siberian high is a cold anticyclone, which is formed when the air sitting over the very cold land mass for a long period is cooled. The air above the surface contracts as it cools leaving space above it which, in turn is filled with new air from above. As the air above subsides, the pressure builds at the surface and often reaches 1,050 millibars or more.

◆ Warm anticyclones

Warm highs can be classed as either permanent or temporary features.

Permanent highs form over the oceans in the subtropics to give stable conditions with fine and sunny weather. They move seasonally and the one that has most influence on UK weather, the Azores high, can give us a good or bad summer depending on its geographical position. If it is well developed and extends north of its general summer position, the UK will probably have a good summer.

Temporary warm highs often start as ridges extending from the Azores high towards the British Isles. They break away from the main system to become a feature in their own right and are more likely to be formed during the summer months.

LOCAL WINDS

Winds that flow around high and low pressure systems are on a large scale that may well affect an area as large as Europe or the whole of northern Russia. However, these winds are often modified by geographical and topographical features in the close surrounding area and give rise to *local winds*. These winds form along the coast when there is a difference in the land and sea temperatures and where there are hills for warm air to climb up and valleys for cold air to rush down. These local winds can give us a good sailing breeze when the gradient wind is light and in areas like the South of France can give a Mistral that is far too strong for comfortable cruising.

◆ Sea breeze

The best sea breezes blow when there is a light offshore wind and near calm conditions in the spring and early summer. At this time of the year the sea is still cold and the land heats up quickly in the Sun giving differential heating of land and sea.

When the land is heated, the air above is warmed and rises away from the surface leaving a low-pressure area over the land. This rising air cools with height and as it cools it gets denser (heavier) and tries to find an easy path back down to Earth just as it did with the bonfire at the beginning of the chapter. The offshore wind helps push it seawards and, as there is already falling air over the cold sea, the cooled air falls back to sea level. Once the air has returned to the sea where the pressure is high it blows back towards the land to complete the circle as in Figure 11.31.

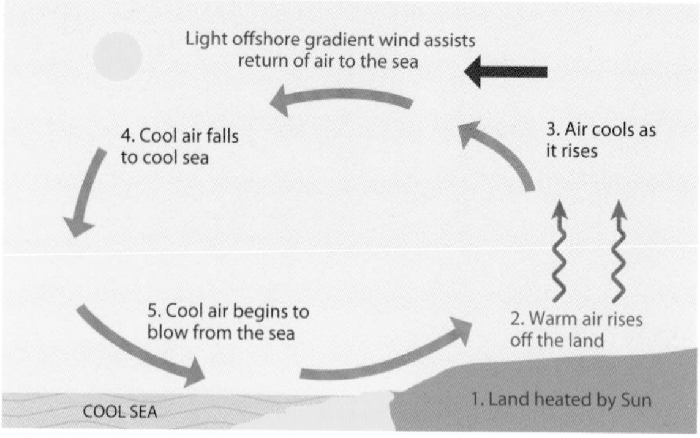

Fig 11.31 A sea breeze begins to blow when warm air rises off the land and is replaced by cooler air coming in from the sea.

This process will probably begin during the mid to late morning; the wind strengthening as the land gets hotter. It will reach a crescendo during the afternoon and veer (in the northern hemisphere) as it speeds up to blow at an angle of about 25 degrees to the shoreline. A well-developed sea breeze can be felt for quite a distance inland and up to 15 miles offshore by the middle of the afternoon.

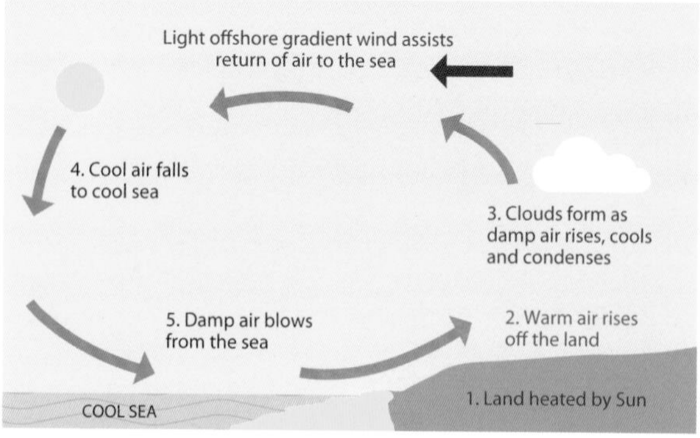

Fig 11.32 A well-established sea breeze can extend to about 15 miles offshore. As the incoming air is damp a line of cumulus cloud will be formed along the shoreline.

The air coming in from the sea passes over enough water to dampen it. When this damp air is heated it then rises. As it rises, it expands and cools again causing condensation to occur to give a line of cumulus cloud along the coastline during the afternoon (Figure 11.32).

The breeze will be accelerated as it bends around headlands and in areas such as the Western Solent where funnelling occurs between the Isle of Wight and the mainland. As there is a strong tidal stream in this area, what began as a gentle drift in the morning can become an exhilarating sail by the end of the afternoon.

The Sun gives the energy to fuel the breeze so, as it loses its power in the early evening, the breeze does not extend so far offshore and the cumulus cloud disappears from the coast. By sunset all is still again so that an evening meal and a bottle of good wine can be enjoyed whilst sitting in the cockpit admiring the sunset!

◆ Land breeze

The land breeze at night is really the reverse of the sea breeze but giving lighter winds over a much shorter distance, usually only a couple of miles offshore. This is because the sea does not heat and cool so quickly as the land and the movement of air is less pronounced.

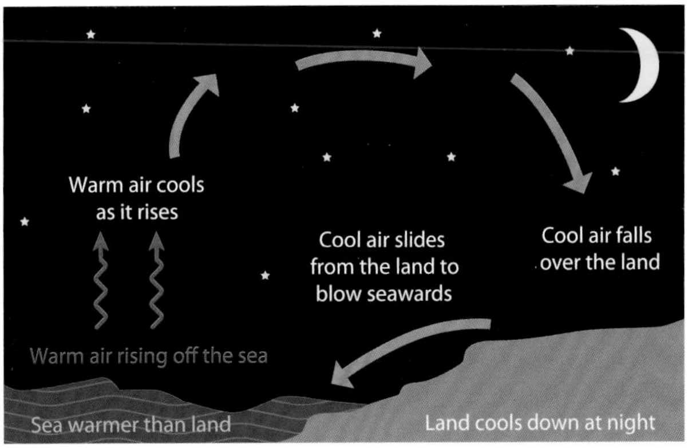
Warm air cools
as it rises
Cool air slides
from the land to
blow seawards
Cool air falls
over the land
Warm air rising off the sea
Sea warmer than land
Land cools down at night

Fig 11.33 The land breeze is not as strong as the sea breeze and extends only a few miles offshore.

The best land breezes occur in the late summer when the sea is warmer and the land cools down quickly in the evenings. Figure 11.33 shows that the air above the land has cooled and become heavier. It sinks and flows out to sea to take the place of the warm air radiating off the sea which, in turn, cools as it rises and flows back towards the land.

COASTAL WINDS

When a wind direction is given in the weather forecast it is for the gradient wind about 600m above the surface where the wind blows more or less along the direction of the isobars. At levels lower than this, surface friction over the sea will slow and back the wind by about 15 degrees and over the land by about 30 degrees.

If the wind blows along the line of a straight coast, there is a significant difference in the wind strength depending on whether the land is on your left or your right when you stand with your back to the wind. Figure 11.34 shows how the winds *converge* and strengthen when the land is on your right and *diverge* and weaken if the land is on your left.

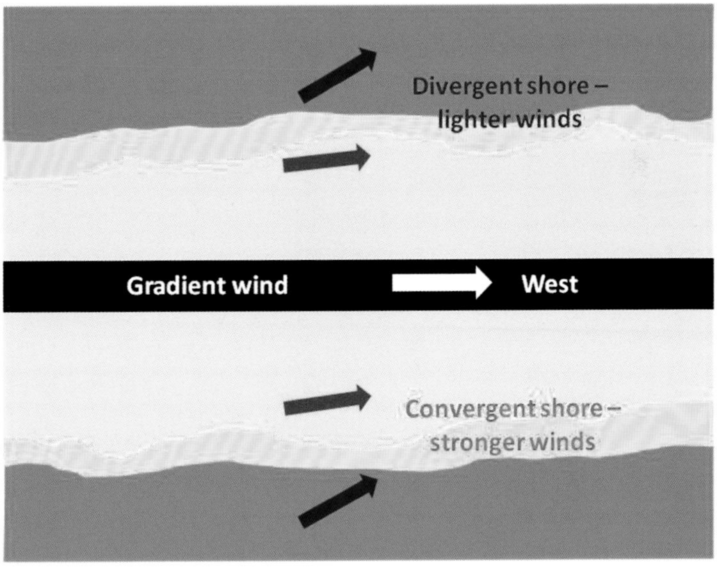
Divergent shore –
lighter winds
Gradient wind
West
Convergent shore –
stronger winds

Fig 11.34 Convergent and divergent winds along a straight shore.

MOUNTAIN (OR SLOPE) WINDS

Hills, long slopes and mountain ranges develop local winds as heating and cooling causes the air to either blow up or down the slopes.

◆ Anabatic wind

An anabatic wind is a wind that blows up the side of a hill or mountain which has been heated by the Sun. Hill ranges close to the sea can cause anabatic winds and the damp air coming in off the sea cools to below its dew point as it rises up and cloud forms on the top of the hill, very much as it does with a sea breeze.

◆ Katabatic wind

A katabatic wind is one that flows down slopes that are in close proximity to glaciers and snowfields or where the land has cooled at night. The cold, dense air slides down the sides of the valley to find the lowest level, usually the sea.

The winds are generally localised but can blow very strongly overnight giving an uncomfortable time to any craft anchored in a bay at the mouth of the valley (Figure 11.35).

Fig 11.35 Katabatic wind. The cool air slides down the hill slopes, funnels through the valley and out to the sea.

I have experienced such winds along the Dorset coast during the early autumn. In this area the land gradually slopes down to the coast from Salisbury Plain to Weymouth, a distance of about 40 miles. With an offshore wind to assist its flow, winds up to force 7 have been experienced on more than one occasion as the cool evening breeze sweeps down the slope and out to sea.

FOG

Dense fog at sea can be a frightening experience, particularly when the bow of your own boat disappears into the gloom whilst in the middle of a busy shipping lane!

Sound from ships' horns becomes diffused in fog and it is difficult to pin-point the exact whereabouts of other craft. Having the knowledge to recognise when conditions are right for the formation of fog could save you a nail-biting time.

We are going to look at the two types of fog that are commonly found at sea and around the coastline.

◆ Advection fog

This fog is also known as *sea fog* and is formed when warm moist air moves over a cold surface, which has a temperature that is lower than the dew point of the air (Figure 11.36).

This situation will give widespread fog and is most common in late spring and early summer when tropical maritime air blows from the south over the (still cold) sea that has not yet reached its summer temperature. A light wind is necessary to blow the air over the surface and to cause a little turbulence but wind of over force 5 will lift the fog off the surface of the water and it will appear as low stratus cloud. The Sun tends to thicken this fog, particularly when it has become deep and well-established and, apart from increased wind speed, the only way it will be cleared is by a change of air mass – to a Polar air stream (Figure 11.37).

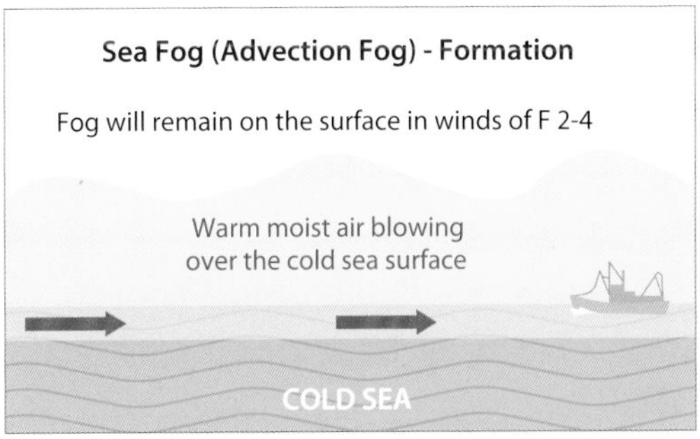

Fig 11.36 Advection or sea fog. This is formed when warm moist air flows across a cold surface such as the sea.

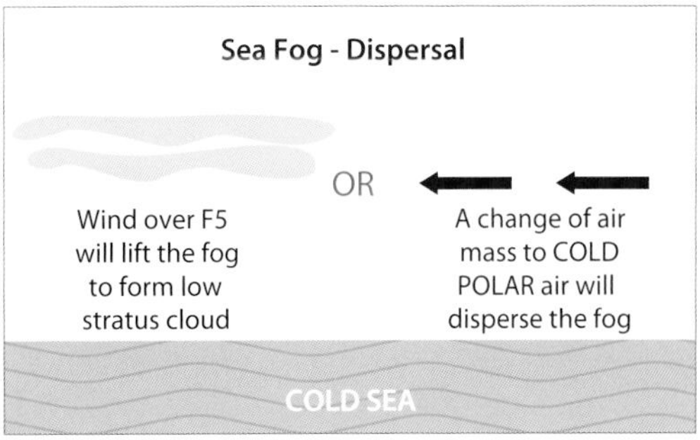

Fig 11.37 Sea fog will disperse if the wind increases to Beaufort force 5 or if the warm moist air stream is replaced by air from a Polar source.

Equipment for measuring the dew point is not normally carried in small craft but the information can be obtained through the Internet from various automatic data collection buoys around the UK. The site is www.ndbc.noaa.gov.

◆ Fog patches

If the dew point of the air is very similar to the sea surface temperature, then the fog will be patchy. Fog banks may be found close to headlands when the tidal stream is running hard over the uneven seabed and the water becomes disturbed, allowing the deep cold water to come to the surface. As the stream slackens, turbulence is reduced and the fog disappears. Once the stream begins to speed up in the other direction, the fog is likely to form once again.

This happens regularly during the summer in the Channel Islands, especially around Alderney which is close to an area where the stream runs at seven or eight knots over an uneven seabed.

◆ Radiation fog

Radiation fog is most commonly found when both the pressure and relative humidity are high in autumn and winter. Clear sunny days warm the land but with no cloud cover at night the land quickly loses heat once the Sun sets. The land cools the humid air above it and condensation occurs to give fog. Rural areas are most affected as the fog accumulates in valleys and across damp moorland whereas in the warmer, drier towns and along motorways, the fog is often thinner.

As the night is usually coldest around dawn the radiation fog will be at its thickest then.

When radiation fog occurs over land close to the coast, the fog slides down the river valleys and out over the sea to give coastal fog over harbours and coastline up to a few miles offshore.

If coastal fog patches are forecast, the visibility will improve the further offshore you go but remember that the fog is likely to form again in the evening along the coast if the pressure remains high.

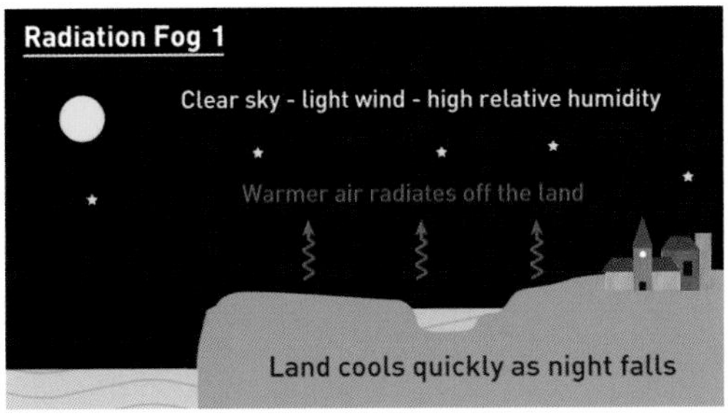

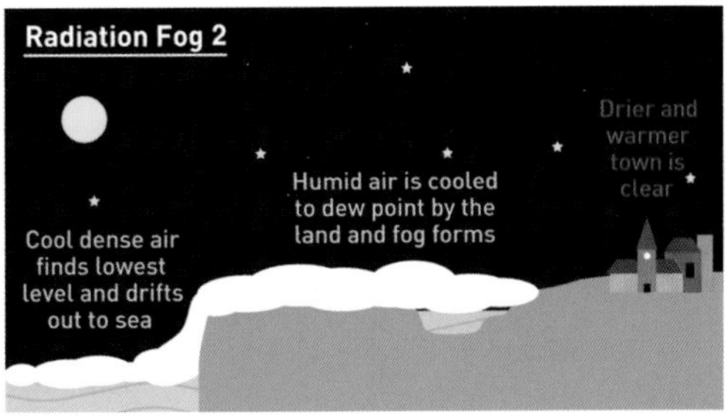

Fig 11.38 Radiation fog is most common in autumn and winter with clear skies and calm conditions.

Once the Sun rises and the land is heated again, the fog usually disperses.

Radiation Fog - Dispersal
Air is warmed and the fog disperses
Land is warmed by the Sun

Fig 11.39 Radiation fog will disperse once the Sun warms the land.

WEATHER FORECASTS

When cruising around the coasts of the UK and Europe it is easy to get detailed weather forecasts and charts from mobile phones, the VHF radio and Navtex. If you have Internet access then a whole stack of information becomes available to you. Navtex is particularly useful when you're abroad as all the information is published in English.

A nautical almanac will give you the times and frequencies of transmissions in its weather section – there is no excuse for not having a forecast. The UK Met Office issues the Shipping Forecast and the Inshore Waters Forecast and as these are used by the UK Coastguard and by Navtex we will look at them first.

◆ Shipping Forecast

The waters around the British Isles are divided up into areas which have names that may be very familiar (Figure 11.41). As the prevailing wind is from the west it is particularly important to listen to the forecast for the sea areas westward of you as this is likely to be the weather that you'll receive later on. Don't be fooled, though: sometimes it comes from the east, just to keep you on your toes!

During the forecast, terms are used to describe winds, visibility and pressure systems and although some, such as 'rather quickly', sound vague, they have very specific meanings which are described in the illustrations that follow.

Time of issue

It is important to know the time of issue when calculating the present position of a weather system and how soon it could arrive. The forecast is for the next 24 hours and can be up to two hours old before it is read.

Gale warning in force at the time of issue

A gale that is described as being 'imminent' (Figure 11.40) can be expected within the next six hours and the weather is often deteriorating when such a warning is received. Although the terms appear vague they describe very specific time periods.

GALE WARNINGS	
When a gale warning is issued there is always an indication of timing	
IMMINENT	**Within 6 hours**
SOON	**6 - 12 hours**
LATER	**More than 12 hours**

Fig 11.40 It may be possible to make the passage to home before the gale hits but remember it is often wiser to stay put.

General synopsis

The weather map is described with geographical positions for pressure centres, troughs and ridges. The words used will allow you to plot the progress of a depression or anticyclone.

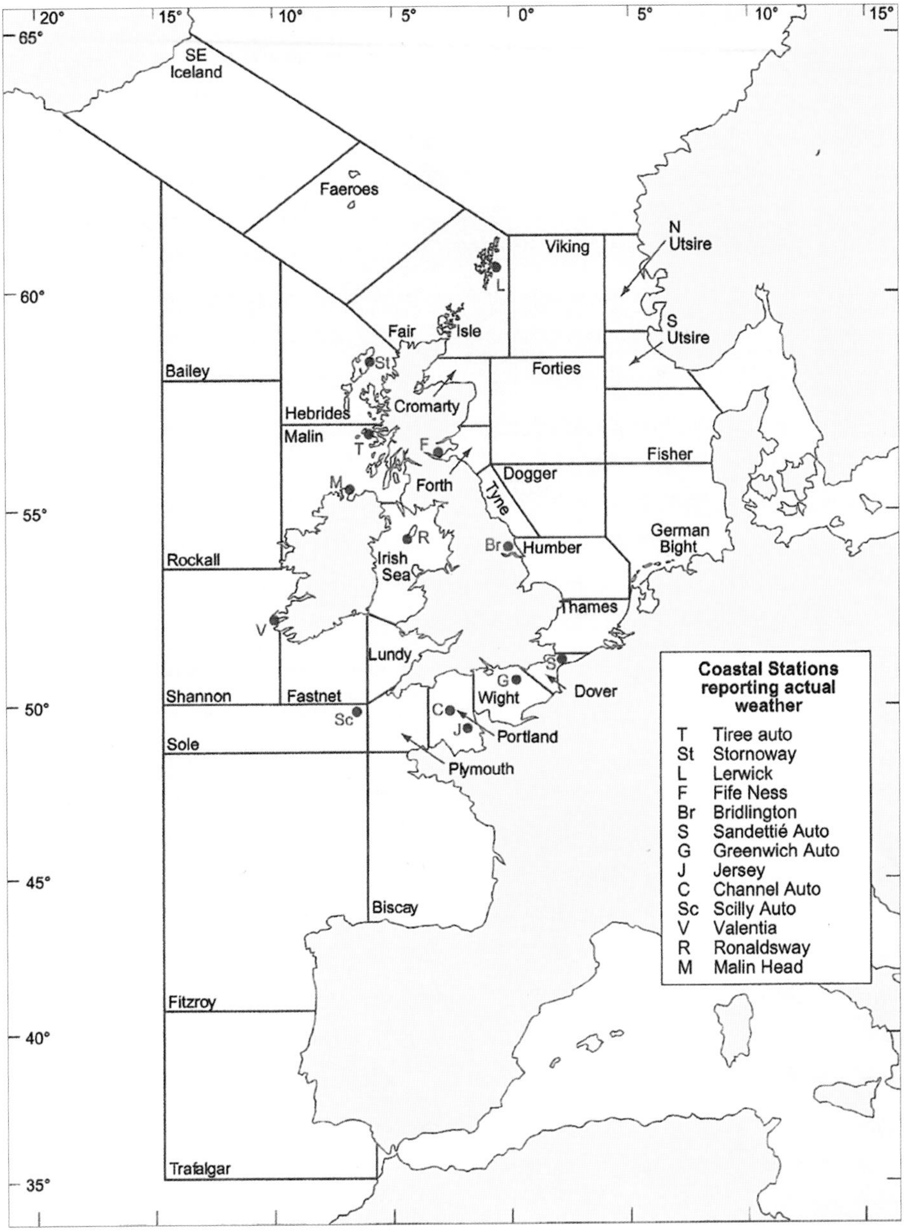

Fig 11.41 Sea areas around the United Kingdom. European area names may be found in a nautical almanac.

Example: Low 978 millibars 600 miles west of Ireland will move slowly north-eastwards to be 200 miles west of area Bailey by 1300 tomorrow. Frontal trough approaching Valentia will move north-eastwards to affect western sea areas.

Sea area forecasts

For each of the sea areas, the expected wind direction and speed is given as a force in the Beaufort scale. Any precipitation will be described and the forecast visibility will be mentioned (Figure 11.43).

Example: Lundy, Fastnet, Irish Sea.
SW 4 or 5 increasing 6 or 7.
Rain then showers.
Moderate, locally poor with fog patches.

PRESSURE SYSTEMS	
	Speed of Movement
SLOWLY	Less than 15 knots
STEADILY	15 – 25 knots
RATHER QUICKLY	25 – 35 knots
RAPIDLY	35 – 45 knots
VERY RAPIDLY	More than 45 knots

Fig 11.42 A depression that moves over 45 knots is likely to be short and sharp!

Coastal station reports

These reports (at 0048 and 0520 only) can be very important in establishing the progress of a front, as information such as the actual wind direction and force, weather, visibility, pressure and pressure tendency is given. A station reporting a barometric pressure that is falling 'more slowly' together with intermittent rain and poor visibility probably indicates that the warm front has passed over recently whereas one that is giving pressure that is falling 'very rapidly' (Figure 11.44) ensures that gale force winds will blow sooner or later – no doubt about it!

VISIBILITY	
GOOD	More than 5 miles
MODERATE	2 - 5 miles
POOR	1000m - 2 miles
FOG	Less than 1000m

Fig 11.43 Good visibility can be any distance between 5 and 35 miles.

◆ Other terms used in the shipping forecast

We have already seen that the wind ahead of a depression which passes to the north of us will back (alter in an anticlockwise direction) but veer as the front goes through (Figure 11.45).

If the centre of a depression is forecast to pass through the centre of a sea area, the wind is described as being 'cyclonic' as the wind changes will obviously differ according to the position of the observer within the area. Some will experience a backing wind ahead of the system and others will find that it veers. Describing the wind shifts as cyclonic covers all eventualities.

PRESSURE CHANGES	
	Change in 3 hrs
STEADY	< 0.1mb
SLOWLY	0.1 to 1.5mb
RISING/FALLING	1.6 to 3.5mb
QUICKLY	3.6 to 6.0mb
VERY RAPIDLY	> 6.0mb

Fig 11.44 A rapidly falling pressure means a strong wind.

OTHER TERMS	
FAIR	No significant precipitation
CYCLONIC	The centre of the depression will move through the sea area and the winds direction changes are difficult to describe.
VEERING	Wind is changing in a CLOCKWISE direction
BACKING	Wind is changing in an ANTICLOCKWISE direction

Fig 11.45 If fair weather is forecast there will be no significant precipitation.

BEAUFORT SCALE			
1	Light airs	1- 3 kn	Ripples without foam crests.
2	Light breeze	4- 6 kn	Small wavelets. Crests do not break.
3	Gentle breeze	7- 10 kn	Large wavelets. Crests begin to break.
4	Moderate breeze	11- 16 kn	Small waves. Frequent white horses.
5	Fresh breeze	17- 21 kn	Moderate waves. Many white horses.
6	Strong breeze	22- 27 kn	Large waves. White foam crests. Some spray.
7	Near gale	28- 33 kn	Sea heaps up, foam from breaking waves blown in streaks. Spray.
8	Gale	34- 40 kn	Moderate waves, crests break into spindrift.
9	Severe gale	41- 47 kn	High waves. Spray affects visibility.
10	Storm	48- 55 kn	Very high waves with overhanging crests. Sea surface looks white.
11	Violent storm	56- 63 kn	Exceptionally high waves. Sea completely covered in foam.

Fig 11.46 The Beaufort wind scale.

◆ Beaufort wind scale

Admiral Sir Francis Beaufort devised this scale in 1808 so that naval captains could use the appearance of the sea to assist with the choice of sails. To this day it is the internationally recognised method of classifying wind speeds and is used in forecasts worldwide.

Remember that the wind strengths given are average wind speeds, not the maximum speed that can be expected. A force 6 may give 20 knots in the lulls but also hefty gusts of 30 knots. The waves which accompany this wind speed are described as large with white foam crests and it is the waves that are a far greater problem than the wind itself – a very demanding challenge for the inexperienced crew of a small boat.

WAVE HEIGHT	metres		metres
CALM	< 0.1m	ROUGH	2.5 - 4m
SMOOTH	0.1 - 0.5m	VERY ROUGH	4 - 6m
SLIGHT	0.5 - 1.25m	HIGH	6 - 9m
MODERATE	1.25 - 2.5m	VERY HIGH	9 - 14m

Fig 11.47 A modern offshore sailing cruiser is classified as being capable of withstanding waves of up to 4 metres in height.

◆ Inshore Waters Forecast

This forecast is for the waters around the UK up to 12 miles offshore and is included in the UK Coastguard's routine Maritime Safety information broadcasts on VHF radio. An announcement is made on Channel 16 which sends listeners to one of the channels reserved for the purpose – 23, 84 or 86. The forecast is read every three hours and renewed every six hours. Twice daily, around breakfast and supper time, an extended forecast is also read. Times of the broadcasts for each region can be found in *Reeds Nautical Almanac*.

In Figure 11.48, you will see that certain areas of the coastline are marked in red where a strong wind warning is in force. The Channel Islands are expected to experience winds of force 6 – the Beaufort force for which a strong wind warning is issued.

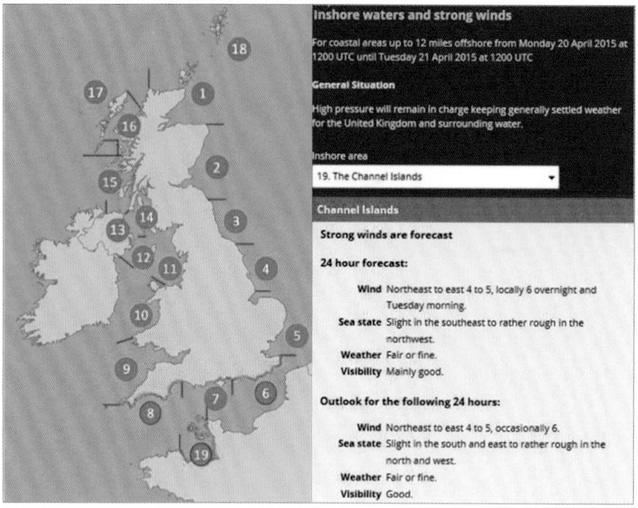

Fig 11.48 Sea areas for the Inshore Waters Forecasts.

◆ Navtex

A Navtex receiver is invaluable as it silently and efficiently records weather information and gale warnings whilst you are occupied berthing the boat in some tricky corner of a marina or getting a good night's sleep! The Navtex receiver uses the medium frequency band and has a range of up to 400 miles. It requires a dedicated antenna which should be mounted low down to avoid spurious reflections from the sea surface and many boatowners mount both the Navtex and GPS antennas on a short mast at the stern of the boat.

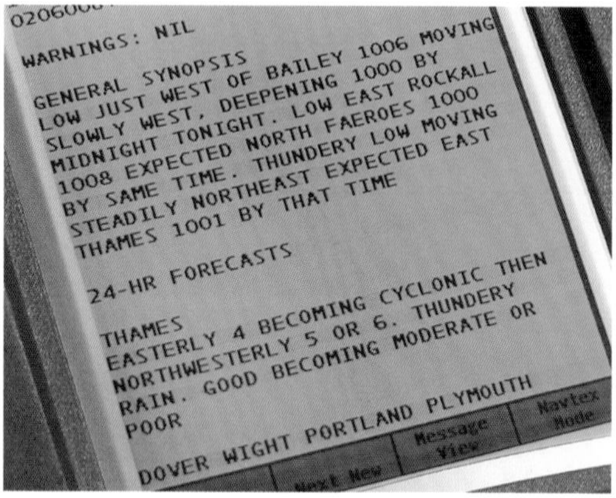

Fig 11.49 A Navtex receiver showing the general synopsis and shipping forecast for area Thames.

All messages are transmitted in English on 518 kHz and a second frequency, 490 kHz, is used for broadcasts in the area national language.

Transmission times are staggered so that there is no interference between stations and full details can be found in the weather section of a yachtsman's nautical almanac. It is sometimes difficult to receive Navtex in a marina where numerous masts affect the signal.

◆ Forecast charts

The UK Met Office issues forecast weather charts for up to five days ahead and an example of a 24-hour forecast is given in Figure 11.50.

The chart shows numerous centres of low pressure with just one anticyclone to the north of Greenland. Hardly summer weather for the UK!

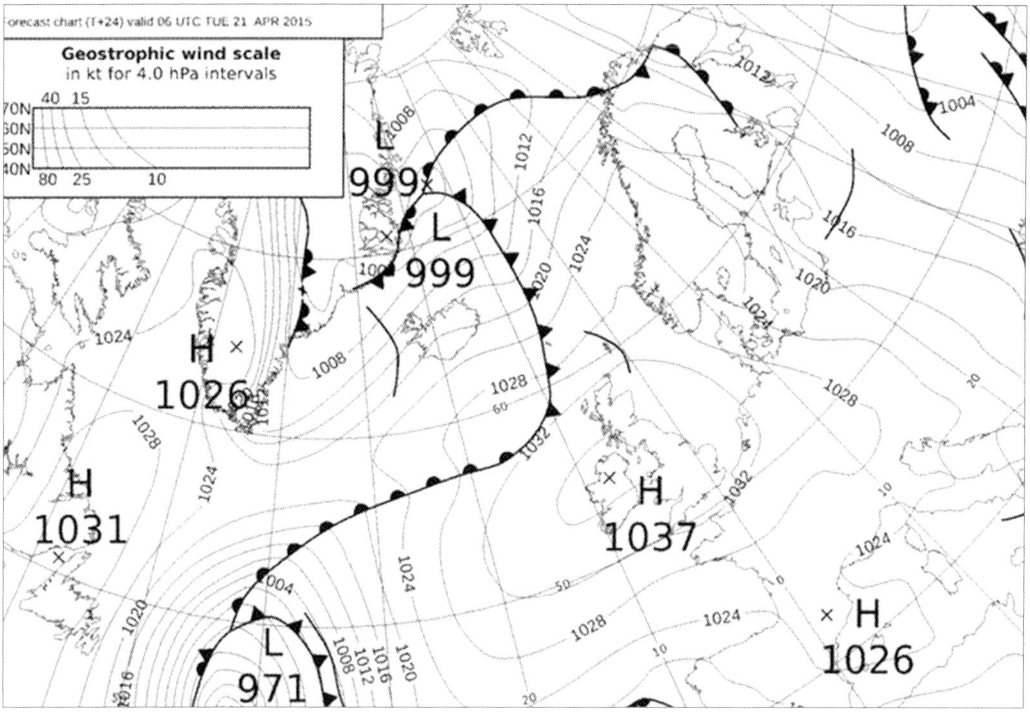

Fig 11.50 This type of forecast chart, which is issued by the UK Met Office, is displayed on notice boards at harbour masters' offices and marinas.

◆ How to measure wind speed on a weather chart

Forecast charts issued by the UK Met Office carry a scale for determining wind speed by measurement across the isobars.

The chart in Figure 11.51 shows an area of high pressure close to 60°N and the distance between the isobars has been measured. This measurement was transferred to the scale at the top of the chart and, starting from the left hand end, was placed on the 60° line. A wind speed of 25 knots was read off the bottom of the scale as highlighted in the illustration.

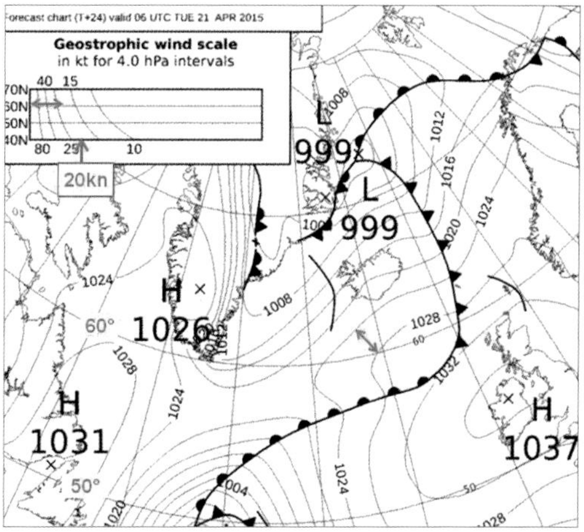

Fig 11.51 The distance across the isobars is measured and the wind speed is then read off the scale at the top of the forecast chart.

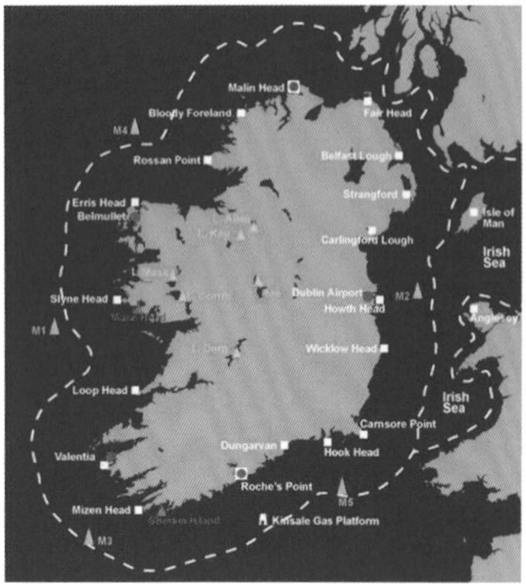

Fig 11.52 Irish Met Office coast station reports.

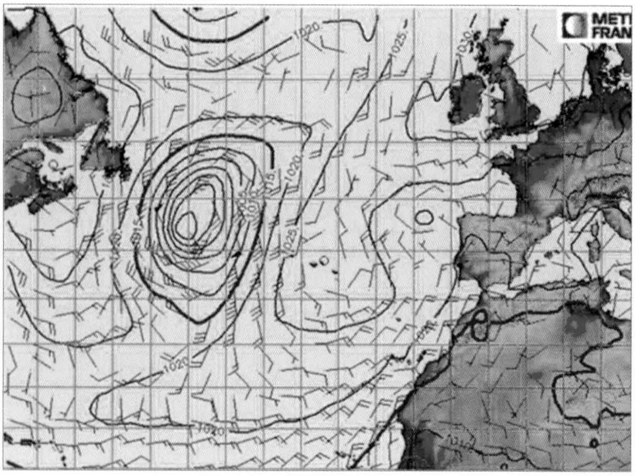

Fig 11.53 Meteo France North Atlantic chart with wind direction and speed.

Forecasts abroad

Most countries in northern Europe give gale and storm warnings in English and in the local language. Figure 11.52 shows Irish coast station reporting points which can easily be found on the Internet.

Most French marinas have television monitors showing data from Meteo France who run an excellent weather service (Figure 11.53).

◆ Weather information on the Internet

With the aid of a laptop computer and a suitable mobile phone, a whole world of weather information is available on the web.

Synoptic charts, infrared satellite images, rain radar, sea and air temperature charts can all be obtained and the UK Met Office has a series of buoys dotted around the UK which report much valuable information including the dew point, which is useful to know when assessing the likelihood of fog whilst on passage.

◆ Useful websites

www.metoffice.gov.uk Shipping Forecast and Inshore Waters Forecast, web cam views and observations from all major UK cities.

www.wetterzentrale.de Weather charts from European weather centres, satellite images, long-range forecasts and a whole lot more.

www.ndbc.noaa.gov This American agency collects data from buoys stationed around the coasts of many countries. The UK buoys can give useful information from places like the Channel Light Vessel off Alderney.

www.meteo.fr Wind charts and five-day forecast for Europe (Inc UK). Wind speed given in km/hour so it may not be as strong as you might think at first glance.

www.bbc.co.uk/weather Good chartlets for wind, pressure, temperature and rain radar for the UK.

www.windfinder.com

Wind, waves & weather Superforecast Ballard Down

Wind statistics | Report | Forecast | Super Forecast | Tides | Webcams | Maps

Last update: 09:28 local time — Show night hours

Local date	Monday, Apr 20														
Local time	07h	08h	09h	10h	11h	12h	13h	14h	15h	16h	17h	18h	19h	20h	21h
Wind direction															
Wind speed (kts)	15	15	13	12	11	9	7	7	7	8	8	8	7	6	8
Wind gusts (kts)	15	15	15	14	13	11	9	9	9	10	10	10	9	9	13
Wave direction															
Wave height (m)	0.8	0.8	0.8	0.8	0.8	0.8	0.8	0.8	0.8	0.8	0.8	0.8	0.7	0.7	0.7
Wave period (s)	16	16	16	16	16	15	15	15	15	15	15	14	14	14	13
Cloud cover															
Relative humidity (%)	87	87	84	79	77	77	79	80	80	81	82	82	83	84	83
Precipitation (mm/h)	0.0	0.0	0.0	0.0	0.0	0.0	0.0	0.0	0.0	0.0	0.0	0.0	0.0	0.0	0.0
Precipitation type															
Air pressure (hPa)	1022	1023	1023	1023	1024	1025	1024	1025	1025	1025	1024	1024	1025	1025	1026
Air temperature (°C)	6	7	8	9	10	11	11	12	12	12	12	12	11	11	11
Feels like (°C)	2	3	4	[illegible]	[illegible]	11	11	12	12	12	12	12	11	11	11

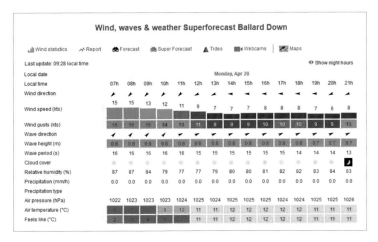

Fig 11.54 Comprehensive forecast for the Dorset coast by Windfinder.

QUESTION PAPER 11 – METEOROLOGY

11.1 Does the wind blow clockwise or anticlockwise around a high pressure area in the northern hemisphere?

11.2 What type of cloud would you associate with squally showers and gusty winds?

11.3 The barometric pressure has risen seven millibars in the last three hours. What wind speed can you expect?

11.4 The sea is forecast to be 'moderate'. What height of waves may you expect?

11.5 When are strong wind warnings issued?

Answers at the back of the book

12 FOG & HEAVY WEATHER

FOG

IN THE PREVIOUS CHAPTER we learned how sea fog forms and how its formation is often dependent on location and the strength of the tidal stream. Sometimes, when a passage has been planned, the odds are weighed up and the decision to go is made even if a risk of fog exists – a decision that might not have been made in the days before GPS and small boat radar became available.

Having an accurate position solves one problem but craft without radar are effectively blind when it comes to collision avoidance. Unless you own a very large flat-sided steel vessel (and not many do), there is no guarantee that a fibreglass boat will be seen by other ships unless it is fitted with an efficient radar reflector. The ship in Figure 12.1 was seen at approximately 400 metres in the middle of the English Channel and there was no way of knowing whether we had been seen on radar.

Fig 12.1 This ship was seen at a distance of about 400 metres in the middle of the English Channel.

Radar sets are fitted with proximity alarms and watch keepers in some merchant ships do not man the radar vigilantly – they can become complacent and assume that all contacts will be identified. In a choppy sea, small boats giving a weak radar return could be hidden by sea clutter and may not trigger the alarm. We will be looking at radar reflectors later in the chapter.

On entering fog there are a number of jobs to be done and a wise skipper will have a checklist of these tasks so that nothing gets forgotten. It will be a busy time and there is no definitive order in which to perform the tasks on the following list.

◆ Fog checklist

1 Adjust speed. Generally this will require a reduction in speed but it may be wise to speed up to clear a busy shipping channel.

2 Before entering the fog, fix position and record it in the log book. Skippers of boats without GPS should take particular note of depth, course and speed so that an accurate EP can be plotted.

3 All members of the crew should dress in warm clothing, waterproofs and lifejackets. Wake

sleeping crew members in case the cabin has to be evacuated quickly as they may feel a bit chilly sitting in the liferaft in their underwear! If crew pop below to get warm, they should stand by the companionway or saloon door.

4 Hoist the radar reflector (if not permanently mounted).

5 Post a lookout in the bows.

6 Consider the use of harness lines by foredeck crew. It is easier to hear other fog signals when away from engine noise. If cockpit or fly bridge crew were unable to see the foredeck crew then clipping on would be sensible.

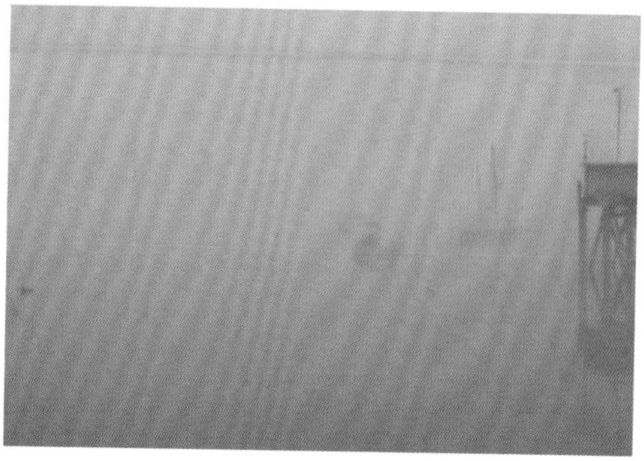

Fig 12.2 In restricted visibility a lookout should stand on the bow in harbours and crowded waterways.

7 Try to maintain silence on deck – distant fog signals could be lost in the chatter. Listening for any period of time is tiring – if there is sufficient crew, rotate the tasks frequently.

8 Switch on the radar and keep a constant watch using an experienced operator. Modern radars are powerful tools and the wisdom of sending a crew member on a radar course is apparent here. The modern set in Figure 12.3 has a colour display on a TFT screen.

9 If there is an Automatic Identification System input to your chart plotter, monitor traffic in your immediate vicinity. Remember that it is only vessels over 300 gross register tons who must use AIS. For smaller vessels it is fitted voluntarily. AIS is explained later in this chapter.

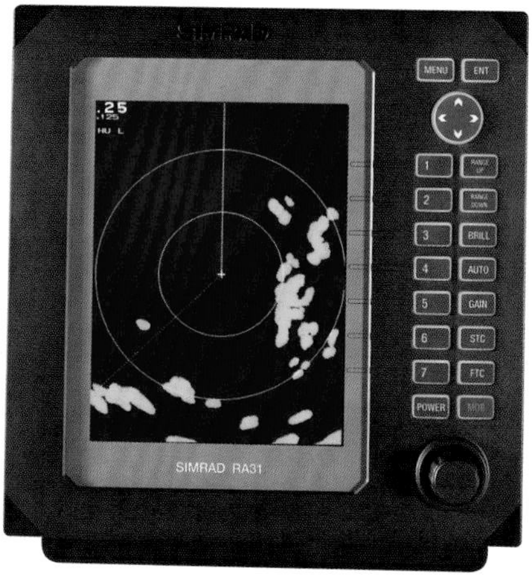

Fig 12.3 Simrad RA 30 colour radar.

10 Have the engine ready for immediate use. If it is already running, throttle back and listen for other ships at regular intervals.

11 Consider a change of destination. If you are in the vicinity of a harbour and commercial shipping, it could be prudent to make for shallow water to reduce the risk of collision, as other craft then encountered would be smaller. If offshore and close to shipping lanes, maintain a steady course and reasonable speed to clear the lanes as soon as possible.

12 Sound the appropriate fog signal:
One prolonged blast at intervals not exceeding 2 minutes if under power.
One short blast and two short blasts if under sail.
Fog horn gas cylinders are emptied quickly so have some other means of sending the fog signal. Lung-powered horns are stocked by many chandlers.

13 Switch on the navigation lights.
Lights mounted on the bow can cause reflections in fog which will affect the lookout's vision if he is too close to the lights. Consider a shield or position the lookout further aft away from the glare.

14 Have a white collision warning flare ready to hand.

15 If close to shallow water, prepare the anchor for immediate use.

16 Ensure that the liferaft is tied to the parent craft and ready for deployment.

17 If no liferaft, prepare the dinghy and tow it astern.

RADAR REFLECTORS

Radar beams pass straight through glassfibre and reflect badly off wood. Engines and cookers are probably the best reflectors on board but they are usually installed too low in the hull to be of any use. It is therefore necessary to carry an additional reflector mounted as high as possible above the fly bridge or on the mast of the yacht.

In a recent in-depth study, reflectors were tested thoroughly and it was found that some reflectors are effective whilst in an upright position but lose efficiency at angles of heel. Both active and passive reflectors were tested.

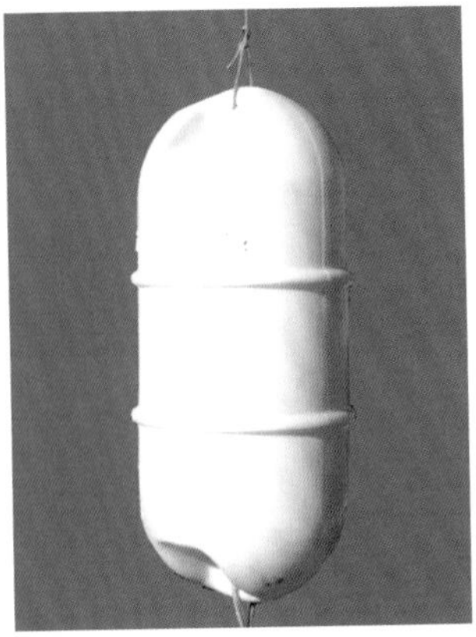

Fig 12.4 Firdell Blipper.

◆ Passive reflectors

Passive reflectors come in many shapes and sizes. Just two types are illustrated here.

Firdell Blipper This reflector can easily be hoisted on a signal halyard if permanent mounting is difficult or on the arch above the fly bridge of a motor cruiser. It uses a helical array and is ideal for RIBs and powerboats that can maintain an upright position.

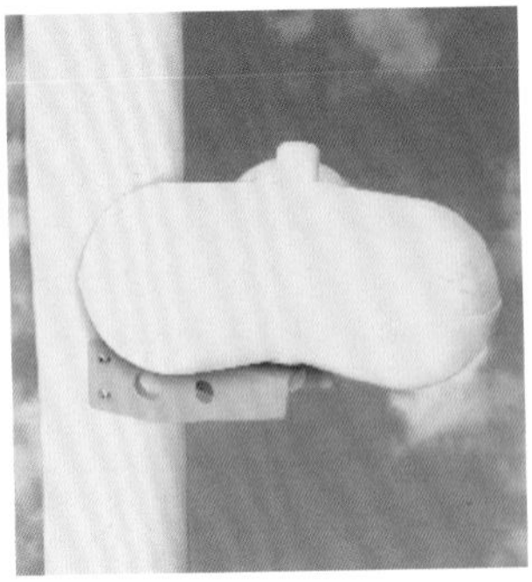

Fig 12.5 Viking Tri-lens.

Viking Tri-lens Using US Department of Defense technology, this reflector is proven to give a good return whatever the sea state or angle of heel. As it weighs approximately 5 kilos, it is best mounted below the spreaders of a sailing yacht to reduce top weight.

◆ Active reflectors (Radar Target Enhancers)

The 'Sea-me' active reflector is a transponder – it 'responds' to the radar beam received from another ship's radar, boosts it, then returns a more powerful signal which gives the impression that it is a larger vessel. It responds to both 3cm and 10cm radar, the two types fitted to merchant ships over 300 GRT. The antenna (illustrated) should be mounted at the top of the mast and requires power. The 'Sea-me' boat may also be fitted with an indicator which shows a red light when a radar beam has been detected.

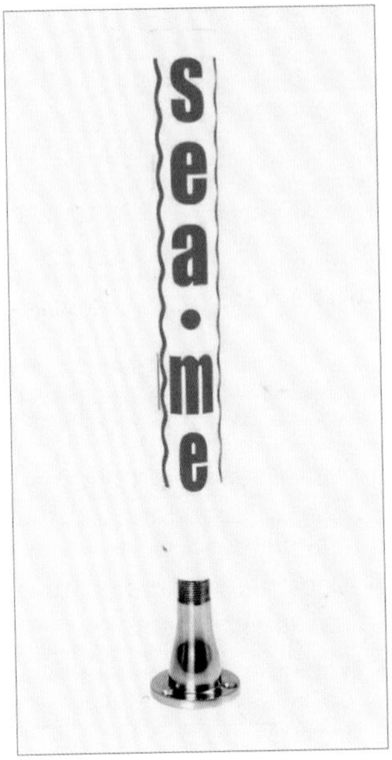

Fig 12.6 Sea-me active reflector.

AUTOMATIC IDENTIFICATION SYSTEM (AIS)

AIS does just what it says on the tin – it is a short-range tracking system for ships in coastal waters, which uses two of the marine band VHF channels. Ships electronically exchange data about position, course and speed with vessel traffic services and other ships. Leisure craft are not forced to fit the equipment but it is so useful that many are installing it to identify themselves to large commercial ships whilst crossing shipping lanes. The data is displayed on a chart plotter or on a dedicated display with a GPS input.

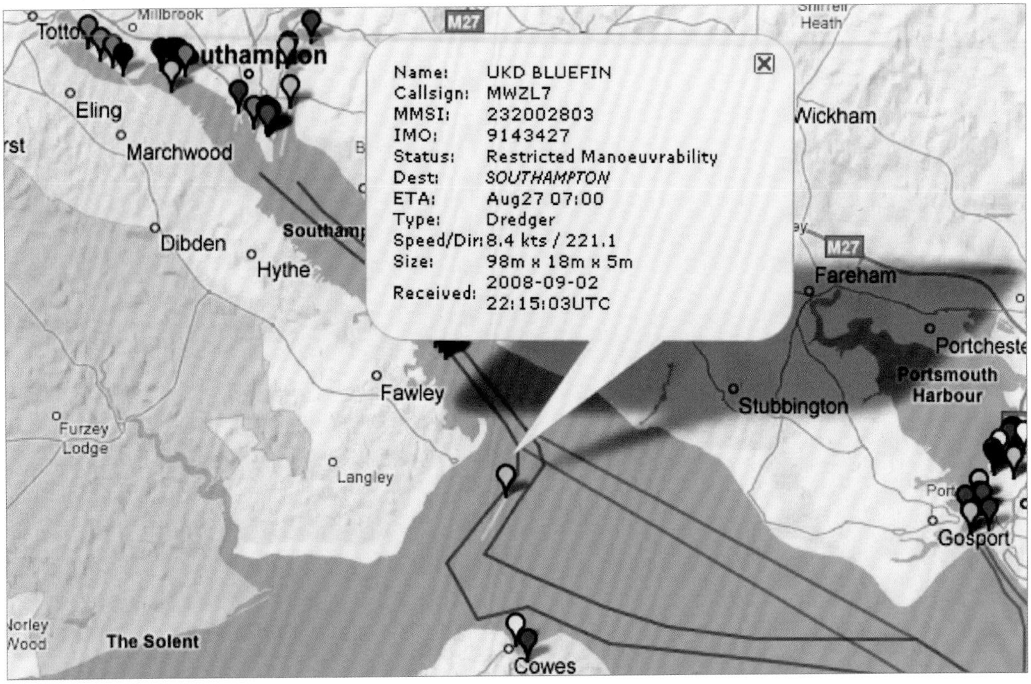

Fig 12.7 Much information is given by a vessel fitted with AIS.

◆ AIS Receiver only

It is possible to get AIS information without transmitting any information yourself. The advantage of this is that the equipment is a lot less expensive but has the great disadvantage that whilst you can see others, they cannot see you. A VHF antenna and a GPS input is required together with the instrument and you are in business. The mock radar type display puts you in the centre of the screen; the geographical position of other craft is taken from the GPS and then displayed.

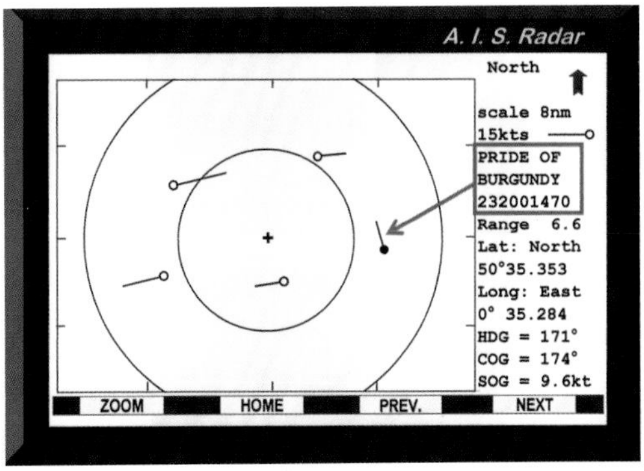

Fig 12.8 AIS receiver only with 'radar' type of display.

DO I CONTINUE?

In order to decide whether you are going to stick to your original plan or seek an alternative destination certain questions need to be answered:

1 Does the destination have a hazard-free, wide entrance or is the approach through a narrow, rock-lined channel?
2 Is radar fitted? If yes, is there someone other than the skipper who is trained to use it? Motor cruisers usually have the radar in clear view of the helmsman but in a sailing yacht the display is often down below and the skipper could lose touch with events on deck if he were below.
3 Is there an accurate position-fixing system such as GPS or a chart plotter interfaced with GPS? If yes, is the accuracy it gives sufficient for close pilotage?

Depending on the answers to all these questions, there are three possible courses of action:
a If a safe anchorage can be found, anchor the boat in relatively shallow water and wait for the fog to lift. This is a wise action when approaching a port entrance, unless it is well known to you or has a relatively easy entrance.
b Standing offshore in deeper water may be the best course of action on an outward passage or if there are inshore hazards. However, it would have to be in an area not used by bigger, faster ships and a constant listening and visual watch would have to be kept.
c Another answer is to close the coast at right angles to one side of the destination. Motor cruisers capable of punching a foul tide might wish to head for the down-tide side so that the final approach is slow and controlled but auxiliary yachts might choose the up-tide side to aim for if the top speed made it impossible to fight the stream.

Whichever side is chosen, the boat can run down a depth contour, preferably one that runs close to the harbour entrance or in through the breakwater. In Figure 12.9 the approach is by a powerboat from down-tide.

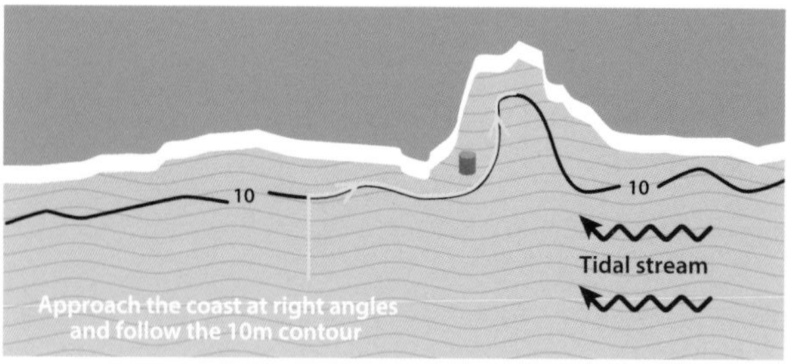

Fig 12.9 Running along a contour line when approaching a harbour in fog.

HEAVY WEATHER

If shipping forecasts and weather reports have been studied, there will usually be some warning of approaching bad weather.

Before setting out into bad weather you need to be absolutely sure that both you and the crew have sufficient experience, knowledge and energy to cope with the forecast weather. Is the boat seaworthy? Could the weather be worse than forecast? If in any doubt stay put where you are – safely tied up in the harbour.

Peer pressure can become very persuasive and it sometimes takes great strength of character to resist taunts of 'Wimp'. The coastguards will be only too willing to tell you sad tales of great daring that resulted in a tragic, but vain, search for survivors. The saying 'There are bold sailors and old sailors but no old, bold ones' is as true today as it ever was.

◆ Wind

Sailing yachts obviously need wind (but only so much for comfort) and motor cruising folk are happier without any at all! Obviously there is a happy medium to be found, and most under sail would be happy with about 14 knots of wind – a Beaufort force 4 whereas the motor yachtsman will be careful to make this passage when the wind is with the tide – not against.

Admiral Beaufort wrote his scale of wind forces to give some guidance to naval captains on which sails to hoist. What they probably didn't appreciate is the enormous increase in pressure on every square metre of sail, as the wind gets stronger. At force 8, the pressure is not just double the strength at force 4, it is over six times

Fig 12.10 This yacht is well reefed but is sailing to windward well in strong winds.

as great, and gusty strong wind conditions can put intolerable loads on sails, rigging and the crew. It is said that force 6, with 25 knots of wind and waves three times as high as those at force 4, is a yachtsman's gale. For the inexperienced sailor it is certainly true and many experienced ones choose to stay in port.

Tasks such as putting in a reef correctly can become difficult as the crew are battered by wind and sea. The fear of sickness can cause reluctance to go below to navigate, prepare meals and to get warm – making it a boat under siege. It is the sea state which causes the problems not the wind itself; the sea can broach and roll the boat, knock it down and swamp it with very little effort – a sobering thought. The wind was blowing a near gale in the Solent when the picture (Figure 12.10) was taken. As these are sheltered waters the waves were small but out at sea the conditions would have been much worse.

◆ True and apparent wind

The true wind is what you feel when you are stationary. If the wind is blowing at 5 knots you feel 5 knots of wind on your face. If you then walk **into** the wind at a speed of 5 knots you will feel 10 knots of wind. Walk at 5 knots **with** the wind behind you and you will feel no wind at all. Heading downwind at 10 knots with the wind blowing 30 knots, you will feel 20 knots, a mere force 5. Turn to head into that 30-knot wind, still managing to log 10 knots, and you will feel 40 knots – force 8/9, quite a difference.

◆ Gusts

It is worth remembering that the Beaufort scale gives the mean wind speed that can be expected and it is quite possible that gusts scaling up into the next force will be experienced. Gusty conditions can be experienced after a cold front has gone through or when sailing near high cliffs or exposed headlands.

◆ Tide races and rips

Conditions can become very much worse close to prominent headlands. When either wind or water has to bend to go around headlands it will speed up. As the nature of the seabed round a headland is usually very uneven, the water has to rise over the obstructions in addition to deviating around it. This causes major disturbances and the water boils and breaks in what is called a 'race' (Figure 12.11).

It is prudent to stay clear of some tidal races even in the calmest weather; in a strong wind and tide it could be suicidal to go through them. The race off Portland Bill is a good example of a particularly evil stretch of water.

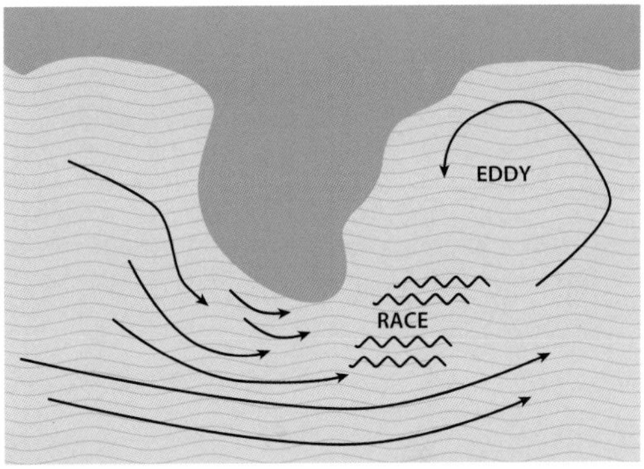

Fig 12.11 Headlands are often affected by a tidal race that forms as water is diverted to move around the promontory.

GETTING READY FOR A BLOW

Stowage down below

In a blow, an unprepared cabin can very quickly look like a battlefield unless care is taken to keep it habitable. Before the weather deteriorates, walk through the boat and check that hatches and ventilators are shut and that the heads are pumped dry.

Saloon bunks can be prepared with lee cloths and bedding so that watch keepers can get some sleep. Clear the chart table, except for the current chart, and have a towel ready near the table so that the navigator can dry his face (and spectacles) to prevent drips on the charts.

Check that tins are in a low stowage – a flying baked bean tin could do untold damage to someone's head. Restock the nibbles box with plain biscuits, flapjacks and glucose sweets.

Think about meals and prepare as much as possible in advance. A large saucepan of stew is always welcome and can easily be topped up with baked beans or tinned vegetables. Lastly, make sure that the bilges are pumped and the washboards ready for use. Now sit back, have a cup of tea and relax for a few minutes before life becomes lively!

Crew

The crew should wear harnesses and lifejackets and should clip on before coming up into the cockpit. Neck towels save wet collars and waterproof hoods often fit better when pulled up over a woolly hat.

Try to get everyone fed before the wind increases too much, and those prone to seasickness are advised to take an anti-seasickness pill earlier rather than waiting for that queasy feeling. If later on people feel seasick give them cold fizzy alkaline drinks, bland biscuits and cold energy-giving foods, as the stomach is more likely to go into spasm with hot food than cold. Flapjack usually stays down but acidic drinks should be avoided.

On deck

Reef the sails or change to smaller storm sails – if in doubt – DO IT. Check that any loose gear on deck is put away, and if the liferaft is kept in a locker, make sure that nothing is on top of it. See that the anchor is well lashed down – anchor and chain have been known to run out and wrap around the propeller shaft during a gale almost causing the loss of the yacht.

◆ Shortening sail

Storm jib

When running before the wind care must be taken that the boat does not become over-canvassed without the skipper noticing that the wind has increased. The subsequent alteration of course into the wind to reef the mainsail can become a tedious, wet and frightening experience for crew not used to foul weather, so keep a weather eye on the anemometer and be aware of increasing boat speed.

Reducing the size of a furling jib in moderate winds is simple because it doesn't require crew on the foredeck but if the wind increases towards gale force it may be necessary to furl it away altogether and rig a smaller, stronger storm jib in its place. This task would be well nigh impossible if no previous thought had been given to a method of attaching the storm jib luff to the forestay especially as many storm jibs use hanks on the luff.

Unfurling and removing the large genoa would be extremely difficult in strong winds but a method has been devised so that the genoa can be furled away and the storm sail hoisted on top of the existing furled headsail.

Figure 12.12 shows that the sail maker has cut a rectangular piece of sailcloth to fit around the forestay. It is fitted with cringles so that the sail can be hanked to the cringles after the cloth has been passed around the furled sail, giving an easy, inexpensive solution to the problem. Some yachts have a spare inner forestay which clips to the shrouds when not in use and then attaches to a D ring on the foredeck. The storm jib, which is brightly coloured so that it can be seen in a rough sea, can then be bent on to this replacement forestay.

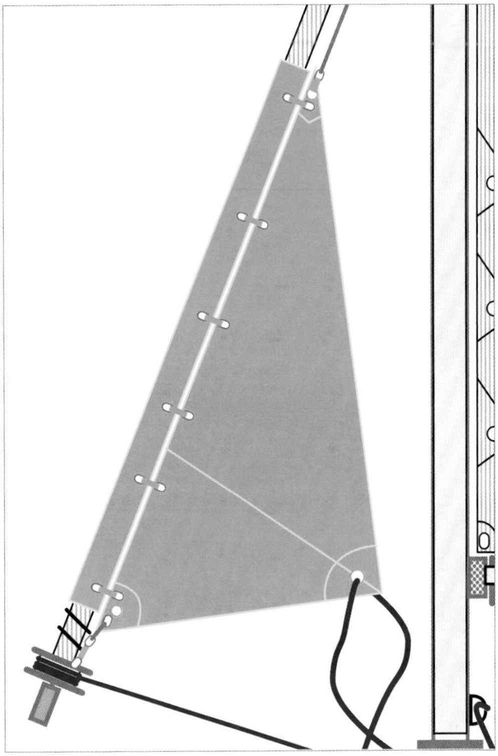

Fig 12.12 The storm jib is hanked on to sailcloth covering the furled headsail.

Storm trysail

In a very strong wind it may not be possible to reef the main sufficiently so a smaller sail, a storm trysail, is used (Figure 12.13). Although this sail is seldom used, it has no real substitute and any yacht venturing offshore is advised to carry one.

As the sail is set loose-footed, the boom should be lowered to the deck on the windward side and lashed down. This not only lowers the centre of gravity but also puts some weight on the windward side to reduce heel angle. It can also give the crew some protection from spray. The luff fits into the mast groove or separate track and should be fitted with slides instead of a boltrope. A boltrope may pull out of the groove, whereas slides should not. The tack downhaul is best taken to the base of the mast – the kicking strap fitting is a good strong point. The sheets should be led through stout blocks on each quarter and then led forward to the main winches. The spinnaker sheet blocks will suffice as long as the trysail sheets are not too thick to go through the cheeks of the blocks. When tacking, the sail and sheets must not be allowed to flog as they could cause injury to cockpit crew.

It is important that the sail is set at a height that will allow a good lead to these blocks, and this often means that it is raised well above the level of the gooseneck where it will be clear of breaking waves. Be prepared to alter the length of the downhaul after the sail has been hoisted.

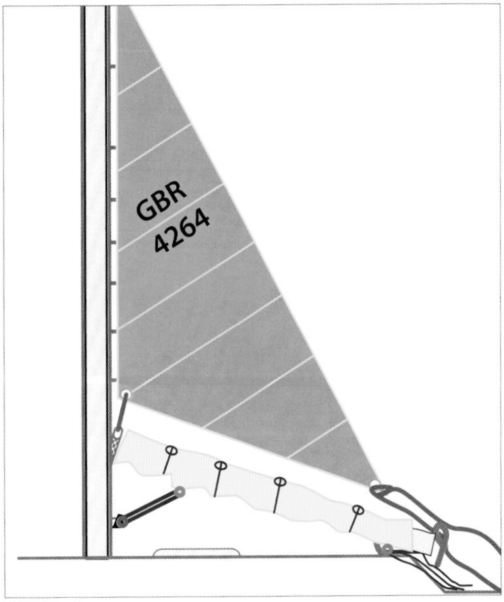

Fig 12.13 The storm trysail is loose-footed with the tack relatively high. The sheets are best led to blocks aft.

◆ Boat handling in rough weather

It would be very easy to fill a whole book on boat handling in rough weather and many great sailors have written of their experiences. Peter Bruce's book *Heavy Weather Sailing* is considered to be the bible for small craft under sail and is strongly recommended as background reading for Yachtmaster candidates.

Motor cruisers that are likely to be out in strong winds will usually have twin screws and trim tabs giving handling characteristics which are very different to sailing yachts.

Books on the subject include: *Boat Handling under Power* by John Mellor and *Heavy Weather Powerboating* by Hugo Montgomery Swan.

QUESTION PAPER 12 – FOG & HEAVY WEATHER

12.1 How often should you sound a fog horn if you are underway?

12.2 List five actions to be taken when preparing for heavy weather.

12.3 Which is the best reflector of radar beams? A wooden boat or a harbour wall?

12.4 In a nautical context, what do the initials AIS stand for?

12.5 Why is it wise to give headlands a wide berth in strong wind conditions?

Answers at the back of the book

13 BUOYANCY & STABILITY

ADVANCES IN COMMUNICATIONS and electronic navigation have meant that more and more people are venturing offshore. The boats they use are various; some choose a planing motor cruiser for a fast passage, others prefer to sail a traditional, heavy, long-keeled yacht. Whichever one is chosen, they will all have different handling characteristics in bad weather.

It is vital for skippers who cruise offshore to know how their boat will behave in a blow and rough seas – the fast one may get you there more quickly, but at what stage will it become unstable? Sailing yachts are built to heel to the wind but motor cruisers may not survive if they lean into a large wave and take water into the engine air intakes. The resultant flooding could cause a sudden and catastrophic loss of buoyancy.

An understanding of the principles of buoyancy and stability, and the reasons why boats float or capsize, is vital for skippers who cruise away from sheltered waters. A knowledge of the hazards which affect stability and buoyancy will, undoubtedly, pay dividends.

BUOYANCY

When any boat is lowered into the water it pushes aside a certain amount of water which has a weight, hence a boat's weight is called *displacement*. The part of the boat that is under the water, the *immersed volume*, is governed by both the density of the water and the boat's weight. A vessel in dense cold salt water will float higher than the same vessel floating in warm fresh water. Commercial vessels have a load line painted on to the hull for both salt and fresh water so that their buoyancy is not compromised by carrying too much cargo. The displaced water has an up thrust (*buoyancy*) which is equal to the weight of the boat. The centre of this displaced water is called the centre of buoyancy. Figure 13.1 shows this.

STABILITY

A boat is considered to be *stable* when it makes every attempt to regain its upright position after it has been rocked or heeled by the wind and waves or disturbed by the movement of the crew around the boat.

Three factors will influence how eager it is to right itself:

Fig 13.1 Centre of buoyancy.

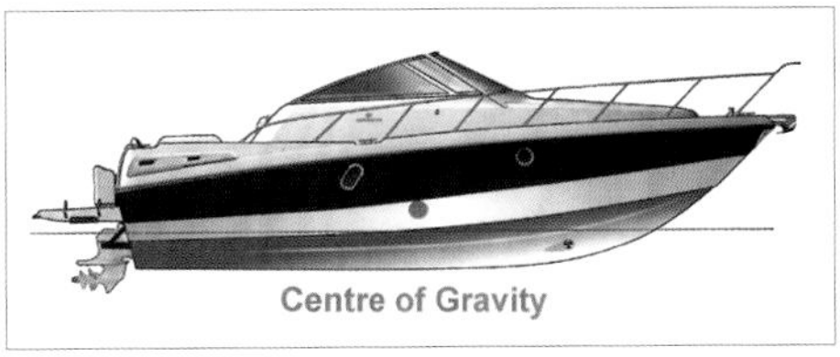

Fig 13.2 Centre of gravity.

- **The centre of buoyancy** The centre of the volume of the water displaced will vary with heel angle, trim and loading.
- **The centre of gravity** This is determined by the boat itself, the position and weight of masts and engine, the height of fly-bridge superstructure and people. The centre of gravity (Figure 13.2) is best if it is low down so don't sit hordes of people on the fly-bridge and make sure you stow the bottles of French wine in the bilge!
- **The mass of the boat** For all practical purposes this equals the weight of the boat.

◆ The righting lever

When a boat is upright, the gravitational force is directly opposed to the buoyancy force. As a stable boat heels, the centre of buoyancy should move sideways more rapidly than the centre of gravity. The shortest distance between the line of buoyancy force and the centre of gravity (mass) is named as the righting lever (Figure 13.3). The longer the lever, the greater the pull back to the vertical. If the heel angle further increases, then the centre of buoyancy repositions so that eventually the lever is lost altogether (Figure 13.4). This point is called the *Angle of Vanishing Stability (AVS)* – the angle at which the boat will invert in calm water.

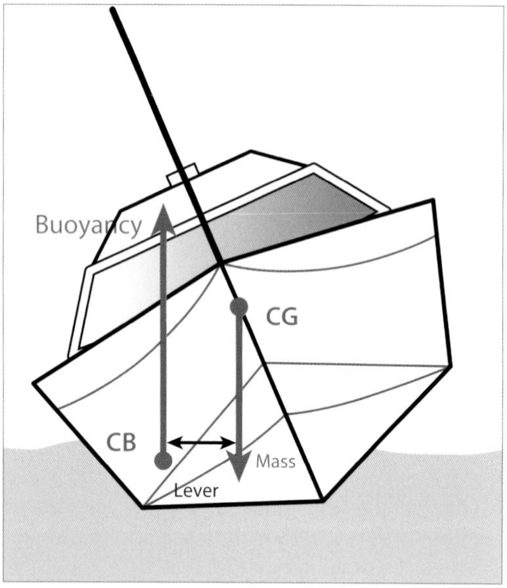

Fig 13.3 The righting lever.

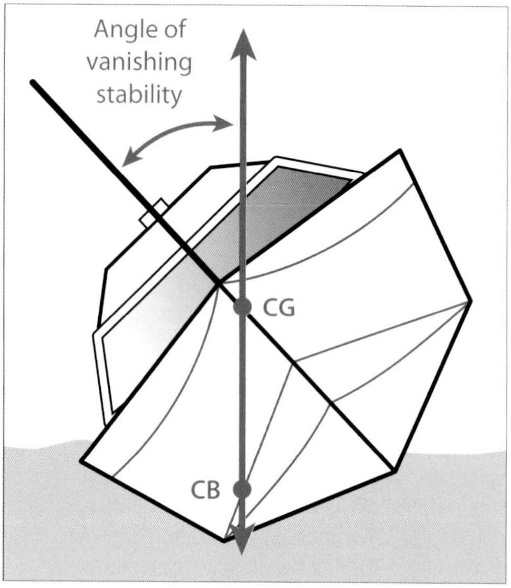

Fig 13.4 The angle of vanishing stability is reached.

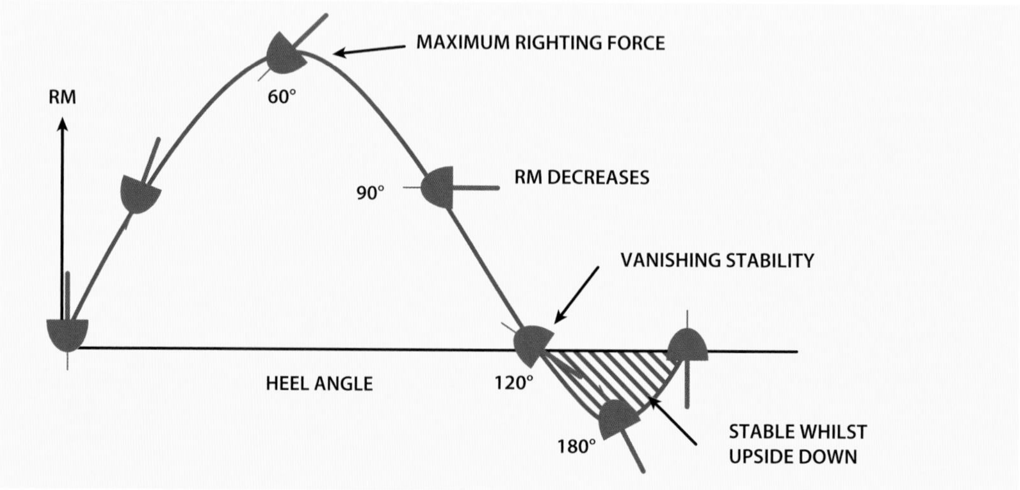

Fig 13.5 The AVS of this yacht is 120° of heel. The boat is stable upside down.

◆ Hull shape

Hull shape is a very important factor. Long-keeled, heavy-displacement yachts with a narrow hull and rounded topsides lose stability at much greater angles than wide light displacement yachts. Some of these more traditionally shaped boats are never stable when upside down – it takes just a small wave to right them.

Wide boats are initially stable but, as most have large shallow cockpits and wide flat decks, once a certain angle is reached they continue to roll over, are stable upside down and are very difficult to right.

◆ Righting moment curves

Boat designers publish righting moment curves for their boats and the curves shown below (Figures 13.6 and 13.7) compare angles for two different yacht types and a motor cruiser.

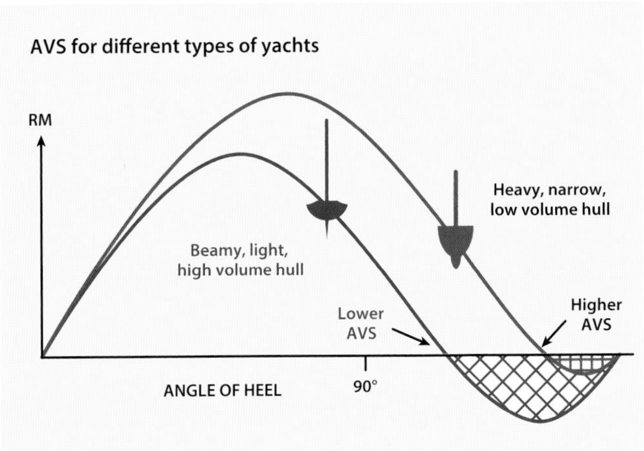

Fig 13.6 Righting moment curve for two distinct hull shapes.

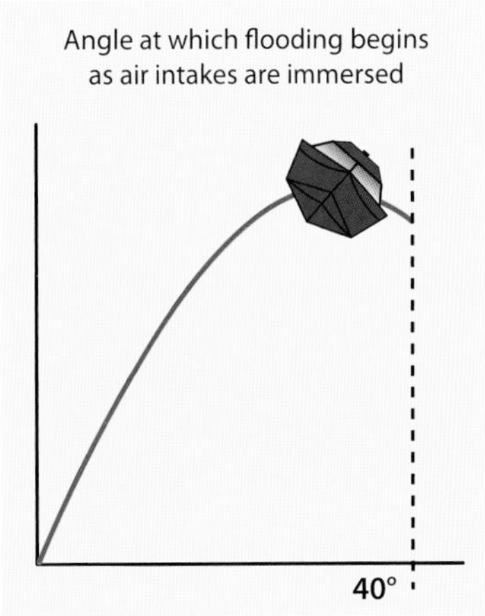

Fig 13.7 In effect the AVS of this boat is only 40° as down flooding occurs at this angle.

RECREATIONAL CRAFT DIRECTIVE (RCD)

All European-built pleasure yachts between 2.5m and 24m have to meet minimum standards of stability and construction. A builder's plate must carry a CE mark to show compliance with one of the following three design categories (Figure 13.8).

Category		Wind	Wave Ht
A	Ocean	> F8	>4m
B	Offshore	< F8	<4m
C	Inshore	< F6	<2m

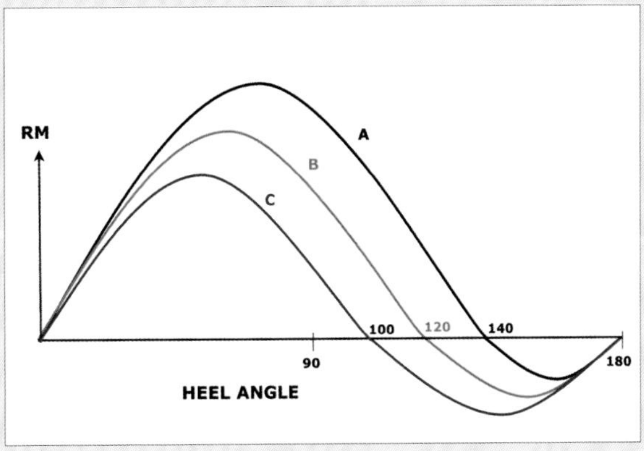

Fig 13.8 Righting moment curves for RCD categories.

STABILITY HAZARDS

◆ Centre of gravity problems

It has been mentioned that the centre of gravity is best if it is low. The AVS, and therefore stability, will be reduced if extra top weight is added thus raising the centre of gravity. In-mast furling mainsails and foresails leave a heavy weight aloft when the sails are reefed and radar scanners add to top weight. Everyone enjoys getting fresh air on the fly bridge of a motor cruiser, but with six people sitting up there when a high speed turn is executed, the effect can be perturbing. Increased waterline length adds to stability; small, shallow-draught boats are most noticeably affected by extra top weight.

◆ Breaking waves

Waves can be fearsome and one that breaks releases an enormous amount of energy relative to its size. A large breaking wave has enough energy to knockdown or invert any boat under 24 metres in length. Steep-sided waves that could break are formed when:

- The wind is blowing against the tide.
- The wind strength has suddenly increased.
- The wind has changed direction significantly causing pyramid waves.
- The seabed shelves and the water shallows when approaching the coast.

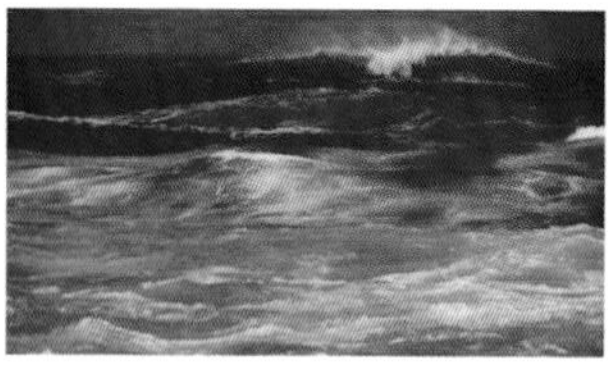

Fig 13.9 Best not to be beam-on to this breaking wave!

A yacht is most likely to be rolled over when caught beam-on to a breaking wave. A wave of a height equivalent to the beam of the boat is capable of inverting it.

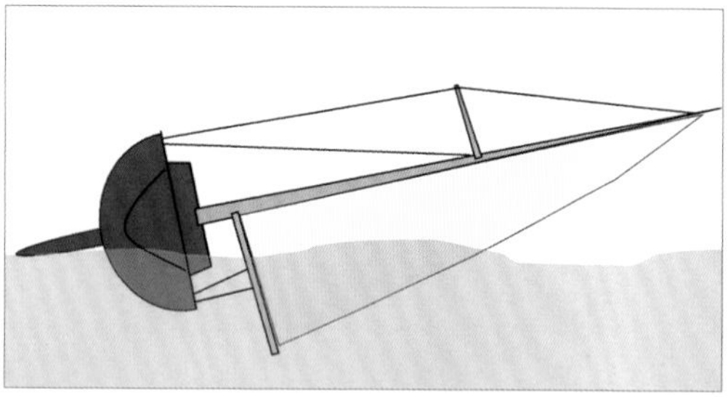

Fig 13.10 Knockdown from strong winds and breaking waves can cause down flooding.

◆ Strong winds

Strong winds can cause 'a knockdown', particularly in sailing yachts and dinghies. Capsize can cause down flooding through open hatches and portlights.

◆ Overloading

Overloading is a hazard in small open boats with no side decks if the load is badly trimmed. Capsize can, and often does, happen. Many a crew has gone ashore in the dinghy in two groups and returned all together. At the very least they all get wet seats but many end up swimming.

◆ Swamping

Boats which fill with water may sink very quickly as buoyancy is lost. Make sure that hatches and doors are securely fastened as flooding into the cabin is not just uncomfortable – it's dangerous.

Look astern if running downwind in heavy weather; if there is any risk of shipping a large wave put the washboards in.

◆ Free surface effect

Excess bilge water rushing from side to side as a boat rolls in a swell has the same effect as extra top weight. Motor cruisers are more vulnerable than yachts as they have large flat engine spaces to flood (see Figure 13.12). The car ferry *Herald of Free Enterprise*, with under two inches of water on her car

Fig 13.11 *Herald of Free Enterprise* lying capsized outside Zeebrugge harbour.

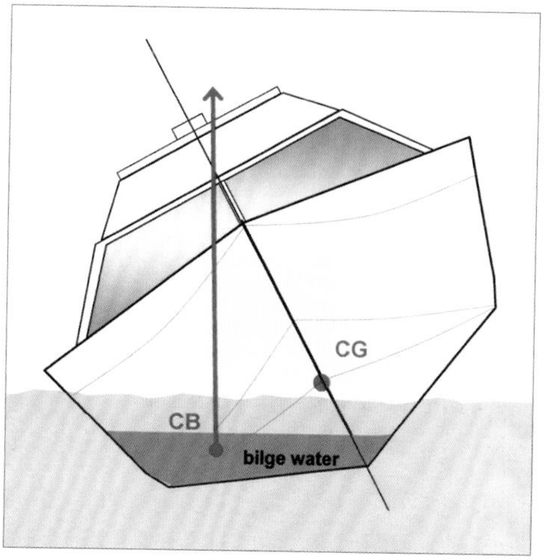

Fig 13.12 (right) Bilge water rushing from side to side has the same effect as extra top weight.

deck, capsized as she heeled to a corner in Zeebrugge harbour with disastrous loss of life. Make sure that bilges are pumped at regular intervals – once an hour in heavy weather.

◆ Resonant rolling

This usually happens when craft are cruising beam-on to the waves and they begin to roll. This roll becomes magnified so much that motor cruisers can immerse engine air intakes on each swing and capsize is a possibility. Try not to take large waves on the beam as illustrated in Figure 13.13.

Yachts can dampen the roll by over-sheeting the spinnaker and running by the lee with gybe preventer set or altering course to avoid the beam sea.

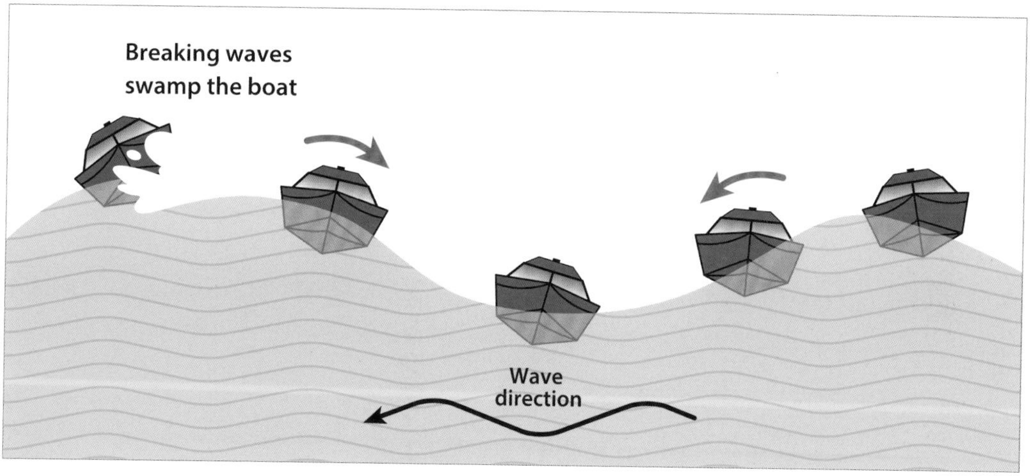

Fig 13.13 Resonant rolling in beam seas may cause capsize.

SUMMARY

DO close hatches and washboards.
DO be aware of your boat's limitations.
DO avoid sailing through tide rips and overfalls in rough weather.
DO pump bilges regularly.

DO NOT get caught beam-on to breaking waves.
DO NOT overload your boat.

QUESTION PAPER 13 – BUOYANCY AND STABILITY

13.1 What is meant by the term AVS?

13.2 Why is resonant rolling more dangerous for a motor cruiser than a yacht?

13.3 What wave height would be sufficient to invert a yacht with a beam of 3m if caught beam-on to the sea?

Answers at the back of the book

14 ANCHORING, MOORING & BERTHING

ONE OF THE JOYS OF BOATING is to spend a warm, quiet evening anchored in a bay like this one in New Zealand and to wake up in the morning to brilliant sunshine.

If the skipper can sleep soundly and not worry about the anchor dragging, it is probably because he has good ground tackle, plenty of chain veered and has chosen a sheltered, uncrowded anchorage.

Fig 14.1 Will this bay make a good anchorage or will the swell make it uncomfortable?

TYPES OF ANCHOR

Boatowners tend to enthuse over a particular type of anchor and condemn the rest as 'fit to be an ornament on the mantlepiece'. Each has its advantages and disadvantages and eventually it comes down to personal choice.

◆ CQR

The CQR anchor (Figure 14.2) is a plough-type anchor which takes its name from the company which first manufactured it. The makers claim that the genuine article is stronger and more reliable because it is forged, and not cast.

- ✓ Good holding in mud and sand.
- ✓ Good power-to-weight ratio.
- ✗ Difficult to stow on deck without chocks.
- ✗ Moving parts can be fouled and also damage fingers.

Fig 14.2 CQR or plough anchor.

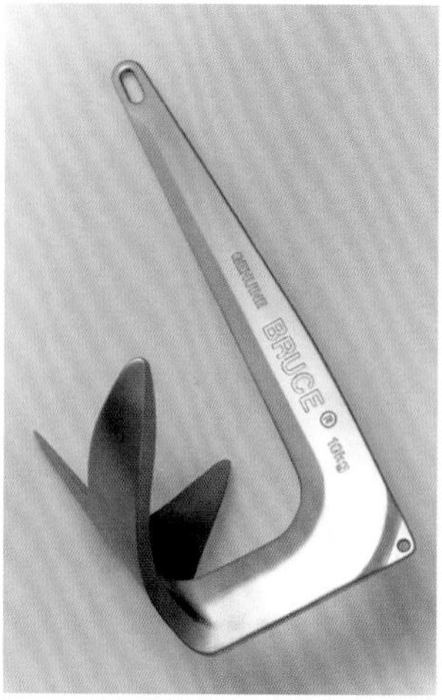

Fig 14.3 Bruce anchor.

◆ Bruce

Originally designed for anchoring oil rigs, it is ever popular (Figure 14.3).

- ✓ Excellent power-to-weight ratio.
- ✓ No moving parts, easy to handle.
- ✓ Easy to break out.
- ✓ Holds well in mud, sand and rock.
- ✓ Stows well on a bow roller.
- ✗ Does not always dig into hard sand and clay easily.

◆ Delta

A very efficient anchor (Figure 14.4).

- ✓ Sets fast and digs deep.
- ✓ Excellent power-to-weight ratio.
- ✓ Does not capsize.
- ✓ Self-righting.
- ✗ Difficult to stow except on bow roller.

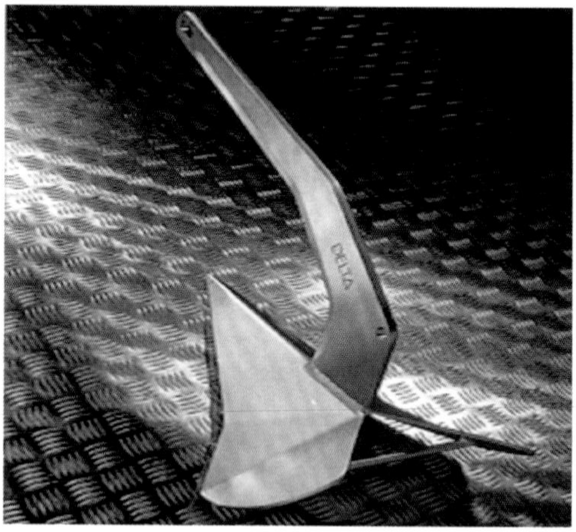

Fig 14.4 Delta anchor.

◆ Danforth

An older type of anchor popular as a kedge as it stows flat in a cockpit locker (Figure 14.5).

- ✓ Good holding in mud and sand.
- ✓ Can be stowed flat.
- ✓ Digs in well.
- ✗ Can be difficult to break out.
- ✗ Moving parts can become fouled.
- ✗ Can damage fingers.

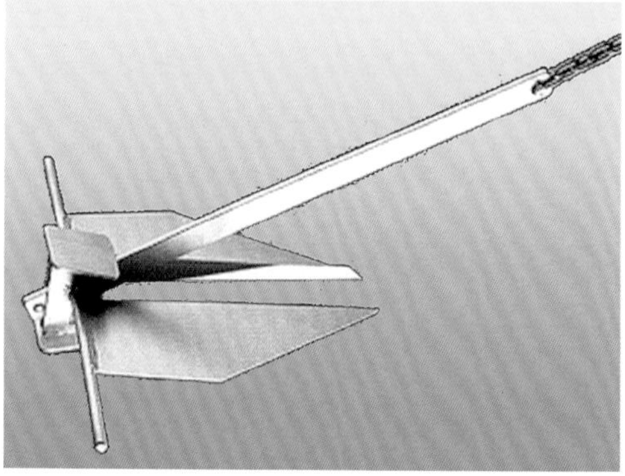

Fig 14.5 Danforth anchor.

◆ Fisherman

The Fisherman anchor is seldom used nowadays but is one of the anchors that can hold on rock (Figure 14.6).

✓ Can be stowed flat (needs room).
✗ Heavy for its holding power.
✗ The upright fluke could hole the boat.
✗ Chain could get caught round the upright fluke and then cause the anchor to break out.

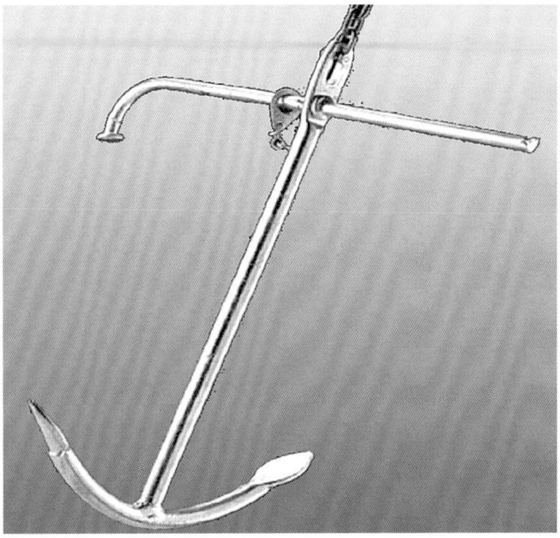

Fig 14.6 Fisherman anchor.

◆ Grapnel

The small grapnel is a very useful anchor for use in an inflatable dinghy as the flukes can be folded so that they don't damage the fabric. It holds well on rock (Figure 14.7).

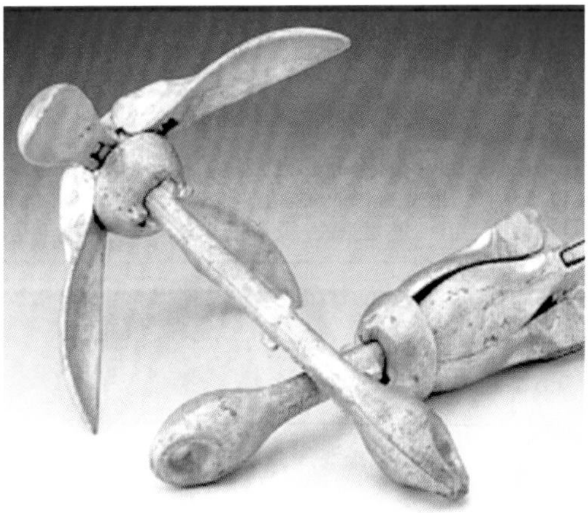

Fig 14.7 Grapnel anchor.

◆ Kedge

A second anchor is carried on all well-equipped cruising boats. It is usually smaller than the main (bower) anchor and one of the kind already mentioned. It is called 'a kedge' or, if you hail from the USA, a 'lunch hook'. Yacht skippers who frequently anchor for short periods often keep the smaller anchor on the bow roller instead of the heavier one. It certainly saves on chiropractor fees if there is no windlass!

◆ Holding power

The best holding is in mud, soft sand and soft clay. Shells, shingle and pebbles are not to be relied upon. Rock is only possible if a fluke gets caught in a crevice and there is always the possibility that it will never break free again! Where there is kelp or weed, the anchor may hook into the kelp only and appear to hold. When the wind picks up and strain on to the chain, the roots of the kelp tear away from the seabed and the anchor drags.

The following table shows recommended weights for main and kedge anchors and diameters for chain and rope.

Length of boat	Anchor mass		Anchor cable diameter			
LOA + LWL / 2	Main	Kedge	Main		Kedge	
			Chain	Rope	Chain	Rope
(metres)	(kg)	(kg)	(mm)	(mm)	(mm)	(mm)
6	8	4	6	12	6	10
7	9	4	8	12	6	10
8	10	5	8	12	6	10
9	11	5	8	12	6	10
10	13	6	8	12	6	10
11	15	7	8	12	6	10
12	18	9	8	14	8	12
13	21	10	10	14	8	12
14	24	12	10	14	8	12
15	27	13	10	–	8	12
16	30	15	10	–	8	12
17	34	17	10	–	8	14
18	38	19	10	–	8	14
19	42	21	12	–	10	14
20	47	23	12	–	10	14
21	52	26	12	–	10	14
22	57	28	12	–	10	16
23	62	31	12	–	10	16
24	68	34	12	–	10	16

1 Chain cable diameter is for short link chain.
2 The rope diameter given is for nylon construction.

GROUND TACKLE

◆ All chain or chain and warp?

The decision whether to use all chain or a chain and warp combination, will depend on a number of factors: the type of boat, the area you cruise, whether you have a bad back and if you have the stowage for one and not the other.

If an anchor is to bite and hold, it must firstly be of a suitable design and of sufficient weight for the boat it is trying to hold. It must have a length of chain attached to the anchor so that chafe from the seabed is minimised and there is enough weight on the bottom to exert a horizontal pull to dig the anchor in. The anchor will break out with a vertical pull when it is time to leave.

All chain is the best choice if you have sufficient stowage and a windlass to assist with raising and lowering the anchor. You will never win any races but a boat that is anchored to chain only usually lies more quietly as the chain dampens movement.

In a racing yacht where excess weight in the bows is a handicap and where stowage space is limited, a good compromise is about ten metres of chain next to the anchor and nylon warp for the remainder. The chain ensures a horizontal pull is still possible and the nylon is used as it stretches by about 20% and reduces snubbing (Figure 14.8).

◆ What length do I need?

The saying 'If in doubt – let it out' is very sound advice. Anchor chain left unused in the locker is about as useful as runway behind you when you are landing in an aircraft! A rough guide to the amount is:

Chain: Four times the maximum expected depth of water.
Chain and warp: Six times the maximum expected depth of water.
Strong wind/strong stream: At least eight times the maximum expected depth of water.

◆ Windlasses

A windlass is a 'must have' device if any appreciable length of chain is to be lowered to or raised from the seabed. They can be electrically, hydraulically or manually operated and on modern craft the whole operation can be done from the fly bridge or cockpit with a remote control device. The Lewmar windlass in the picture (Figure 14.9) is a powered gypsy winch for chain. It does not have an additional drum for rope. In most craft it is necessary to run the engine in neutral when the windlass is under load to avoid flattening the battery.

Fig 14.8 Anchor chain spliced to nylon line.

◆ Stowage

As a boat enters and leaves the harbour or when it is manoeuvring in a confined space, it is probably at its most vulnerable to engine failure or a rope around the propeller so the main anchor should be ready for use at short notice. Most boats keep it stowed on the bow roller so that it may be released quickly with the chain led into a deck locker or over a windlass drum.

Some craft have deck lockers so that the deck remains clear of equipment but check that the anchor is secured so that it does not damage the side of the hull. Make sure that it can be manoeuvred into place around headsail furling gear.

Try not to bury the kedge anchor under all manner of equipment in the cockpit locker – imagine trying to extract it in a hurry!

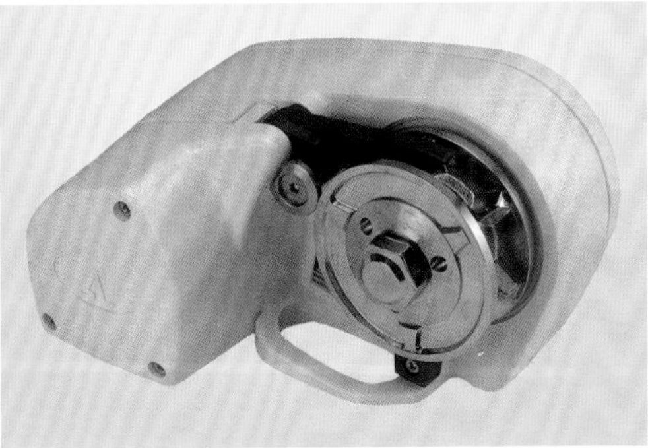

Fig 14.9 The Lewmar windlass makes life easy when weighing anchor.

ANCHORING

◆ Where to anchor

There are a number of factors to be considered before deciding on a suitable anchorage and it is a good plan to have a checklist ready so that nothing is overlooked.

1 Will the bay be sheltered from the present and forecast wind direction?
2 Could the wind funnel down a valley or hill to make the anchorage uncomfortably rough during the night? (See section on katabatic wind in Chapter 11).
3 Nature of the seabed? Is the holding good?
4 Out of shipping channel and out of strong tidal stream?
5 Free from underwater obstructions?
6 Is there enough space for the boat to swing without hitting other boats with different swinging characteristics?
7 Will I have sufficient depth at low water? What will be the maximum depth so that I can calculate the amount of chain required?
8 Can I get out in the dark without hitting any unlit rocks or obstructions?
9 Is the anchorage close to a landing stage if I want to eat out?

◆ Preparing the anchor

Prepare the anchor before you reach the intended anchorage – remove any lashings.

Check the depth and tell the foredeck crew how much cable will be required. The anchor cable should be marked at five-metre intervals with paint or soft pieces of strong material tied through the chain links. Do not fasten electrical cable ties to the chain links as a marker because they are vicious and dangerous to the hands if the chain is allowed to run out quickly.

As the boat approaches the desired spot, slow the boat until it is no longer making way through the water. Lower, don't drop, the anchor to the bottom and as the boat falls back, pay out the chain. (In slack stream and light winds it may be necessary to motor *very gently* astern.) When sufficient chain is lowered, secure it to a strong foredeck cleat or Samson post and dig in the anchor by going gently astern. If the boat suddenly sheers round on a taut cable, this is a sign that it is securely anchored.

When the boat has settled, set a deep and shallow alarm on the depth sounder and an 'out of position' alarm on a GPS or chart plotter; radar can also be used. If these are not fitted, bearings or transits should be taken and checked to make sure that the anchor is not dragging.

Finally, raise an anchor ball at the bow if it is light or use an anchor light at night.

◆ Laying a second anchor

Occasionally it is necessary to lay a second anchor when there is a strong wind or you wish to stop the boat swinging into a close neighbour. The trick is to position the two anchors well forward from the bows, with not too wide an angle, say 45°, between them (Figure 14.10). By taking in more on one line and slackening the other, the boat can either be kept clear of the other boat or head-to-wind as the wind veers.

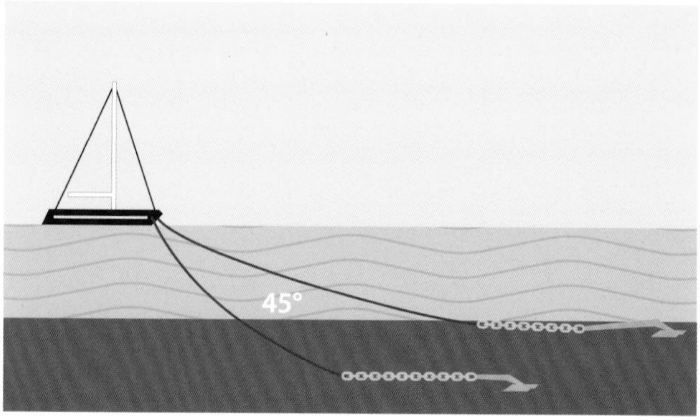

Fig 14.10 A second anchor can be laid to reduce the swing and to give extra holding power in a blow.

◆ Trip line

Most well made anchors have a small hole in the crown so that a light trip line can be attached. It is important to rig a trip line if there is any danger of the anchor becoming fouled because it may be the only way to extricate the anchor from under a cable or chain (Figure 14.11).

The end that is not secured to the anchor can be attached to a small plastic buoy or brought back on board at the bow.

If the anchor is fouled the trip line can be used to drag the anchor out backwards.

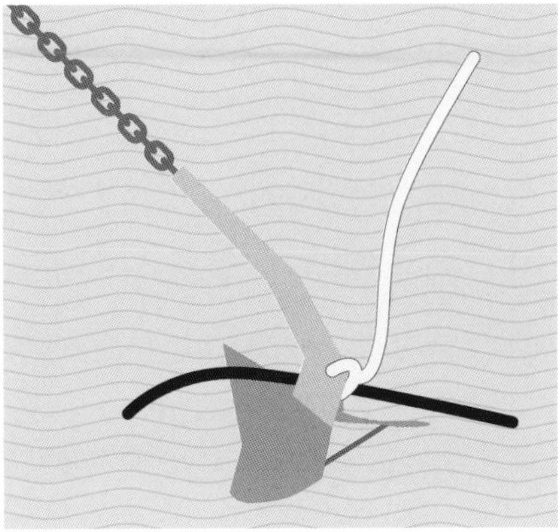

Fig 14.11 The trip line can be used to help free the main anchor.

BERTHING

The photo Figure 14.12 shows yachts rafted up alongside a pontoon in Weymouth. This raft is long and the outboard boats do not have lines long enough to reach the shore. Consequently the raft is free to move around at the seaward end and if the wind got up it could drift into the next row.

The ropes used for berthing will depend upon the size and type of the boat but as a guide a 10 metre boat would most likely carry 12mm or 14mm lines for mooring warps. Polyester rope is ideal for the purpose, as it has some stretch but not too much.

Fig 14.12 Yachts rafted up alongside a harbour wall.

Figure 14.13 shows lines, which should be rigged when berthed alongside a tidal wall. The two blue ropes on the inside boat are very short and will require constant attention as the tide drops or else they will become bar taut. A longer bow and stern line would need little adjustment as the tide falls. The springs on the inside boat are an ideal length.

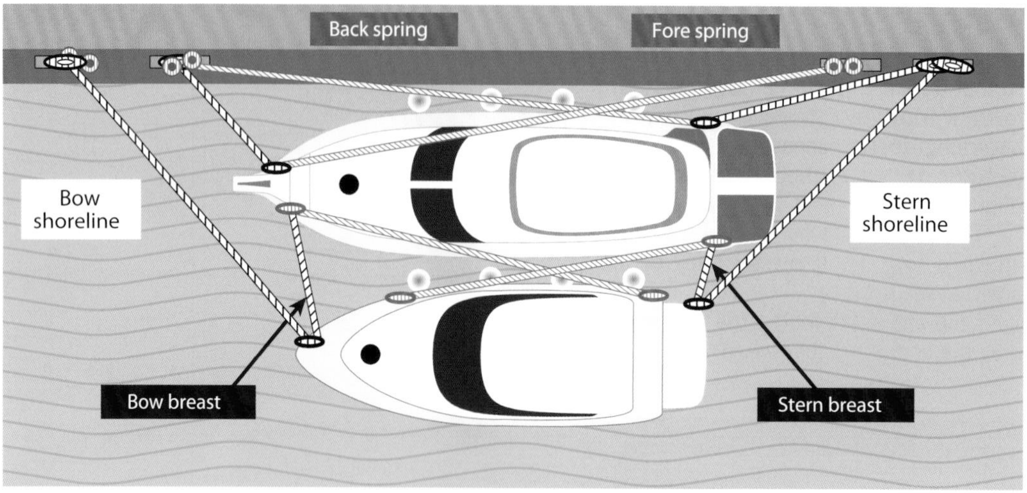

Fig 14.13 The outboard boat rigs lines to the shore to relieve the strain on the inside boat.

Points to remember when making fast alongside:

1 If lying alongside another boat, it is bad manners to rely on the other boat's ropes especially if she is smaller. Shore lines should always be rigged unless you are staying for a very short time and the owner of the inboard boat tells you not to bother.
2 Mast spreaders should be staggered to avoid clashing in a swell.
3 Rig fenders so that neither hull gets damaged.
4 Rig springs. Check whether the owner of the other boat dislikes his winches being used to secure mooring lines – some do!
5 When crossing another boat's deck, walk around the bow section as quietly as possible – not across the cockpit. It is also courteous to seek permission first if the owner is aboard.

Fig 14.14 How NOT to do it!

Try not to tramp dirt or mud across the boat and if others are crossing your decks make sure that a sail is not left where people could slip on it.

6 A spinnaker pole laid on deck when in harbour can get kicked as other crews cross the decks and the resulting noise down below can be very disturbing. If possible move it further aft so that you get some peace.

7 Remove halyards from the mast and clip them out to the rail to prevent them slapping on the mast or, alternatively, rig frapping lines.

MEDITERRANEAN MOOR

Where there is little rise and fall of tide, such as in the Mediterranean, it is common to moor the stern to the quayside after dropping a bow anchor to hold the boat off. The chain on the bow should be free to run as the boat goes astern. It is also wise to fender the transom well in case of an accident! The speed whilst going astern should just be sufficient to maintain steerage way and to keep the boat going in a straight line.

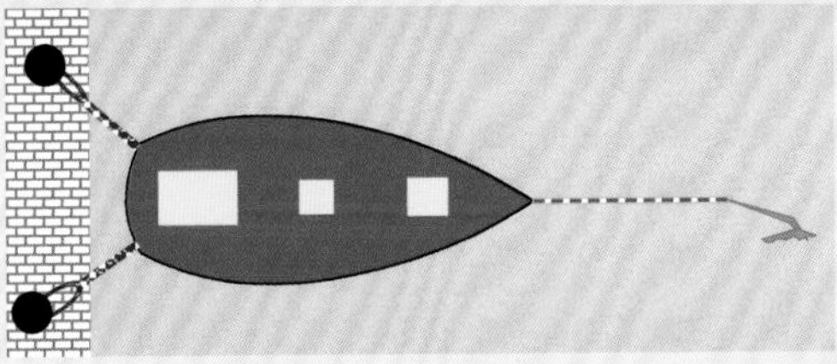

Fig 14.15 Mediterranean Moor.

QUESTION PAPER 14 – ANCHORING, MOORING & BERTHING

14.1 What is a trip line?

14.2 The forecast is for E4 winds veering S5 later. Which of the anchorages in Figure 14.16 would you consider suitable for:

a a two-hour lunch stop?

b an overnight stay?

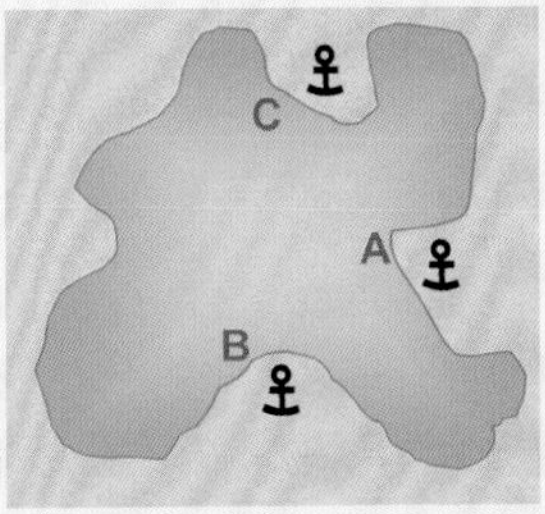

Fig 14.16 Which is the sheltered anchorage?

14.3 List three things to remember when rafting up on another boat.

14.4 What is the recommended weight for the main anchor on a 10m boat?

14.5 It is HW and you are about to anchor for the night with all chain in 5m of water. What is the minimum amount of chain you will use?

Answers at the back of the book

15 PASSAGE PLANNING

A PASSAGE PLAN is just like a pilotage plan, but on a much larger scale and over a longer time period; the pilotage comes at each end and the passage is in the middle. However, some pre-planning is needed if the crew are to work a sensible watch system, get food and rest when off watch and arrive at the other end thinking that they would quite like to cruise with the skipper again. It's like running a hotel – the guests never seem to notice when things run well but they soon mumble and grumble when they don't!

Before embarking on some ambitious plan, it is best to jot down some first thoughts:

- What will the weather do?
- How far is it?
- What is the likely speed?
- How long will it take?
- Is the boat suitable?
- Can eight-year-old Jamie cope with the distance or must we go at night so that he can sleep?
- Are the rest of the crew experienced enough to stand a watch on their own?
- Are there any shipping lanes to cross or other dangers en route?

All these factors will govern whether the proposed passage is possible and once these questions are answered you can get down to the finer points.

◆ Weather

The wind strength will most likely be the deciding factor on whether you go or not, so study the weather trends for several days before the trip. Download some forecast charts from the Internet – a five-day forecast will always be subject to variation but will give you an indication of how settled or unsettled the pattern is. If the forecast is unfavourable you may decide to postpone the trip or alter the destination; a long hike to windward is never popular with family crews at the beginning of a holiday. Better to have a shorter 'shakedown' passage so that the crew can find their sea-legs.

The weather chart in Fig 15.2 shows an unsettled situation with a north-westerly airstream and a depression to the west of the British Isles. A careful study of the forthcoming weather will be needed before any decisions to go are made.

Some useful Internet weather sites

1 **www.metoffice.gov.uk**

2 **www.bbc.co.uk/weather/coast**

3 **www.windfinder.com**

4 **www.wetterzentrale.de**

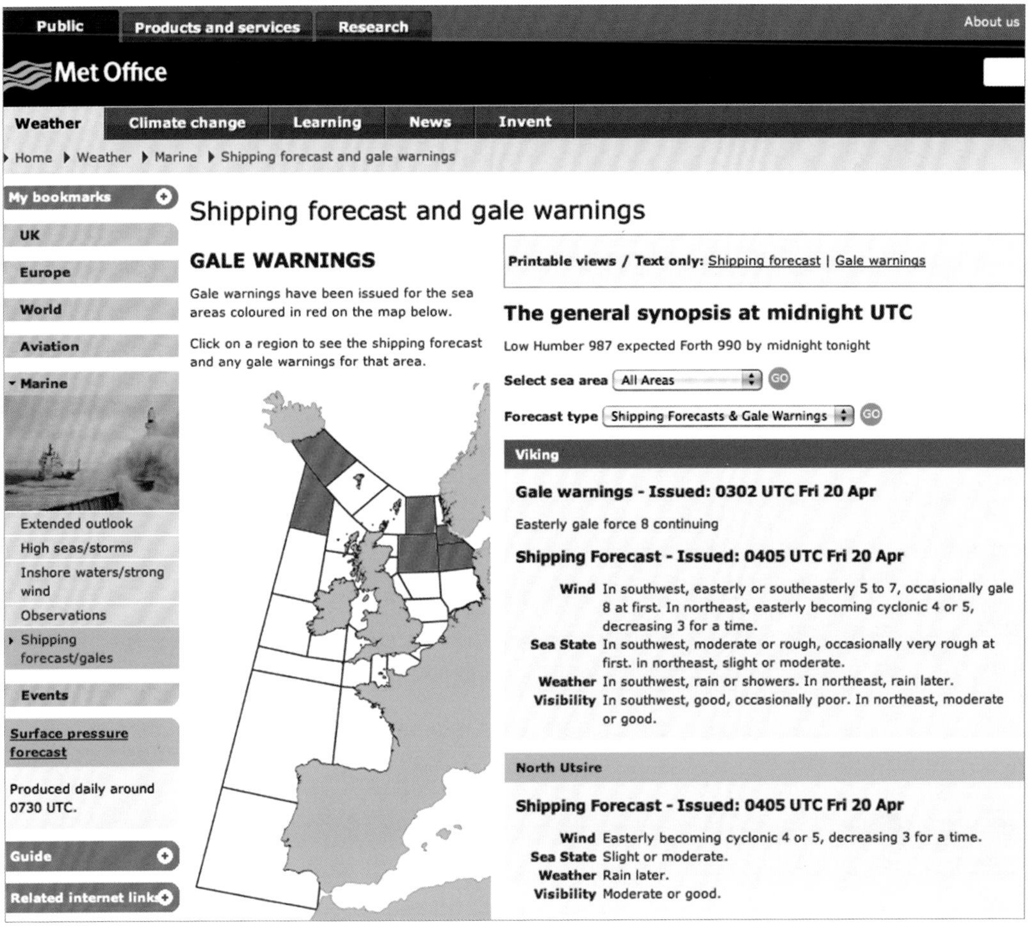

Fig 15.1 Shipping Forecast from the UK Met Office.

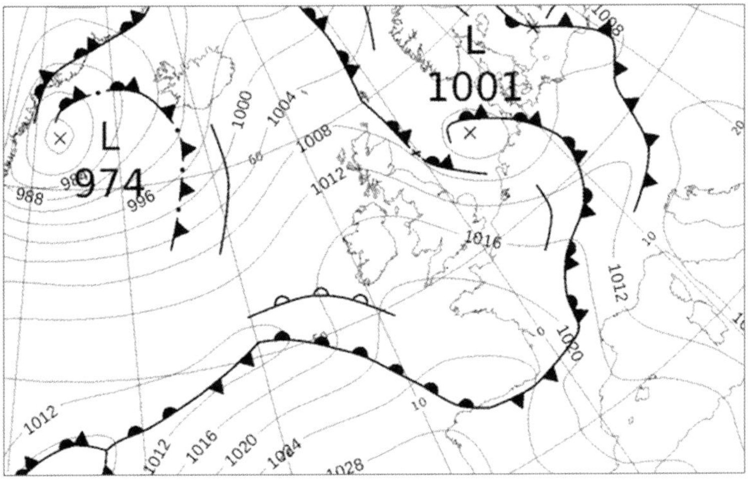

Fig 15.2 Synoptic chart of the North Atlantic.

◆ Ports of refuge and alternative destinations

Whilst planning the cruise, make sure that you have singled out a port en route that could be used as a 'bolt hole' if the weather deteriorates unexpectedly. The one you choose should be easy to enter at all states of the tide, have a clearly marked entrance, be well lit and provide good shelter once inside – large commercial ports are usually the best bet.

Also, look up details of ports before and beyond your destination, just in case the crew want to push on a little further or call it a day sooner than expected.

On any passage it is wise to decide upon a point of no return – is it quicker to go on rather than back? Sometimes this decision has to be made when crew become seasick, the weather gets worse or the tidal stream turns foul.

◆ Range under power

Check that you have sufficient fuel for more than the whole distance so that alternate ports can be reached with ease. Many small, quaint harbours do not have a fuelling berth alongside although the local garage will supply it in cans – by no means ideal when hundreds of gallons may be required!

◆ Charts and pilot books

You will need a small-scale chart, which covers the whole distance and a large-scale one for the destination and any tricky parts of the route. Ideally, the small-scale one should be waterproof so that if foul weather clothing dampens it, the top surface will not get scuffed. A word of warning here – try not to leave both the small- and the large-scale charts lying on top of each other whilst you plot on the chart. Many a navigator has come unstuck by working on the top chart but measuring distance from the scale on the one underneath! Keep the large-scale charts in the chart table until they are needed.

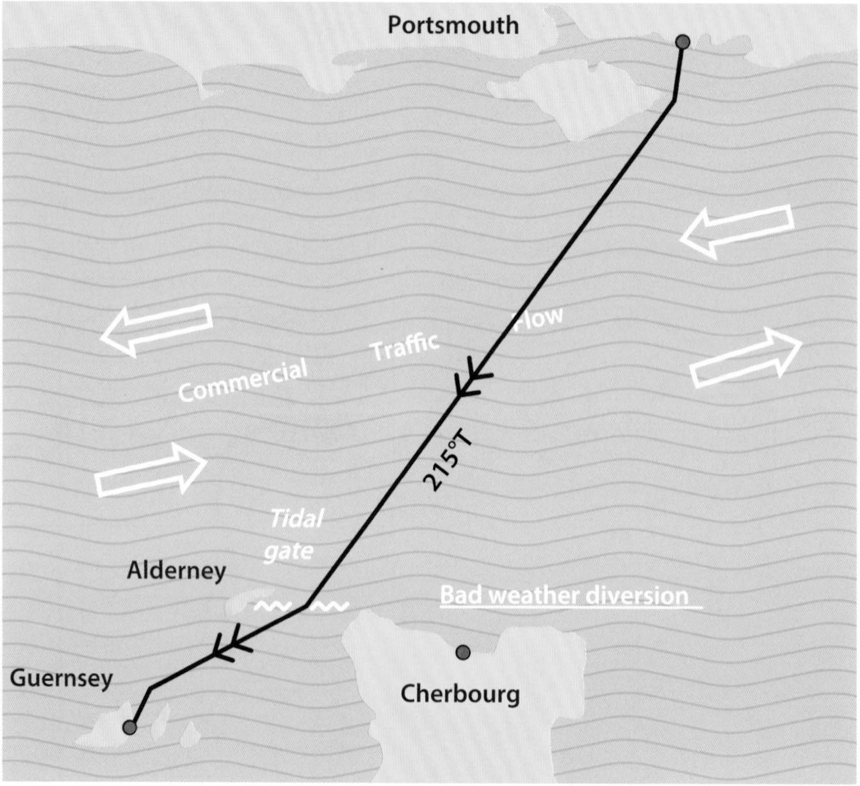

Fig 15.3 A sketch map of an outline passage plan from Portsmouth to Guernsey.

Erase old workings first and check that there have not been any major changes to the chart – remember the UKHO website lists all the corrections.

Having the whole journey on one chart will enable you to draw a line from departure point to destination, measure distance and eventually plot a course to steer. Figure 15.3 shows a passage from Portsmouth to Guernsey where it is important to arrive in the Alderney area at the start of the favourable stream to Guernsey.

Most pilot books have passage notes and photographs in addition to harbour information. The Admiralty *Sailing Directions* are famous for such notes and advise the best route around prominent headlands and tidal races. The accompanying photographs of headlands, lighthouses and offshore dangers are especially helpful.

◆ Tidal heights and tidal streams

Now is the time to look at both the tidal heights and tidal streams. Is there enough water at the destination at all states of the tide, or does it have a locked marina where the gates are only open for a couple of hours either side of HW? Is there a tidal 'gate' en route (see Figure 15.3) where it would be impossible to make any headway against a very strong stream? Does the departure port have free access at all times or is it necessary to leave a locked marina and then wait on a pontoon for a fair stream? At what time will the sea be most calm around a headland or in a tide race?

◆ Dangers en route

Warship exercise areas and gunnery ranges can seriously disturb a pleasant cruise and can often mean a wide detour around the danger area. Phone the nearest coastguard to find out if the range will be active during the journey.

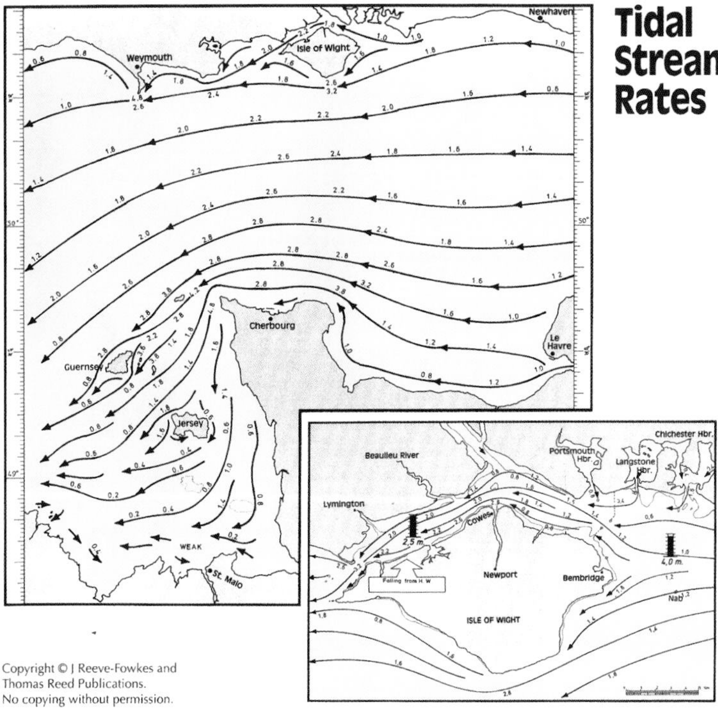

Tidal Stream Rates

5 hours after HW Cherbourg **+5**

Time (to be inserted)

Stream Rate Conversion Table

Pencil-in height of HW Cherbourg
Read from column below pencil mark

Mean Rate Figure from Chart ▼	4.8	5.0	5.2	5.4	5.6	5.8	6.0	6.2	6.4	6.6	6.8	
0.2	0.1	0.1	0.2	0.2	0.2	0.2	0.2	0.2	0.3	0.3	0.3	0.3
0.4	0.2	0.3	0.3	0.3	0.4	0.4	0.4	0.5	0.5	0.5	0.6	0.6
0.6	0.4	0.4	0.5	0.5	0.6	0.6	0.6	0.7	0.7	0.8	0.8	0.9
0.8	0.5	0.5	0.6	0.7	0.7	0.8	0.9	1.0	1.0	1.1	1.2	1.2
1.0	0.6	0.7	0.8	0.8	0.9	1.0	1.1	1.2	1.3	1.4	1.5	1.5
1.2	0.7	0.8	0.9	1.0	1.1	1.2	1.3	1.4	1.5	1.6	1.7	1.9
1.4	0.8	0.9	1.1	1.2	1.3	1.4	1.6	1.7	1.8	1.9	2.0	2.2
1.6	0.9	1.1	1.2	1.4	1.5	1.6	1.8	1.9	2.1	2.2	2.3	2.5
1.8	1.0	1.2	1.4	1.5	1.7	1.8	2.0	2.1	2.3	2.5	2.6	2.8
2.0	1.2	1.3	1.5	1.7	1.9	2.0	2.2	2.4	2.6	2.7	2.9	3.1
2.2	1.3	1.5	1.7	1.9	2.1	2.2	2.4	2.6	2.8	3.0	3.2	3.4
2.4	1.4	1.6	1.8	2.0	2.2	2.5	2.7	2.9	3.1	3.3	3.5	3.7
2.6	1.5	1.8	2.0	2.2	2.4	2.7	2.9	3.1	3.3	3.6	3.8	4.0
2.8	1.6	1.9	2.1	2.4	2.6	2.9	3.1	3.3	3.6	3.8	4.1	4.3
3.0	1.8	2.0	2.3	2.5	2.8	3.1	3.3	3.6	3.8	4.1	4.4	4.6
3.2	1.9	2.2	2.4	2.7	3.0	3.3	3.5	3.8	4.1	4.4	4.7	4.9
3.4	2.0	2.3	2.6	2.9	3.2	3.5	3.8	4.1	4.4	4.7	5.0	5.3
3.6	2.1	2.4	2.7	3.1	3.4	3.7	4.0	4.3	4.6	4.9	5.2	5.6
3.8	2.2	2.6	2.9	3.2	3.6	3.9	4.2	4.5	4.9	5.2	5.5	5.9
4.0	2.3	2.7	3.0	3.4	3.7	4.1	4.4	4.8	5.1	5.5	5.8	6.2
4.2	2.5	2.8	3.2	3.6	3.9	4.3	4.7	5.0	5.4	5.8	6.1	6.5
4.4	2.6	3.0	3.3	3.7	4.1	4.5	4.9	5.3	5.6	6.0	6.4	6.8
4.6	2.7	3.1	3.5	3.9	4.3	4.7	5.1	5.5	5.9	6.3	6.7	7.1
4.8	2.8	3.2	3.6	4.1	4.5	4.9	5.3	5.7	6.2	6.6	7.0	7.4
5.0	2.9	3.4	3.8	4.2	4,7	5.1	5.5	6.0	6.4	6.9	7.3	7.7
5.2	3.0	3.5	4.0	4.4	4.9	5.3	5.8	6.2	6.7	7.1	7.6	8.0
5.4	3.2	3.6	4.1	4.6	5.0	5.5	6.0	6.5	6.9	7.4	7.9	8.3
5.6	3.3	3.8	4.3	4.7	5.2	5.7	6.2	6.7	7.2	7.7	8.2	8.6
5.8	3.4	3.9	4.4	4.9	5.4	5.9	6.4	6.9	7.4	7.9	8.5	9.0
6.0	3.5	4.0	4.6	5.1	5.6	6.1	6.7	7.2	7.7	8.2	8.7	9.3
6.2	3.6	4.2	4.7	5.3	5.8	6.3	6.9	7.4	8.0	8.5	9.0	9.6
6.4	3.8	4.3	4.9	5.4	6.0	6.5	7.1	7.7	8.2	8.8	9.3	9.9
6.6	3.9	4.4	5.0	5.6	6.2	6.7	7.3	7.9	8.5	9.0	9.6	10.2
6.8	4.0	4.6	5.2	5.8	6.4	6.9	7.5	8.1	8.7	9.3	9.9	10.5
7.0	4.1	4.7	5.3	5.9	6.6	7.2	7.8	8.4	9.0	9.6	10.2	10.8

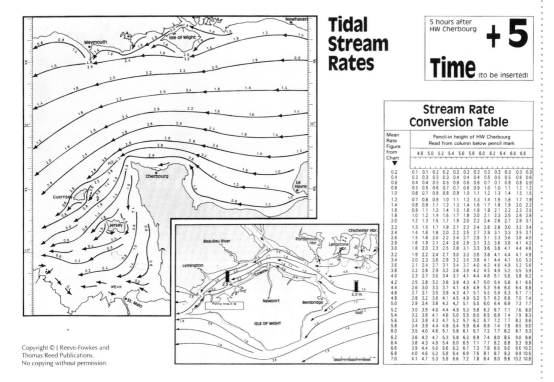

Fig 15.4 A page from the Reeve-Fowkes tidal stream atlas showing a favourable stream for Guernsey when approaching from the north.

If there is a separation scheme en route, try to keep away from it if possible. Small craft are allowed to cross on a heading at right angles to the traffic flow but coping with heavy commercial traffic can be very stressful and may mean that the skipper cannot get adequate rest if an inexperienced crew is on watch.

◆ Watch-keeping

If a passage of more than six hours is planned, it is important that you divide your crew into watches even if there are just two people on board. A twelve-hour passage asks to be divided into four x three hour stints which will ensure that the off-watch crew get about two and a half hours' sleep at a time with the remaining half hour being used for chart work and a meal. The skipper can be part of this system if the crew is small, and outside it if there are sufficient crew; whatever routine is chosen it is vital that the skipper rests whenever possible as he may be needed if an emergency arises.

If you are skipper make sure that you leave written instructions in the log if you wish to be woken up at a certain time. I well remember the time when a 'kind' member of the crew left me asleep for longer than requested – the resulting skirmish into a rocky area to the east of Cherbourg remains imprinted on my memory for ever!

GOING FOREIGN

◆ UK Customs regulations

Yachtsmen from European Union countries can move freely within the community, provided that taxes such as Customs duty and VAT have been paid in one of the EU countries. However if you have crew members who are not EU nationals, even though they checked into the UK at a customs airport, it will be necessary to contact customs officers on arrival in the destination EU country. Islands such as the Canaries, Isle of Man and the Channel Islands are not part of the European Union and boats going directly to these islands will need to complete Customs form C1331 Part 1 on leaving the UK and Part 2 on return (see Figure 15.5).

Home Office
UK Border Agency

Leaving the United Kingdom (UK)
Pleasure craft on non-EU voyages

Part 1

- Before your departure you must complete sections i and ii and show any duty-free stores on the reverse of the form.
- You should sign and date the Declaration and send Part 1 to the address shown on the reverse.
- If you will be stopping at another location in the EU before proceeding to your final destination, you do not need to complete Part 1 of this form.

Home Office
UK Border Agency

Arriving in the United Kingdom (UK)
Pleasure craft on non-EU voyages

Part 2

- On arrival, ensure that sections i and iii have been completed.
- Follow the reporting procedure on the back of this form.
- If you are visiting the UK, keep Part 1 on board until you leave.
- If you are returning to the UK without having reached a non-EU port, write 'Voyage Abandoned' across this page and send it to where you sent Part 1.

i General *Complete in capital letters*	Nationality of yacht
Name and address of owner	Colour of hull
	Length (metres) Tonnage
Name and address of person responsible (if not owner)	Call sign
	Normal moorings

Fig 15.5 Part 1 of Customs form C1331 must be either posted or submitted on line before you leave the UK and Part 2 must be completed after return.

Whatever your destination, it is prohibited to import goods such as knives, drugs, trees and shrubs, meat products and potatoes, to mention just a few. It is easy to forget the bag of potatoes in a locker and the cooked meat in the fridge when returning to the UK.

Full details of the numerous regulations and a downloadable copy of form C1331 may be found on the HM Revenue and Customs website www.hmrc.gov.uk and any advice can be obtained from the National Advice Line number: 0845 010 9000.

◆ Documentation

Before cruising abroad, make sure that you take the originals (not photocopies) of the following documents:

Ship Radio Licence / Ship Portable Ra

United Kingdom of Great Britain & Northern Ireland, the Chan
Royaume-Uni de Grande Bretagne et d'Irlande du Nord, les Iles A
Vereinigte Königreich von Großbritannien und Nordirland, die Kan

Wireless Telegraphy Act 2006

Note: This Licence is valid only if the vessel and Lic details of the Licence and shall continue in force un surrendered by the Licensee or revoked by Ofcom.

Section 1

Licence details

Licence Class	Ship Rad
Licence number	1-8450-
Licensee's name	Mr P No
Licensee's address	16 Orkn Cosham PORTS PO6 3U United K
Mailing address	16 Orkn Cosham PORTS PO6 3U
Name of vessel (Applicable only for a Ship Radio Licence)	AFRITA
Call sign (Applicable only for a Ship Radio Licence)	2YGD
MMSI (Applicable only for a Ship Radio Licence)	234797
MMSI for VHF DSC portable radio	
"T" number identification (Applicable only for a Ship Portable Radio Licence)	
Date of issue	26-FEB

CERTIFICATE OF BRITISH REGISTRY

The Merchant Shipping Act 1995
The Merchant Shipping (Registration of Ships) Regulations 1993, as amended

PARTICULARS OF SHIP

Name Of Ship	AFRITA OF ARNE		
Official Number	386749	Radio Call Sign	2YGD
IMO Number / HIN		Port	COWES
Type Of Ship	PLEASURE YACHT		
Method Of Propulsion	SAIL & MOTOR		
Engine Make & Model	VOLVO PENTA MD 2020		
Total Engine Power	20.00 kW		
Length	9.84 metres	Breadth	3.20 metres
Depth	1.61 metres		
Gross Tonnage	8.09	Net Tonnage	0.00
Registered Tonnage	8.09		
Year of Build	1979		
Name of Builder	MARINE PROJECTS LTD		
Country of Build	UNITED KINGDOM		

This Certificate was issued on 18 June 2007 at 9:22

This Certificate expires on 17 June 2012

Fig 15.6 The certificate of British Registry (or Small Craft Registry) and a Ship's Radio Licence must be on board the vessel when going outside the UK.

Charter agreement

If you are chartering the boat, don't forget to take the charter agreement or a letter of authority from the owner.

Ship's log

Current SOLAS (Safety of Life at Sea Convention) regulations require that any voyage should be planned and a record of the passage entered into the ship's log. Typical log entries are shown in Figure 15.7.

Registration certificate

British-owned craft may be registered under the Merchant Shipping Act 1995 and those proceeding abroad are required to carry either Part 1 (Full Registration) or Part 3 (Small Ships Registration) details of which can be obtained from: UK Ship Register-RSS, Anchor Court, Keen Road, Cardiff CF24 5JW. E-mail: part1_registry@mcga.gov.uk or ssr_registry@mcga.gov.uk.

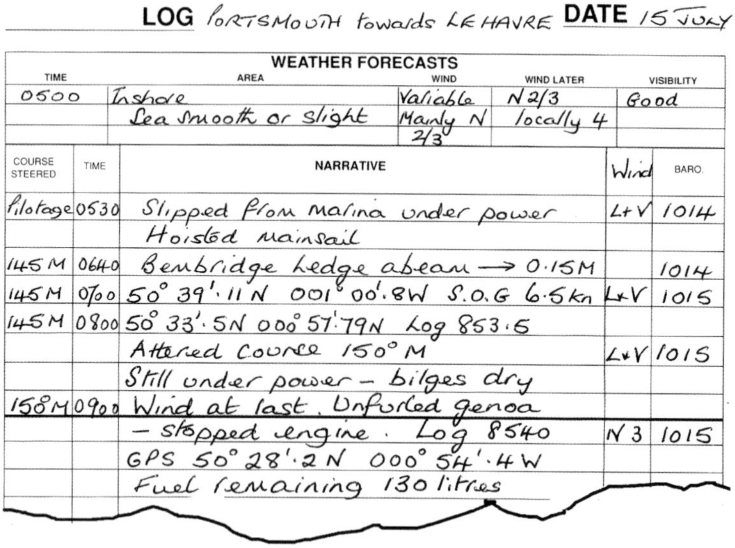

LOG Portsmouth towards Le Havre DATE 15 July

WEATHER FORECASTS

TIME	AREA	WIND	WIND LATER	VISIBILITY
0500	Inshore	Variable	N 2/3	Good
	Sea smooth or slight	Mainly N 2/3	locally 4	

COURSE STEERED	TIME	NARRATIVE	Wind	BARO.
Pilotage	0530	Slipped from marina under power	L+V	1014
		Hoisted mainsail		
145 M	0640	Bembridge Ledge abeam → 0.15M		1014
145 M	0700	50° 39'.11N 001° 00'.8W S.O.G 6.5kn	L+V	1015
145 M	0800	50° 33'.5N 000° 57'.79N Log 853.6		
		Altered course 150° M	L+V	1015
		Still under power – bilges dry		
158 M	0900	Wind at last. Unfurled genoa		
		– stopped engine. Log 8540	N 3	1015
		GPS 50° 28'.2N 000° 54'.4W		
		Fuel remaining 130 litres		

Fig 15.7 Extract from the log of a yacht on passage from Portsmouth to Le Havre.

Insurance

If you intend to cruise outside the limits stated in the policy, your insurer should be told and extra cover arranged. UK marine insurance policies usually cover the coastal waters of the UK and the European coast from Brest to Elbe, so a cruise down into Biscay would need further cover. Third party insurance is essential and many marinas require £2,000,000 or more cover.

Ship's radio licence

The original should be carried on board at all times together with the Radio Operator's Certificate of Competence and Authority to Operate.

International Certificate of Competence (ICC)

Those British Citizens or bona fide UK residents who wish to cruise in the inland waters of Europe must have an International Certificate of Competence and should apply to the RYA for one even though they may already have a Yachtmaster Offshore Certificate. The ICC has translations so that local lock keepers can understand the details of the qualification but the YM Offshore Certificate does not. The ICC can be awarded to those who already hold a suitable seagoing qualification such as a Day Skipper practical certificate or to those who pass a test at an RYA Training Centre.

◆ Foreign Customs

Most other EU countries follow a similar routine to the UK but Holland and Belgium require a vessel to report on arrival even if coming from another EU country.

◆ Flag etiquette

Burgee

A burgee is a small triangular flag signifying that the boatowner is a member of a particular club or association. It is flown day and night when the owner is on board either at the masthead or, if this is not convenient because of instrumentation, at the starboard spreaders.

Ensign

The red ensign is the national maritime flag of the UK but others (white, blue, blue defaced, red defaced) can be flown on boats whose owners are members of certain yacht clubs and associations. A special warrant has to be held on board the vessel and the ensign can only be flown when the owner is aboard and the club burgee is hoisted.

The ensign should be flown at all times when the boat is at sea but in harbour it is worn from 0800 (0900 in winter) until sunset.

Fig 15.8 French and Guernsey courtesy flags.

Courtesy flag

When visiting a foreign country it is normal practice to hoist the ensign of the country you are visiting at the starboard spreader from the time you enter their territorial waters until you leave. Territorial waters can extend up to 12 miles offshore. The French tricolour and the Guernsey flag are shown in Figure 15.8.

Q flag

When you require customs clearance for any reason, you should hoist the Q flag (plain yellow) once in territorial waters and keep it hoisted until customs formalities are complete. Remember that the Channel Islands and the Isle of Man are not part of the EU and, although the rules vary slightly from island to island, it is both courteous and wise to hoist this flag where it can be seen when arriving in the islands. In Guernsey, for example, customs forms are given to visiting yachts on entering the harbour and any formalities are quickly completed.

NAVIGATION & TACTICS ON THE DAY

Although adequate preparation is usually the key to success, it will not be possible to work out the course to steer in advance of the day until you can be sure of the actual wind direction and speed; this knowledge will then make it possible to make an informed guess as to possible boat speed. For cross-Channel passages, it will then be necessary to calculate the amount of tidal stream in each direction before finally plotting a course to steer. This course will more than likely have to be revised as the wind fluctuates but when making a landfall where there is a strong cross-tide it always pays to set a course which takes you a mile or two up-tide of your destination. The crew will not look kindly to spending the end of a long day just down-tide of the best restaurant in town!

If the wind dictates a course just free of close-hauled, it is a wise move to harden up a few degrees for a few hours so that a heading windshift does not mean that you have to tack. If the header never happens, you can ease sheets and enjoy!

◆ Lee bowing

Your favourite port may be directly to windward on the day and if you are determined to stick to the original plan it could be a great advantage to have an appreciation of how taking the tidal stream on your lee bow could help you reach your goal more easily.

This is particularly important on a long cross-tide passage, of say 12 hours, where the tidal stream changes direction halfway. The diagram in Figure 15.9 shows the dramatic difference in the course made towards the wind.

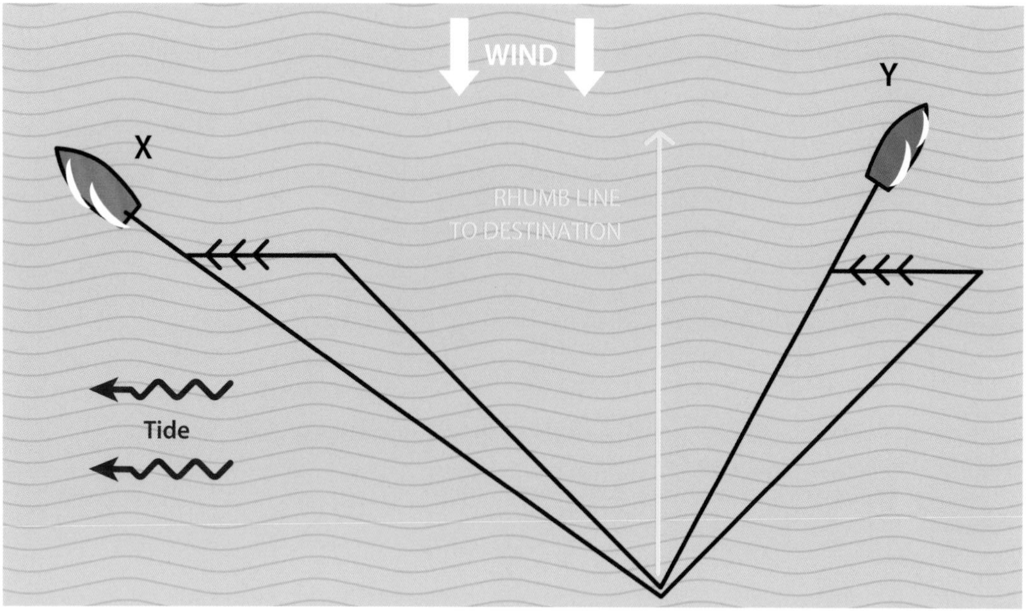

Fig 15.9 Yacht X is taking the tide on the windward bow whereas Yacht Y is gaining ground by putting his lee bow to the tidal stream.

Both yachts in the diagram start from the same position but Yacht X turns on to the starboard tack to take the tide on his windward bow whilst Yacht Y goes off on port tack with the tidal stream hitting the bow on his leeward side.

Yacht Y makes more progress to windward than Yacht X. When the tide turns, Yacht Y can tack on to starboard and continue lee bowing. If Yacht X is foolish enough to tack as the stream turns, he will again be disadvantaged.

The crew of Yacht Y will be living it up in the hot spots of some delightful foreign port when Yacht X is still slogging it out at sea.

Photo: Peter Noice.

QUESTION PAPER 15 – PASSAGE PLANNING

15.1 Are you required to complete Customs form C1331 when an EU port is the intended destination?

15.2 From whom could you obtain information about any activity on a gunnery range?

15.3 Do Customs officials in EU countries accept photocopies of the ship's documents?

15.4 Will tide taken on the leeward bow assist or hinder progress to windward?

Answers at the back of the book

16 SAFETY & SURVIVAL

YACHT CHANDLERIES are full of brightly coloured safety equipment of every description but none of it is any use if the crew do not know where it is stowed or how to use it. Safety is a state of mind as well as equipment and this section covers items that should be covered in any safety briefing to old and new crew alike. Captains of passenger aircraft refer to a checklist before leaving the ground and the same procedure should be used for boats so that nothing gets forgotten. A suggested safety-briefing checklist is shown in Appendix C.

PERSONAL SAFETY

Crew who are not kitted out properly can become wet, cold, miserable and seasick which is certainly not a safe state to be in! It is the skipper's responsibility to ensure that the crew have adequate clothing and personal safety equipment.

The man shown in Figure 16.1 is well clad and, with the addition of hat and gloves, would remain warm and dry offshore.

Fig 16.1 Dressed for offshore sailing. Photo: Rick Tomlinson.

Minimum requirements:

1 Waterproof non-slip footwear.
2 Warm layers of clothing and a change.
3 Hat, gloves, socks and towelling scarf.
4 Lifejacket of approved type.
5 Safety harness and line with quick release fastening (often combined with the lifejacket).
6 Knife and spike on a lanyard.

◆ Lifejackets

Lifejackets come in a variety of shapes, sizes and methods of inflation. In order to be described as a lifejacket the equipment has to be capable of turning an unconscious casualty into the face-up position with chin above the water. It also has to have a mouth top-up inflation tube, a whistle, reflective tape and a lifting strop. Children's lifejackets are most likely to be part air/part foam as illustrated in Fig 16.2.

Most adult crew members prefer to wear the less restricting 'all air' waistcoat type which may have oral or automatic inflation. All jackets are labelled according to how much weight they can support. At one time it was considered that 150 Newtons were sufficient to do the job but now a variety of sizes are offered with the 190 Newton size as a favourite for offshore use. Crotch straps should be considered essential as they prevent the jacket from riding up over the face when inflated and, as a floating person automatically turns head to wind, a spray hood will prevent drowning.

Neither these items nor lights are supplied as standard with the less expensive lifejackets, so make sure you buy one that is suitable for you.

The jacket illustrated in Figures 16.3 and 16.4 is a top-of-the-range jacket by Crewsaver.

Fig 16.2 Child's lifejacket with integral buoyancy and crotch straps.

Dinghy sailors who risk entrapment under the boat in the event of a capsize are advised to wear a manually inflated jacket. Care should be taken to keep the inflation toggle readily accessible.

Lifejackets should be inspected annually to check that the lungs are still airtight and that stitching has not become rotten in the sun. It is best to take the jackets to a registered safety centre for checking. Hammar inflation devices have an expiry date printed on them, so keep a check to see that they are still in date.

◆ Harness lines

Any lifejacket that is fitted with a safety harness will have a large ring on the front, to which a harness line should be attached.

Clipping on is advised:

- In rough weather when working out of the cockpit.
- At night in any weather when not sitting down in the cockpit and at all times in rough weather outside the cabin.
- When alone on deck (this includes being at the helm) whatever the weather. This is especially important if the autopilot is engaged; a person could fall overboard without anyone below knowing.

Fig 16.3 Crewsaver 190 Newton Ergofit jacket.

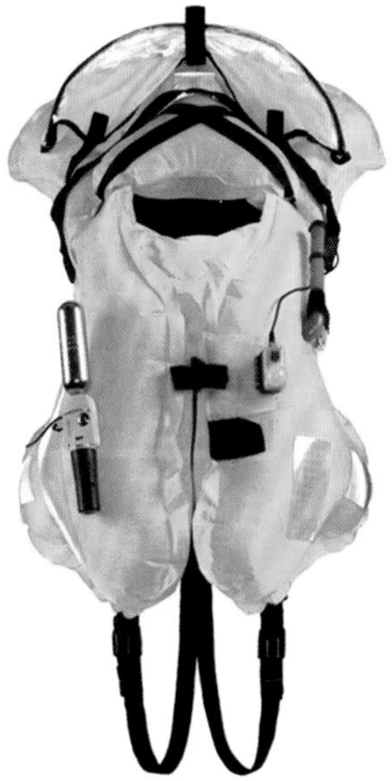

Fig 16.4 Inflated Ergofit jacket. Note the light and the spray hood.

It must be the skipper's decision whether harnesses are worn in fog when the risk of collision and rapid sinking is probably at its highest. However, trying to find a person in the water in foggy conditions could prove extremely difficult.

The safety line should be attached to:
- Strong points, usually D rings or U bolts.
- Webbing lines rigged from stern to bow on each side of the boat (jackstays).
- Shrouds (if no risk of a knockdown).
- Around the mast.

DO NOT clip on to guardrails, as they are seldom strong enough to take the weight of a falling body.

Fig 16.5 Crewsaver harness line with elasticated cover.

MAN OVERBOARD

Sometimes, despite all sensible precautions, a crew member may fall overboard.

This is not the time to botch together some sort of rough and ready plan for getting the boat back to them and for lifting them from the water. Shocked, trained crew have a fair chance of recovering the person safely and quickly; shocked, untrained ones are highly likely to fail. There is no substitute for a well-practised drill where everyone on board knows which tasks need to be done.

The preferred method will depend upon conditions, type of boat, the ability of the helmsman and number of persons on board. Many yachts go offshore with a couple as crew and, hopefully, they will have planned how the remaining person will rescue someone from the water. Rescue equipment needs to be readily available and the plan to be suitable for the single-handed.

For night use the lifebuoy (and the dan-buoy) should have retro-reflective tape and a light; white parachute flares could also be used to illuminate the area. The lights attached to the lifebuoys are best with a fixed, non-flashing light as there is a better chance of it being spotted as it bobs up and down in a choppy sea.

Three well proven recovery methods follow but whichever is chosen, the following actions should be taken:

1 Shout 'Man Overboard' to alert the crew.

2 Delegate someone to point at the casualty.

3 If possible: press the MOB button on the GPS. If sufficient crew send a DSC distress alert.

◆ MOB method 1 – yacht under sail with serviceable engine

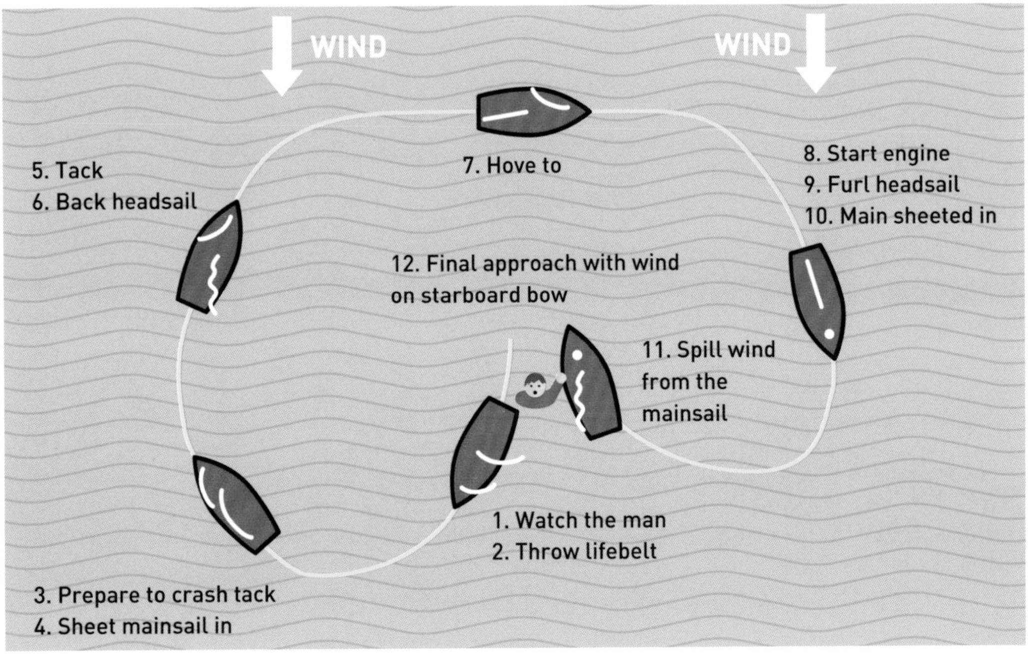

Fig 16.6 Method for sailing yacht with a serviceable engine.

1	Point to the man
2	Throw a lifebelt or dan-buoy if possible.
3	Prepare to 'crash' tack.
4, 5 & 6	Haul the mainsail in tightly as you tack but leave the headsail sheet as it is.
7 & 8	Check for ropes in the water then start the engine.
9 & 10	Furl or lower the headsail keeping the mainsail sheeted in so that the shocked and unwary cannot get injured by the boom.
11 & 12	Turn towards the wind until the boat is approx 50° off the wind. Approach under power and free the main sheet to stop it driving the boat. Bring the man alongside to leeward and close to the boat's point of pivot (usually just forward amidships). Stop the boat and stop the engine once the casualty is alongside.

◆ MOB method 2 – yacht sailing with no serviceable engine

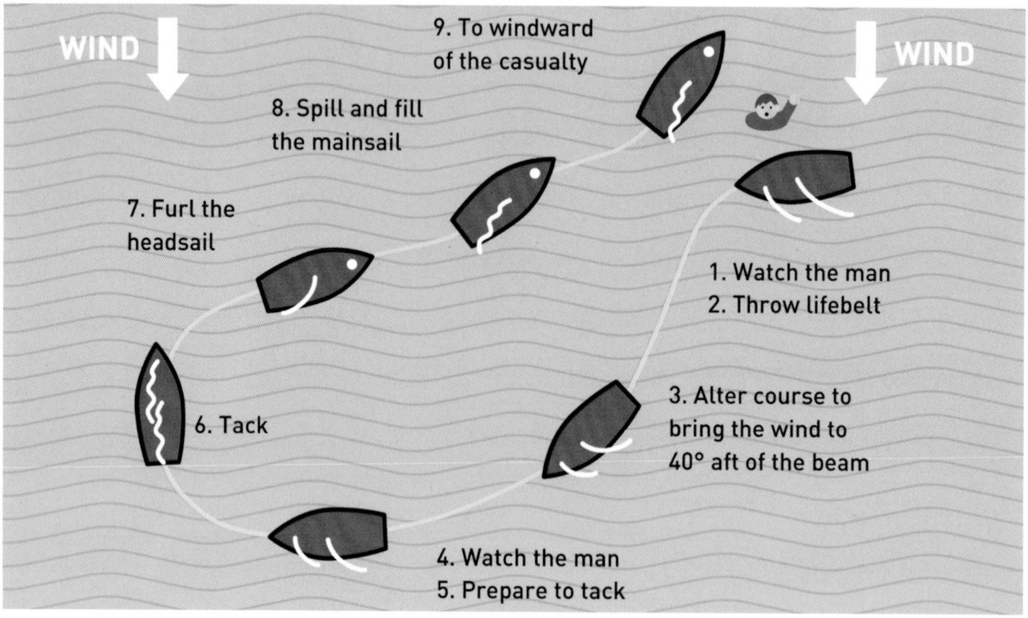

Fig 16.7 Method for returning to the casualty in a yacht with an unserviceable engine.

1 Whatever the point of sailing, turn on to a course with the wind slightly aft of the beam (say 120° to 130° off the bow).

2 Sail on for a sufficient distance to enable the boat to tack and return at slow speed under full control.

3 After tacking, test to see if the mainsail empties when the mainsheet is released.

4 *If the mainsail can be emptied:*
Sight the casualty through the leeward shrouds and aim to arrive slightly to windward of his position with the boat stopped. During the final approach, the mainsail can be filled or spilled as a 'throttle' to give any drive needed.

If the mainsail CANNOT be emptied:
Drop slightly to leeward for a few seconds then test again for a spilling main.

◆ MOB method 3 – motor cruiser or yacht under power

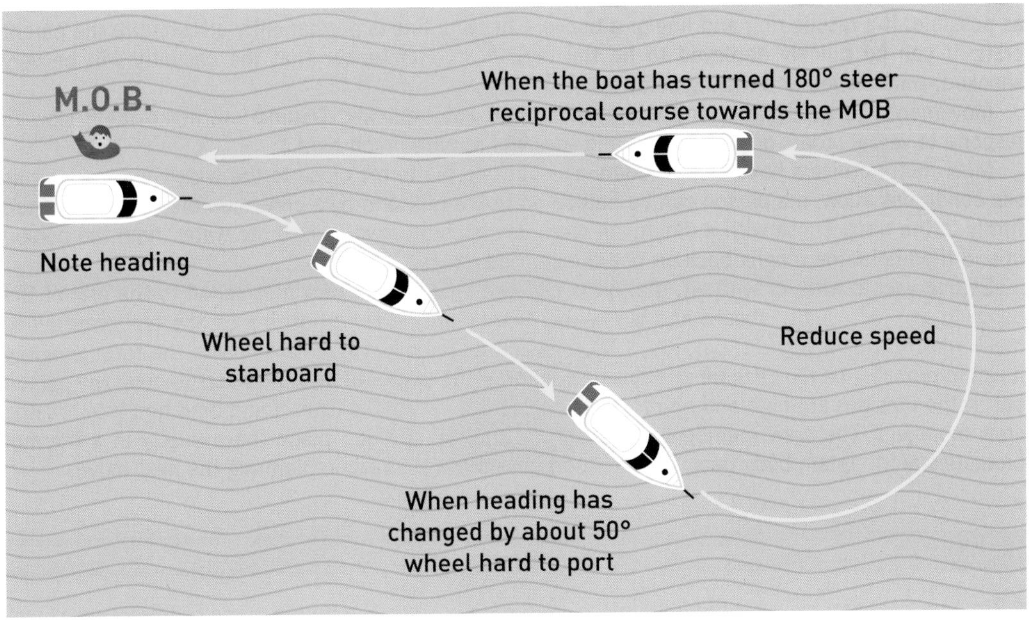

Fig 16.8

1. As soon as the person goes overboard, note the course.
2. Put the helm over to starboard and alter course by 50°.
3. When on a course of plus 50° put the helm hard over the other way – to port.
4. When you are on a reciprocal of the original course cut the throttles.
5. The casualty should be in the area ahead.

◆ AIS Beacon

Locating a man in rough sea conditions at night has always been a problem but a great step forward is the Smartfind AIS beacon. It is compact, waterproof and buoyant and can be carried by individual crew members for deployment if they are unfortunate enough to fall into the water. When activated, the beacon transmits a unique identity number and a GPS position to the vessel which the casualty has come from. The information it transmits has a typical 4 mile range and can be viewed using standard AIS equipment such as Class A and Class B transponders and a wide selection of receive only AIS units. The exact location and the bearing and distance to that location will be transmitted and displayed continuously for a minimum of 24 hours.

Fig 16.9 The Smartfind S20 AIS beacon.

◆ Recovery

Once the boat is alongside the casualty, it is imperative that they are attached to the craft as soon as possible. If a rescue ring and line or a buoyant heaving line is permanently attached to the parent craft, it can be quickly deployed to tie the person on. Remember that the casualty will be very shocked, waterlogged and feeling cold.

Movement will be difficult and energy will drain away quickly. Trauma will make them slow to respond to verbal orders or suggestions and they will require much help.

Most motor cruisers have stern ladders and bathing platforms close to the water and, as long as sea conditions allow, the person can be helped on to the platform by a crew member who is attached firmly to the boat. Those with a dinghy on stern davits could lower it into the water, haul the person in and then hoist the dinghy back on board using the davits.

Sailing yachts with, or without, platforms can use a halyard or tackle attached to the end of the boom to haul a casualty aboard and it may be beneficial to cut the lashing on the top guardrail to make what will be a very difficult job, a little easier. As most headsails are now of the furling variety it would probably be too difficult and too slow to lower the large sail into the water to hoist the person out. If the topsides are high and all else fails consider inflating the liferaft and haul him into it using crew members. The crew members can then bail the raft dry and place the casualty in a thermal protective aid to retain body heat. This method buys some time while planning the next move.

FIRE

A fire on a boat can be very alarming indeed, particularly when the hull is made of fibreglass which, when it burns, gives off dense black smoke, toxic fumes and quickly loses buoyancy.

The first defence against fire is to avoid it happening in the first place:

- Don't smoke down below or store fuels such as petrol below decks.
- Frying should be restricted and pans not left unattended.
- Make sure that there are no curtains above the gas cooker.
- Don't put used matches into the rubbish bin while still hot.
- Check electrical wiring for chafe within the engine space as shorting could cause the plastic insulation to catch fire.
- Fit a smoke detector, especially in quarter cabins near the engine and galley.

◆ What does fire need?

Fire requires three elements for it to take hold and spread:

- **Fuel**
- **Oxygen**
- **Heat**

If you remove any one or more of the three then the fire will be eliminated.
This can be achieved by:

- Removing the fuel source by turning off the fuel or getting rid of combustible material.
- The oxygen can be removed by smothering.
- The heat can be removed by cooling.

◆ Types of fire

Class A

Carbonaceous materials such as paper, wood and textiles.
Class A fires can be deep seated and might smoulder for some time when they appear to be out. There is a danger of re-ignition.

Class B

Flammable liquids such as petrol, diesel, solvents, cooking oil and paint.

Class C

Flammable gas such as butane and propane.

◆ Fire extinguishers

All fire extinguishers are coded with:

- **A letter** denoting the category of fire they are most suited to fight.
- **A number** indicating the size of fire, ie 5A, 27A, 55A etc.

Extinguishers should be sited:

- Near cabin entrances and hatches so that the occupants can escape and then fight the fire from outside. (Especially important where quarter cabins are close to the engine and galley.)
- Inside the engine space – discharging automatically. Figure 16.10 shows the auto capsule on this type.

OR

- Close to the engine space – discharged manually into engine space using a small closable aperture in the casing, which can remain closed to reduce oxygen.
- In the cockpit locker – larger than the ones in the cabins.

FIRE ON BOARD – ACTION TO TAKE

If, despite precautions, a fire breaks out:

- Shout 'FIRE' to alert everyone. Get all crew members up on deck.
- If possible, close the hatches to reduce airflow but do not lock them.
- Aim a fire extinguisher at the base of the fire or, if appropriate, smother with a fire blanket.
- Turn off any gas or fuel, which could feed the fire and move any gas cylinders, spare fuel containers or pyrotechnics away from the area of the fire.
- Put on lifejackets.
- If the fire looks as though it might get out of control, send a distress alert and message and prepare to abandon to the liferaft.

◆ Types of fire extinguisher

ABC dry powder (Figure 16.11)

Suitable for Class A, B and C fires. The powder reacts chemically with the fire, knocks the flame down quickly and can find its way into very small spaces. Unfortunately, it is very messy but its advantages outweigh the disadvantages making it the most versatile type of extinguisher to have on a boat.

Water

This acts by cooling and is always in plentiful supply with the aid of a bucket.
Effective on Class A fires involving wood, paper and textiles.
It is good for damping down a recently extinguished fire once electrical power has been turned off.
It must not be used on electrical or hot fat fires.

Foam

Foam can be used on boats but it is more limited in its application. It does not have the fluid properties of powder and therefore does not get into every nook and cranny. It operates by cooling and smothering and is also very messy.

Aerosol generators

This type of aerosol emits a very fine powder and gas and leaves little or no mess. It is effective and considered suitable for the engine space.

Carbon dioxide

Carbon dioxide is not considered suitable for small craft because of the risk of suffocation in confined spaces. A large amount is also needed to extinguish modest fires.

Fig 16.10 (above) Firemaster extinguisher for installation in an engine space.

Fig 16.11 (right) Firemaster dry powder extinguishers.

◆ Fire blanket

The fire blanket (Figure 16.12) should be mounted within easy reach of the cooker but not where it would mean reaching over the stove to deploy it.

It should be wrapped over the hands to avoid burnt knuckles and held to protect the fire fighter's chest and face.

Fig 16.12 Firemaster fire blanket.

GAS COOKERS

Most recreational craft carrying gas cylinders will use butane gas in Europe and propane if blue water cruising, as propane is available worldwide; many motor cruisers cook with electricity and carry no gas at all. Unfortunately gas is both highly flammable and heavier than air meaning that it will sink into the bilges if there is a gas leak. If gas were to collect in this area overnight there could be an explosion immediately if a naked flame was used in the morning.

Boats built to European specifications have a dedicated compartment for gas bottles that allows any leaked gas to drain overboard and many also have gas detectors installed. If extra gas bottles are carried they should be stowed on deck – not in a cockpit locker.

As well as having flame failure devices on gas cookers, there should be a gas shut-off valve close to the cooker and at the gas bottle; it is important to turn the one near the cooker off when the cooker is not in use. The tap on the bottle should be turned off when leaving the boat and overnight.

DO NOT burn off the gas remaining in the pipe as a gas and air mixture is far more explosive than gas alone.

Pipes from the bottle are part rigid and part flexible and it is important to check for chafe on the flexible rubber hoses at the cooker end of the installation; as the cooker swings on its gimbals, it can easily chafe on the surrounding woodwork.

Gas leak

If there is a gas leak:

1 Extinguish all flames.
2 Turn off the engine, if running, because the alternator makes sparks.
3 Once the engine has stopped, turn off the battery isolator switches, thereby ensuring that equipment such as automatic electric bilge pumps are turned off.
4 Ventilate the boat.
5 Bail the gas out of the bilge with a plastic cup and a bucket.

SEACOCKS

This valve, which is designed to allow seawater to pass into the engine and waste to be expelled overboard, is the biggest threat to watertight integrity and is probably one of the most neglected pieces of equipment on a boat. Annual servicing is essential and plastic piping attached to them should be secured with two jubilee clips for safety. If the boat is to be left, you should shut all seacocks but commercial charter yachts, (which are constantly attended), leave them open in the fear that a charterer may start the engine with the engine water intake valve closed. Seacocks are less likely to let you down if they are opened and closed regularly; ones left untouched eventually seize and cannot be closed.

Make sure that you know where all the seacocks are located. It makes for a very undignified scramble if water starts pouring in and you don't know where they all are!

Two designs of valve are common and are illustrated in Figure 16.13. It becomes very obvious when the tapered valve fails because the handle will not move but the gate valve can sometimes sheer inside – the wheel still turns without anything happening.

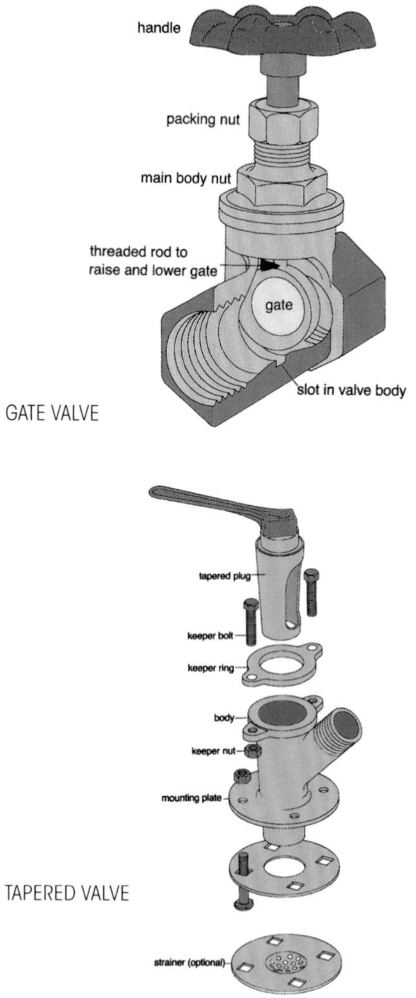

Fig 16.13 A gate valve and a tapered valve seacock.

Fig 16.14 First aid manual

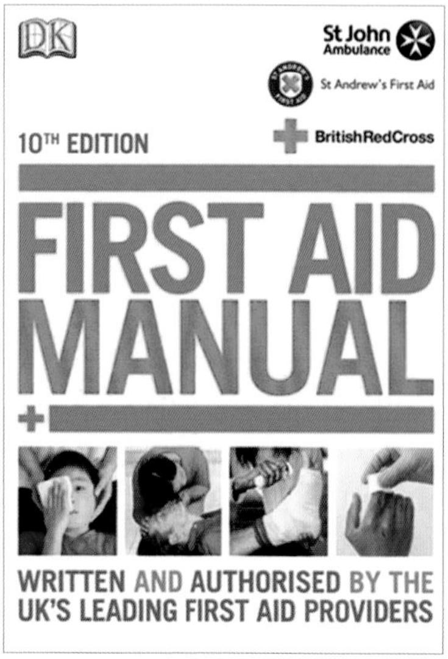

FIRST AID BOX

Suggested contents for a first aid box are shown in Appendix A.

First aid agencies, such as St John Ambulance, St Andrew's and Red Cross, jointly print a colourful and very comprehensive book on first aid and a current manual should be stored with the boat's first aid box. Contents of the box need to be checked regularly as engineers frequently 'borrow' items such as plastic gloves when servicing the engine. Rusty scissors, leaking tubes of antiseptic cream and dirty strips of adhesive plaster do not inspire confidence in the injured! It is sensible to have two boxes, one for major injuries and the other for everyday use.

EQUIPMENT FOR AN OFFSHORE YACHT

The equipment recommended for a sailing yacht or motor cruiser going offshore is listed in Appendix B.

SAFETY BRIEFING CHECKLIST

A list of items to be covered in a safety brief is shown in Appendix C.

PYROTECHNICS

Flares are carried as a back up for the VHF radio, for guiding rescuers to your exact position and to illuminate persons in the water. They should be kept in a waterproof container similar to the one shown in Figure 16.17, stowed away from damage and where they can be grabbed quickly. The cockpit locker is often the best place as it is close to the liferaft stowage. The whole crew should be aware of the location. The container should have a lanyard attached to it so that it can be tied on to the liferaft should abandonment be necessary. It is a good idea to stow a pair of gardening gloves in the flare box as handheld flares get quite hot.

REMEMBER NEVER TO POINT FLARES AT ANOTHER PERSON

◆ Types of flare

Red handheld flare – Distress (Figure 16.15)

- Use within sight of land or rescuers.
- Burns for 1 minute.
- Point downwind. Hold up and outboard.
- Do not look directly at the burning flare.

Red parachute flare – Distress (Figure 16.16)

- Use for long-range distress signalling – small parachute suspends red burning flare.
- Height: 300m if fired vertically, 200m if fired at 45°.
- Burns for 40 seconds.
- Stand with back to the wind and fire slightly downwind if the cloud is a reasonable height but at an angle of 45° if the cloud base is below 300m (1,000 feet).

Orange smoke flare – Distress

There are two types:

1. Handheld smoke, which burns for 1 minute.
2. Buoyant canister, which burns for 3 minutes.

   Instructions for use:
   - Drop the canister into the water downwind of the boat (you may become an orange survivor if you launch it on the windward side!).
   - Point the handheld smoke downwind.

White handheld – Illuminating – NOT distress

- Burns for 1 minute.
- Point downwind. Hold up and outboard.
- Do not look directly at the burning flare.

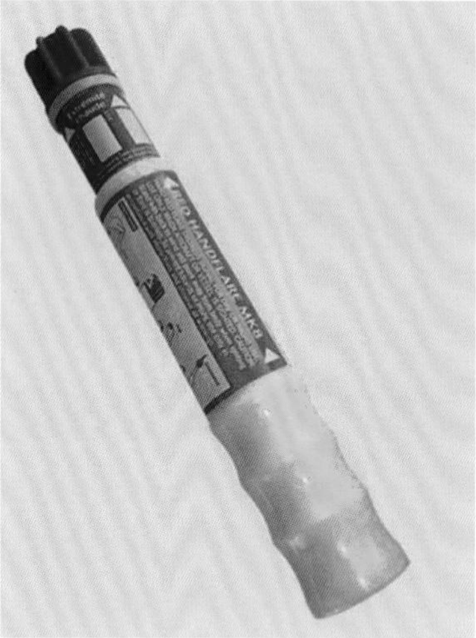
Fig 16.15 Pains Wessex handheld red distress flare.

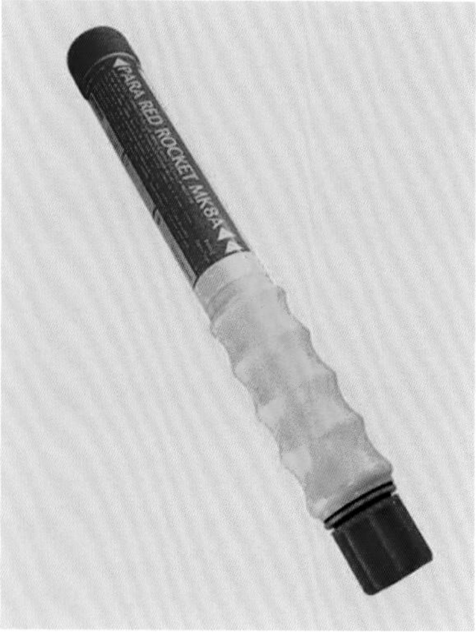

Fig 16.16 Pains Wessex red parachute distress flare.

◆ Expiry date and disposal

Each flare will be stamped with an expiry date, which should give four seasons' use if purchased early in the year. Out-of-date flares lose their colour and if they have not been stored in dry conditions, the compacted combustible medium breaks apart. With handheld flares this means that dangerous burning material could drop on to feet or boat when flares are ignited. Some chandlers will accept old flares for return to the manufacturer but if this is not possible contact your nearest coastguard who will tell you who to contact in your area. This may mean that you have to drive some distance to keep your appointment at the disposal point.

Warning: It is illegal to dump flares in the sea or to let them off on bonfire night.

◆ Minimum recommended flare packs

Inshore – less than 3 miles from land

2 orange hand smokes
2 red hand flares

Coastal – up to 7 miles from land

2 red hand flares
2 red parachute flares
2 orange hand smokes

Offshore – over 7 miles from land (Fig.16.17)

4 red parachute rockets
4 red hand flares
2 buoyant orange smokes

For collision warning

4 white hand flares

Important note: It is certainly worth considering the addition of up to 4 white illuminating parachute flares for use at night if someone goes overboard. In tests it was found that the reflective strips on waterproof jackets show up extremely well when the area is illuminated with these flares.

Fig 16.17 Hansson offshore flare pack in waterproof container.

LIFERAFT

UNLESS THE BOAT IS ON FIRE, OR SINKING FAST, DON'T GET INTO THE LIFERAFT.
You will stand a greater chance of being rescued, and suffer less from hypothermia in a flooded boat than in a flimsy rubber raft. However, it is extremely important that you and your crew all know how to launch, inflate and board the raft.

Don't keep the raft alongside for any length of time after it has been inflated as it may flip over in a strong wind and the painter, which has a weak link to prevent it going down with the ship, may part before you have boarded.

◆ Before abandoning

1 Send out a DSC distress alert and Mayday voice message giving your position and number of crew (see Chapter 17).
2 Wear plenty of warm clothing and foul weather gear. Don't forget a hat, as heat is lost quickly from the head. Keep your boots on – they will act as insulation.
3 Put on lifejackets.
4 Take a pre-prepared grab bag containing:
Flares, water, thermal protective aids, spare spectacles, any medication, ship's papers, passports and lastly something funny to cheer the crew up (a Mike Peyton book of nautical cartoons).
5 A handheld radio could greatly assist communication with rescuers and if an EPIRB is available it should be activated and attached to the raft.

◆ Launching

1 Make sure the painter is attached to a strong point.
2 Release the fastenings, which secure the raft to the boat and launch it to windward if the boat is on fire, but otherwise to leeward.
3 When it is in the water, take in all the slack on the painter and then give a sharp tug. This should inflate the raft (Figure 16.18).

◆ Boarding the raft

1 Try not to jump into the raft; if possible, board from a ladder or the stern platform. The heaviest and strongest person should board first, in case people need to be pulled into the liferaft from the water.
2 Cut the painter with the knife stored by the liferaft entrance.
3 When the liferaft is fully boarded, distribute the weight as evenly as possible and paddle away from the boat.

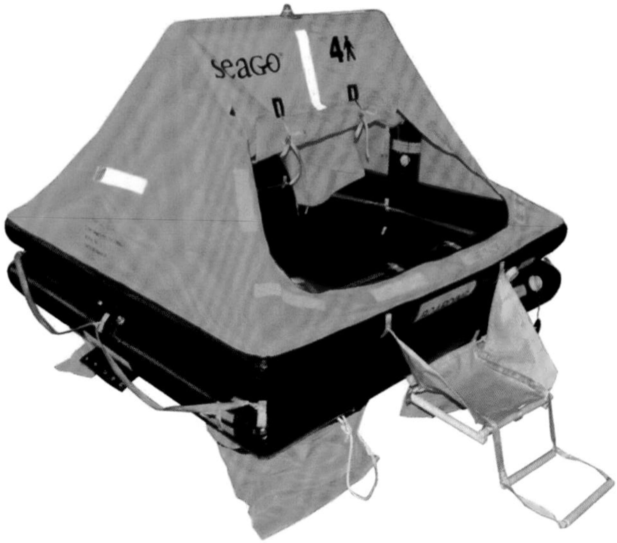

Fig 16.18 Seago 4 x man ISO 9650.1 liferaft.

◆ Surviving

1 Stream the drogue. The raft depends upon this drogue for its stability so this must be done as soon as possible.
2 Unplug the light in daylight to save battery power.
3 Close the canopy.
4 Open the survival pack and issue seasickness pills, even to those who are never normally sick, as the motion in a liferaft is unpleasant.
5 Check for leaks and treat any injuries.
6 Post a lookout.
7 Inflate the double floor for insulation.
8 Activate the EPIRB.
9 Do not issue any water for the first 24 hours unless an injured person is losing blood. Do not drink seawater or urine.
10 **BELIEVE THAT YOU WILL SURVIVE.**

4 × MAN ISO LIFERAFT	
LIST OF CONTENTS	
1 × pair of oars	1 × bailer
2 × sponges	2 × red hand held flares
1 × waterproof torch, spare batteries	1 × whistle
1 × pack seasickness tablets	1 × drogue
1 × floating knife	1 × pair scissors
1 × repair clamp	1 × rescue quoit
1 × lifesaving signal card	2 × repair bungs
1 × bellows hand pump	

Fig 16.19 List of safety equipment for an ISO 9650.1 liferaft.

SURVIVAL

Traumatised survivors often deteriorate into a zombie state and the skipper will have to take very positive control of those in the raft if they are to survive. Bailing the raft dry and inflating the floor will need organisation in the confined space but it must be done as this will help protect the occupants from the cold. Give each person a job and make him or her responsible for some aspect of a routine. A watch system should be introduced, however long rescue is likely to take. Order and self-discipline will help survival and nautical quizzes and community singing have been known to raise crew morale.

For longer-term survival it will be necessary to devise methods of collecting water as protein food such as fish cannot be digested without extra water.

◆ Lifeboat rescue

The RNLI is a voluntary organisation whose aim is to save lives. Although they often tow broken vessels to a place of safety, they are not obliged to do so.

When a lifeboat is deployed to assist you, it is likely that a member of the lifeboat crew will board your craft to help with handling and communications. He is more experienced in rescue techniques than you are so it is best to defer to him as the expert and do as he suggests.

He will want to attach a towline to a strong point, which could be the windlass if you have one. He may rig a bridle that encircles the boat.

SEARCH & RESCUE

◆ SAR helicopter

HM Coastguard co-ordinate helicopter search rescue in the UK and Channel Islands and if a helicopter is tasked to you, it greatly helps if you and your crew know what to do.

It is easier to effect a rescue from a fast-moving motor cruiser with large open cockpit than it is from a sailing yacht. The high speed means that the helicopter uses less power than it would in a hover, and the absence of a mast means that the helicopter can fly overhead to drop the winchman directly on to the deck without using a secondary line, called the *hi-line.*

The boat may have to identify itself, if close to a number of other craft, and this can be done with a name displayed on a brightly coloured piece of canvas or with a handheld smoke flare. The rescue crew will not appreciate having a parachute flare fired at the helicopter at any time!

Fig 16.20 An HM Coastguard search and rescue helicopter exercising with a willing volunteer. The hi-line has been dropped on to the yacht in preparation for the diver's descent.

The actions are as follows:

1 Make sure that all loose items on deck are secured.
2 The helicopter pilot will call you on VHF and give you a briefing before making a final approach. Listen to his instructions and he will ask you if you have any questions.
3 Sailing yachts will probably be told to start the engine. Depending on the length of the rescue helicopter, which determines how much down-draft affects the yacht, you may be told to either keep the sails you are currently using or to furl the headsail and deep reef the mainsail. It stabilises the yacht if the sail remains hoisted and tips the mast away from the helicopter thus allowing a clearer approach. Occasionally you will be told to lower all sails.
4 *If under sail* you will probably be told to sail close-hauled on the port tack on a steady heading. The door and the pilot are on the starboard side of the aircraft as in Figure 16.20, which is why the port tack is chosen.
   If under power you will be given a course and speed to maintain.
5 A bucket and line should be made available for stowage of the rope hi-line. Make sure that the crew member handling the hi-line wears protective gloves to avoid rope burns.
6 Allow the hi-line to earth itself on the deck or in the water once it has been lowered.
7 The gloved crew should take in the slack on the hi-line and maintain sufficient firmness to prevent the winchman swinging as he is lowered to the deck. At no time must this line be attached to a person or to the boat.
8 The winchman will indicate when he wishes to be hauled down on to the deck. The noise will be extremely loud and he will use hand signals to direct the boat's crew.

◆ Search and rescue signals

The International Maritime Organisation requires all craft, whatever their size, to carry a card showing international signals that are likely to be used during rescue by aircraft and officials on the shore. Figure 16.21 a & b (pages 171 and 172) give these signals.

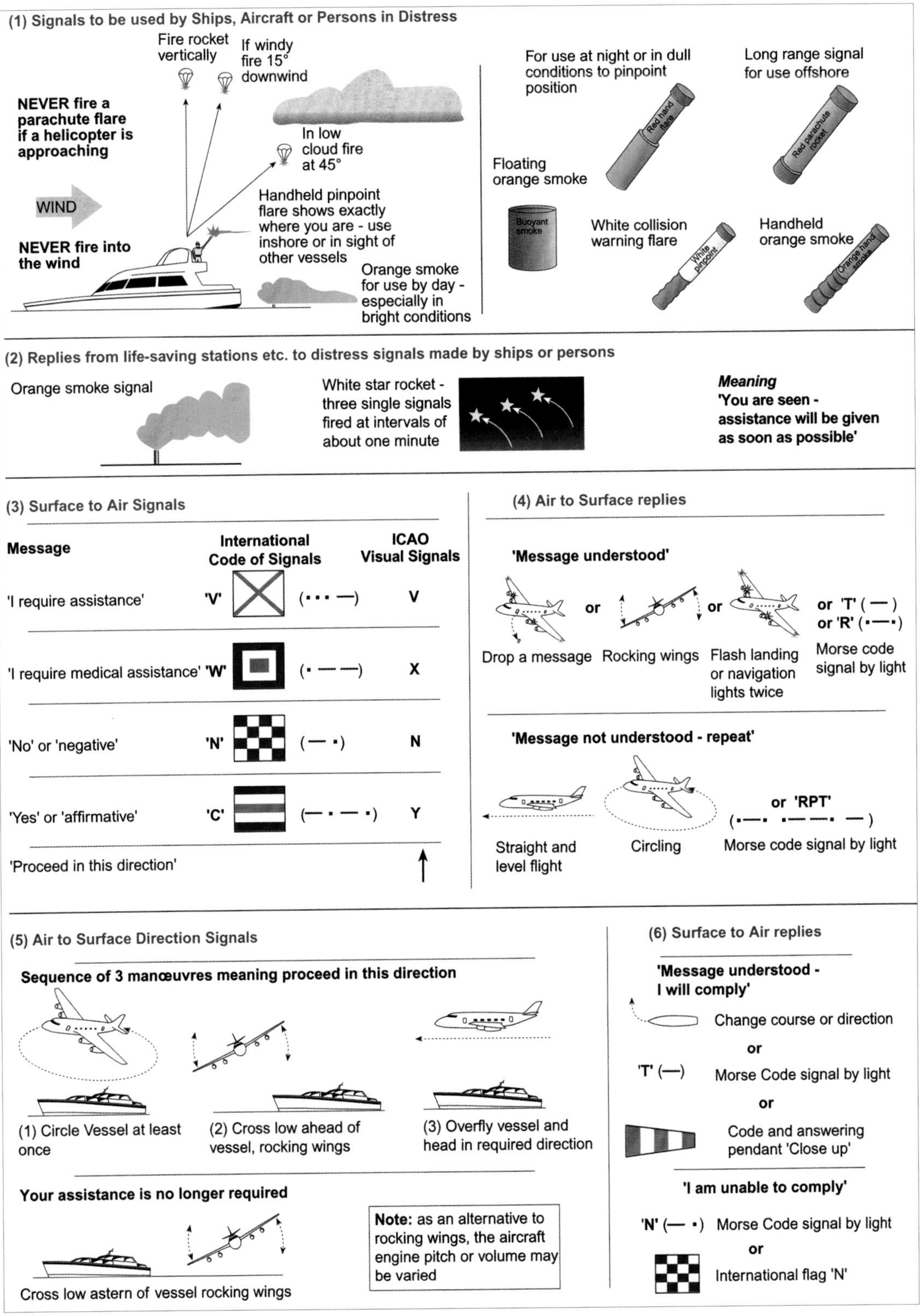
(1) Signals to be used by Ships, Aircraft or Persons in Distress
Fire rocket vertically
If windy fire 15° downwind
NEVER fire a parachute flare if a helicopter is approaching
In low cloud fire at 45°
WIND
NEVER fire into the wind
Handheld pinpoint flare shows exactly where you are - use inshore or in sight of other vessels
Orange smoke for use by day - especially in bright conditions
For use at night or in dull conditions to pinpoint position
Red hand flare
Long range signal for use offshore
Red parachute rocket
Floating orange smoke
Buoyant smoke
White collision warning flare
White pinpoint
Handheld orange smoke
Orange hand smoke
(2) Replies from life-saving stations etc. to distress signals made by ships or persons
Orange smoke signal
White star rocket - three single signals fired at intervals of about one minute
Meaning
'You are seen - assistance will be given as soon as possible'
(3) Surface to Air Signals
Message
International Code of Signals
ICAO Visual Signals
'I require assistance' 'V' (• • • —) V
'I require medical assistance' 'W' (• — —) X
'No' or 'negative' 'N' (— •) N
'Yes' or 'affirmative' 'C' (— • — •) Y
'Proceed in this direction' ↑
(4) Air to Surface replies
'Message understood'
Drop a message
or
Rocking wings
or
Flash landing or navigation lights twice
or 'T' (—)
or 'R' (• — •)
Morse code signal by light
'Message not understood - repeat'
Straight and level flight
Circling
or 'RPT'
(• — • • — — • —)
Morse code signal by light
(5) Air to Surface Direction Signals
Sequence of 3 manœuvres meaning proceed in this direction
(1) Circle Vessel at least once
(2) Cross low ahead of vessel, rocking wings
(3) Overfly vessel and head in required direction
Your assistance is no longer required
Cross low astern of vessel rocking wings
Note: as an alternative to rocking wings, the aircraft engine pitch or volume may be varied
(6) Surface to Air replies
'Message understood - I will comply'
Change course or direction
or
'T' (—)
Morse Code signal by light
or
Code and answering pendant 'Close up'
'I am unable to comply'
'N' (— •) Morse Code signal by light
or
International flag 'N'

Fig 16.21a Distress and life-saving signals.

(7) Landing signals for the guidance of small boats with crews or persons in distress. By night white lights or flares are used instead of white flags.

		Other signals	*Meaning*
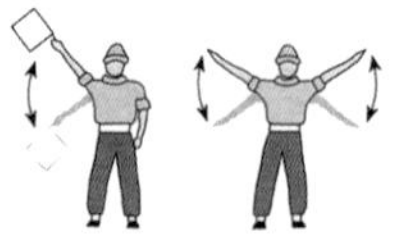	**Vertical** motion of a white flag) or of the arms	International Code letter **'K'** (— • —) by light or sound	**'This is the best place to land'** (An indication of direction may be given by a steady white light or flare at a lower level)
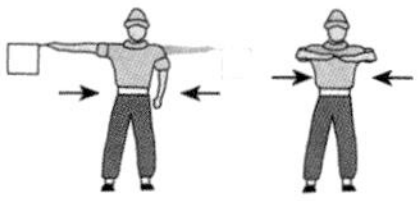	**Horizontal** motion of a white flag or of the arms extended horizontally	International Code letter **'S'** (• • •) by light or sound	**'Landing here is highly dangerous'**
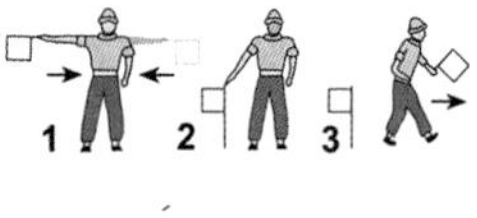	**Horizontal** motion of a white flag followed by **2**. placing the white flag in the ground and **3**. by carrying another white flag in the direction to be indicated.	**1**. Signalling the code letter **'S'** (• • •), followed by the code letter **'R'** (• — •) if the better landing place is more to the right in the direction of the approach, or **2**, by the code letter **'L'** (• — • •) if the better landing place is more to the left in the direction of approach	**'Landing here is highly dangerous. A more favourable location for landing is in the direction indicated'**

(8) Signals to be made in connection with the use of shore apparatus for life-saving

Signal	*Meaning*	**Signal**	*Meaning*
Vertical motion of a white flag (or white light or flare by night) or of the arms 	**In general:** 'affirmative' Specifically: 'rocket line is held - tail block is made fast - hawser is made fast - man is in the breeches buoy - haul away'	**Horizontal** motion of a white flag (or white light or flare by night) or of the arms 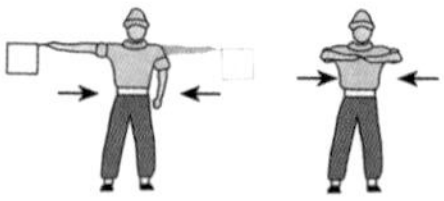	**In general:** negative. Specifically : slack away - stop hauling

(9) Signals to be used to warn a ship which is standing into danger

International Code flag **'U'** 

or **'NF'** 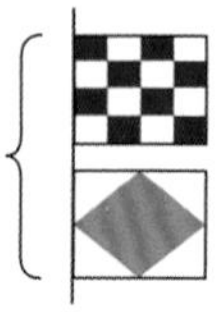

International Code signal **'U'** by light or sound • • —

(10) Signals used by Sub-Aqua divers

'I am OK'

'I need assistance'

Fig 16.21b Distress and life-saving signals continued.

QUESTION PAPER 16 – SAFETY & SURVIVAL

16.1	List four things you should do once you have boarded the liferaft.
16.2	A vessel is seen to be flashing a torch towards you at night – the sequence is two short flashes followed by one long flash. What does this signal indicate?
16.3	List four engine spares that should be carried for a marine diesel.
16.4	How many parachute flares should be carried on an offshore yacht?
16.5	Why is it important to stream the liferaft drogue as soon as possible after boarding?

Answers at the back of the book

17 COMMUNICATIONS, GMDSS & DISTRESS

VHF RADIO

WHEN WE WISH TO TALK WITH a friend on shore we make a quick call on the mobile phone and only the friend hears what we say. At sea, communications are conducted differently as many callers have to share the few channels allocated for ship to ship use and all calls can be heard by others listening on the chosen channel. To avoid total confusion it is necessary to impose a disciplined calling system, and communication has to be brief.

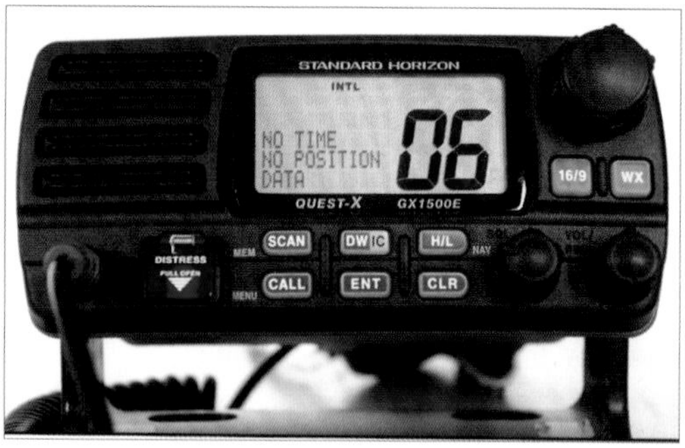

Fig 17.1 Standard Horizon 1500E VHF DSC radio.

Potential operators are required to pass a practical and written test to obtain the Short Range Certificate. In the UK the Royal Yachting Association is the examining body for this certificate and their website gives details of available teaching centres.

The radio also has to be licensed in order that the boat may be allocated with a unique international call sign and, if it is fitted with Digital Selective Calling (DSC for short), a nine-figure identity number known as an MMSI. This licence is free of charge if it is obtained online from ofcom.org.uk but a charge is made for postal applications. The International Telecommunications Union (ITU) keeps a searchable record of all call signs and MMSIs at www.itu.int/mars. All crew members should be encouraged to use the set under supervision and be able to send a distress message to the rescue services in the event of a serious emergency.

Later in this chapter we shall learn about the Global Maritime Distress and Safety System, which affects the way craft contact each other on VHF radio.

◆ VHF range

The range of VHF is limited to line of sight, so the antennae should be mounted as high as possible. An offshore motor cruiser, with the antennae mounted 4 metres above the waterline, could expect to speak to a Coastguard, with an aerial 100 metres high, at a range of about 25 miles; a sailing yacht between 30 and 40 miles, provided that the yacht is upright and not pounding to windward.

Fig 17.2 Icom handheld radio.

◆ Channels

There are nominally 59 channels allocated to marine VHF (on the frequencies between 156.00 and 174.00 MHz for those seeking technical details).

These channels are divided into four groups for: **Ship-to-Ship, Port Operations, Ship Movement** and **Public Correspondence**. The last group is hardly worth worrying about in the UK as there are no longer any BT coast radio stations operating a ship to shore service. This is due to the ever increasing use of mobile phones and satellite communication. Some other European countries, including Eire, still offer a limited service, details of which may be found in *Reeds Almanac.*

IMPORTANT CHANNELS

CHANNEL	16	Distress, safety and calling
CHANNEL	6, 8, 72, 77	Ship-to-ship (Ch 6 being the primary channel)
CHANNEL	13	Bridge-to-bridge communication on matters of navigational safety
CHANNEL	67	*UK only:* HM Coastguard Small Craft safety
CHANNEL	80	*UK only:* Marina berthing
CHANNEL	M /37	Racing and yacht club safety boats
CHANNEL	11,12,14	Typically for Port Operations. A nautical almanac or pilot book will give port channels.
CHANNEL	70	On some older sets it is possible to select this channel for voice communication. It must **NOT** be used for this purpose as it is reserved for sending the digital alerts within the GMDSS. With new sets it can not be selected or is blocked.

◆ Simplex and Duplex operation

Simplex uses one channel and one antenna and, as the name suggests, it is the simple system used in most small craft. A press to talk button on the microphone has to be used to switch between transmit and receive; it is impossible to speak and listen at the same time. Some people may argue that this is not a bad thing! All but one of the commonly-used channels listed above are Simplex channels.

Duplex is more complex and requires either two antennas or a single more complicated one. It uses two frequencies, which allows normal two-way conversation but is generally only installed in larger motor cruisers and ships.

Small craft using a Simplex system may use a Duplex channel provided that one side of the communication is with a marina fitted with the correct equipment.

GLOBAL MARITIME DISTRESS & SAFETY SYSTEM (GMDSS)

During the 1970s, ships grew larger and crews got smaller. It was no longer economical to employ professional radio officers to keep watch around the clock and radio receivers were installed on the bridge in the hope that the watch-keeping officers would hear other craft in distress. Unfortunately, some distress calls were missed and the International Maritime Organisation (IMO) felt it had to act. The Global Maritime Distress and Safety System was the result and by 1999, all ships of over 300 gross register tons, and those carrying 13 passengers or more (classed as 'compulsory fit'), had to have at least two methods of sending and receiving distress messages and carry certain other equipment. (See details at the end of the chapter.)

GMDSS uses four coverage areas, only three of which are of interest and are shown in the illustration Figure 17.3. The area A4, which covers the Polar regions, is not shown because small boats have yet to be fitted with ice skates!

A1	Coverage of VHF coast stations (between 30 and 40 miles for a 15m mast).
A2	Coverage of MF coast stations (about 150 miles).
A3	Coverage of Inmarsat geo-stationary satellites (between 70°N and 70°S).
A4	Polar regions above 70°N and 70°S.

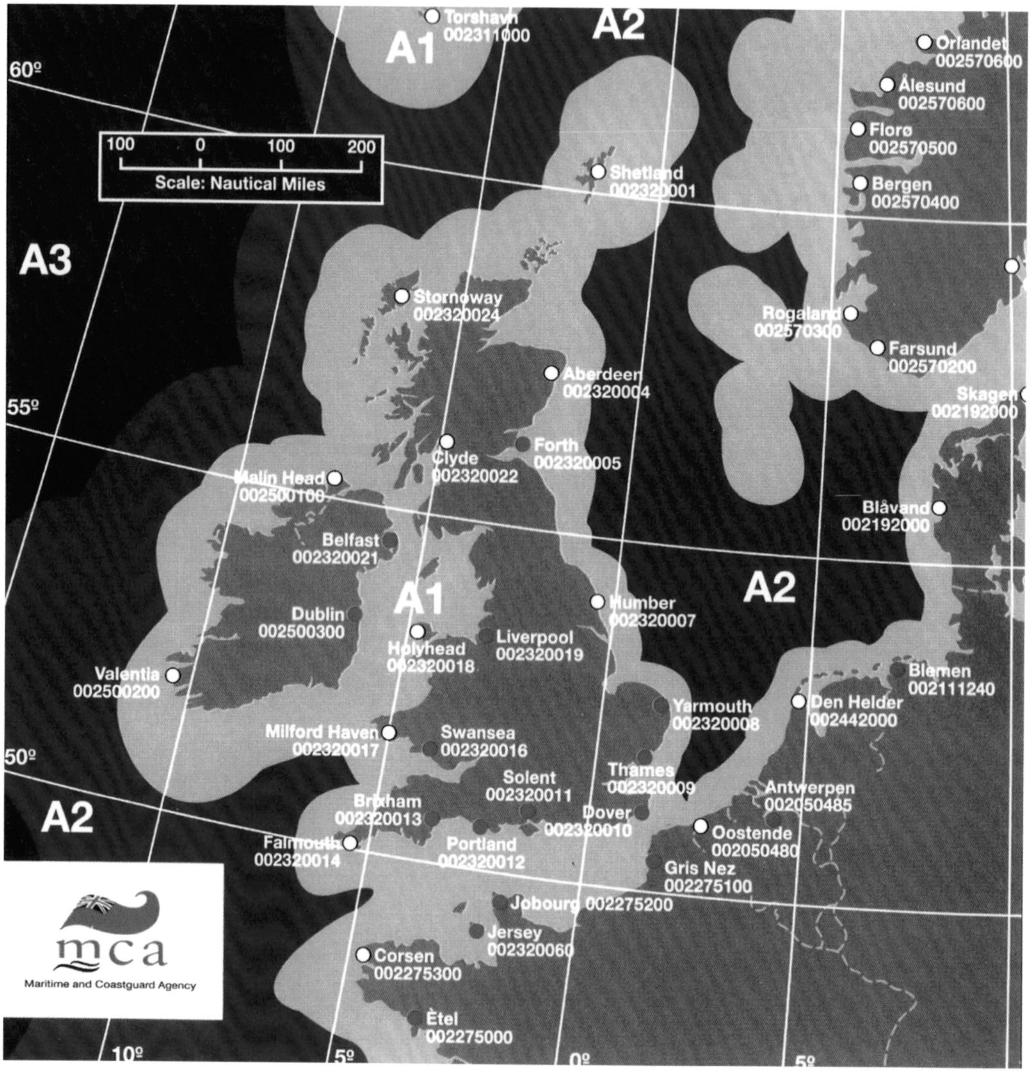

Fig 17.3 The coast stations of the UK and Ireland are fully fitted with digital selective calling equipment. Each station has an MMSI number beginning with a double zero if it controls search and rescue in the region.

DIGITAL SELECTIVE CALLING (DSC)

As the GMDSS idea developed, technology also advanced to provide radio sets that used Digital Selective Calling: the system used in radio pagers and mobile phones. When switched on, the set keeps an automatic listening watch on Channel 70 even though it is tuned to listen on another channel. When a vessel requires immediate assistance a digital alert is sent which activates a strident audio alarm in all other craft fitted with DSC. Their radios are then automatically switched to Channel 16, ready to receive a voice message. Even better, the set is designed to interface with GPS so that it can send a text message giving the stricken vessel's position and the time that disaster struck.

Once this digital alert has been sent, all DSC sets within range of the casualty will automatically be switched to Channel 16 to await the voice Mayday which will follow 15 seconds later. All maritime rescue centres in Europe are fitted with DSC and the map in Figure 17.3 shows their geographical positions together with their MMSIs. Inexpensive DSC sets are readily available in marine chandleries and HM Coastguard urge owners to fit the equipment.

◆ Distress (Mayday)

The Mayday call is used when:

There is GRAVE AND IMMINENT DANGER to a Person, Vessel, Aircraft or Other Vehicle and they require IMMEDIATE ASSISTANCE.

If fitted with DSC, you should send a digital distress alert by pressing the **RED** distress button once and then again for a further 5 seconds – the screen will inform you when the alert has been transmitted. After 15 seconds or a digital acknowledgement, proceed with the voice call and message using Channel 16 (Figure 17.4). Those without DSC miss this step but thereafter the routine is the same for all.

Now operate the press-to-talk switch and speak SLOWLY.

Fig 17.4 Simrad RD68 DSC radio with the sliding cover to the distress button clearly visible on the right-hand side of the set.

1	*Distress call 3 times*	**Mayday, Mayday, Mayday**
2	*Name of vessel*	**This is Yacht Banjo, Banjo, Banjo**
	Call sign & MMSI	**Call sign: two alpha bravo charlie. MMSI: 235899982**
3	*Mayday message*	**Mayday Banjo two alpha bravo charlie. MMSI 235899982**
4	*Position*	**Position 225 degrees true from Needles light three miles**
5	*Nature of distress*	**Struck a submerged object and sinking**
6	*Assistance required*	**I require immediate assistance**
7	*Other information*	**Four persons on board. No liferaft**
8	*End of message*	**Over**

Once a reply is received, pass on any further information by preceding each message with the word '**Mayday**'.

It is important to keep to this very rigid format as English is not the primary language for many merchant seaman and most crews are taught to listen for certain specific phrases.

Remember that people will be trying to write down your distress message and the average yachtsman can never find the pencil where he last left it! If you rush through reading latitude and longitude – the most important information of all – you could well be swimming before the rescue services find you.

◆ Urgency (Pan Pan)

This type of call is used when there is an urgent message concerning the safety of a vessel or person but where IMMEDIATE assistance is not required; medical advice and those requiring a tow might be good examples.

DSC-fitted craft sound an **URGENCY** alert before a voice message is spoken; those without go straight to Channel 16, high power.

This call is slightly different from the Mayday call as it is addressed to someone in particular, usually HM Coastguard as he has the best access to the emergency services.

Operate the press-to-talk switch and say:

1	*Urgency call (3 times)*	**Pan pan, Pan pan, Pan pan**
2	*Address (up to 3 times)*	**Solent Coastguard**
		Solent Coastguard
		Solent Coastguard
3	*Name of boat*	**This is Motor Yacht Tango, Tango, Tango**
	Call sign and MMSI	**Call sign: two yankee golf delta. MMSI: 235899981**
4	*Position*	**Position is five zero degrees two six minutes north**
		Zero one degrees four one minutes west
5	*Nature of urgency*	**Require urgent medical advice for sick crew**
6	*End of message*	**Over**

HM Coastguard stations have equipment that enables those needing advice to speak directly with a doctor in a hospital. The coastguard will tell you which channel he wishes you to use.

◆ Safety (Sécurité)

A Sécurité call may be made by all craft to give important navigational or weather information but in practice is used only by Coast Stations. A yacht skipper with an urgent message about a semi submerged container is strongly advised to contact a Coast Station about the problem so that a greater area can be covered by the subsequent Coast Station's Sécurité call.

The Sécurité call is transmitted on Channel 16. The message is sent on an alternative channel so that *16 is kept clear* for emergencies.

A digital alert is used only for new gale warnings and urgent navigational warnings, not routine weather information.

◆ Intership working (speaking to another boat)

If fitted with DSC

Select '**Routine call**' and either **key in the MMSI** or **select the number** from the stored directory, similar to a mobile phone. Chose a vacant inter-ship channel ie 6,8,72,77 and operate the call button.

If not fitted with DSC

Select Channel 16, wait for it to become vacant then make initial contact.

Arrange to transfer to a vacant intership channel as soon as possible. Note that it is forbidden to chat about the fortunes of your favourite football team over the radio – your mobile phone is for chatting.

OTHER SAFETY EQUIPMENT

◆ 406MHz Emergency Position Indicating Radio Beacon (EPIRB)

There are several different types of EPIRB but the one required for the GMDSS transmits on 406MHz. It is portable, waterproof and battery-operated and is released either manually or by a hydrostatic release unit (Figure 17.6), which deploys automatically when the vessel sinks to a predetermined depth.

Once activated, the EPIRB sends a signal containing the casualty's identity code to a Polar orbiting search and rescue satellite within the COSPAS/SARSAT system.

The satellite stores the signal until it can send it down to an available Earth station, which in turn passes the signal to other centres. Finally, HM Coastguard in Falmouth tells the appropriate rescue co-ordination centre that they have a 406 alert.

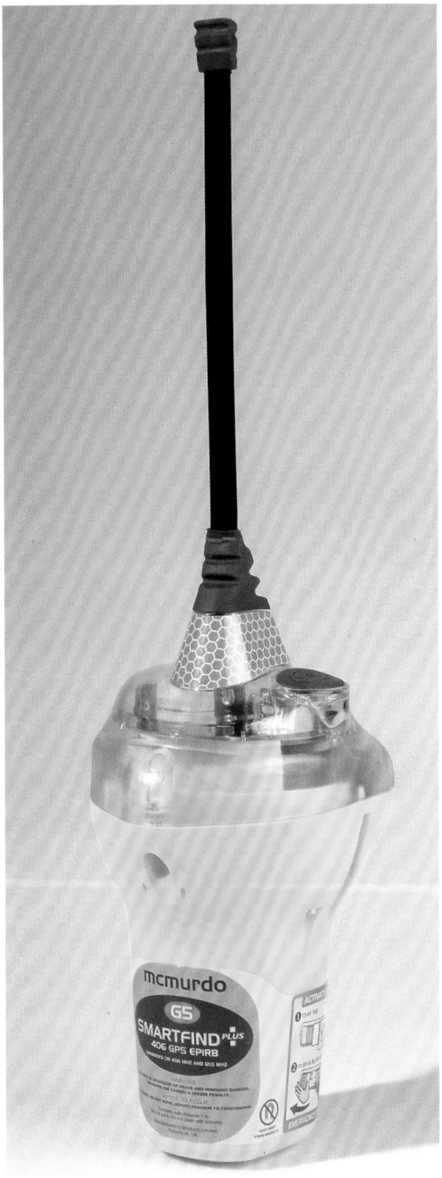

Most EPIRBs are now fitted with GPS (Figure 17.5) which makes it simple for rescuers to be given a position to within 100m by the mission control centre. Older versions which use 121.5MHz as a homing frequency are now obsolete.

A hand-held personal locator beacon which uses 406MHz and GPS is now readily available and can be kept in the pocket of crew members in case they go overboard whilst offshore.

Registry

All 406MHz EPIRBs in the UK are registered with HM Coastguard at their national registry in Falmouth and it is now a legal requirement to register them. If the equipment is temporarily lent to someone else, Falmouth must be informed of the change so that they don't look for the wrong boat.

Fig 17.5 (left) The McMurdo 406MHz EPIRB is fitted with GPS.

Fig 17.6 (below) Hydrostatic release unit for EPIRB.

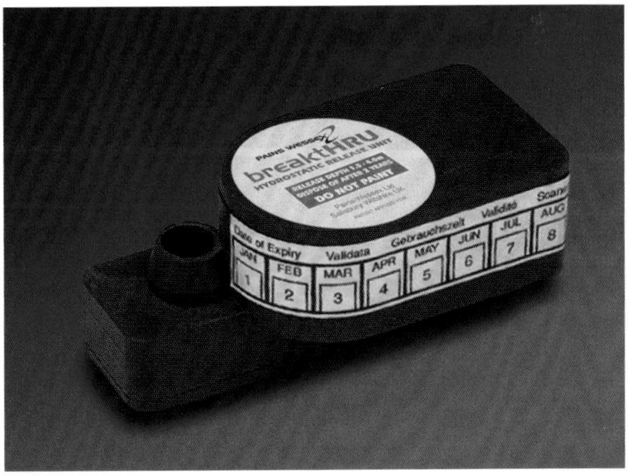

Fig 17.7 McMurdo personal location beacon.

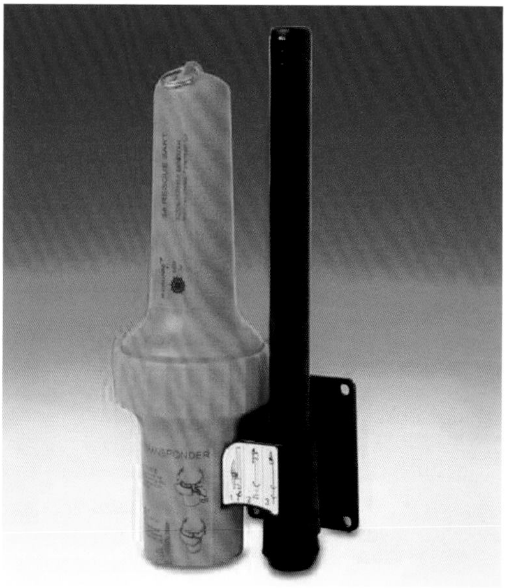

Fig 17.8 Search and Rescue (Radar) Transponder.

Accidental activation

If an EPIRB is accidentally activated, don't try to drown it or pretend it is not yours. It should be turned off to save its battery for any future activation and every attempt should be made to inform the nearest coastguard.

◆ Search and Rescue Transponder (SART)

The SART, which is shown in Figure 17.8, is used as a locating and homing device once the EPIRB has done its job. The SART is taken into the liferaft as the crew abandons ship and then attached to the raft by means of a telescopic pole, giving it a height of approximately 1 metre above sea level. Very similar to the Racon, it remains passive until it is triggered by a 3cm radar transmission.

The rescue craft's radar will show a line of dots on the casualty's bearing. As the casualty is closed, these dots change to arcs and then to concentric circles at about half a mile range. Figure 17.9 illustrates how the display changes as the rescue craft closes in on the casualty.

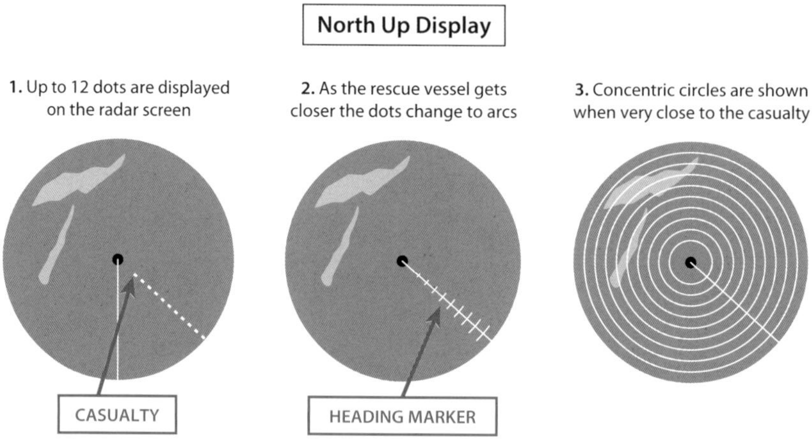

Fig 17.9 Typical display from a Search and Rescue Transponder.

Typical ranges are 30 miles from a rescue helicopter at 3,000 feet and 5 miles for a ship.

It is important that an inflatable radar reflector is not deployed with a SART, as this would block the radar beam.

◆ Navtex

Navtex is the part of the worldwide GMDSS that provides weather forecasts, navigational warnings and search information. The information, which is received automatically, can be displayed on a paper roll or as text, depending on equipment type; the one shown in Figure 17.10 uses a text display. Sets have a range of up to 400 miles and the more modern ones operate on the two medium frequencies, 518kHz and 490kHz so that both English and local language information can be received.

Navtex requires a dedicated antenna, which should be mounted low down to prevent reflection from the sea.

Fig 17.10 The McMurdo Smartfind GMDSS Navtex displays weather forecasts and navigational warnings as text.

◆ Inmarsat

Inmarsat is a satellite communications system, which also forms part of the GMDSS. The four geo-stationary satellites cover the area from 70°S to 70°N and are capable of relaying voice, telex, fax and data as well as sending weather forecasts and navigational warnings. Typified by the large white dome, it has proved invaluable for those venturing across oceans in relatively small craft. Inmarsat C restricts the user to text only.

QUESTION PAPER 17 – COMMUNICATIONS, GMDSS & DISTRESS

17.1 For which of the following should a distress alert be sent?

- **a** A person with a broken arm
- **b** A boat which has run aground and is pounding heavily in strong wind conditions
- **c** Another vessel, which appears to be on fire sighted

17.2 For what purpose would you use VHF Channel 67?

17.3 What action should you take if you inadvertently activate your EPIRB?

17.4 Would you expect the details of a new gale warning to be given on Channel 16 or a working channel?

17.5 What type of DSC alert would you send when relaying the distress message of another vessel?

Answers at the back of the book

18 ANTI-COLLISION RULES – the highway code

THE INTERNATIONAL REGULATIONS FOR PREVENTING COLLISIONS AT SEA are just what they say they are – global rules to limit the possibility of one ship hitting another.

Any aspiring Yachtmaster Offshore candidate **must** have a thorough knowledge of The Regulations and for this reason they have been printed in full in this chapter. Learning them by heart is probably unnecessary but every seafarer should be knowledgeable enough to abide by the spirit of the Rules, as there is little or no time to delve into the rulebook when confronted with lights, shapes and sound signals in a crowded commercial harbour.

Notes have been added at the end of each rule highlighting sections that are particularly significant to small power and sailing craft.

It is worth noting that:

Rules 4 to 10	Apply in any condition of visibility.
Rules 11 to 18	Are for vessels in sight of one another – when one can be observed visually from the other – not by radar alone.
Rule 19	Is for vessels who cannot observe each other visually but who may have been able to do so on radar only.

INTERNATIONAL REGULATIONS FOR PREVENTING COLLISIONS AT SEA

PART A: GENERAL

◆ Rule 1 Application

(a) These Rules shall apply to all vessels upon the high seas and in all waters connected therewith navigable by seagoing vessels.

(b) Nothing in these Rules shall interfere with the operation of special Rules made by an appropriate authority for roadsteads, harbours, rivers, lakes or inland waterways connected with the high seas and navigable by seagoing vessels. Such special Rules shall conform as closely as possible to these Rules.

(c) Nothing in these Rules shall interfere with the operation of any special Rules made by the Government of any State with respect to additional station or signal lights, shapes or whistle signals for ships of war and vessels proceeding under convoy, or with respect to additional station or signal lights or shapes for fishing vessels engaged in fishing as a fleet. These additional station or signal lights, shapes or whistle signals shall, so far as possible, be such that they cannot be mistaken for any light, shape or signal authorized elsewhere under these Rules.

(d) Traffic separation schemes may be adopted by the Organization for the purpose of these Rules.

(e) Whenever the Government concerned shall have determined that a vessel of special construction or purpose cannot comply fully with the provisions of any of these Rules with respect to the number, position, range or arc of visibility of lights or shapes, as well as to the disposition and characteristics of sound-signalling appliances, such a vessel shall comply with such other provisions in regard to the number, position, range or arc of visibility of lights or shapes, as well as to the disposition and characteristics of sound-signalling appliances, as her Government shall have determined to be the closest possible compliance with these Rules in respect of that vessel.

Notes to Rule 1

(a) *Although the Rules do not apply to landlocked lakes and reservoirs, most local authorities adopt them in by-laws.*
(b) *Inland waterway systems often have an additional or substitute set of rules and signals; European rivers such as the Rhine are good examples where CEVNI (Code Européen des Voies de la Navigation Intérieure) rules are adopted.*
(c) *The annual summary of* Admiralty Notices to Mariners *has details of any known changes for lighting convoys in time of war (or not lighting them would be more appropriate!)*
(d) *New traffic separation schemes are often introduced as a result of fuel tanker accidents. France and Spain have been particularly badly affected in the vicinity of major headlands. It is therefore vital that both electronic and paper charts are kept up to date so that ships in new schemes are not impeded.*
(e) *Warships, due to their construction, often cannot carry the prescribed lights. Submarines, for example, sometimes appear like small craft as the lights are carried close together on the sail and many conventional warships of over 50 metres in length are fitted with just one mast instead of two.*

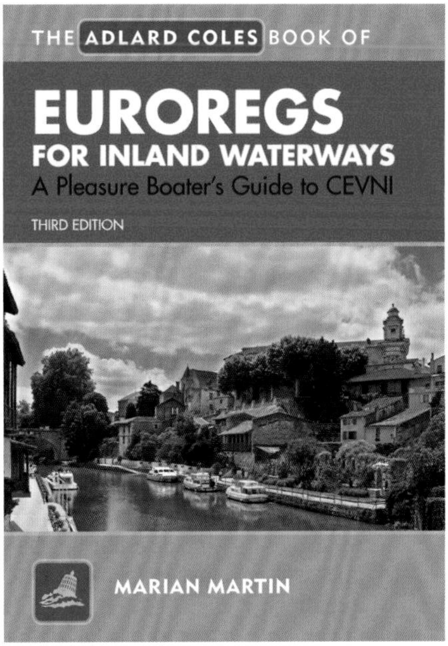

Fig 18.1 *The Adlard Coles book of Euroregs for Inland Waterways.*

◆ Rule 2 Responsibility

(a) Nothing in these Rules shall exonerate any vessel, or the owner, master or crew thereof, from the consequences of any neglect to comply with these Rules or of the neglect of any precaution, which may be required by the ordinary practice of seamen, or by the special circumstances of the case.
(b) In construing and complying with these Rules due regard shall be had to all dangers of navigation and collision and to any special circumstances, including the limitations of the vessels involved, which may make a departure from these Rules necessary to avoid immediate danger.

Notes to Rule 2

Obeying the Rules to the letter will not always prevent a collision; good seamanship and common sense may also be required under special circumstances even if it means departing from the Rules. Whatever the situation, it is the responsibility of all to avoid a close-quarters situation developing; the stand-on vessel cannot continue its course and speed regardless. It is useless to shake your fist at the transgressor screaming 'I had right of way' whilst your damaged boat sinks under you!

◆ Rule 3 General definitions

For the purpose of these Rules, except where the context otherwise requires:

(a) (a) The word 'vessel' includes every description of watercraft, including non-displacement craft, WIG craft and seaplanes, used or capable of being used as a means of transportation on water.

(b) The term 'power-driven vessel' means any vessel propelled by machinery.

(c) The term 'sailing vessel' means any vessel under sail provided that propelling machinery, if fitted, is not being used.

(d) The term 'vessel engaged in fishing' means any vessel fishing with nets, lines, trawls or other fishing apparatus which restrict manoeuvrability, but does not include a vessel fishing with trolling lines or other fishing apparatus which do not restrict manoeuvrability.

(e) The word 'seaplane' includes any aircraft designed to manoeuvre on the water.

(f) The term 'vessel not under command' means a vessel which through some exceptional circumstance is unable to manoeuvre as required by these Rules and is therefore unable to keep out of the way of another vessel.

(g) The term 'vessel restricted in her ability to manoeuvre' means a vessel which from the nature of her work is restricted in her ability to manoeuvre as required by these Rules and is therefore unable to keep out of the way of another vessel. The term 'vessels restricted in their ability to manoeuvre' shall include but not be limited to:
  - (i) a vessel engaged in laying, servicing or picking up a navigation mark, submarine cable or pipeline;
  - (ii) a vessel engaged in dredging, surveying or underwater operations;
  - (iii) a vessel engaged in replenishment or transferring persons, provisions or cargo while underway;
  - (iv) a vessel engaged in the launching or recovery of aircraft;
  - (v) a vessel engaged in mine-clearance operations;
  - (vi) a vessel engaged in a towing operation such as severely restricts the towing vessel and her tow in their ability to deviate from their course.

(h) The term 'vessel constrained by her draught' means a power-driven vessel which, because of her draught in relation to the available depth and width of navigable water, is severely restricted in her ability to deviate from the course she is following.

(i) The word 'underway' means that a vessel is not at anchor, or made fast to the shore, or aground.

(j) The words 'length' and 'breadth' of a vessel mean her length overall and greatest breadth.

(k) Vessels shall be deemed to be in sight of one another only when one can be observed visually from the other.

(l) The term 'restricted visibility' means any condition in which visibility is restricted by fog, mist, falling snow, heavy rain storms, sandstorms or any other similar causes.

(m) The term *Wing-In-Ground (WIG) craft* refers to a multimodal craft which, in its main operational mode, flies in close proximity to the surface by utilising surface-effect action.

Notes to Rule 3

(c) Sailing yacht skippers need to be aware that the boat becomes a power-driven vessel once the engine is running and in gear.

(d) Anglers fishing with rods from a vessel drifting with the tide in a main fairway cannot claim priority as a 'fishing vessel'.

(f) A 'vessel not under command' is not one where either the skipper is absent from his place of duty or the only person onboard is asleep!

(g) These are vessels which are restricted in their ability to manoeuvre because of their work. Once the job is complete they remove special shapes and revert to being a normal power-driven vessel.

(i) This part of Rule 3 is significant because vessels not under command, vessels restricted in their ability to manoeuvre and fishing vessels *extinguish their side lights, stern light and masthead light when they are under way but not making way through the water.*

PART B: STEERING AND SAILING RULES

SECTION I: CONDUCT OF VESSELS IN ANY CONDITION OF VISIBILITY

◆ Rule 4 Application

Rules in this Section apply in any condition of visibility.

◆ Rule 5 Look-out

Every vessel shall at all times maintain a proper look-out by sight and hearing as well as by all available means appropriate in the prevailing circumstances and conditions so as to make a full appraisal of the situation and of the risk of collision.

Notes to Rule 5

The requirement to keep a good look-out is paramount and Rule 5 is both short and concise; single-handed sailors who retire below decks to sleep are, to put it bluntly, breaking the Rules. Radar is also mentioned and, if fitted and operational, should be used.

Skippers should pay particular attention to blind arcs that can occur. Large deck-sweeping genoas, for instance, may mask another yacht approaching from leeward. In wet and windy weather the area to windward is also vulnerable when the crew are huddled into their jacket hoods, whereas facing into the wind would mean getting water down their necks.

Motor yachts have an even bigger problem in bad weather when the inside steering position is used. Superstructure can mask the view astern and this area is often cluttered with dinghies on davits. Engine noise and sound signals from an approaching ship may also not be heard behind closed wheelhouse doors.

Good night vision is vital if dim lights and hazards are to be spotted in darkness. A torch or cigarette lighter used carelessly can ruin night vision for up to half an hour.

◆ Rule 6 Safe speed

Every vessel shall at all times proceed at a 'safe speed' so that she can take proper and effective action to avoid collision and be stopped within a distance appropriate to the prevailing circumstances and conditions.

In determining a safe speed the following factors shall be among those taken into account:

(a) By all vessels:
- (i) the state of visibility;
- (ii) the traffic density including concentrations of fishing vessels or any other vessels;
- (iii) the manoeuvrability of the vessel with special reference to stopping distance and turning ability in the prevailing conditions;
- (iv) at night the presence of background light such as from shore lights or from back scatter of her own lights;
- (v) the state of wind, sea and current, and the proximity of navigational hazards;
- (vi) the draught in relation to the available depth of water.

(b) Additionally, by vessels with operational radar:
- (i) the characteristics, efficiency and limitations of the radar equipment;
- (ii) any constraints imposed by the radar range scale in use;
- (iii) the effect on radar detection of the sea state, weather and other sources of interference;
- (iv) the possibility that small vessels, ice and other floating objects may not be detected by radar at an adequate range;
- (v) the number, location and movement of vessels detected by radar;
- (vi) the more exact assessment of the visibility that may be possible when radar is used to determine the range of vessels or other objects in the vicinity.

Notes to Rule 6

It is difficult to quantify what is a safe speed as every situation is different. Generally an excess of speed has been the cause of many a collision. At night it can be difficult identifying an unfamiliar harbour entrance with its many confusing lights whereas a reduction in speed could give adequate time to resolve pilotage problems.

The planing motor cruiser whose wash swamps and capsizes a small dinghy is obviously going too fast, as is a sailing yacht romping into a crowded harbour with large spinnaker set.

However, on rare occasions, it may be necessary to speed up to ensure safety. A yacht bobbing around in the middle of a traffic separation lane at minimum speed would undoubtedly be safer if the engine were started enabling it to clear the lane more quickly.

◆ Rule 7 Risk of collision

(a) Every vessel shall use all means appropriate to the prevailing circumstances and conditions to determine if a risk of collision exists. If there is any doubt such risk shall be deemed to exist.

(b) Proper use shall be made of radar equipment if fitted and operational, including long-range scanning to obtain early warning of risk of collision and radar plotting or equivalent systematic observation of detected objects.

(c) Assumptions shall not be made on the basis of scanty information, especially scanty radar information.

(d) In determining if risk of collision exists the following considerations shall be among those taken into account:

- (i) such risk shall be deemed to exist if the compass bearing of an approaching vessel does not appreciably change;
- (ii) such risk may sometimes exist even when an appreciable bearing change is evident, particularly when approaching a very large vessel or a tow or when approaching a vessel at close range.

Notes to Rule 7

The first part of this Rule emphasises the need for care when assessing whether there is a risk of collision. It stresses that decisions should not be made from scanty information, particularly that gained from radar. If there is doubt as to whether a risk of collision exists then it must be assumed that a risk does exist. *The last two sentences explain how to assess the risk.*

Figure 18.2 shows two ships converging where the compass bearing doesn't alter, with the inevitable result – a collision. Fast merchant ships can cover up to five miles in ten minutes so it is important to take compass bearings at about one minute intervals to see whether the bearing changes. It is wise to take a bearing towards the stern of a large ship if you are hoping to pass astern of her.

As long as a steady course is held, it is possible to make a quick check for a steady bearing situation by lining up the closing ship with a stanchion or something similar and the experienced can often make a judgement by eye. However, never rely completely on this method – a compass bearing is the answer.

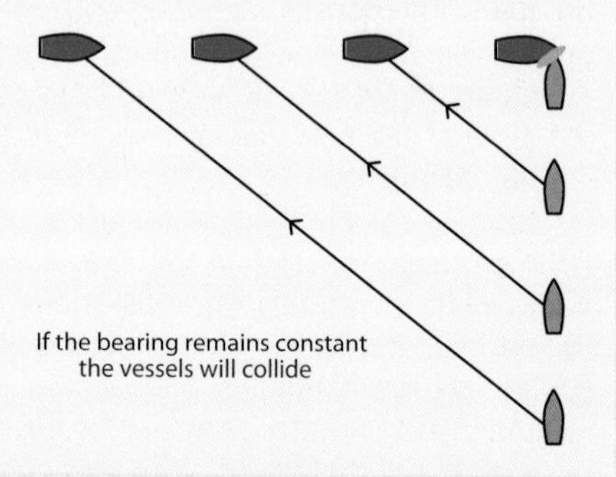
If the bearing remains constant
the vessels will collide

Fig 18.2 A hand bearing compass should be used to take bearings of the other vessel to determine whether a risk of collision exists.

◆ Rule 8 Action to avoid collision

(a) Any action taken to avoid collision shall, if the circumstances of the case admit, be positive, made in ample time and with due regard to the observance of good seamanship.

(b) Any alteration of course and/or speed to avoid collision shall, if the circumstances of the case admit, be large enough to be readily apparent to another vessel observing visually or by radar; a succession of small alterations of course and/or speed should be avoided.

(c) If there is sufficient sea room, alteration of course alone may be the most effective action to avoid a close-quarters situation provided that it is made in good time, is substantial and does not result in another close-quarters situation.

(d) Action taken to avoid collision with another vessel shall be such as to result in passing at a safe distance. The effectiveness of the action shall be carefully checked until the other vessel is finally past and clear.

(e) If necessary to avoid collision or allow more time to assess the situation, a vessel shall slacken her speed or take all way off by stopping or reversing her means of propulsion.

(f) (i) A vessel which, by any of these Rules, is required not to impede the passage or safe passage of another vessel shall, when required by the circumstances of the case, take early action to allow sufficient sea room for the safe passage of the other vessel.

(ii) A vessel required not to impede the passage or safe passage of another vessel is not relieved of this obligation if approaching the other vessel so as to involve risk of collision and shall, when taking action, have full regard to the action which may be required by the Rules of this part.

(iii) A vessel the passage of which is not to be impeded remains fully obliged to comply with the Rules of this part when the two vessels are approaching one another so as to involve risk of collision.

Notes to Rule 8

Paragraph (a) of this Rule is almost a summary of the rest. Avoiding action should be taken early; not at the last minute. It should be clearly obvious to the other ship and above all it should be sensible and seamanlike – it should not create a new danger with another vessel.

At night the best way to show another vessel that you have changed course is to show him a different aspect of your boat: a different-coloured navigation light.

◆ Rule 9 Narrow channels

(a) A vessel proceeding along the course of a narrow channel or fairway shall keep as near to the outer limit of the channel or fairway which lies on her starboard side as is safe and practicable.

(b) A vessel of less than 20 metres in length or a sailing vessel shall not impede the passage of a vessel which can safely navigate only within a narrow channel or fairway.

(c) A vessel engaged in fishing shall not impede the passage of any other vessel navigating within a narrow channel or fairway.

(d) A vessel shall not cross a narrow channel or fairway if such crossing impedes the passage of a vessel which can safely navigate only within such channel or fairway. The latter vessel may use the sound signal prescribed in Rule 34 (d) if in doubt as to the intention of the crossing vessel.

(e) (i) In a narrow channel or fairway when overtaking can take place only if the vessel to be overtaken has to take action to permit safe passing, the vessel intending to overtake shall indicate her intention by sounding the appropriate signal prescribed in Rule 34 (c) (i). The vessel to be overtaken shall, if in agreement, sound the appropriate signal prescribed in Rule 34(c) (ii) and take steps to permit safe passing. If in doubt she may sound the signals, prescribed in Rule 34 (d).

(ii) This Rule does not relieve the overtaking vessel of her obligation under Rule 13.

(f) A vessel nearing a bend or an area of a narrow channel or fairway where other vessels may be obscured by an intervening obstruction shall navigate with particular alertness and caution and shall sound the appropriate signal prescribed in Rule 34 (e).
(g) Any vessel shall, if the circumstances of the case admit, avoid anchoring in a narrow channel.

Notes to Rule 9

As no definition of a 'narrow channel' is given, the appropriate action depends on the type and size of vessel using the channel.

Generally speaking, there is usually enough depth for a motor cruiser or sailing yacht to navigate outside a buoyed channel used by deep draught vessels. The onus is on vessels of under 20 metres and sailing vessels to keep out of the way.

◆ Rule 10 Traffic separation schemes

(a) This Rule applies to traffic separation schemes adopted by the Organisation and does not relieve any vessel of her obligation under any other Rule.
(b) A vessel using a traffic separation scheme shall:
 (i) proceed in the appropriate traffic lane in the general direction of traffic flow for that lane;
 (ii) so far as practicable keep clear of a traffic separation line or separation zone;
 (iii) normally join or leave a traffic lane at the termination of the lane, but when joining or leaving from either side shall do so at as small an angle to the general direction of traffic flow as practicable.
(c) A vessel shall, so far as practicable, avoid crossing traffic lanes but if obliged to do so shall cross on a heading as nearly as practicable at right angles to the general direction of traffic flow.
(d) (i) A vessel shall not use an inshore traffic zone when she can safely use the appropriate traffic lane within the adjacent traffic separation scheme. However, vessels of less than 20 metres in length, sailing vessels and vessels engaged in fishing may use the inshore traffic zone.
 (ii) Notwithstanding subparagraph (d) (i), a vessel may use an inshore traffic zone to or from a port, offshore installation or structure, pilot station or any other place situated within the inshore traffic zone or to avoid immediate danger.
(e) A vessel other than a crossing vessel or a vessel joining or leaving a lane shall not normally enter a separation zone or cross a separation line except:
 (i) in cases of emergency to avoid immediate danger;
 (ii) to engage in fishing within a separation zone.
(f) A vessel navigating in areas near the terminations of traffic separation schemes shall do so with particular caution.
(g) A vessel shall so far as practicable avoid anchoring in a traffic separation scheme or in areas near its terminations.
(h) A vessel not using a traffic separation scheme shall avoid it by as wide a margin as practicable.
(i) A vessel engaged in fishing shall not impede the passage of any vessel following a traffic lane.
(j) A vessel of less than 20 metres in length or a sailing vessel shall not impede the safe passage of a power-driven vessel following a traffic lane.
(k) A vessel restricted in her ability to manoeuvre when engaged in an operation for the maintenance of safety of navigation in a traffic separation scheme is exempted from complying with this Rule to the extent necessary to carry out the operation.
(l) A vessel restricted in her ability to manoeuvre when engaged in an operation for the laying, servicing or picking up of a submarine cable, within a traffic separation scheme, is exempted from complying with this Rule to the extent necessary to carry out the operation.

Notes to Rule 10

Traffic separation schemes were designed to keep large ships away from each other in areas of heavy converging traffic – definitely not the place for small craft to linger.

Paragraph (c) advises that craft shall not cross a separation scheme unless absolutely necessary, but if forced to, must cross as quickly as possible. This can be most easily achieved with a right-angled heading which not only presents a square-on aspect to ships within the lane, it speeds up the crossing as shown in Figure 18.3.

Although the rules do not prohibit a yacht from sailing across the lanes, in light airs it is probably best to start the engine and motor across.

Vessel A *is crossing correctly with the heading at 90° to the lane.*

Vessel B *has turned into the tidal stream to track at 90°. He takes longer to cross the lane and presents a quarter aspect to the traffic flow.*

Sailing yachts and motor cruisers under 20m cannot expect ships within the lane to give way and Rule 10 (j) is specific on this point.

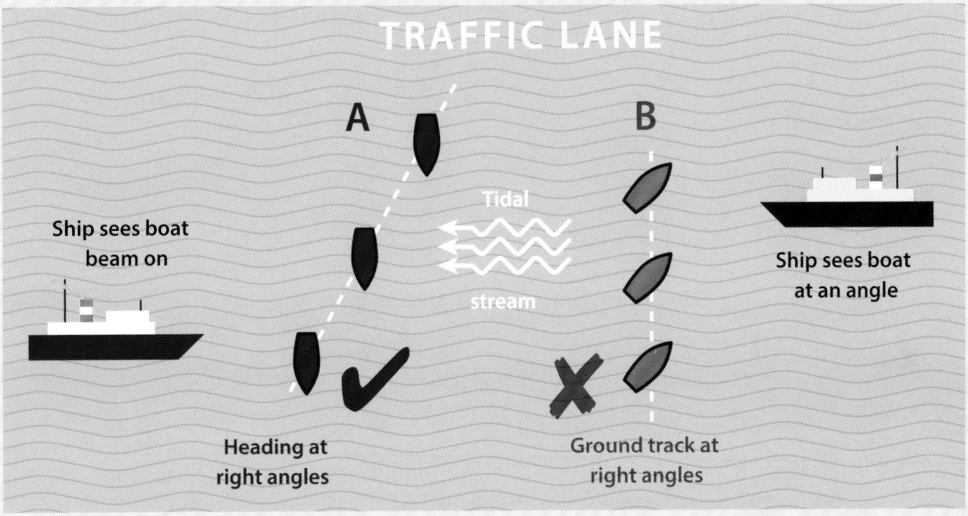

Fig 18.3 Vessel A is crossing the lane correctly as she is showing a beam aspect to the traffic in the lane.

SECTION II: CONDUCT OF VESSELS IN SIGHT OF ONE ANOTHER

◆ Rule 11 Application

Rules in this Section apply to vessels in sight of one another.

◆ Rule 12 Sailing vessels

(a) When two sailing vessels are approaching one another, so as to involve risk of collision, one of them shall keep out of the way of the other as follows:
  - (i) when each has the wind on a different side, the vessel which has the wind on the port side shall keep out of the way of the other;
  - (ii) when both have the wind on the same side, the vessel which is to windward shall keep out of the way of the vessel which is to leeward;
  - (iii) if a vessel with the wind on the port side sees a vessel to windward and cannot determine with certainty whether the other vessel has the wind on the port or the starboard side, she shall keep out of the way of the other.

(b) For the purposes of this Rule the windward side shall be deemed to be the side opposite that on which the mainsail is carried or, in the case of a square-rigged vessel, the side opposite to that on which the largest fore-and-aft sail is carried.

Notes to Rule 12

(a) (i)

Yacht A has the wind on the port side and is therefore the give-way vessel. She eases sheets and bears away to pass astern of Yacht B (Figure 18.4).

(a) (ii)

In Figure 18.5, both yachts have the wind on the port side. Yacht A is the windward boat so gives way to Yacht B by bearing away to pass astern.

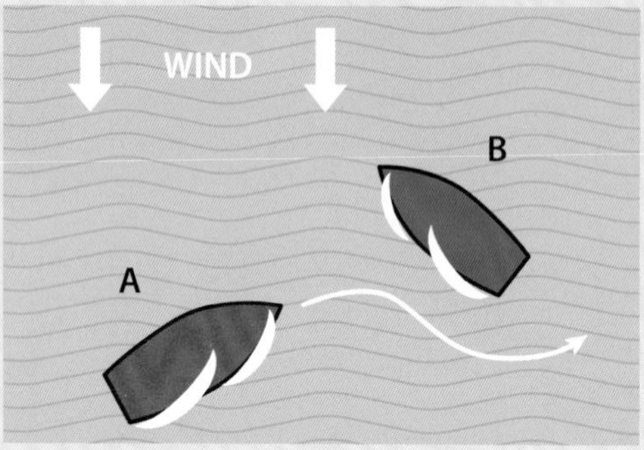

Fig 18.4 Yacht A has the wind on port side so gives way to Yacht B.

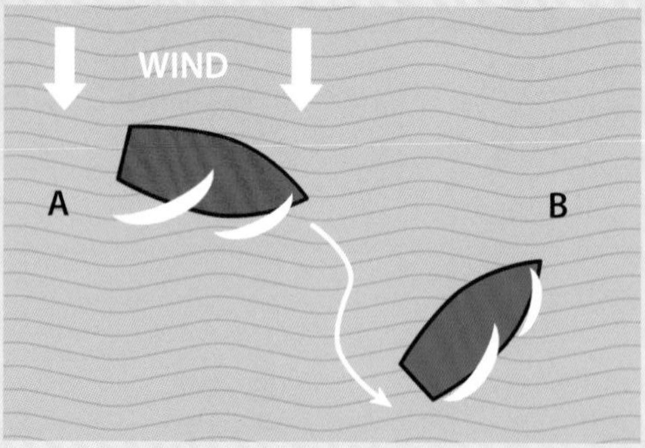

Fig 18.5 Yacht A is the windward boat and therefore gives way to Yacht B.

◆ Rule 13 Overtaking

(a) Notwithstanding anything contained in the Rules of Part B, Sections I and II any vessel overtaking any other shall keep out of the way of the vessel being overtaken.
(b) A vessel shall be deemed to be overtaking when coming up with another vessel from a direction more than 22.5 degrees abaft her beam, that is, in such a position with reference to the vessel she is overtaking, that at night she would be able to see only the stern light of that vessel but neither of her sidelights.
(c) When a vessel is in any doubt as to whether she is overtaking another, she shall assume that this is the case and act accordingly.
(d) Any subsequent alteration of the bearing between the two vessels shall not make the overtaking vessel a crossing vessel within the meaning of these Rules or relieve her of the duty of keeping clear of the overtaken vessel until she is finally past and clear.

Notes to Rule 13

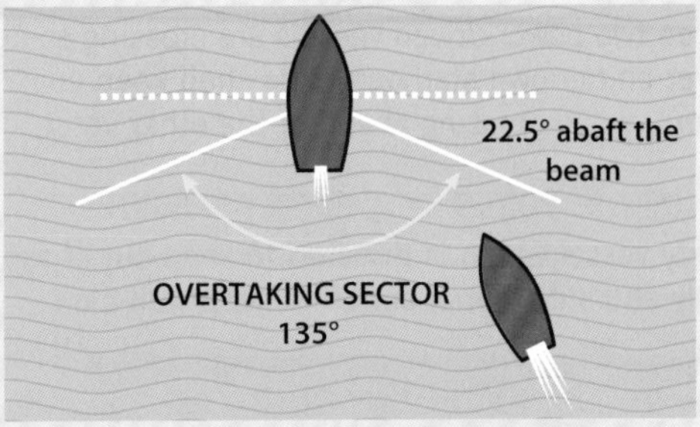

Fig 18.6 The overtaking arc covers an angle of 135° at the stern.

Rule 13 over-rides all the other steering and sailing rules and applies equally to both power and sail. Even a vessel 'not under command' or one 'restricted in its ability to manoeuvre' loses priority when overtaking another craft.

In (b) the overtaking sector which covers an angle of 135° is illustrated in Figure 18.6. This is the angle covered by the sternlight.

Part (d) of Rule 13 lays down that a vessel shall remain the overtaking vessel until it is completely clear of the one being overtaken. Many years ago a spectacular collision happened south of the Isle of Wight when a very large crude oil carrier crossed the bows of a smaller tanker it had overtaken. The resultant fire burned for many days.

As a courtesy, power vessels should, if possible, overtake a sailing yacht on its leeward side to avoid taking its wind.

◆ Rule 14 Head-on situation

(a) When two power-driven vessels are meeting on reciprocal or nearly reciprocal courses so as to involve risk of collision each shall alter her course to starboard so that each shall pass on the port side of the other.

(b) Such a situation shall be deemed to exist when a vessel sees the other ahead or nearly ahead and by night she could see the masthead lights of the other in a line or nearly in a line and/or both sidelights and by day she observes the corresponding aspect of the other vessel.

(c) When a vessel is in any doubt as to whether such a situation exists she shall assume that it does exist and act accordingly.

Notes to Rule 14

This Rule should not really cause many problems but in reality it is not uncommon to see boats altering the wrong way in the hope of avoiding trouble.

It is the phrase 'nearly reciprocal courses' in paragraph (a) that gives trouble.

Figure 18.7 gives an example of a classic situation when confusion and chaos could occur if the wrong decision were made.

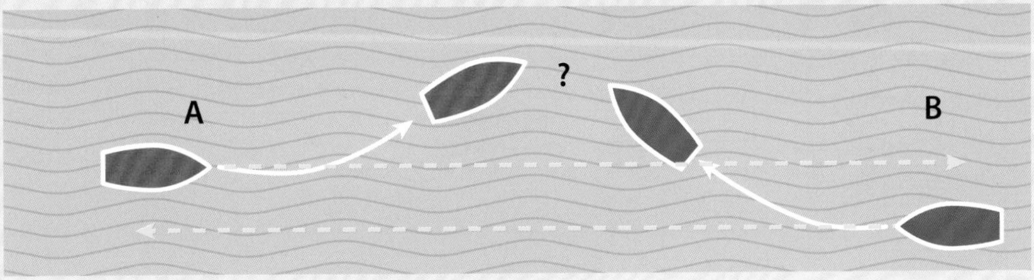

Fig 18.7 Vessel A should have turned to starboard to avoid a collision.

◆ Rule 15 Crossing situation

When two power-driven vessels are crossing so as to involve risk of collision, the vessel which has the other on her own starboard side shall keep out of the way and shall, if the circumstances of the case admit, avoid crossing ahead of the other vessel.

◆ Rule 16 Action by give-way vessel

Every vessel which is directed to keep out of the way of another vessel shall, so far as possible, take early and substantial action to keep well clear.

Note to Rule 16

This Rule is simply a repeat of Rule 8 – stressing the importance of this Rule and the requirement to take early and positive action to avoid a collision.

◆ Rule 17 Action by stand-on vessel

(a) (i) Where one of two vessels is to keep out of the way the other shall keep her course and speed.
   (ii) The latter vessel may however take action to avoid collision by her manoeuvre alone, as soon as it becomes apparent to her that the vessel required to keep out of the way is not taking appropriate action in compliance with these Rules.

(b) When, from any cause, the vessel required to keep her course and speed finds herself so close that collision cannot be avoided by the action of the give-way vessel alone, she shall take such action as will best aid to avoid collision.

(c) A power-driven vessel which takes action in a crossing situation in accordance with sub-paragraph (a) (ii) of this Rule to avoid collision with another power driven vessel shall, if the circumstances of the case admit, not alter course to port for a vessel on her own port side.

(d) This Rule does not relieve the give-way vessel of her obligation to keep out of the way.

Notes to Rule 17

Small craft find difficulty with this Rule particularly at night when offshore in an area thick with merchant ships. There is always nagging doubt as to whether the watch keepers on the merchant ship have seen such a small boat over the wave tops or whether the automatic radar alarm has been triggered on the ship.

The Rule allows the stand-on vessel to take action instead of resolutely standing into danger; for peace of mind it is wise to follow advice and take early action.

Getting too close to a ship such as the one shown in Figure 18.8 is foolhardy as the view forward of the bow is so severely restricted.

The Rule instructs stand-on vessels, who take avoiding action, not to turn to port towards a vessel on the port side and this is very sound advice; if the give-way vessel alters course late he will probably turn to starboard, so turning away from him means a turn into clear water.

Fig 18.8 This ship is heavily laden and will take a few miles to stop. The officer on the bridge will be unable to see traffic up to a mile ahead because his view is restricted by the containers.

◆ Rule 18 Responsibilities between vessels

Except where Rules 9, 10 and 13 otherwise require:

(a) A power-driven vessel underway shall keep out of the way of:
  (i) a vessel not under command;
  (ii) a vessel restricted in her ability to manoeuvre;
  (iii) a vessel engaged in fishing;
  (iv) a sailing vessel.

(b) A sailing vessel underway shall keep out of the way of:
  (i) a vessel not under command;
  (ii) a vessel restricted in her ability to manoeuvre;
  (iii) a vessel engaged in fishing.

(c) A vessel engaged in fishing when underway shall, so far as possible, keep out of the way of:
  (i) a vessel not under command;
  (ii) a vessel restricted in her ability to manoeuvre.

(d) (i) Any vessel other than a vessel not under command or a vessel restricted in her ability to manoeuvre shall, if the circumstances of the case admit, avoid impeding the safe passage of a vessel constrained by her draught, exhibiting the signals in Rule 28.
  (ii) A vessel constrained by her draught shall navigate with particular caution having full regard to her special condition.

(e) A seaplane on the water shall, in general, keep well clear of all vessels and avoid impeding their navigation. In circumstances, however, where risk of collision exists, she shall comply with the Rules of this part.

(f) (i) A WIG craft, when taking off, landing and in flight near the surface, shall keep well clear of all other vessels and avoid impeding their navigation.
  (ii) A WIG craft operating on the water surface shall comply with the Rules of this part as a power driven vessel.

SECTION III: CONDUCT OF VESSELS IN RESTRICTED VISIBILITY

◆ Rule 19 Conduct of vessels in restricted visibility

(a) This Rule applies to vessels not in sight of one another when navigating in or near an area of restricted visibility.

(b) Every vessel shall proceed at a safe speed adapted to the prevailing circumstances and conditions of restricted visibility. A power-driven vessel shall have her engines ready for immediate manoeuvre.

(c) Every vessel shall have due regard to the prevailing circumstances and conditions of restricted visibility when complying with the Rules of Section I of this Part.

(d) A vessel which detects by radar alone the presence of another vessel shall determine if a close-quarters situation is developing and/or risk of collision exists. If so, she shall take avoiding action in ample time, provided that when such action consists of an alteration of course, so far as possible the following shall be avoided:
  (i) an alteration of course to port for a vessel forward of the beam, other than for a vessel being overtaken;
  (ii) an alteration of course towards a vessel abeam or abaft the beam.

(e) Except where it has been determined that a risk of collision does not exist, every vessel which hears apparently forward of her beam the fog signal of another vessel, or which cannot avoid a close-quarters situation with another vessel forward of her beam, shall reduce her speed to the minimum at which she can be kept on her course. She shall if necessary take all her way off and in any event navigate with extreme caution until danger of collision is over.

Notes to Rule 19

Remember that all previous manoeuvring rules are for vessels in sight of one another but this one assumes that there is no visual contact other than by radar.

More and more small boats are now fitting radar, but it does require training to use it efficiently. Many a radar-assisted collision has happened because the crew could not calculate the true course and speed of a close radar contact.

Rule 19 requires a vessel to slow down or stop if a fog signal is heard forward of the beam and to have an engine ready for urgent manoeuvres.

Lastly, Rule (d) (i) tells vessels to avoid turning towards a vessel on, or aft of, the beam.

PART C: LIGHTS AND SHAPES

◆ Rule 20 Application

(a) Rules in this Part shall be complied with in all weathers.
(b) The Rules concerning lights shall be complied with from sunset to sunrise, and during such times no other lights shall be exhibited, except such lights as cannot be mistaken for the lights specified in these Rules or do not impair their visibility or distinctive character, or interfere with the keeping of a proper look-out.
(c) The lights prescribed by these Rules shall, if carried, also be exhibited from sunrise to sunset in restricted visibility and may be exhibited in all other circumstances when it is deemed necessary.
(d) The Rules concerning shapes shall be complied with by day.
(e) The lights and shapes specified in these Rules shall comply with the provisions of Annex I to these Regulations.

◆ Rule 21 Definitions

(a) 'Masthead light' means a white light placed over the fore and aft centreline of the vessel showing an unbroken light over an arc of the horizon of 225 degrees and so fixed as to show the light from right ahead to 22.5 degrees abaft the beam on either side of the vessel.
(b) 'Sidelights' means a green light on the starboard side and a red light on the port side each showing an unbroken light over an arc of the horizon of 112.5 degrees and so fixed as to show the light from right ahead to 22.5 degrees abaft the beam on its respective side. In a vessel of less than 20m in length sidelights may be combined in one lantern carried on the fore and aft centreline of the vessel.
(c) 'Sternlight' means a white light placed as nearly as practicable at the stern showing an unbroken light over an arc of the horizon of 135 degrees and so fixed as to show the light 67.5 degrees from right aft on each side of the vessel.
(d) 'Towing light' means a yellow light having the same characteristics as the 'sternlight' defined in paragraph (c) of this Rule.
(e) 'All round light' means a light showing an unbroken light over an arc of the horizon of 360 degrees.
(f) 'Flashing light' means a light flashing at regular intervals at a frequency of 120 flashes or more per minute.

◆ Rule 22 Visibility of lights

The lights prescribed in these Rules shall have an intensity as specified in Section 8 of Annex I to these Regulations so as to be visible at the following minimum ranges:
(a) In vessels of 50 metres or more in length:
- a masthead light, 6 miles;
- a sidelight, 3 miles;
- a sternlight, 3 miles;

- a towing light, 3 miles;
- a white, red, green or yellow all-round light, 3 miles.

(b) In vessels of 12 metres or more in length but less than 50 metres in length:
- masthead light, 5 miles;
- except that where the length of the vessel is less than 20 metres, 3 miles;
- a sidelight, 2 miles;
- a sternlight, 2 miles;
- a towing light, 2 miles;
- a white, red, green or yellow all-round light, 2 miles.

(c) In vessels of less than 12 metres in length:
- a masthead light, 2 miles;
- a sidelight, 1 mile;
- a sternlight, 2 miles;
- a towing light, 2 miles.

(d) In inconspicuous, partly submerged vessels or objects being towed:
- a white all-round light, 3 miles.

◆ Rule 23 Power-driven vessels underway

(a) A power-driven vessel underway shall exhibit:
  (i) a masthead light forward;
  (ii) a second masthead light abaft of and higher than the forward one; except that a vessel of less than 50 metres in length shall not be obliged to exhibit such light but may do so;
  (iii) sidelights;
  (iv) a sternlight.

(b) An air-cushion vessel when operating in the non-displacement mode shall, in addition to the lights prescribed in paragraph (a) of this Rule, exhibit an all-round flashing yellow light.

(c) A WIG craft only when taking off, landing and in flight near the surface shall, in addition to the lights prescribed in paragraph (a) of this rule, exhibit a high-intensity all-round flashing red light.

(d) (i) A power-driven vessel of less than 12 metres in length may in lieu of the lights prescribed in paragraph (a) of this Rule exhibit an all-round white light and sidelights;
  (ii) a power-driven vessel of less than 7 metres in length whose maximum speed does not exceed 7 knots may in lieu of the lights prescribed in paragraph (a) of this Rule exhibit an all-round white light and shall, if practicable, also exhibit sidelights;
  (iii) the masthead light or all-round white light on a power-driven vessel of less than 12 metres in length may be displaced from the fore and aft centreline of the vessel if centreline fitting is not practicable, provided that the sidelights are combined in one lantern which shall be carried on the fore and aft centreline of the vessel or located as nearly as practicable in the same fore and aft line as the masthead light or the all-round white light.

Note to Rule 23

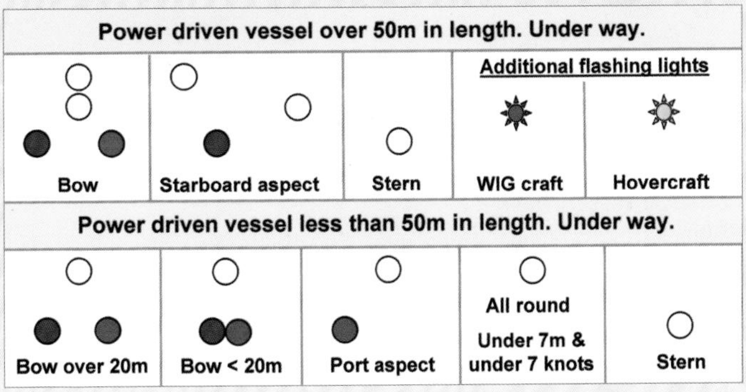

Fig 18.9 Rule 23. Lights for power driven vessels.

◆ Rule 24 Towing and pushing

(a) A power-driven vessel when towing shall exhibit:
  (i) instead of the light prescribed in Rule 23 (a) (i) or (a) (ii), two masthead lights forward in a vertical line. When the length of the tow, measuring from the stern of the towing vessel to the after end of the tow exceeds 200 metres, three such lights in a vertical line;
  (ii) sidelights;
  (iii) a sternlight;
  (iv) a towing light in a vertical line above the sternlight;
  (v) when the length of the tow exceeds 200 metres, a diamond shape where it can best be seen.

(b) When a pushing vessel and a vessel being pushed ahead are rigidly connected in a composite unit they shall be regarded as a power-driven vessel and exhibit the lights prescribed in Rule 23.

(c) A power-driven vessel when pushing ahead or towing alongside, except in the case of a composite unit shall exhibit:
  (i) instead of the light prescribed in Rule 23 (a) (i) or (a) (ii), two masthead lights forward in a vertical line;
  (ii) sidelights;
  (iii) a sternlight.

(d) A power-driven vessel to which paragraphs (a) or (c) of this Rule apply shall also comply with Rule 23 (a) (ii).

(e) A vessel or object being towed, other than those mentioned in paragraph (g) of this Rule, shall exhibit:
  (i) sidelights;
  (ii) a sternlight;
  (iii) when the length of the tow exceeds 200 metres, a diamond shape where it can best be seen.

(f) Provided that any number of vessels being towed alongside or pushed in a group shall be lighted as one vessel,
  (i) a vessel being pushed ahead, not being part of a composite unit, shall exhibit at the forward end, sidelights;
  (ii) a vessel being towed alongside shall exhibit a sternlight and at the forward end, sidelights.

(g) An inconspicuous, partly submerged vessel or object, or combination of such vessels or objects being towed, shall exhibit:
  (i) if it is less than 25 metres in breadth, one all-round white light at or near the forward end and one at or near the after end except that dracones need not exhibit a light at or near the forward end;
  (ii) if it is 25 metres or more in breadth, two additional all-round white lights at or near the extremities of its breadth;
  (iii) if it exceeds 100 metres in length, additional all-round white lights between the lights prescribed in sub paragraphs (i) and (ii) so that the distance between the lights shall not exceed 100 metres;
  (iv) a diamond shape at or near the aftermost extremity of the last vessel or object being towed and if the length of the tow exceeds 200 metres an additional diamond shape where it can best be seen and located as far forward as is practicable.

(h) Where from any sufficient cause it is impracticable for a vessel or object being towed to exhibit the lights or shapes prescribed in paragraph (e) or (g) of this Rule, all possible measures shall be taken to light the vessel or object towed or at least to indicate the presence of such vessel or object.

(i) Where from any sufficient cause it is impracticable for a vessel not normally engaged in towing operations to display the lights prescribed in paragraph (a) or (c) of this Rule, such vessel shall not be required to exhibit those lights when engaged in towing another vessel in distress or otherwise in need of assistance. All possible measures shall be taken to indicate the nature of the relationship between the towing vessel and the vessel being towed as authorized by Rule 36, in particular by illuminating the towline.

Note to Rule 24

Key: < = less than
> = more than

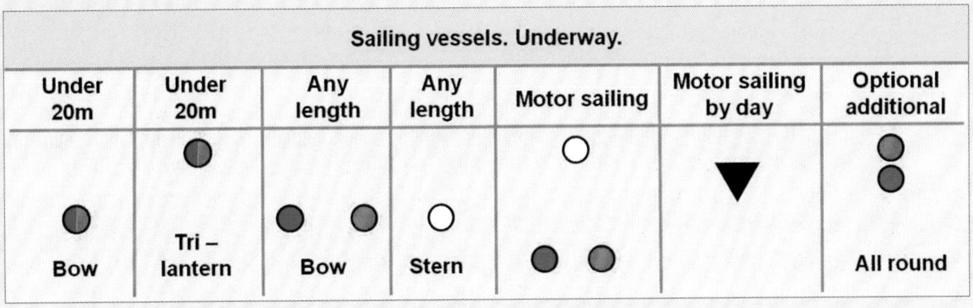

Fig 18.10 Rule 24. Lights and shapes for towing vessels.

◆ Rule 25 Sailing vessels underway and vessels under oars

(a) A sailing vessel underway shall exhibit:
  (i) sidelights;
  (ii) a sternlight.

(b) In a sailing vessel of less than 20 metres in length the lights prescribed in paragraph (a) of this Rule may be combined in one lantern carried at or near the top of the mast where it can best be seen.

(c) A sailing vessel underway may, in addition to the lights prescribed in paragraph (a) of this Rule, exhibit at or near the top of the mast, where they can best be seen, two all-round lights in a vertical line, the upper being red and the lower green, but these lights shall not be exhibited in conjunction with the combined lantern permitted by paragraph (b) of this Rule.

(d) (i) A sailing vessel of less than 7 metres in length shall, if practicable, exhibit the lights prescribed in paragraph (a) or (b) of this Rule, but if she does not, she shall have ready at hand an electric torch or lighted lantern showing a white light which shall be exhibited in sufficient time to prevent collision.
  (ii) A vessel under oars may exhibit the lights prescribed in this Rule for sailing vessels, but if shedoes not, she shall have ready at hand an electric torch or lighted lantern showing a white light which shall be exhibited in sufficient time to prevent collision.

(e) A vessel proceeding under sail when also being propelled by machinery shall exhibit forward where it can best be seen a conical shape, apex downwards.

Note to Rule 25

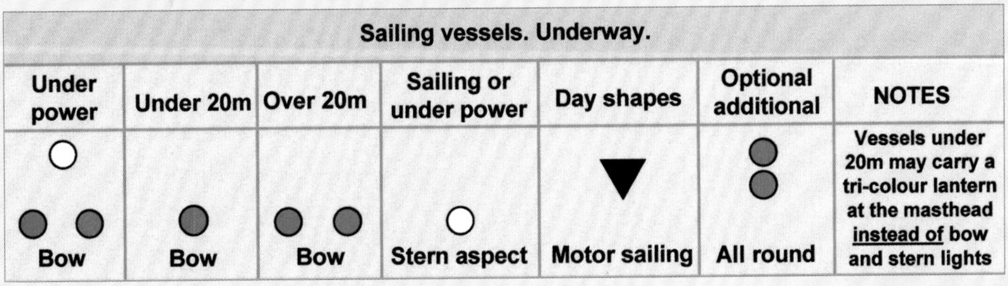

Fig 18.11 Rule 25. Lights and shapes for sailing vessels.

◆ Rule 26 Fishing vessels

(a) A vessel engaged in fishing, whether underway or at anchor, shall exhibit only the lights and shapes prescribed in this Rule.

(b) A vessel when engaged in trawling, by which is meant the dragging through the water of a dredge net or other apparatus used as a fishing appliance, shall exhibit:

- (i) two all-round lights in a vertical line, the upper being green and the lower white, or a shape consisting of two cones with their apexes together in a vertical line one above the other;
- (ii a masthead light abaft of and higher than the all-round green light; a vessel of less than 50 metres in length shall not be obliged to exhibit such a light but may do so;
- (iii) when making way through the water, in addition to the lights prescribed in this paragraph, sidelights and a stern light.

(c) A vessel engaged in fishing, other than trawling, shall exhibit:

- (i) two all-round lights in a vertical line, the upper being red and the lower white, or a shape consisting of two cones with apexes together in a vertical line one above the other;
- (ii) when there is outlying gear extending more than 150 metres horizontally from the vessel, an all-round white light or a cone apex upwards in the direction of the gear;
- (iii) when making way through the water, in addition to the lights prescribed in this paragraph, sidelights and a sternlight.

(d) The additional signals described inn Annex II to these regulations apply to a vessel engaged in fishing in close proximity to other vessels engaged in fishing.

(e) A vessel when not engaged in fishing shall not exhibit the lights or shapes prescribed in this Rule, but only those prescribed for a vessel of her length.

Note to Rule 26

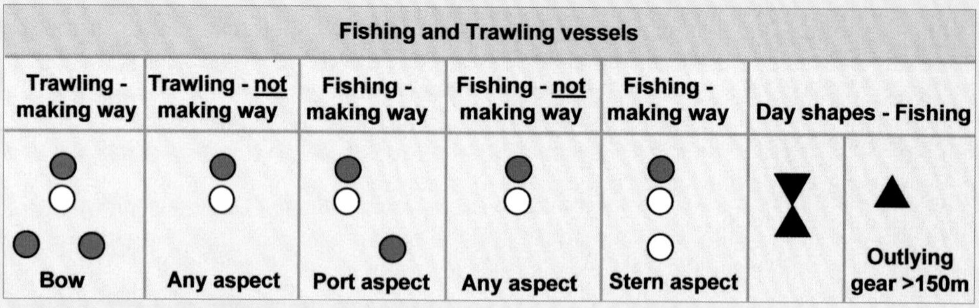
Fishing and Trawling vessels
Trawling - making way
Trawling - not making way
Fishing - making way
Fishing - not making way
Fishing - making way
Day shapes - Fishing
Bow
Any aspect
Port aspect
Any aspect
Stern aspect
Outlying gear >150m

Fig 18.12 Rule 26. Lights and shapes for fishing vessels.

◆ Rule 27 Vessels not under command or restricted in their ability to manoeuvre

(a) A vessel not under command shall exhibit:

- (i) two all-round red lights in a vertical line where they can best be seen;
- (ii) two balls or similar shapes in a vertical line where they can best be seen;
- (iii) when making way through the water, in addition to the lights prescribed in this paragraph, sidelights and a sternlight.

(b) A vessel restricted in her ability to manoeuvre, except a vessel engaged in mine clearance operations, shall exhibit:

- (i) three all-round lights in a vertical line where they can best be seen. The highest and lowest of these lights shall be red and the middle light shall be white;
- (ii) three shapes in a vertical line where they can best be seen. The highest and lowest of these shapes shall be balls and the middle one a diamond;

(iii) when making way through the water, a masthead light or lights, sidelights and a sternlight, in addition to the lights prescribed in sub-paragraph (i);
(iv) when at anchor, in addition to the lights or shapes prescribed in sub-paragraphs (i) and (ii), the light, lights or shape prescribed in Rule 30.

(c) A power-driven vessel engaged in a towing operation such as severely restricts the towing vessel and her tow in their ability to deviate from their course shall, in addition to the lights or shapes prescribed in Rule 24 (a), exhibit the lights or shapes prescribed in sub-paragraphs (b) (i) and (ii) of this Rule.

(d) A vessel engaged in dredging or underwater operations, when restricted in her ability to manoeuvre, shall exhibit the lights and shapes prescribed in subparagraph (b) (i), (ii) and (iii) of this Rule and shall in addition, when an obstruction exists, exhibit:
(i) two all-round red lights or two balls in a vertical line to indicate the side on which the obstruction exists;
(ii) two all-round green lights or two diamonds in a vertical line to indicate the side on which another vessel may pass;
(iii) when at anchor the lights or shapes prescribed in this paragraph instead of the lights or shape prescribed in Rule 30.

(e) Whenever the size of a vessel engaged in diving operations makes it impracticable to exhibit all lights and shapes prescribed in paragraph (d), of this Rule, the following shall be exhibited;
(i) three all-round lights in a vertical line where they can best be seen. The highest and lowest of these lights shall be red and the middle light shall be white;
(ii) a rigid replica of the International Code Flag 'A' not less than 1 metre in height. Measures shall be taken to ensure its all-round visibility.

(f) A vessel engaged in mine clearance operations shall in addition to the lights prescribed for a power-driven vessel in Rule 23 or to the lights or shape prescribed for a vessel at anchor in Rule 30 as appropriate, exhibit three all-round green lights or three balls. One of these lights or shapes shall be exhibited near the fore mast head and one at each end of the fore yard. These lights or shapes indicate that it is dangerous for another vessel to approach within 1000 metres of the mine clearance vessel.

(g) Vessels of less than 12 metres in length, except those engaged in diving operations, shall not be required to exhibit the lights and shapes prescribed in this Rule.

(h) The signals prescribed in this Rule are not signals of vessels in distress and requiring assistance. Such signals are contained in Annex IV to these Regulations.

Note to Rule 27

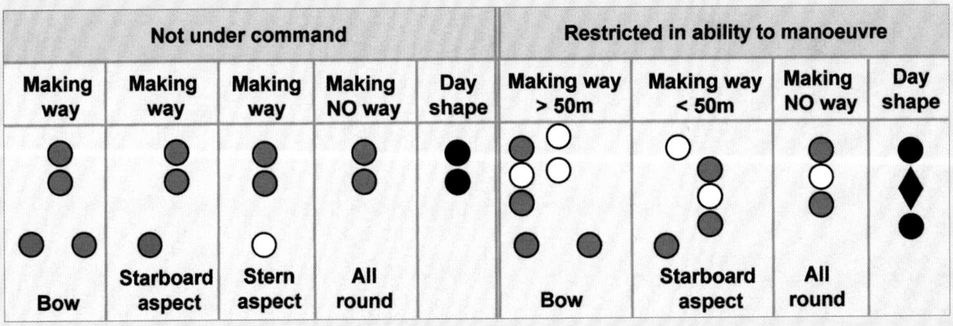
Not under command
Restricted in ability to manoeuvre
Making way
Making way
Making way
Making NO way
Day shape
Making way > 50m
Making way < 50m
Making NO way
Day shape
Bow
Starboard aspect
Stern aspect
All round
Bow
Starboard aspect
All round

Fig 18.13 Rule 27. Lights and shapes for Not Under Command and Restricted in Ability to Manoeuvre.

◆ Rule 28 Vessels constrained by their draught

A vessel constrained by her draught may, in addition to the lights prescribed for power-driven vessels in Rule 23, exhibit where they can best be seen three all-round red lights in a vertical line, or a cylinder.

Note to Rule 28

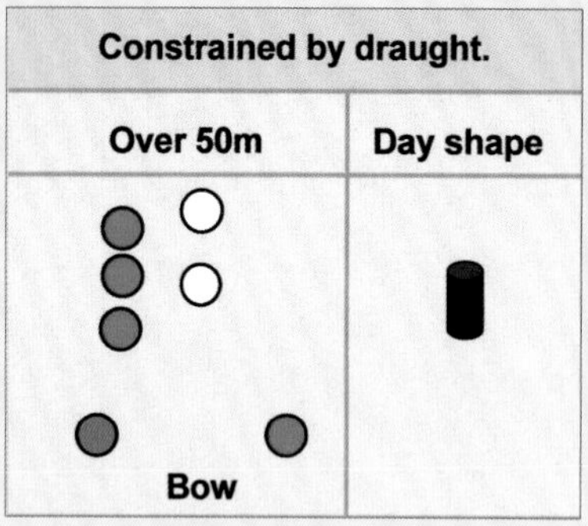

Fig 18.14 Rule 28. Lights and shapes for vessels constrained by their draught.

◆ Rule 29 Pilot vessels

(a) A vessel engaged on pilotage duty shall exhibit:
- (i) at or near the masthead, two all-round lights in a vertical line, the upper being white and the lower red;
- (ii) when underway, in addition, sidelights and a sternlight;
- (iii) when at anchor, in addition to the lights prescribed in sub-paragraph (i), the light, lights or shape prescribed in Rule 30 for vessels at anchor.

(b) A pilot vessel when not engaged on pilotage duty shall exhibit the lights or shapes prescribed for a similar vessel of her length.

Note to Rule 29

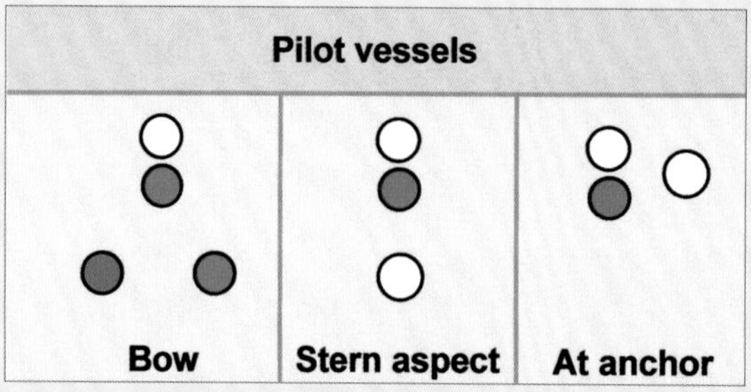

Fig 18.15 Rule 29. Lights for pilot vessels.

◆ Rule 30 Anchored vessels and vessels aground

(a) A vessel at anchor shall exhibit where it can best be seen:
   (i) in the fore part, an all-round white light or one ball;
   (ii) at or near the stern and at a lower level than the light prescribed in subparagraph (i), an all-round white light.

(b) A vessel of less than 50 metres in length may exhibit an all-round white light where it can best be seen instead of the lights prescribed in paragraph (a) of this Rule.

(c) A vessel at anchor may, and a vessel of 100 metres and more in length shall, also use the available working or equivalent lights to illuminate her decks.

(d) A vessel aground shall exhibit the lights prescribed in paragraph (a) or (b) of this Rule and in addition, where they can best be seen:
   (i) two all-round red lights in a vertical line;
   (ii) three balls in a vertical line.

(e) A vessel of less than 7 metres in length, when at anchor, not in or near a narrow channel, fairway or anchorage, or where other vessels normally navigate, shall not be required to exhibit the lights or shape prescribed in paragraphs (a) and (b) of this Rule.

(f) A vessel of less than 12 metres in length, when aground, shall not be required to exhibit the lights or shapes prescribed in sub-paragraphs (d) (i) and (ii) of this Rule.

Note to Rule 30

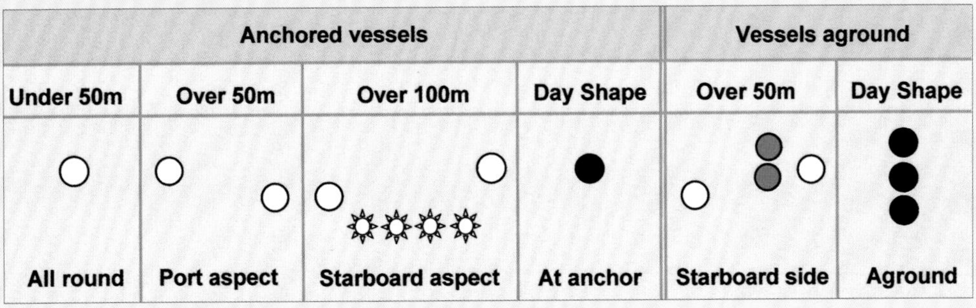
Anchored vessels
Vessels aground
Under 50m
Over 50m
Over 100m
Day Shape
Over 50m
Day Shape
All round
Port aspect
Starboard aspect
At anchor
Starboard side
Aground

Fig 18.16 Rule 30. Lights and shapes for anchored vessels and vessels aground.

◆ Rule 31 Seaplanes

Where it is impracticable for a seaplane or a WIG craft to exhibit lights and shapes of the characteristics or in the positions described in the Rules of this part, she shall exhibit lights and shapes as closely similar in characteristics and position as is possible.

PART D: SOUND AND LIGHT SIGNALS

◆ Rule 32 Definitions

(a) The word 'whistle' means any sound signalling appliance capable of producing the prescribed blasts and which complies with the specifications in Annex III to these Regulations.

(b) The term 'short blast' means a blast of about one second's duration.

(c) The term 'prolonged blast' means a blast of from four to six seconds' duration.

◆ Rule 33 Equipment for sound signals

(a) A vessel of 12m or more in length shall be provided with a whistle, a vessel of 20m or more in length shall be provided with a bell in addition to a whistle, and a vessel of 100m or more in length shall, in addition, be provided with a gong, the tone and sound of which cannot be confused with that of the bell. The whistle, bell and gong shall comply with the specifications in Annex III to these regulations. The bell or gong or both may be replaced by other equipment having the same respective sound characteristics, provided that manual sounding of the required signals shall always be possible.

(b) A vessel of less than 12 metres in length shall not be obliged to carry the sound signalling appliances prescribed in paragraph (a) of this Rule but if she does not, she shall be provided with some other means of making an efficient sound signal.

Notes to Rule 33

Para (a): Craft over 12m in length must be fitted with a bell and a whistle. The whistle must have a range of at least 0.5 nautical mile.

Para (b): For boats under 12m there is no such requirement and 'an efficient sound signal' is not defined. Portable fog horns are readily available at the chandlery and the anchor signal could consist of a saucepan and a soup ladle.

◆ Rule 34 Manoeuvring and warning signals

(a) When vessels are in sight of one another, a power-driven vessel underway, when manoeuvring as authorized or required by these Rules, shall indicate that manoeuvre by the following signals on her whistle:
one short blast to mean 'I am altering my course to starboard';
two short blasts to mean 'I am altering my course to port';
three short blasts to mean 'I am operating astern propulsion'.

(b) Any vessel may supplement the whistle signals prescribed in paragraph (a) of this Rule by light signals, repeated as appropriate, whilst the manoeuvre is being carried out:
   (i) these light signals shall have the following significance:
   one flash to mean 'I am altering my course to starboard';
   two flashes to mean 'I am altering my course to port';
   three flashes to mean 'I am operating astern propulsion';
   (ii) the duration of each flash shall be about one second, the interval between flashes shall be about one second, and the interval between successive signals shall be not less than ten seconds;
   (iii) the light used for this signal shall, if fitted, be an all-round white light, visible at a minimum range of 5 miles, and shall comply with the provisions of Annex I to these Regulations.

(c) When in sight of one another in a narrow channel or fairway:
   (i) a vessel intending to overtake another shall in compliance with Rule 9 (e) indicate her intention by the following signals on her whistle:
   two prolonged blasts followed by one short blast to mean 'I intend to over take you on your starboard side';
   two prolonged blasts followed by two short blasts to mean 'I intend to overtake you on your port side'.
   (ii) the vessel about to be overtaken when acting in accordance with Rule 9 (e) (i) shall indicate her agreement by the following signal on her whistle:
   one prolonged, one short, one prolonged and one short blast, in that order.

(d) When vessels in sight of one another are approaching each other and from any cause either vessel fails to understand the intentions or actions of the other, or is in doubt whether sufficient action is being taken by the other to avoid collision, the vessel in doubt shall immediately indicate such doubt by giving at least five short and rapid blasts on the whistle. Such a signal may be supplemented by a light signal of at least five short and rapid flashes.

(e) A vessel nearing a bend or an area of a channel or fairway where other vessels may be obscured by an intervening obstruction shall sound one prolonged blast. Such signal shall be answered with a prolonged blast by any approaching vessel that may be within hearing around the bend or behind the intervening obstruction.

(f) If whistles are fitted on a vessel at a distance apart of more than 100 metres, one whistle only shall be used for giving manoeuvring and warning signals.

Notes to Rule 34

Para (a): It is worth noting that a large heavy vessel with its engines going astern in an attempt to crash stop will continue to travel forwards for a few miles, not just yards.

Para (d): It is not unusual to hear up to nine short and rapid blasts coming from a ship's whistle when the captain is extremely irate with another craft.

Manoeuvring and warning signals					
— 1 short blast	— — 2 short blasts	— — — 3 short blasts	— — — — — Min 5 short & rapid blasts	——— 1 long blast	NOTES Long blast = 4 to 6 seconds Short blast = 1 second
Altering course to starboard	Altering course to port	Operating astern propulsion	I do not understand your intentions	Approaching a blind bend	

Fig 18.17 Rule 34. Manoeuvring and warning signals.

◆ Rule 35 Sound signals in restricted visibility

In or near an area of restricted visibility, whether by day or night, the signals prescribed in this Rule shall be used as follows:

(a) A power-driven vessel making way through the water shall sound at intervals of not more than 2 minutes one prolonged blast.

(b) A power-driven vessel underway but stopped and making no way through the water shall sound at intervals of not more than 2 minutes two prolonged blasts in succession with an interval of about 2 seconds between them.

(c) A vessel not under command, a vessel restricted in her ability to manoeuvre, a vessel constrained by her draught, a sailing vessel, a vessel engaged in fishing and a vessel engaged in towing or pushing another vessel shall, instead of the signals prescribed in paragraphs (a) or (b) of this Rule, sound at intervals of not more than 2 minutes three blasts in succession, namely one prolonged followed by two short blasts.

(d) A vessel engaged in fishing, when at anchor, and a vessel restricted in her ability to manoeuvre when carrying out her work at anchor, shall instead of the signals prescribed in paragraph (g) of this Rule sound the signal prescribed in paragraph (c) of this Rule.

(e) A vessel towed or if more than one vessel is towed the last vessel of the tow, if manned, shall at intervals of not more than 2 minutes sound four blasts in succession, namely one prolonged followed by three short blasts. When practicable, this signal shall be made immediately after the signal made by the towing vessel.

(f) When a pushing vessel and a vessel being pushed ahead are rigidly connected in a composite unit they shall be regarded as a power-driven vessel and shall give the signals prescribed in paragraphs (a) or (b) of this Rule.

(g) A vessel at anchor shall at intervals of not more than one minute ring the bell rapidly for about 5 seconds. In a vessel of 100 metres or more in length the bell shall be sounded in the forepart of the vessel and immediately after the ringing of the bell the gong shall be sounded rapidly for about 5 seconds in the after part of the vessel. A vessel at anchor may in addition sound three blasts in succession, namely one short, one prolonged and one short blast, to give warning of her position and of the possibility of collision to an approaching vessel.

(h) A vessel aground shall give the bell signal and if required the gong signal prescribed in paragraph (g) of this Rule and shall, in addition, give three separate and distinct strokes on the bell immediately before and after the rapid ringing of the bell. A vessel aground may in addition sound an appropriate whistle signal.

(i) A vessel of 12m or more but less than 20m in length shall not be obliged to give the bell signals prescribed in paragraphs (g) and (h) of this Rule. However, if she does not, she shall make some other efficient sound signal at intervals of not more than 2 minutes.

(j) A vessel of less than 12m in length shall not be obliged to give the above mentioned signals but, if she does not, shall make some other efficient sound signal at interval of not more than 2 minutes.

(k) A pilot vessel when engaged in pilotage duty may in addition to the signals prescribed in paragraphs (a), (b) or (g) of this Rule sound an identity signal consisting of 4 short blasts.

Notes to Rule 35

Sound signals in restricted visibility				
—	— —	— - -	— - - -	- - - -
1 long blast	2 long blasts	1 long + 2 short blasts	1 long + 3 short blasts	4 short blasts
Power driven vessel making way	Power driven vessel underway but stopped	NUC + RAM + CBD + Fishing + Sail + Towing	Towed vessel or last vessel in a tow	Pilot vessel on duty (additional)
At intervals of not more than 2 minutes				When appropriate

Fig 18.18 Rule 35. Sound signals in restricted visibility.

Anchored vessels			Vessels aground in restricted visibility		
Vessels under 100m	Vessels over 100m	All sizes	Vessels under 100m	Vessels over 100m	All sizes
Bow	+ GONG Bow Stern	- — - On whistle	3 strokes Ringing 3 strokes	3 strokes Ringing + GONG 3 strokes	- — - On whistle
Rapid ringing for 5 seconds every minute	Rapid ringing on bell and gong for 5 seconds every minute	Optional when necessary	Every minute		Optional when necessary

Fig 18.19 Rule 35. Sound signals for anchored vessels and vessels aground in restricted visibility.

◆ Rule 36 Signals to attract attention

If necessary to attract the attention of another vessel any vessel may make light or sound signals that cannot be mistaken for any signal authorized elsewhere in these Rules, or may direct the beam of her searchlight in the direction of danger, in such a way as not to embarrass any vessel. Any light to attract the attention of another vessel shall be such that it cannot be mistaken for any aid to navigation. For the purpose of this Rule the use of high intensity intermittent or revolving lights, such as strobe lights, shall be avoided.

◆ Rule 37 Distress signals

When a vessel is in distress and requires assistance she shall use or exhibit the signals described in Annex IV to these Regulations.

PART E: EXEMPTIONS

These exemptions are of no real interest to pleasure craft as they concern technical details of lights and shapes, so are not included in this chapter.

ANNEX I

Annex I covers technical details for lights and shapes and has been omitted.

ANNEX II

◆ Additional signals for fishing vessels in close proximity

1 *General*
The lights mentioned herein shall, if exhibited in pursuance of Rule 26(d), be placed where they can best be seen. They shall be at least 0.9 metre apart but at a lower level than lights prescribed in Rule 26(b) (i) and (c) (i). The lights shall be visible all round the horizon at a distance of at least 1 mile but a lesser distance than the lights prescribed by these Rules for fishing vessels.

2 *Signals by trawlers*
(a) Vessels when engaged in trawling, whether using demersal or pelagic gear may exhibit:
(i) when shooting their nets: two white lights in vertical line;
(ii) when hauling their nets: one white light over one red light in a vertical line.
(iii) when the net has come fast upon an obstruction: two red lights in a vertical line.
(b) Each vessel engaged in pair trawling may exhibit:
(i) by night, a searchlight directed forward and in the direction of the other vessel of the pair;
(ii) when shooting or hauling their nets or when their nets have come fast on an obstruction, the lights prescribed in 2(a) above.

3 *Signals for purse seiners*
Vessels engaged in fishing with purse seine gear may exhibit two yellow lights in a vertical line. These lights shall flash alternately every second and with equal light and occultation duration. These lights may be exhibited only when the vessel is hampered by its fishing gear.

Notes to Annex II

2(b): Trawlers working together as a pair are not an uncommon sight off the French and Portuguese coasts and are often surprisingly far apart. Crew on night watch need to be well-briefed if sailing close to fishing fleets.

3: Fishing vessels, using purse seine gear, steam round in a large circle laying net marked by yellow floats at the surface. When the circle is complete, the rope on the surface is tightened in like a drawstring purse so that the fish (and any unsuspecting boats!) are trapped inside.

ANNEX III

Annex III concerns complicated technical details for sound signals and is not included in this chapter. However, the following note is worthy of attention:

> ***Note to Annex III***
> *The larger the ship the deeper the fog signal. (And before you ask – no, you may not make your 12m yacht sound like a super tanker to frighten everyone else away!)*

ANNEX IV

◆ Distress signals

1 The following signals, used or exhibited either together or separately, indicate distress and need of assistance:

(a) a gun or other explosive signal fired at intervals of about a minute;
(b) a continuous sounding with any fog-signalling apparatus;
(c) rockets or shells, throwing red stars fired one at a time at short intervals;
(d) a signal made by radiotelegraphy or by any other signalling method consisting of the group ••• – – – ••• (SOS) in the Morse code;
(e) a signal sent by radiotelephony consisting of the spoken word 'Mayday';
(f) The International Code Signal of distress indicated by NC;
(g) a signal consisting of a square flag having above or below it a ball or anything resembling a ball;
(h) flames on the vessel (as from a burning tar barrel, oil barrel, etc);
(i) a rocket parachute flare or a hand flare showing a red light;
(j) a smoke signal giving off orange-coloured smoke;
(k) slowly and repeatedly raising and lowering arms outstretched to each side;
(l) a distress alert by means of digital selective calling (DSC) transmitted on
  (i) VHF Channel 70, or
  (ii) MF/HF on the frequencies 2187.5kHz, 8414.5kHz, 4207.5kHz, 6312kHz, 12577 kHz or 16804.5 kHz;
(m) a ship-to-shore distress alert transmitted by the ship's Inmarsat or other mobile satellite service provider ship earth station;
(n) approved signals transmitted by radiocommunication systems, including survival craft radar transponders.

2 The use or exhibition of any of the foregoing signals except for the purpose of indicating distress and need of assistance and the use of other signals which may be confused with any of the above signals is prohibited.

3 Attention is drawn to the relevant sections of the International Code of Signals, the Merchant Ship Search and Rescue Manual and the following signals:

(a) a piece of orange coloured canvas and either a black square and circle or other appropriate symbol (for identification from the air);
(b) a dye marker.

> ***Notes to Annex IV***
> *There is no mention of hoisting a sail or an ensign upside down in this section as, contrary to popular belief, these are not internationally recognised distress signals.*
>
> *1(k): It is always worth using the binoculars to get a closer look at a person who appears to be waving to you; it may be someone onshore cut off by the tide or a windsurfer in distress.*
>
> *1(i) & (j): Flares are explained and illustrated in Chapter 16.*

QUESTION PAPER 18 – ANTI-COLLISION RULES

18.1 What do the Rules say about keeping a lookout?

18.2 How would you assess whether a risk of collision exists?

18.3 What day shape should a vessel at anchor display?

18.4 In fog you hear one prolonged blast followed by four short blasts. What type of vessel is it?

18.5 List seven distress signals, listed in Annex IV of the Rules, that could reasonably be sent by a 10m boat within 12 miles of the coast.

Answers at the back of the book

19 BENDS & HITCHES

◆ Buntline coil

The rope in Figure 19.1 may be coiled either clockwise or anticlockwise as it is a sheathed, not laid, rope. After the initial coils take three or four turns of rope around the coil. Lastly take a loop of rope through the coil before pulling it over the top.

Fig 19.1 Coiling a rope for stowage in a locker.

◆ Reef knot

Used for joining lines of equal thickness and for tying up the bunt of a sail when reefing (Figure 19.2).

◆ Round turn and two half hitches

Used for fixing a rope to a ring and the base of a cleat. It is a versatile knot that can be undone under load and never locks (Figure 19.3).

Fig 19.2 Reef knot.

Fig 19.3 Round turn and two half hitches.

◆ Figure of eight

This prevents a rope from running through an eye or block. The knots are not put in the end of spinnaker sheets and guys as they may need to run out through the block if the boat is over-pressed (Figure 19.4).

◆ Bowline

Used for making a non-slip loop at the end of a line. Also used for placing over a cleat or bollard when mooring alongside and for a safety line around a casualty in the water (Figure 19.5).

Fig 19.4 Figure of eight.

Fig 19.5 Bowline.

◆ Single sheet bend

Can be used for joining ropes of unequal thickness. Useful when two mooring warps need to be joined temporarily. For longer term use, the rope ends should be seized with twine (Figure 19.6).

◆ Double sheet bend

Joins two ropes of unequal thickness. It is more secure than a single sheet bend. The ends should be seized with whipping twine if the knot is to be left for any length of time. Suitable for joining two shore lines (Figure 19.7).

Fig 19.6 Single sheet bend.

Fig 19.7 Double sheet bend.

◆ Clove hitch

For fixing a rope to a spar when there is equal pull on the two ends. Suitable as a temporary adjustable knot for attaching fenders when coming alongside. For longer term use, a half hitch should be added for security as the knot may slip (Figure 19.8).

◆ Rolling hitch

Used for fixing a rope to a spar or for taking the load off a trapped rope. If the pull is to the left the rope will lock on to the spar; if pulled to the right it will slide along (Figure 19.9).

Fig 19.8 Clove hitch.

Fig 19.9 Rolling hitch.

◆ Securing a rope to a cleat

When securing a rope to a cleat, a round turn is used followed by two or three figure of eight turns, and finished with a round turn which is jammed behind the figure of eight turns. There is no need to use a locking hitch – the knot is secure as it stands.

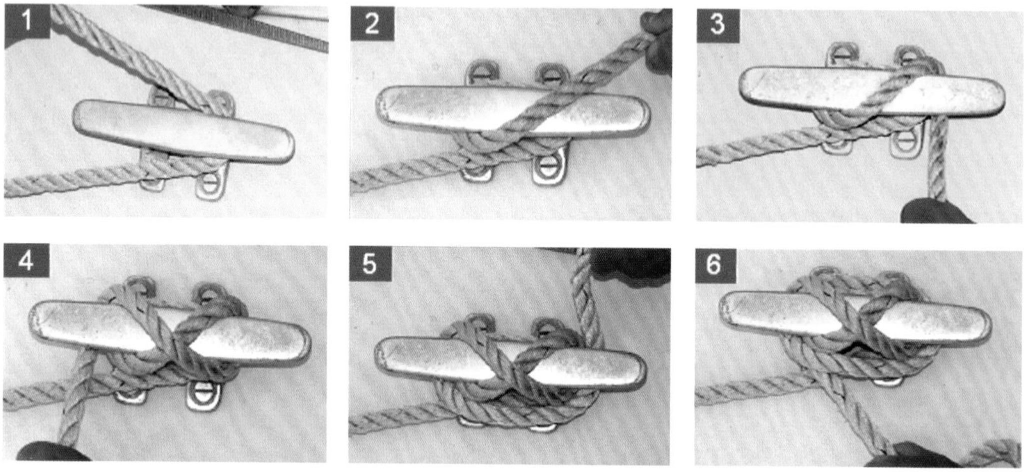

Fig 19.10 Securing a rope to a cleat.

QUESTION PAPER 19 – BENDS & HITCHES

19.1 Which knot would you use to make a non-slip loop in the end of a rope?

19.2 You wish to secure to ring with a knot that can be undone under load. Which knot would you use?

19.3 Why would you not put a stopper knot in the end of spinnaker sheets?

19.4 Which knot would you use for tying up the bunt of a sail after reefing?

Answers at the back of the book

ANSWERS TO QUESTIONS

CHAPTER 1 – CHARTS & POSITIONS

1.1 Transverse Mercator projection is used because it distorts land masses less than other projections and there are usually large blocks of land on harbour plans.

1.2 Chart book 5011 – Symbols and Abbreviations.

1.3 WGS 84.

1.4 Raster charts are copies of paper charts and no further information is given as you zoom in; the hardware plotter changes to another large-scale chart to give further detailed information. Raster charts are less expensive to produce and the UKHO give a good correction service and worldwide coverage.

Vector charts have the data in layers and, as you zoom in, another layer of information is presented. Vector charts use less computer memory, allow alarms to be set and those which conform to IMO standard S57 are accepted for use on commercial ships without a paper chart as a backup.

CHAPTER 2 – THE COMPASS

2.1 Printed on the chart close to the centre of the compass rose.

2.2 Low down in the vessel, and as far as possible from magnetic influences (wiring carrying a large current, electric motors and ferrous objects) and where it will not suffer damage.

2.3 **a** 178°T + 3°W = 181°M **b** 345°T + 7°W = 352°M
c 245°T - 5°E = 240°M **d** 002°T - 9°E = 353°M

2.4 **a** 086°M - 4°W = 082°T **b** 235°M + 10°E = 245°T
c 358°M + 6°E = 004°T **d** 000°M - 3°W = 357°T

2.5 Yes, electronic compasses do suffer from deviation but once correctly set up will correct themselves automatically.

2.6 **a** 038°C No dev = 038°M **b** 000°C - 1°W = 359°M
c 242°C - 3°W = 239°M **d** 190°C + 1°E = 191°M

CHAPTER 3 – ELECTRONICS

3.1 Speed over the ground.

3.2 **a** Cross Track Error
b Time to go to waypoint.

3.3 **a** Material **b** Aspect **c** Texture **d** Shape **e** Size

3.4 Radar ranges.

3.5 **a** Variable Range Marker
b Electronic Bearing Line

CHAPTER 4 – FINDING THE POSITION

4.1 Position: On the 20 metre line at 48° 42'.7N 2° 05'.8W.

4.2 Position: 48° 39'.8N 2° 10'.4W.

4.3 Position: 48° 43'5N 2° 00'.8W.

4.4 The GPS can be used to fix position with:
a Latitude and longitude.
b Bearing and distance to a waypoint.
c Spider's web for plotting bearing and distance to a waypoint.
d Cross track error ladder.

Fig A.4 Plots for questions 4.1, 4.2, 4.3.

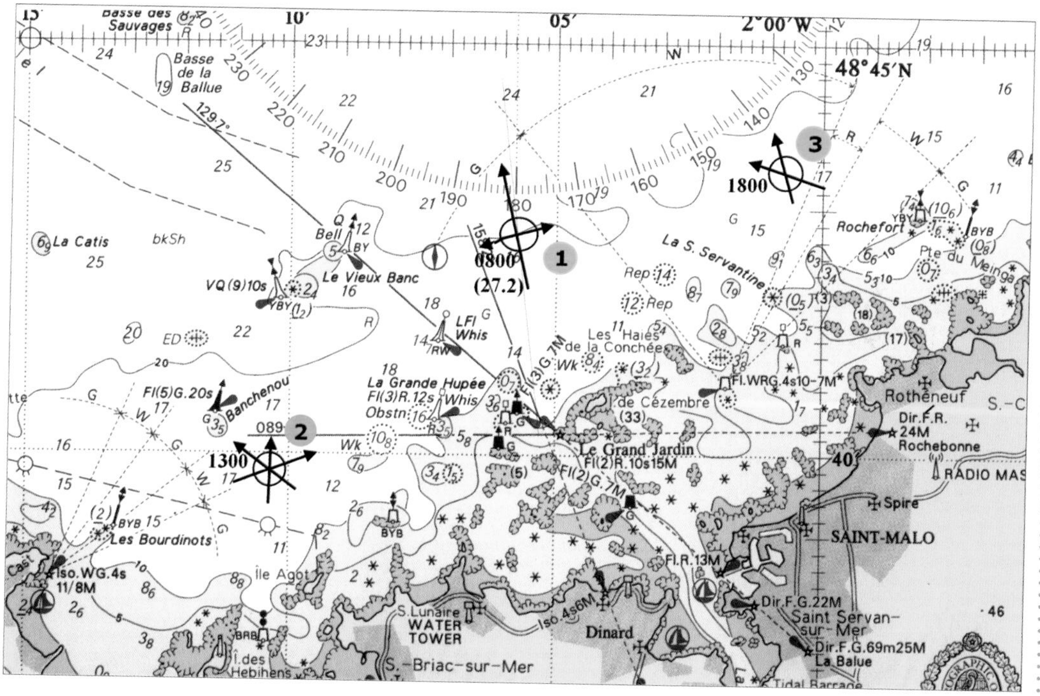

CHAPTER 5 – TIDAL HEIGHTS

5.1 5.3m.

5.2 St Malo HAT = 13.6m MHWN = 9.5m Difference = 4.1m
Charted clearance height + difference = 24.1m
Height of mast above waterline (air draught) = 18.5m
Clearance = 5.6m. A safe clearance under a power cable.

5.3 0745 French Standard Time.

5.4 By interpolation LW Lymington is: LW Portsmouth 1.6 – 0.4m = 1.2m

5.5 From figure 5.11: Height of tide St Helier 7.5m
Fall to LW (3.7m) = 3.8m
Water required = Fall 3.8m + Draught 2.0m = 5.8m
Depth of water at 1240 = 6.8m
Clearance is therefore 1.0m

CHAPTER 6 – TIDAL STREAMS

6.1 126°T 1 knot.

6.2 The stream would be slackest at HW +5 = 1330 to 1430.

6.3 1.8 knots.

6.4 HW -2 0700 to 0800 = 315°T 3.5kn.

6.5 Deep water.

CHAPTER 7 – ESTIMATED POSITION

7.1 Course steered 175°M less 3°W variation = 172°T.
COG = 164°T and SOG = 12kn.

7.2 Course steered 355°M less 3°W = 352°T less 5° leeway = 347°T.
The yacht passes to the east of the east cardinal beacon at a distance of 0.6M.

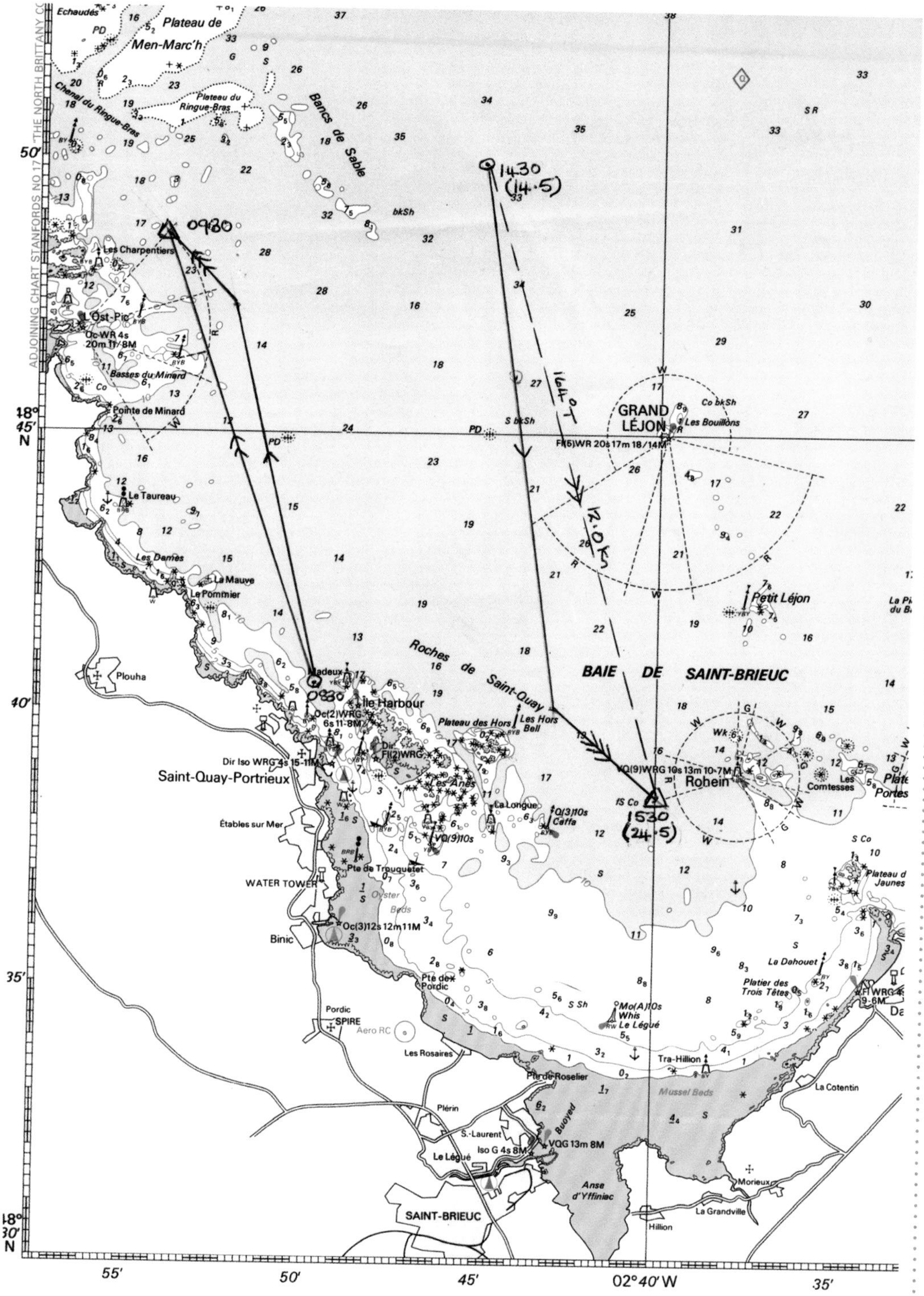

Fig A.7 Plots for answers to questions 7.1, 7.2.

CHAPTER 8 – COURSE TO STEER

8.1 **a** Course to steer 211°T = 214°M.
b SOG = 6.6kn.

8.2 **a** This is a half hour vector triangle. Plot 1.25 miles of tide and 9 miles of distance covered.
Course to steer 136°T = 139°M.
b ETA = Distance to entrance 7.1 miles ÷ SOG 15.8 x 60 = 27min = 0927.

8.3 Course to steer 127°T = 130°M + 10° L/W = 140°M. (Aim into the south wind.)

CHAPTER 9 – LIGHTS & BUOYAGE

9.1 Leave them to port as they are fixed marina pontoons, harbour walls etc.

9.2 2 x black spheres.

9.3 **a** Flashing 4 yellow. The others have lights that could be used for a white light so are not allowed.

9.4 A white light flashing in groups of two during a 15second period. The centre of the light is 45m above mean high water springs and the nominal range is 18 nautical miles. It also has a fixed red light.

9.5 A safe water mark.

CHAPTER 10 – PILOTAGE

10.1 Clearing bearings are bearings used to clear a danger. If the boat sails within the area defined by the bearings then the danger is avoided. They are used, for example, when wishing to enter a harbour with off-lying dangers and a strong cross-tidal stream.

10.2 Do not proceed except outside the main channel.

10.3 A transit is when two objects are seen in line to give a position line.

10.4 Almanac, pilot book, chart plotter, harbour master and tourist board. On the reverse side of some small craft charts.

10.5 You should enter Portsmouth on the western side using the Small Boat Channel. Proceed to Ballast Beacon and leave it close to port. Call QHM on Ch 11 and ask permission to cross the main channel to Gunwharf Quays. When permission is granted, cross the main channel at 90° at not more than 10 knots through the water, keeping a good lookout.

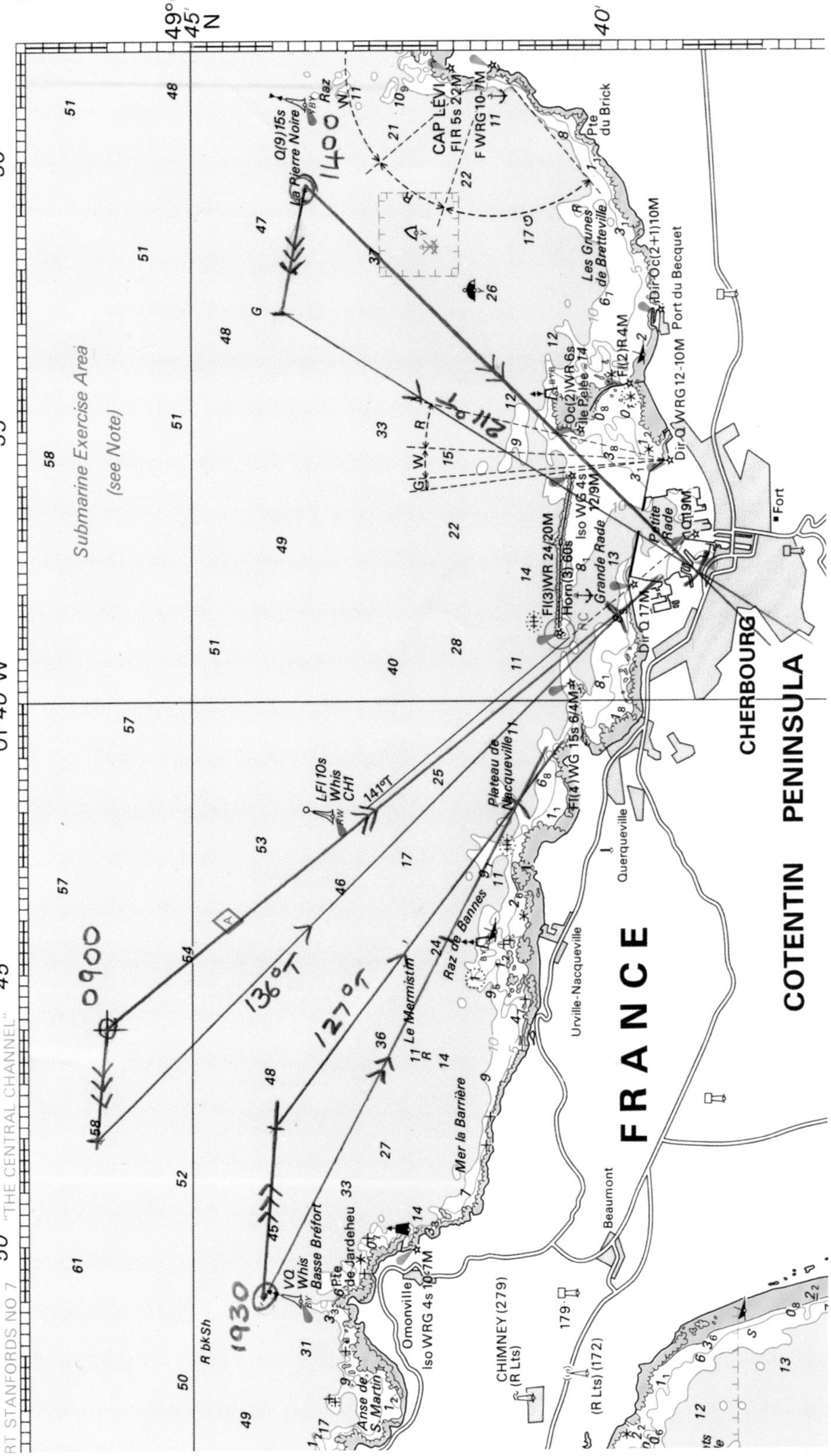

Fig A.8 Plots for answers to questions for chapter 8.

CHAPTER 11 – WEATHER TO GO – OR NOT TO GO

11.1	The wind blows clockwise around a high pressure in the northern hemisphere.
11.2	Cumulonimbus clouds would be associated with squally showers and gusty winds.
11.3	A rise or fall of seven millibars in 3 hours will give a certain gale F8.
11.4	The waves will be between 1.25m to 2.5m high.
11.5	When the wind is expected to reach Force 6.

CHAPTER 12 – FOG & HEAVY WEATHER

12.1	At intervals not exceeding two minutes.
12.2	Any five from: Close hatches and ventilators, prepare food in advance, reef early, crew to wear harnesses and lifejackets, lash anchor down, take seasickness pills.
12.3	A harbour wall.
12.4	Automatic Identification System.
12.5	The seabed around a headland is often very uneven and strong tidal streams running over the seabed can cause dangerously rough conditions.

CHAPTER 13 – BUOYANCY & STABILITY

13.1	Angle of vanishing stability. If a boat heels to its AVS, the righting moment is zero and it could either invert or right.
13.2	A motor cruiser will take in water through the engine air intakes at low heel angles; subsequent flooding will lead to buoyancy loss. Any water lying in the bilge will also slop from side to side and increase the heeling angle.
13.3	A wave 3m high.

CHAPTER 14 – ANCHORING, MOORING & BERTHING

14.1 A trip line is a light line that is attached to an eyelet on the crown of the anchor so that the anchor can be pulled free of an obstruction on the seabed should it become ensnared.

14.2 **a** Anchorage B or C will give protection for a short stop.
b Anchorage C will give protection at all times.

14.3 Any three from:
Rig shore lines.
Check that the spreaders will not touch the rigging of the other boat.
Stop halyards from slapping on the mast.
Walk around the bow.
Place fenders to protect the hulls.
Rig springs.

14.4 13kg.

14.5 20 metres.

CHAPTER 15 – PASSAGE PLANNING

15.1 No. However, if you have a non-EU person on board you will have to inform a Customs officer at the destination port.

15.2 The coastguard station closest to the range or other danger areas keep details of firing times.

15.3 No.

15.4 Tide taken on the leeward bow will assist progress to windward.

CHAPTER 16 – SAFETY & SURVIVAL

16.1 Any four from:
Cut the painter, distribute weight evenly, stream the drogue, bail the raft dry, close the canopy, post a lookout, inflate the floor, check for leaks, issue seasickness tablets.

16.2 This is a U in Morse code which means that you are standing into danger.

16.3 Drive belt, oil filter, water pump impeller, first fuel filter, fine fuel filter, spare oil.

16.4 Four parachute flares.

16.5 The drogue is vital to preserve the liferaft's stability – it holds it down in the water and prevents the wind flipping it over and reduces drift.

CHAPTER 17 – COMMUNICATIONS, GMDSS & DISTRESS

17.1 The vessel in b) should issue a DSC distress alert.

17.2 Channel 67 is the channel used by the UK Coastguard for small craft safety.

17.3 The EPIRB should be allowed to continue transmitting until the nearest Maritime Rescue Co-ordination Centre (in UK, HM Coastguard) has been informed and permission granted for it to be switched off. If you are well offshore where communication to a Coastguard may be a lengthy process, turn the EPIRB off as you may well need it later. Keep trying to contact the nearest Coastguard.

17.4 A working channel after the announcement on Channel 16.

17.5 An All Ships Urgency alert.

CHAPTER 18 – ANTI-COLLISION RULES

18.1 Every vessel shall at all times maintain a proper lookout by sight and hearing as well as by all available means appropriate in the prevailing circumstances and conditions.

18.2 Take a compass bearing on an approaching vessel. If the bearing does not appreciably change then a risk of collision exists.

18.3 A black ball hoisted in the forepart of the vessel.

18.4 A pilot vessel on duty, underway.

18.5 Any seven from:
- Continuous sounding of a fog horn.
- SOS sent by light or by sound.
- Repeatedly raising and lowering of the arms.
- A radio telephone alarm signal (DSC Distress alert).
- A radio transmission including the word "Mayday".
- Something round over something square or vice versa.
- Signal transmitted by an EPIRB.
- A red parachute rocket or a red hand held flare.
- An orange smoke signal.
- The International code signal NC.

CHAPTER 19 – BENDS & HITCHES

19.1	A bowline.
19.2	Round turn and two half hitches.
19.3	Stopper knots are not generally placed in the end of spinnaker sheets and guys in case the lines need to be released in a hurry when the boat becomes over-pressed.
19.4	A reef knot.

GLOSSARY OF SAILING TERMS

Abeam (on the beam)	At right angles to the fore-and-aft line of the boat.
Ahead	The direction directly in front of the boat.
Aloft	Above deck level; up the mast.
Anchor buoy	Small buoy attached to the tripping line on the crown of an anchor.
Anchor light	A white all-round light hoisted up the mast or positioned at the top of the mast.
Anchor roller	A roller at the bow of a vessel over which the anchor cable is run.
Astern	Direction directly behind the boat.
Back	The wind backs when its direction shifts in an anticlockwise direction.
Bar	An area near the mouth of a river where the water flow causes silting, resulting in a shallow patch.
Batten	A stiff slat used to control the curve of a sail.
Batten pocket	A pocket on a sail where the batten is inserted.
Beam	The width of a boat.
Beam reach	A point of sailing with the apparent wind on the beam.
Bear away	To alter course away from the wind.
Bearing	The direction, normally measured in degrees, from the observer to the object described.
Beat	To sail on alternate tacks towards a position that is upwind of the boat.
Bilge	The area of a boat underneath the cabin sole where bilge water collects.
Bilge pump	A hand or electrical water pump designed to empty the bilge.
Binnacle	A structure near the helmsman's position housing the compass and often instrumentation.
Black ball	An IRPCS shape. A single ball hoisted on a vessel indicates that it is at anchor.
Boat hook	A hook on a pole used to pick up mooring buoys etc. Using it to hold on to other boats is unpopular!
Boom vang	A device for pulling the boom down in order to flatten the mainsail.
Bottle-screw	A screw fitting on guardrails, shrouds and stays; used to tension the wire.
Breast ropes	Mooring lines run at right angles to the fore and aft line of the vessel.
Broach	When a heavy following sea causes the boat to slew round towards the wind. In a sailing boat this can result in a large angle of heel.
Broad reach	A point of sailing between running and beam reaching.
Broken water	An isolated area of the sea with small breaking waves. Often caused by a rough seabed and strong tidal flow.
Bulkhead	A partition built across the width of the hull.
Burgee	A small triangular flag flown to indicate membership of a sailing club or organisation.
Cable	A distance of one tenth of a nautical mile. Approx 185 metres.
Calm	A state when the sea is smooth with little or no wind.
Cast off	An instruction to release or let go a rope or line.
Centre of buoyancy	Geometric centre of that part of the hull that is below the waterline.
Centre of gravity	A theoretical position where the weight of the vessel appears to be centred.

Chain plate	A metal strip on the hull to which the shrouds are attached.
Chart datum	The level from which depth soundings are measured. It is close to the minimum height of low water springs.
Cleat	A fitting, normally on deck, for securing lines and ropes.
Clew	The lower aft corner of a sail.
Clew outhaul	A line attached to the clew of a mainsail to tension the foot.
Close hauled	A point of sailing as close to the wind as possible.
Cocked hat	A triangle formed on the chart when three position lines are drawn. Gives some indication of the size of the measurement error.
Course made good	The course over the seabed. The resultant of heading, tidal movement and leeway.
Current	Movement of water caused by geographical features, eg the Gulf Stream.
Deck log	Book in which all events and navigational data are recorded.
Deviation	The error between the reading on a compass and the correct magnetic bearing.
Displacement	The weight of the craft. Equal to the weight of water displaced.
Distance made good	The distance covered over the seabed.
Drag (an anchor)	A condition when the anchor slides over the seabed.
Drift	The distance the boat is carried by the tidal stream in a fixed time.
Ease-out	To let out a rope or sheet by a small amount.
Ebb	The tidal stream that occurs when the tidal height of water is falling.
EBL	Electronic Bearing Line on a radar display.
Echo sounder	An instrument that measures the depth of water by using sound waves.
EPIRB	Emergency Position Indicating Radio Beacon.
Fairlead	A fitting on the edge of a deck to reduce chafe when mooring lines are led over the deck edge.
Fairway	A passage of deeper water permitting entry to a port or river.
Fix	The position of the boat obtained from compass bearings or electronic means.
Flood	The tidal stream that occurs when the tidal height of water is rising.
Fog	Visibility of less than 1,000 metres.
Foot	The lower edge of a sail.
Foresail	A sail set on the forestay or inner forestay.
Fractional rig	A yacht in which the forestay is attached to the mast between the spreaders and the top of the mast.
Frap	To secure the halyards away from the mast in order to prevent them rattling against the mast in a wind.
Freeboard	The distance between water level and deck level.
Furl	To roll a sail – normally applies to a headsail.
Genoa	A large headsail that overlaps the mainsail.
Geographical range	The geographical range of a light is the theoretical distance at which an observer at a height of 15 feet could see the light provided that the nominal range is sufficient.
Go about (to)	To tack. To move the bow through the wind and set the sail on the other side.
Goose wing (to)	To set the mainsail and headsail on opposite sides of the boat when running downwind.
Gooseneck	A fitting that secures the boom to the mast.
Great Circle	A line on the surface of the Earth with the same circumference as the Equator. The shortest route between two points on the Earth's surface.
Ground (to)	To touch the seabed. To run aground.

Gunwale	The bulwark along the upper side of the boat.
Gybe	To turn the boat so that the stern passes through the wind permitting the sails to be set on the other side.
Halyard	The wire or rope used to hoist a sail.
Harden up	To alter course towards the wind.
Haze	A meteorological condition where visibility is between 1,000m and 2,000m.
Heading	The direction in which the boat is pointing.
Headsail	A sail set forward of the mast.
Headway	Moving through the water in the direction the bow is pointing.
Heave-to	To stop the boat at sea without lowering the sails. In a motor cruiser to stop the engine at sea.
Height of tide	The vertical distance between the actual height of water and the level of Chart Datum.
Hoist	To raise an object such as a sail using a halyard.
IALA	International Association of Lighthouse Authorities.
IALA A	A system of buoyage used in all areas other than the USA and Pacific Rim.
IALA B	A system of buoyage used in the USA and Pacific Rim.
In irons	A condition where the boat has stopped making way with sails flapping and is head to wind.
Isobar	A line joining points of equal pressure on a meteorological chart.
Isophase	A light characteristic consisting of equal lengths of light and darkness.
Jib	A triangular headsail set on the forestay.
Kedge anchor	A small anchor, often kept in a locker, for anchoring for a short time.
Ketch	A two masted yacht where the after mast is for'd of the rudder post.
Kicking strap	A device for pulling the boom down in order to flatten the mainsail.
Leach	The after edge of a sail.
Lee	The direction downwind.
Leeward	The opposite side of a boat to that from which the wind is blowing.
Leeway	The angle, caused by the wind, between heading and water track.
LOA	Maximum length of the craft. Length overall.
Local time	The time you would see on a clock at the place specified.
Log	An instrument for measuring distance through the water. (See also Deck log.)
Luff	The front edge of a sail.
Luff (to)	To alter course towards the direction of the wind.
LWL	Length of the craft measured on the waterline.
Making way	A boat is 'making way' when it is moving through the water.
Mast – deck stepped	A mast that sits on top of the coachroof.
Mast – keel stepped	A mast that passes through the coachroof and sits on the keel.
Masthead rig	The forestay is attached to the top of the mast. (See also fractional rig.)
MHWN	Mean high water neaps.
MHWS	Mean high water springs.
Mizzen mast	The aftermost mast in a yawl or ketch.
MLWN	Mean low water neaps.
MLWS	Mean low water springs.
Nautical mile	A unit of distance based on 1 minute of latitude (approx 1,852m).
Neap tide	A tide where the tidal range is small and streams are at their weakest.

No Go Zone The sector within which a yacht cannot sail.
Nominal range The nominal range of a light is dependent on the intensity of the light in meteorological visibility of 10 miles. Note that this takes no account of the curvature of the Earth. This range is shown on charts.
North-up mode A stabilised radar picture when North is at the top of the screen.
Not under command A vessel that through some exceptional circumstance is unable to manoeuvre as required by the Rules.

Occulting light The light is on for longer than it is off.
On the bow A sector within 45° either side of the bow.
On the quarter A sector within 45° either side of the stern.
Open When two leading marks are not in line they are described as open.
Outhaul A means of pulling a mainsail towards the end of the boom.
Overfalls Turbulent sea caused by a sudden change in water depth. Effect increases in a strong tidal stream.
Overtaking light The 135° white light at the stern.

Painter The line used to secure or tow a dinghy.
Pay out To ease out a line or rope slowly.
Period The time a navigational light takes to complete one cycle.
Pile A strong timber driven into the ground in order to provide a boat berth. Normally in pairs.
Pinch To attempt to sail so close to the wind that boat speed is reduced.
Piston hanks Metal fittings for attaching a headsail to the forestay.
Plot To transfer a position to the chart.
Pooped A dangerous condition where a following sea breaks over the stern of the boat.
Port The left-hand side of the boat when looking forward.
Port tack A point of sailing with the mainsail filled on the starboard side of the boat (wind from port).
Position line A line drawn on the chart giving one component of a fix.
Preventer A line rigged to secure the boom and prevent an accidental gybe.
Pulpit Metal frame round the bow at deck level, to protect the working crew.
Pushpit Metal frame across the stern at deck level, to protect the crew.

Range of tide The difference between water height at HW and water height at LW.
Reach A point of sailing between close hauled and running free.
Reefing (to reef) To reduce the area of a sail.
Registered tonnage A measure of the volume of the craft – not the weight. Originally used for taxation purposes.
Relative wind The wind you feel. The result of true wind and boat movement.
Rhumb line A line that crosses each meridian of latitude at a constant angle on a Mercator chart. Not the shortest route.
Riding turn Occurs when the turns on a winch become crossed and then jam.
Running by the lee When the wind is blowing from the same side of the boat as the mainsail. There will be the possibility of a gybe.

Sail ties Lengths of light line or tape used to secure a sail to the boom after lowering.
Schooner A yacht in which the after mast is taller than the main mast.
Sea anchor A device used to hold the head of the boat into wind when neither sailing nor anchored.
Sea clutter A control on a radar display that reduces unwanted beam reflections caused by waves close to the ship.

Set The direction towards which the tidal stream flows.
Sheet A control rope attached to the clew of a sail (or boom in the case of the mainsheet).
Shorten sail To reef the sails or change to sails of a smaller size.
Sill A wall or dam across the entrance to a harbour or marina.
Speed made good The speed of the vessel over the ground.
Spring tide A tide where the tidal range is large and streams are at their strongest.
Springs Ropes rigged to prevent a boat from moving forward or aft when secured alongside.
Stanchions Metal poles that support the guardrail lines.
Starboard The right-hand side of the boat when looking forward.
Starboard tack A point of sailing with the mainsail filled on the port side of the boat (wind from starboard).
Steaming light Alternative name for masthead light. Used when a vessel is driven by power.
Stern light See overtaking light.
Storm A wind of, or exceeding, Beaufort force 10.
Storm jib A small headsail set in strong winds.
Swashway A channel of deeper water, normally into a harbour or river.

Tack To change course through the wind and set the sails on the other side.
Tell-tails Small pieces of wool or cloth on the luff of a sail to indicate the path of the wind over the sail.
Thames Tonnage A measure of the volume of the craft – not the weight. Originally used for taxation purposes.
Tidal range The vertical distance between the level of low water and high water.
Tide The vertical rise and fall of the water level.
Topping lift A line from the masthead to the end of the boom, used to support the boom when the mainsail is lowered.
Traffic Separation Scheme An area of one-way traffic lanes where special rules apply.
Transducer The unit of an instrument system that converts depth, speed etc into electrical signals.
Transit Two objects are 'in transit' when they are seen one behind the other.
Transom The flat part of the hull across the stern.
Traveller A metal car on a track that allows the mainsheet lower end to move across the boat from one side to the other.
Tri-coloured light A red, green and white light at the masthead, which may *replace* the lower red and green lights and overtaking light, *when under sail.*
Trip line A light line between the crown of an anchor and the anchor buoy.
Trysail A small, heavy sail used to replace the mainsail in very strong winds.

Underway A ship is underway if it is not attached to the seabed.
Up and down The state of the anchor cable, when being weighed, just before it breaks out of the seabed.

Veer To pay out an anchor cable or a rope.
VRM Variable Range Marker on a radar display.

Wear (to) To change tacks by moving the stern of the boat through the wind.
Weigh (the anchor) To raise the anchor.
Withies Small sticks or saplings used in rivers to mark the deeper water.

Yawing Swinging from side to side of the set course.
Yawl A two-masted yacht where the after mast is aft of the rudder post.

APPENDIX A

MEDICAL EQUIPMENT FOR A CRUISING YACHT

Item	Recommended	Quantity
First Aid Book	St John current edition	1
Adhesive elastic bandage	7.5cm x 4m	1
Tubular gauze bandage	20m length with applicator	1
Disposable gloves	Latex free vinyl	5 prs
Adhesive dressings	Assorted sterile	20
Sterile bandages	Medium No 1 (12 x 10cm)	2
	Large No 2 (20 x 15cm)	2
	Extra large No 3 (28 x 20cm)	1
Triangular bandages	About 90cm x 127cm	4
Adhesive sutures (Steristrip)	75mm adhesive strips	6
Gauze dressings	Sterile, paraffin	10
Sterile gauze swabs	Pkt of 5. (7.5cm x 7.5cm)	1 pkt
Equipment for mouth-to-mouth resuscitation	Pocket face mask with valve	1
Scissors	Stainless steel or disposable	1
Burn bags	Plastic	1
Safety pins	Rustless, medium	6
Clingfilm wrap	Roll	1 roll
Space blanket	Pkt	1

MEDICINES FOR A CRUISING YACHT

Anti-angina preparations	Glyceryl Trinitrate Capsules	3
Seasickness and anti-emetic	Hyoscine hydrobromide 0.3mg	60
	or Cinnarizine 15mg	60
Anti-diarrhoeals	Loperamide 2mg capsules	30
Antiseptic wipes	Pre-impregnated wipes	1 pkt
Analgesics and	Paracetamol 500mg tablets	50
anti-inflammatory agents	and Ibuprofen 400mg tablets	50

Note: Some of the listed equipment, bandages and medicines carry a 'best before' date.

Container

The container used to carry all the First Aid equipment should be durable and waterproof.

APPENDIX B

RECOMMENDED EQUIPMENT FOR OFFSHORE CRUISING BOATS

*** = Not required in motor cruisers.

An approved liferaft to carry all persons on board; stowed where it can be launched quickly. (A half-inflated dinghy can be carried but in anything but sheltered waters, it is totally inadequate.)

Two lifebuoys, with battery light (not flashing) and drogue.

Dan-buoy with self-igniting light ***.

Rescue quoit with 30m buoyant line.

Boarding ladder.

Two strong buckets with strong handles and lanyards.

At least two multi-purpose fire extinguishers of suitable type and capacity.

Fire blanket near cooker.

Spare bulbs for navigation lights.

An anchor of sufficient size, and enough chain and/or warp for all expected depths and conditions.

A second smaller anchor as a spare.

One fixed and one portable bilge pump.

An approved, up-to-date pack of flares containing: 4 red parachute flares, 4 red hand held flares, 2 buoyant orange smoke.

Radar reflector.

First aid kit and book in waterproof box (See Appendix A).

Waterproof torch and spare batteries.

Safety harness anchor points, one located near the main hatch for use as the crew step into the cockpit ***.

Strong guardrails. Lifelines in yachts.

A method of securing and releasing the doors and deck hatches (and washboards in yachts) from inside and outside the cabin.

The name of the boat or radio call sign should be displayed on the dodgers or on a piece of canvas ready to display on the coachroof.

A method of securing all equipment such as batteries, cookers and other heavy gear liable to do damage in heavy weather.

Radio receiver suitable for receiving weather forecasts.

Marine band VHF radio ideally fitted with Digital Selective Calling.

Electronic navigational system such as GPS or chart plotter.

A steering compass readable by the helmsman and hand-bearing compass.

Reliable clock or watch.

Distance log.

Echo sounder.

Lead line.

Up-to-date charts, tidal tables, pilot books etc.

Navigational plotting instruments.

General tool kit.

Bolt croppers ***.

Engine spares including:

Water pump impeller, engine drive belts, spare oil and fuel filters, spare oil(s), coolant, stern gland grease (as recommended by the engine manufacturer).

A separate battery used only for engine starting.

Rope suitable for towing another craft.

Emergency water supply.

Inflatable dinghy or rigid tender.

Mainsail capable of being deeply reefed or a trysail; a storm jib ***.

Fog horn and spare air bottle.

EPIRB if cruising beyond coastal waters.

Gas alarm/detector (if gas used on board).

APPENDIX C

SAFETY BRIEFING CHECKLIST

◆ Below decks

Gas
- Heavier than air – precautions.
- Gas taps – whereabouts and usage.
- Gas bottles – location.
- Routine before & after using cooker & gas spillage.

Fire Prevention
- No smoking down below or near sails.
- Cooker – no chip pans.
- Curtains away from cooker.
- Gas and smoke alarms.

Fire Extinguishers & Fire Blanket
- Location – fore cabin, saloon, aft cabins, engine.
- Explain types.
- Method of operation.

Galley
- Pour boiling water into mugs in the sink.
- Wear foul weather trousers when cooking at sea.
- Put kettle spout in fore and aft line at sea.

First Aid Box
- Everyday box & serious injury box – location.
- Tell skipper when items used.
- Anybody First-Aid trained?

Heads & Seacocks
- Heads operating procedure.
- Location of all seacocks.

VHF Radio – Main & Handheld
- How to switch on and squelch. Use of DSC Distress button.
- Changing channels & press to transmit switch.
- Show distress card.

Flares & Emergency Radio Aerial
- Where stowed & type carried.
- How to use.

Lifejackets and Harnesses
- All crew members to fit.
- Whistle, inflation toggle, light, top-up tube, crotch straps.
- Light operation.
- When to wear – when told by Skipper, fog, risk of collision, abandoning ship, heavy weather, in the dinghy, if they want to.
- Clip on points.
- Procedure for exiting companionway in heavy weather.
- Where stowed. Accessibility at sea.

◆ Above decks

Heaving line
- Location & operation.

Lifebelts, Drogues & Dan-buoy
- Location, use & test lights.

Liferaft
- Securing points – painter attached.
- When & how to launch.
- How to board.
- Contents.

Engine
- Batteries.
- Throttle/gear position.
- Starting/stopping.

◆ Miscellaneous

Slips and Falls
- One hand for yourself and one for the boat.
- Highlight danger of BOOM.

Winch and Line Safety
- Never release a jammer (clutch) without first taking a turn round the winch.
- Keep fingers clear of line under load on winch.
- Do not leave winch handles in the winch.

With grateful thanks to Hamble School of Yachting.

APPENDIX D

COASTAL SKIPPER & YACHTMASTER THEORY SYLLABUS

This is an advanced course in navigation and meteorology for candidates for the Yachtmaster Coastal and Yachtmaster Offshore Certificate. The syllabus makes some provision for the revision of subjects in the elementary course but those who have not acquired the knowledge set out in the elementary course are unlikely to be able to assimilate the subjects covered in the advanced course in the time available.

SUBJECT	BROAD DETAIL TO BE COVERED
Position	Dead reckoning and estimated position Satellite-derived position Use of waypoints to fix position Radar fixes Techniques of visual fixing Fixes using a mixture of position lines Relative accuracy of different methods of position fixing Areas of uncertainty
The Magnetic Compass	Allowance for variation Change of variation with time and position Causes of deviation Compass checks for deviation (but not correction) Allowance for deviation Different types of compasses
Tides	Causes of tides – Springs and Neaps Tide tables – sources Tide levels and datum Standard and secondary ports Tidal anomalies (Solent etc.)
Tidal Streams	Sources of tidal information Tidal stream information in sailing directions and Yachtsman's Almanacs Allowance for tidal streams in computing a course to steer Tide rips, overfalls and races Tidal observation – buoys, beacons

Buoyage	IALA system buoyage in Region A Limitations of buoys as navigational aids
Lights	Characteristics Ranges – visual, luminous and nominal Rising and dipping distances Light lists
Pilotage	Harbour regulations and control signals Methods of pre-planning Clearing lines Use of soundings Transits and leading lines
GPS and Chart Plotters	Principles of operation and limitations of use Raster and vector charts Datum Importance of confirmation of position by an independent source and keeping a separate record of position Importance of paper charts
Echo Sounders	Principles of operation and limitations of use
Logs (speed & distance)	Principles of operation and limitations of use
Deck Log	The importance of the log as the yacht's official document Layout of log, hourly and occasional entries
Meteorology	Basic terms, the Beaufort scale Air masses Cloud types Weather patterns associated with pressure and frontal systems Sources of forecast information Ability to interpret a shipping forecast, weather fax and weather satellite information Land and sea breezes Sea fog Use of a barometer as a forecasting aid
Rule of the Road	A sound knowledge of the IRPCS, except Annexes 1 & 3

Safety at Sea	Personal safety, use of lifejackets, safety harnesses & lifelines Fire prevention and fire fighting Distress signals Coastguard and Boat Safety Scheme Preparation for heavy weather Liferaft and helicopter rescue Understanding of capabilities of vessel and basic knowledge of stability
Navigation in Restricted Visibility	Precautions to be taken in fog Limitations to safe navigation imposed by fog Navigation strategy in poor visibility
Passage Planning	Preparation of charts and notebook for route planning and use at sea Customs regulations as they apply to yachts Routine for navigating in coastal waters Strategy for course laying Use of and visual confirmation of waypoints and routes Use of weather forecast information for passage planning strategy Sources of local and national regulations
Marine Environment	The responsibility to minimise pollution and protect the marine environment

INDEX